Vivid and encyclopaedic in his description of organizational purpose, Ellsworth helps leaders truly understand the tremendous impact that knowing who you are has on where you go and how you get there. In these globally turbulent times, any thoughtful leader will benefit greatly from this book.

—**Jerry I. Porras**
Lane Professor of Organizational Behavior and Change,
Stanford Business School
co-author of *Built to Last:*
Successful Habits of Visionary Companies

A truly unique effort. I know of no other book that takes for its centerpiece the concept of purpose and then refracts it so meaningfully through the prism of the modern corporation. Ellsworth argues forcibly for a strong point of view and moral imperative in the corporation, brilliantly presenting a book of immense importance.

—**Warren Bennis**
Distinguished Professor of Business,
University of Southern California
co-author of *Geeks and Geezers:*
How Era, Values and Defining Moments Shape Leaders

The unique strength of Richard Ellsworth's book is that it presents the business enterprise in *all* its dimensions—as an *economic* institution; as a *human* organization; and as an embodiment of *values*—and carries all three dimensions in both clear theory and practical application.

—**Peter F. Drucker**
Clark Professor of Social Science,
Claremont Graduate University

Reexamining the view that the overriding purpose of a corporation is to increase shareholder wealth, this book challenges corporations to integrate product development, customer satisfaction, employee productivity, and shareholder satisfaction to both remain competitive in the world economy and contribute to the betterment of the community. *Leading with Purpose* exemplifies Ellsworth's ability to identify and analyze abstract philosophical conceptions in a way that is useful to practicing managers.

—George C. Lodge
Harvard Business School

Ellsworth links the literature of current management practice to the findings of economists and political scientists who study the global environment, making the argument that purpose is at the core of a company's global competitiveness and managers have a moral as well as a fiduciary responsibility in the corporation. The strong, clear voice that comes through in this work is one that should be heard more often in business schools. *Leading with Purpose* is a major contribution on an issue of immense importance and provides an effective counterweight to the rational and analytic frameworks that often drive our MBA programs and executive classrooms.

—Christopher A. Bartlett
Thomas D. Casserly Professor of Business Administration,
Harvard Business School

LEADING WITH PURPOSE

LEADING

WITH PURPOSE The New Corporate Realities

Richard R. Ellsworth

STANFORD BUSINESS BOOKS
An Imprint of Stanford University Press

Stanford University Press
Stanford, California
©2002 by Richard R. Ellsworth

Printed in the United States of America on acid-free, archival-quality paper

Library of Congress Cataloging-in-Publication Data

Ellsworth, Richard R.
  Leading with purpose : the new corporate realities /
Richard R. Ellsworth.
      p.   cm.
Includes bibliographical references and index.
  ISBN 0-8047-4385-1 (cloth : alk. paper)
  1. Leadership. 2. Business planning.   3. Organizational effectiveness.
4. Competition, International.   5. Industrial
management. I. Title.
  HD57.7 .E42 2002
  658.4'092—dc21   2002007221

Original Printing 2002

Last figure below indicates year of this printing:
11   10   09

Designed by Rob Ehle.
Typeset by BookMatters in 10/13.5 Sabon.

For Ginger Veirs Ellsworth
(1943–2001)

Whose curiosity and keen eye for beauty enabled me to see what otherwise would have been unseen,
Whose capacity for selfless love and unassuming courage gave me comfort and strength,
Whose passion and joy of life made her an extraordinary teacher of us all.

Contents

Preface

This is a book about corporate purpose—the organization's raison d'être—and its effect upon competitive performance, individuals, and executive leadership. It was written for practicing managers and serious students of management who seek to understand the roots of outstanding competitive performance and the leadership required to achieve it.

The concept of corporate purpose has long been central to the ideas of classic and contemporary management thinkers and scholars of leadership, such as Chester Barnard, Christopher Bartlett, Warren Bennis, James MacGregor Burns, Jim Collins, Peter Drucker, Charles Handy, Jerry Porras, Philip Selznick, and Peter Senge. However, despite its importance, corporate purpose has yet to be examined in depth. This book is designed to fill this void.

While the classic management authors generally agree that the corporation's primary purpose is to produce goods and services, not to maximize profits, most recent authors do not argue one purpose is superior to others. This book does and provides the strategic and human reasons why—supported by examples. The book's range is broad—spanning from purpose's effect on the meaning derived from work, strategy, and the way of managing, to the competitive consequences of different ideologies among global competitors, to the philosophical, historical, and cultural roots and psychological effects of different purposes. This comprehensive perspective is designed to aid managers in preventing myopic thinking regarding the purpose of their corporations.

This book represents a confluence of two streams of ideas emanating from my teaching, research, and work as a corporate executive. In essence, I have been concerned about the issues addressed in this book for thirty years. From my work as a corporate treasurer and then as a general manager of a group of business units, I became increasingly aware of how divergent the worlds of the capital markets and product markets can be, and how readily management-imposed financial policies can constrain competitive strategy. From my work on executive leadership, it became clear that central to outstanding leadership is the manager's responsibility to define the organization's purpose in such a way as to provide direction to strategy, to bring meaning to the work of others, to infuse the organization with value, and consequently to stimulate commitment and action. From my work on capital markets, financial policies, and competitive strategy, it became evident that there is often conflict between the policies and processes that internalize a purpose of maximizing shareholder wealth and the strategic actions required to provide customers with sustained value and to achieve long-term competitive superiority. Furthermore, the globalization of business has brought intensified competition from competitors who play by very different rules. Corporate purposes vary significantly across countries as differences in the institutional structure, culture, and government policies shape the relationship between financial institutions and corporations.

The concerns that have propelled this book have intensified in recent years. Today too many companies give lip service to the customers being their number one priority and employees as being their most valuable asset, yet they pursue a purpose of shareholder wealth maximization that subordinates the interest of customers to those of shareholders and treats employees as expendable means to these financial ends. This organizational schizophrenia results in a purpose focused on the capital market (shareholders), which often conflicts with strategies oriented toward product markets and with employees' values. Consequently, many people experience difficulty finding meaning in their work, and most corporations are failing to realize their potential to make people's lives better—the lives of the people who use their products, work within their boundaries, and invest in their future. For "employees" the deep longings of the human spirit—the desire for a life rich in meaning, passion, creativity, and a sense of belonging—are being left unsatisfied. The result is a hollowness of work.

Fortunately, pathfinding American firms have shown a better way:

harmony and wholeness among a firm's customer-focused purpose, strategy, and the values of individual employees unleash considerable human energy and creativity that significantly enhance performance. Their leaders recognize the moral dimension of purpose and the need for courage to make the choices and set the priorities that create strong institutions, even when these acts run counter to prevailing conventional opinion. This book attempts to capture the essence of the thinking behind this pathbreaking way.

The book's central thesis is that a customer-focused corporate purpose provides the key to outstanding performance and to enhancing the lives of those the company serves and of those who serve it. This will be even truer in the intensely competitive knowledge-based markets of the future. At a time when allegiance to shareholder wealth creation is reaching fad proportions, this book provides compelling strategic, managerial, and moral arguments for moving from a shareholder-focused corporate purpose to one focused on customers.

My over twenty years of experience in teaching at the Harvard Business School and the Peter F. Drucker Graduate School of Management at Claremont Graduate University—particularly teaching executives—have reinforced these concerns. I have witnessed how these issues generate vigorous debate and deeply move people as few other management issues do. Managers resonate strongly with these ideas and conclusions, and they long to find environments in which their work can become more meaningful.

It is my hope that this book will enable readers to lead more effectively through a deepened understanding of why the substantive content of corporate purpose makes such a difference. I hope they come away with a richer appreciation of the reasons alternative formulations of purpose have significantly differing competitive impacts; with an enhanced ability to judge the merits of the arguments underlying each of these different purposes and to appreciate their historical and philosophical roots; and with the ability to constructively challenge the many unquestioned, but erroneous, conventional wisdoms supporting the current prevalent American ideology and to comprehend the often subtle link between valued purposes, meaningful work, motivation, and knowledge creation. Ultimately my hope is that as leaders readers will learn how to develop a sense of purpose within their organization that unleashes human creativity and initiative in the service of a noble cause.

The book is divided into four parts. Part I examines how the substance of an organization's purpose makes a profound difference to a firm's competitive performance (Chapter 1) and to the lives of people in the organization. The reasons are grounded in the meaning individuals derive from work that serves valued ends (Chapter 2) and the powerful effect of purpose on strategy (Chapter 3) and the way of managing (Chapter 4). Corporate purpose's importance rests in the fact that it both expresses the organization's most fundamental value—why it exists—and is the end to which strategy is directed. Furthermore, the meaning people find in serving a purpose that embodies a noble ideal increases their commitment and loyalty and, as the boundaries between the self and the cause blur, enhances knowledge creation. In a world in which the coin of competition is knowledge, this linkage has profound strategic implications.

To better understand the arguments for a purpose of shareholder wealth maximization, Part II critiques the logic of "shareholder value-based management" and the relationship of the firm to the equity markets (Chapter 5). The validity of extending traditional concepts of property rights to share ownership is explored in Chapter 6, concluding that the separation of stock ownership from the responsibility for and managerial control over corporate actions makes traditional property rights arguments inapplicable to the underlying assets of a corporation. The traditional argument for a shareholder-dominated purpose is based on the assumption it furthers individual autonomy. But in today's corporation, individual fulfillment and the realization of the ideals of individualism are profoundly influenced by the firm's purpose, as shown in Chapter 7. But the people whose sense of self are most affected by the corporation are the employees and customers, rather than the shareholders. Therefore, a constructive individualism rooted in a meaningful customer-focused purpose is advocated—one that enhances self-fulfillment and the creativity and initiative that are the wellsprings of innovation. By challenging many of the conventional wisdoms surrounding the shareholder wealth maximization ideology, the book aids readers in developing their own well-grounded philosophy.

Part III examines the implications of corporate purpose in a global economy, where companies must compete with firms with fundamentally different views of purpose that reflect distinct national histories and philosophical ideas. Chapter 8 explains the realities of U.S. international competitiveness, while Chapter 9 explores the cultural, historical, and philosophical roots of the ideologies that shape the purposes of companies in Germany, Japan, Korea, and other Asian countries. Globalization vastly expanded the playing field, creating a Darwinian struggle for dominance among free-market ideologies. This section helps the reader understand the essence of this struggle and the importance in a global arena of the ability of purpose to retain its significance and motivational power across national boundaries (which a shareholder-focused purpose fails to do).

Part IV explores the implications of corporate purpose for leaders, arguing in Chapter 10 that infusing an organization with a worthy purpose is an essential responsibility of leadership—an act that is at once strategic and moral. In today's environment, it is often an act of courage. As the organization's ultimate end value, corporate purpose provides the foundation for the shared values that define organizational character, raise moral aspirations, and enhance performance.

In addressing these issues, ideas are integrated from a wide range of thought: from strategy, management, and executive leadership to history, cultural anthropology, philosophy, theology, and psychology. These ideas are woven together with examples from leading companies to demonstrate the superior value of a customer-focused purpose.

Acknowledgments

On such a long journey as the one that has led to this book, I owe great debts to the many people who helped me develop and refine my understanding of corporate purpose. I owe a special debt to the students in my classes, whose thought-provoking insights, probing questions, examples from their own experience, and excitement in discussing these issues not only improved the ideas in the book but also strengthened my motivation and commitment to write it.

I benefited greatly from the insights and constructive challenges to my thinking provided by my colleagues at the Peter F. Drucker Graduate School of Management at Claremont Graduate University who read early versions of the manuscript. Peter Drucker not only provided very helpful and practical comments on the manuscript but also maintained a constant interest in my work and gave me important encouragement at critical junctures along the way. I am particularly grateful to colleagues with whom I have cotaught courses on subjects related to the ideas in this book: Mihaly Csikszentmihalyi (with whom I have taught "Leadership and the Making of Meaning"), Vijay Sathe ("The Strategy Course"), and Richard Smith ("Strategy and Finance"). I learned much from each of them. My relationship with Mihaly

Csikszentmihalyi proved particularly fruitful in expanding my thinking regarding the psychological roots of purpose and meaning. Vijay Sathe's continuing interest from the inception of this work, his constant encouragement, and his detailed comments on the original manuscript proved invaluable. The keen and creative mind of Jean Lipman-Blumen, who shares with me the directorship of the Institute for Advanced Studies in Leadership, has never failed to stimulate my thinking; her willingness to share a disproportionate share of the burden of running the institute during "crunch times" greatly aided my ability to sustain my work on the manuscript.

I am indebted to others who read and provided discerning comments on the manuscript: Joseph Badaracco Jr., Christopher Bartlett, Warren Bennis, David Jemison, Harold Leavitt, George Lodge, Nicola Sabin, and Jerry Porras. Their constructive observations and suggestions, as well as their encouragement, helped me to refine my thinking and clarify my presentation in many critical areas. In addition, my many hours of discussing these ideas with Christopher Bartlett, who has been on an intellectual journey similar to mine, proved both stimulating and reassuring in ways that solidified my resolve and confidence in my work. George Lodge's work on ideology and his willingness to help deepen my understanding of the ideological foundations of different formulations of corporate purpose contributed to shaping important segments of this work.

I also am grateful to my students at Claremont who worked directly on this research: to Stephen R. Moffett, who as part of his senior thesis did the initial work in quantifying the relationship between purpose and performance; to Shankar Basu, whose doctoral dissertation shed light on the effect of purpose on objectives and strategic decisions at Toyota Motor Corporation; to my research assistants Krishnaswami Raman, Tuong Tran, Ravi Mathai, and Dosik Kim, who helped develop the data that enlightened the inquiry. I am also appreciative of early financial support of this project provided by Deloitte & Touche as a Deloitte & Touche Research Fellow.

Finally, my greatest debt is to my wife, Ginger. I will be forever grateful for her steadfast encouragement, abiding love, and willingness to endure considerable sacrifice to enable me to pursue my passion for my work. The spirit and clarity of purpose with which she approached her teaching are emblematic of the best of the ideas in this book. I deeply regret that she did not see the final fruit of this work in which she played such a central role. Without her support, it would have never become a reality.

Introduction: The New Realities of Corporate Purpose

Perfection of means and confusion of ends seem to characterize our age.
—*Albert Einstein*[1]

This is a book about the stranglehold an outdated—but, ironically, an increasingly accepted—ideology has on business performance; about the integral link between corporate purpose, competitive advantage, and work that brings meaning and enrichment to lives; and ultimately about the responsibilities of executive leadership to define noble ends for collective efforts. It explores a central truth underlying the creation of great companies capable of exceptional and sustained achievement. The leaders of these companies have long known that providing value to customers—not the maximization of shareholder wealth—is fundamentally why their organizations exist and that this purpose is key to their companies' outstanding performance. This linkage between customer-focused purposes and performance will be even truer in the intensely competitive, knowledge-based global markets of the future.

We live in a new age. Economic and social forces are converging in ways never before experienced by humankind. Throughout the world, the tumultuous pace of change is shaking the very foundation of enterprises. The forces of change are many and each challenges the traditional view of the fundamental purpose of American corporations. The globalization of markets has brought companies with fundamentally different corporate purposes into direct, daily competition. The creation and management of knowledge have become the central sources of competitive advantage, displacing past advantages of capital and labor costs. In America, fueled by concerns over ineffective corporate governance, hostile takeovers, and often-ruthless corporate downsizing, an active debate persists over whom corporations primarily exist to serve. These forces have contributed to a sense among employees that they are expendable parts in a corporate machine. Many feel they have become means to ends they do not value. The result has been an alarming erosion of loyalty among the key source of competitive advantage—the company's people. Consequently, at work many people have turned their focus inward, away from the common good to their own narrow self-interest. Simultaneously, American capital-market institutions are scrambling to exert greater influence over corporate management to assure the shareholders' primacy among the companies' competing constituent interests.

Amid this tumult, the traditional sources of senior management's influence—authority and formal management systems—have lost much of their ability to motivate, direct, and control behavior in organizations. In their stead, twenty-first-century leaders will increasingly need to rely on the power of a clear mission, an understood strategy, and shared values to guide decisions and motivate people to achieve outstanding results. Purpose takes on much of its importance precisely because each of these sources of influence requires—indeed is founded upon—a clear concept of purpose. Conversely, leadership's failure to define a clear purpose—or the propagation of a purpose with little value to people within the company, such as the maximization of shareholder wealth—explains much of the tension, conflict, and ambivalence that inflict American companies today.

These realities reflect an age of paradox. Each of the following fundamental yet provocative contradictions is rooted in corporate purpose and will be addressed in the pages that follow:

- Long-term shareholders are *not* best served when a company puts the shareholders' interests above all others. Instead, they benefit most when customers are made the primary reason for the firm's existence and employees are given priority ahead of shareholders.
- Similarly, employees' interests are *not* best served when the corporation's purpose places top priority on their interests. Instead, the highest level of individual development and the greatest happiness are derived from serving ends beyond the self—ends that employees value, that enable them to feel they are "making a difference," and consequently that bring increased meaning to their lives through work.

- The value a company creates for society is not synonymous with its shareholder wealth creation. Most critical for society is the firm's sustained *total* value-generating ability, not the value created for shareholders alone, but also for customers, employees, and communities.

- Maximizing discounted net present value returns on investment is not the same as—and can conflict with—achieving greater competitiveness. Therefore, profits are best treated as a means to competitive advantage, not an end in themselves.

- At a time when the benefits of capital-market discipline are widely touted, the reality is that for most firms the discipline administered by the competitive product market is swifter, surer, more direct, more in harmony with the needs of competitiveness, and therefore more constructive and effective. By paying primary attention to capital market pressures, managers can undermine their company's ability to respond to the more critical competitive pressures emanating from the product market.

- A leader's high moral standards of behavior do not—as is commonly thought—constrain the pragmatic actions necessary to secure outstanding competitive performance. To the contrary, they enhance long-term competitiveness by creating an environment that raises the organization's members to their better selves, thereby enhancing commitment, innovation, and cohesiveness.

This book is dedicated in part to a greater understanding of the implications these paradoxes have for corporate leadership. How leaders respond to the challenges of this new age will profoundly influence people's lives and the competitive performance of organizations.

Although there are persuasive moral and social arguments for moving away from a shareholder-focused corporate purpose, the pragmatic strategic benefits of replacing this purpose with a customer-centered purpose alone are compelling. The strategies of customer-focused companies usually result in a level of competitiveness that significantly outstrips equally capable shareholder-focused rivals. Within the firm, the purpose of maximizing shareholder wealth has failed to energize employees—those individuals whose knowledge and effort create the competitive advantages of today and the future. For many, it has also failed to bring meaning to their work lives. Consequently, there is a bankruptcy of spirit in many American companies. The remedy begins with a purpose that defines ends that people find meaningful and worthy of their commitment.

The pragmatic economic ends of competitive advantage and enhanced wealth creating capacity are inextricably linked to the moral quality of the firm's purpose in two fundamental ways. First, wealth creation, properly defined, is a moral good that should be maximized. But corporations create value for many more people than shareholders alone. Value is received by customers in the form of higher quality and more functional and lower-priced products and services; by employees through their compensation and more secure and meaningful jobs in which they can grow, develop, and find greater personal meaning for their lives; and by communities through the consequences of the firm's economic activities. Measures of corporate wealth creation need to incorporate the impact on all of these constituents.

Second, the competitive consequences of corporate purpose flow in part from the meaning organizational members find in their work and much of this power comes from the moral dimensions of purpose. The knowledge, cooperation, commitment, and hard work of individuals are the stuff from which competitive advantage is formed. When the corporate purpose stands for a cause in which its members believe, it activates their higher motivations and deeper commitment. The result is often heroic contributions to the firm's competitive success.

Understanding the Critical Role of Corporate Purpose

Corporate purpose sits at the confluence of strategy and values. It expresses the company's fundamental value—the raison d'être or overriding reason for existing. It is the end to which strategy is directed. Without a clear purpose that reinforces the organization's other espoused values and gives meaning and direction to strategy, the firm will eventually wither under competitive pressure from companies with purposes that provide greater coherence.

The Role of Corporate Purpose

In turbulent times such as these, corporate purpose can be both a source of stability and an impetus to proactive change. In fact, Lew Platt, former chairman and CEO of Hewlett-Packard, considers instilling an appropriate purpose into the organization to be "the real challenge before every business leader today." At the heart of this challenge is finding "a way to change quickly enough to remain competitive while still giving your people enough continuity that they feel comfortable or, if not comfortable, that at least they're not terrified all the time."[2] A clearly articulated and properly formulated purpose—one that members of the organization understand and value—provides continuity and constancy while placing the need to adapt to changing customer needs at the heart of the company's shared values. Properly defined, corporate purpose should rarely, if ever, change. This permanence of ends provides continuity amid strategic change. Since the purpose is never completely realized, it acts as a powerful antidote to complacency, stimulating the need to change. It can furnish the reason change is necessary; when the purpose is valued by members of the organization, it can do so in ways that are meaningful to those who must implement the change, thus evoking their commitment. However, a vague purpose—or one not valued by the company's people—loses these powers to provide organizational cohesion during times of change.

Corporate purpose defines the contribution management seeks to make to its various constituents—the corporation's owners, employees, and customers and the communities in which the company does business. Corporate purpose specifies a firm's ultimate priority among its responsibilities, be that priority the maximization of shareholder wealth, satisfying customer needs, providing for the employees' welfare, or serving the national or community interest. In this sense corporate purpose is irreducible except for spiritual reasons for the existence of organized human endeavors.

Needless to say, the full power of corporate purpose is rendered when it is aligned with the essential nature of man's being. Purpose can bring an uplifting moral quality to a company's mission. In doing so, it appeals to the organizational members' higher instincts, unifying their personal aspirations and their work and unleashing greater initiative and commitment in service of corporate ends.

By defining the basic end values for which a company stands—the values that bind the members of a company together—corporate purpose is at the core of what Richard Pascale and Anthony Athos call the "superordinate goals" that define "the overarching purposes to which an organization and its members dedicate themselves." These "spiritual or significant meanings and shared values" provide "the guiding concepts" that unite people within an organization in a common cause.[3]

What Should the Purpose Be?

To provide these benefits, not any formulation of purpose will do. Its substance matters critically.

Contrary to widely held belief, the *ultimate* reason we create businesses is not to make a profit. Profit is a necessary factor for producing product and services and for creating wealth—a means not an end in itself. Nor is the ultimate purpose to make a product or service. One must ask, "Why make a profit or provide a particular product or service? Does it make any difference to corporate performance whether the answer is creating wealth for shareholders, satisfying the needs of customers, providing people with satisfying and fulfilling work, or serving society or the nation?" This book's thesis is that the answer makes a profound difference—a difference to corporate performance, to human satisfaction, and to the wealth of society.

To be more effective than alternative formulations of purposes, the chosen corporate purpose should do the following:

- Provide the greatest focus on achieving competitive advantage
- Lay the best foundation for achieving harmony among the purpose, strategy, goals, and shared values
- Motivate managers to create the maximum level of total value—not just value for one particular constituent
- Heighten the motivation of members of the organization, subordinating narrow self-interest to corporate ends and enhancing the firm's ability to create knowledge
- Be seen by employees around the globe as a worthy and meaningful end to serve, and serving this end, potentially raise employees' moral aspirations
- Promise to enhance the legitimacy of the corporation's actions in society

Only a purpose of serving customers' interests, followed closely by attending to the needs of employees, satisfies each of these criteria.

A customer-focused purpose is aligned with both the strategic needs of the competitive product market and the employees' welfare. It provides the foundation for strategies and objectives directed toward winning in global markets and the quality of ends that can rekindle people's commitment to their work. An ultimate corporate purpose of maximizing shareholder wealth does none of this as well as does a customer focus.

The choice of this raison d'être and its reflection in action deeply influence competitive strategy. The selection of the customers' needs as the dominant priority vitally affects the outcome of critical, character-defining corporate decisions that shape strategies, commit resources, and build core competencies. In a world of global competition among firms with differing views of purpose, this sense of ultimate priority is of critical importance to competitive success.

The most common purpose of American companies—to maximize shareholder wealth—is threatened with competitive obsolescence by a purpose that places the highest priority on the long-run health of the enterprise and on serving the needs of customers, and in this way best serving society. This is not a new idea. Leading management thinkers have long recognized the importance of purpose. Classic management scholars, such as Chester Barnard, Peter Drucker, Philip Selznick, and Kenneth Andrews, never lost sight of the centrality of purpose. For them, purpose is at the core of effective management. It has both a moral and a pragmatic business dimension. In the 1970s Peter Drucker observed that a company's purpose "must lie outside the business itself. In fact, it must lie in society since business enterprise is an organ of society. There is only one valid definition of business purpose: *to create a customer.*"[4] In other words, corporations fundamentally exist to produce goods and services that serve the needs of present and future customers better than competitors do. Drucker considers purpose the starting point in understanding what a business is. He sees corporate purpose as critical to successful performance, concluding, "That business purpose and business mission are so rarely given adequate thought is perhaps the most important cause of business frustration and failure."[5]

Chester Barnard was one of the first management thinkers to articulate a comprehensive view of the importance of purpose to effective management. To him the formulation of purpose is one of three essential executive functions—and critical to the other two (providing a system of communication and securing the efforts essential to the organization's success). The purpose of any organization, he believed, is service to its customers. By providing the "objective of cooperation," this purpose becomes "the coordinating and unifying principle" in organizations, guiding individual actions.[6] When people believe in the cause defined by the purpose and believe in its feasibility, purpose becomes a powerful stimulus to individual willingness to cooperate and contribute effort to the organization. To Barnard, "An objective purpose that can serve as the basis for a cooperative system is one that is *believed* by the contributors (or potential contributors) to it to be the determined purpose of the organization. The inculcation of belief in the real existence of a common purpose is an essential executive function."[7] Common purpose gives meaning to the environment, is a powerful force for coherence among activities throughout the organization, and motivates individuals to forgo immediate self-gratification to further the aims of the organization. It is essential to effective and efficient corporate performance.

Philip Selznick, in his pathbreaking work on leadership, concluded that defining institutional purpose, "building purpose into the social structure of the enterprise," and consequently "transforming a neutral body of men into a committed polity" are central tasks of leadership.[8] The "institutional embodiment of purpose" shapes "the 'character' of the organization" by "joining immediate goals to ultimate values."[9] To him, there is "no sharp division between the tasks of defining mission and embodying purposes. Each entails a self-assessment, an appreciation of internal pressures and external demands. This self-knowledge leads to the formulation of truly guiding aims and methods."[10] When organizational purpose reflects the values of individual members, the organization becomes "infused with value." It becomes valued for itself and the ends it represents. Consequently, the individual's daily activity becomes filled with meaning and purpose. The result is deep commitment and loyalty and a readiness to defend the organization because of the values it embodies.

Purpose clarifies which decisions are critical and informs how these decisions should be made. Critical decisions, in Selznick's view, are those that define the character of the organization, its values, and the mission to which it is committed. The two purposes of serving customers and maximizing shareholder wealth embody different values and therefore mold different organizational character. Because of its ambiguous nature, a purpose calling for the "balancing constituents' interests" gives little form to organizational character.

Kenneth Andrews (who was the spokesman for a larger group of individuals concerned with general management and strategy at the Harvard Business School in the 1960s and 1970s) links corporate purpose to the moral aspirations of the members of the organization. He concludes that purpose should define the "human needs the organization would find satisfaction in serving."[11] For Andrews, as for Drucker, corporate purpose does not reside in maximizing shareholder wealth.

Similarly, W. Edwards Deming, in his seminal work on quality, followed the simple principles of putting the customers' needs first and placing the product before profits. For Deming, quality comes from people who believe in the corporate ends and are entrusted to work positively for the common good.

Common themes run through the reflections of these leading management thinkers. To be effective and to be a stimulus to competitive behavior, the members of the organization must believe the corporate purpose; it must be built into the social structure of the enterprise; and it must be capable of transforming a "neutral body" of people into a committed group and to direct their actions. To achieve these objectives, the corporate purpose must be clear, consistently implemented, and constantly reinforced. It must be one in which people have faith and see value—as the organization's ultimate value, it must possess a quality capable of eliciting belief and defining the organization's character and direction.

Yet even though the central importance of corporate purpose has long been recognized, it receives inadequate attention in practice and management research. What is taught in most, if not all, American business schools represents indoctrination into an unquestioned ideology of maximizing the shareholders' wealth. Although the central role of purpose is often acknowledged in courses on strategic management, the focus quickly digresses to teaching about economic goals, competitive strategies, and rubrics for maximizing the return on investment with little attention to the purposes served. However, the intensity and nature of the new competitive forces are of necessity rekindling attention to corporate purpose. Recent studies of companies with outstanding performance records—studies by leading thinkers such as Christopher Bartlett, Sumatra Ghoshal, Charles Handy, James Collins, and Jerry Porras— have placed purpose back at the center of management thought.

Purpose and the New Realities of Competition

The global currents of change buffeting corporations are enhancing corporate purpose's importance to competitive success. The following five trends are particularly powerful:

1. The coin of competitive advantage is rapidly evolving to knowledge.
2. Loyalty and commitment are increasingly essential to knowledge-based competitive advantage.
3. The sources of managerial influence are changing.
4. Firms with different concepts of corporate purpose are competing head to head.
5. Returns on investment are under competitive pressure.

Each one of these trends is changing the face of competition and collectively will determine competitive advantage in the twenty-first century. Corporate purpose directly affects an organization's ability to respond constructively to each of these currents.

The Coin of Competitive Advantage Is Rapidly Evolving to Knowledge

The terms of competition are dramatically shifting. Technological advancements have caused the labor-cost advantages of the past to give way to capital- and knowledge-based advantages. Even in the low-wage developing world, rising living standards and the substitution of capital for labor have eroded labor-cost advantages. As capital advantages are transformed into highly automated plants filled with complex computerized equipment that replaces labor, not only do labor-cost advantages diminish, but also the knowledge possessed by the fewer remaining workers becomes more important. Even in industries in which capital has not significantly replaced labor, global companies can rapidly move their manufacturing facilities to countries with low labor costs. The substitution of capital for labor and the rapid access to low labor costs mean that competitive advantages based on lower labor costs are fleeting. More important, as access to capital has become more and more equal throughout the developed world, intellectual capital has supplanted financial capital in competitive importance. Capital retains its competitive importance more from management's willingness to invest than from the availability of capital. Capital availability itself is unlikely to provide sustainable advantages in today's world.

Labor is an indigenous, tangible resource, which at any point of time is pretty much a given. Capital, on the other hand, although tangible, is not indigenous. The decision to procure and commit capital is the result of human decisions influenced by cultural beliefs, institutional relationships, and management's values, beliefs, and priorities. Consequently, the capital advantages go not just to companies from countries with a lower cost of capital; even more important, those firms willing and able to invest capital efficiently—often at lower returns than those of their competitors—capture the advantages. Purpose affects the willingness to invest. A company driven to maximize shareholder wealth will carefully restrict investments to those with returns above the cost of capital. However, companies with purposes to serve customers, to serve the national interest and/or employees (such as many European and Asian companies), or to serve society in general will be motivated to make investments to promote growth with less emphasis on the level of the financial returns from these investments. When they do so, they often capture the investment initiative from their shareholder-focused competitors, with significant competitive consequences.

This is exactly what happened in the semiconductor industry in the 1980s and early 1990s, as Japanese and then Korean manufacturers outinvested U.S. producers. In 1975 all of the world's leading merchant producers of integrated circuits were American. However, within a decade, Japan's share of the world semiconductor market passed that of the United States. The rapid Japanese market share increase in semiconductors came largely at the expense of U.S. manufacturers. Initially, American firms attributed the Japanese gains to unreasonable pricing (dumping charges were filed) and to their investment in projects offering little prospect of a reasonable return. Slowly, American producers became aware that Japan enjoyed another critical advantage—a knowledge-based advantage. Japanese superiority in manufacturing processes, which generated substantially fewer defective chips, could not be replicated by investment alone. Whereas American firms could quickly adapt to building world class "fabs," gaining comparable skill in the actual manufacturing processes took years. Consequently, by 1989 only one American company remained among the world's top ten producers. By 1994, as U.S. firms gained greater process skills, three more American companies had climbed back into the top ten, and five of the top ten firms were Japanese and one was Korean. The U.S. semiconductor market share, aided by American dominance in high-value microprocessors, exceeded Japan's for the first time since 1985. By the mid-1990s, Korean firms, led by Samsung, had gained world leadership in memory chips, after a prodigious investment campaign.

Today, knowledge provides the primary source of sustainable advantage. Competitors can quickly replicate capital-based advantages. Capital migrates readily across national boundaries and from firm to firm. Seeking low labor costs, global companies can choose to site or source production anywhere in the world, tapping the physical dexterity, effort, and endurance of the world's best workers. Only knowledge-creation abilities have difficulty transferring across corporate boundaries.

Most service and manufacturing businesses are essentially knowledge-based businesses. In all businesses, the activities requiring greater levels of knowledge to stay competitive are many and varied: the plant worker's skill in operating numerically controlled machinery and in originating cost-saving and quality-enhancing ideas; the salesperson's know-how in creatively identifying, communicating, and serving customer needs; the researcher's expertise in developing new products and processes; and the manager's ability to cope with ambiguity and uncertainty in directing, coordinating, and motivating fellow workers to achieve excellence. The force that drives costs lower and increases the functionality and quality of the products and services is the application of the knowledge of the firm's members at all organizational levels. In manufacturing and service businesses alike, the knowledge advantages go to those with the most highly skilled, committed, and effectively coordinated people.

This shift in competitive advantage raises issues of how best to gain and trap knowledge within a firm. Not all forms of knowledge provide equal competitive advantages. Knowledge gained by individual experience and training is often skill oriented. These skills and the people who possess them can migrate rather quickly in response to economic incentives. Knowledge that provides the most sustained source of competitive advantage does not migrate easily to other companies. It is either protected by government action, such as patents, or infused in the organization's social structure and possessed collectively by many of its members, such as proprietary production processes. Knowledge gained from collective experience—from working together in groups—becomes institutionalized within the group and transfers slowly and with difficulty. No one person knows what the group as a whole knows; often much of the uniqueness of this institutionalized know-how concerns the process by which the group learns and creates new knowledge. This "embedded knowledge" cannot be obtained through reverse engineering, pirating of employees, consultants, or books.[12] As Joseph Badaracco has shown, it can be developed only over long periods of time, and this learning takes place within numerous individuals and is woven into the social fabric of the organization.

The future belongs to those with the greatest ability and willingness to deploy capital, to create and leverage knowledge, and to realize the latent potential of their employees. The nature of a corporation's purpose directly influences the firm's motivation to develop these abilities.

Loyalty and Commitment Are Essential
to Knowledge-Based Competitive Advantage

The increasing importance of knowledge to competitive performance requires the company to have the ability both to attract talented people with new ideas and to maintain continuity in relationships among individuals within the organization. It also demands that individuals give more of them-selves—their intellectual skills as well as physical effort and a willingness to constantly improve their skills through education and training. Ironically, just as the commitment, initiative, and loyalty of employees are increasing in competitive importance, America is experiencing a serious weakening of the traditional bonds of loyalty and commitment between employees and their companies.

For many Americans, work no longer provides the meaning to their lives it once did. In many ways this is a consequence of management's reac-tions to intense capital-market pressures, which have caused shareholder interests to be placed ahead of those of customers and employees. Hostile takeovers, senseless mergers, corporate downsizing, and an intensified emphasis on the creation of shareholder wealth as the aim of work (partic-ularly as manifested in a preoccupation with near-term earnings) have caused many people to feel betrayed by the organizations to which they have dedi-cated significant portions of their lives. In companies where this has hap-pened, the demoralized employees clearly do not share knowledge or learn as readily as the committed membership of otherwise equal competitors. Cor-porate purpose has turned hollow and meaningless, giving rise to cynicism regarding senior management's motivations and abilities and to estrangement from work. In addition, these companies risk their potential competitive advantage walking out the door, siphoning off valuable knowledge and breaking up knowledge-creating groups.

Corporate purpose can play a critical role in attracting high-caliber people and in reinvigorating feelings of loyalty. Purpose imbued with a quality that organizational members find worthwhile and meaningful can command loyalty and commitment—the company embodies ends that are personally valued and deserve promotion and defense. Such a purpose can even help justify necessary corporate actions—such as layoffs—that could otherwise tear at the fabric of loyalty.

The Sources of Managerial Influence Are Changing

The dizzying pace of change, rapid technological innovation, the increasing complexity of doing business, and the rising intensity of competition require a significant rethinking of traditional ways of managing. The past heavy reliance on authority of position and on professional management systems is no longer adequate to guide decentralized decision making and to motivate people. These techniques of professional management must give way to an increasing emphasis on the alignment of corporate purpose, mission, and shared values. When purpose imbues mission and values with a quality and moral tone, they become sources of powerful motivation, direction, and organizational coherence.

Firms with Different Concepts of Corporate Purpose Are Competing Head to Head

The increasing homogeneity of markets throughout the world and the rapid spread of technology have created truly global industries. Daily, competitors from different cultures collide with one another in the marketplace. No longer do American companies have unquestioned dominance over world trade, dictating the rules by which worldwide competition takes place. Nor do they continue to enjoy the luxury of competing almost exclusively with other American companies—companies guided by essentially similar views of how to compete and sharing the same shareholder-focused view of corporate purpose.

Not only has the playing field been vastly expanded, but today's competitors also play by a variety of rules, including how the game is scored. These divergent ideas about how to win in today's markets often result from domestic differences in ingrained beliefs and values and the structure of the institutional relationships among government, business, and financial institutions. In part this reflects varying beliefs about what the ultimate purpose of corporate activity is.

These differences significantly affect the terms of competition, and thus corporate performance, as firms with divergent concepts of their ultimate ends battle over the same markets. For example, if a company's purpose is to maximize shareholders' wealth, it will most often seek to maximize returns on investment to serve this aim. This practice can necessitate the curtailment of product development or market penetration initiatives that promise long-term competitive benefits but generate inadequate discounted rates of return on investment today. In essence, the needs of the product market are subordinated to the needs of the capital market. However, if the purpose is to serve the needs of customers, employees, or the national interest (as is the case for many international competitors), then reinvestment in R&D, cost-reduction projects, or more efficient distribution beyond the point of optimal returns (as measured by the capital markets in terms of discounted present value *today*) might be required. In this case, the reward will be improved market share and strengthened core competencies, but not necessarily increased returns. Of course, profits remain critically important, not as an end, but rather as means to serving the customer and as a measure of the firm's efficiency and effectiveness in doing so.

One of the great competitive strengths derived from a customer-focused purpose is the dominant focus it places on the product markets. This purpose brings a harmony and coherence to strategies, goals, and values throughout the organization. Outstanding leaders use this laserlike focus to derive competitive benefits by developing capabilities, fostering commitment and initiative, and deploying resources in ways not possible when strategies and operational goals must be rationalized with a capital-market purpose.

These different corporate purposes reflect different views of a corporation's role in a free-market economy. With the triumph of capitalism over socialism, the focus of the debate has shifted to which of the competing forms of capitalism will emerge victorious in the future. For reasons of economic logic and human motivation, capitalist societies that direct their enterprises' primary attention to the product market rather than the capital market will be the victors. Companies focused principally on shareholders, rather than customers and competitors, will be at an increasing competitive disadvantage in the future.

Returns on Investment Are Under Competitive Pressure

Coinciding with the development of this new game is a downward pressure on return on investment caused by a global influx of capital investments—many of them producing returns American managers would consider far below their standards. In the global fight for increased market share, the continued deployment of more capital at lower returns will accelerate the shift to knowledge- and capital-based competitive advantages. This will create an acute competitive dilemma for firms espousing a purpose of maximizing shareholder wealth—how to achieve high returns in a declining-return environment populated with competitors willing to make competitiveness-enhancing investments at returns that erode near-term shareholder wealth.

These pressures have already begun. Since World War II the United States has faced three waves of attack from foreign competitors. First came the Europeans led by West Germany. Next came Japan. Then came the third wave—the Asian Tigers consisting of Korea, Taiwan, Hong Kong, Singapore, and Malaysia. On the horizon is the threat of a fourth wave that has the potential to swamp the three preceding ones—China. In 2000 the five Asian Tigers, if combined, represented the United States' largest trading partner in goods outside of NAFTA ($233 billion of trade); Japan was second at $212 billion, and China was third at $116 billion. Also in 2000, the U.S. trade deficit with China reached $83.8 billion, surpassing Japan to become America's largest deficit trading partner.

China poses a particularly vexing competitive challenge. The combination of exceptionally low wages and a high propensity for capital investment produces an economy with exceptionally fast export growth. During the 1990s, Chinese exports grew at a rate of 14 percent per year.[13] Because of the enormous population, for the foreseeable future China has a nearly perfectly elastic labor market with an essentially unlimited supply of people willing to work for little more than three dollars per day. This alone gives Chinese goods a considerable advantage over those produced in developed countries in the East and the West. In addition, China has invested at a dizzying pace. In the late 1990s, its manufacturing capacity was estimated to be nearly double its actual production.[14] This overcapacity resulted in a flood of low-priced Chinese goods on the world market ($184 billion worth in 1998), forcing the prices down in competing countries. Not only has this reduced inflationary pressure worldwide, but also for many of China's closest competitors, such as Thailand, Indonesia, Korea, the Philippines, and Malaysia, it has necessitated a devaluation of their currencies and helped trigger the "Asia Crisis" of the late 1990s.

Except for China, these waves of foreign competition are all made up of basically capitalist countries. Yet when compared to the United States, each of these countries has fundamentally different cultures, financing conventions, and corporate relationships with their sources of capital and with the government. For example, Confucian thought heavily influences each of these Asian countries. Accordingly, many of their companies emphasize the importance of loyalty and the harmony of individuals and institutions with the needs of the broader society. A sense of duty to family and society is often deeply rooted in the corporate psyche. The consequence of these differences is divergent views of corporate purpose. In practice these differences result in varying beliefs that define the relationships of the firm to society, elicit differing intensities of commitment to the organization's ends, and determine the level of return on invested capital that is deemed necessary and appropriate. Companies with a demonstrated willingness to invest capital at lower returns than those deemed acceptable by U.S. firms have dominated each of these waves of competition. In fact, for many of these companies, return on investment measures have little influence on investment decisions.

The result of these successive waves is twofold. First, more capital is entering the world marketplace, as the major Asian countries save and invest at a prodigious pace. Second, different corporate objectives across countries, which are facilitated by, and in many cases driven by, contrasting views of the purpose of corporations, have led to an increasing number of strong competitors that place growth and market share goals ahead of returns. In our increasingly global society, when highly competent and efficient firms are willing to invest large amounts of capital at returns that are low by American standards, the simple law of supply and demand means that returns will be under downward pressure throughout the world. In this environment, a competitor whose purpose shackles its willingness to invest and its ability to motivate employees will be at a severe disadvantage.

This is precisely what is happening. Spurred on by national governments, further motivated by the threatened entry of China into key industries, and facilitated by a lesser importance placed on return on investment, companies in many of these countries have captured international market share from American manufacturers by pursuing "substandard" investments. If this trend continues—and there is little to indicate that it will not, with China (and eventually possibly Eastern Europe, Russia, India, Latin America, and others) looming in the background—then the return on manufacturing investments will continue to experience downward pressure.

These declining returns have been accompanied by increasing pressure on American managers from U.S. capital-market institutions. The pressure is for financial performance—usually near-term performance. But in many cases (similar to the past experience in automobiles, machine tools, consumer electronics, and memory chips) higher returns today can only be bought with the declining investment and market shares that erode tomorrow's competitiveness and returns because of decaying product differentiation and waning scale and scope economies.

The strongest manifestation of this capital-market pressure is encompassed in what is euphemistically called "the battle for corporate control." This term in itself indicates the fundamental importance of the stakes. The hostile takeover is the most visible form of this "battle." But it is also being played out more subtly in shareholder activism, particularly in the efforts of some large public-sector pension funds to have a greater influence over management decisions.

Purpose and Competitive Change

Although often unrecognized, a common element influences the effect each of these five forces has on the competitiveness of individual corporations. It is corporate purpose. The choice of purpose deeply affects a company's response to these competitive forces and determines the degree strategies and goals diverge from those of rivals driven by different purposes. The increasing significance of both capital and knowledge to competitiveness highlights the importance of corporate purpose. Purpose will determine whether and to what degree returns on capital will be subordinated to actions designed to better serve customers and consequently to achieve greater competitiveness. Furthermore, purpose can be a stimulus to commitment and a source of motivation for employees, causing them to work harder and smarter and more creatively. Since employees possess the knowledge-based core competence of most firms, the competitive benefits are obvious. A corporate purpose that embodies ends that employees consider worthwhile—a

purpose that infuses an organization with the belief that the aim of its product or service (and thus of the employees' work) is to satisfy valued human
needs—has the power to bring greater meaning to employees' work and thus
to their lives. It is a simple fact that few people find personal meaning in
enhancing the wealth of usually remote, faceless, ever-changing shareholders.
However, other ends, such as directly serving human needs—particularly the
needs of customers and fellow employees—can be related tangibly to individual effort at all organizational levels.

The Future Purpose of American Corporations

Despite the vast economic and social changes of the last quarter century, most Americans continue to view the marketplace, and our corporations' role in it, in much the same way as we did in the 1950s and 1960s. But
the world has fundamentally changed, and so must our response to it.

We stand at a moment in history poised to make a fundamental shift
in our thinking about corporate purpose. The "constellation of beliefs, values and techniques" shared by managers and the public at large is in a state
of change.[15] Our traditional explanations of strategy and competitive behavior are proving inadequate. Discontent and dissatisfaction with the current
state of affairs is widespread. Opinions and actions in response to this state
are becoming polarized. This discontent and polarization, coupled with the
evolving competitive forces, provide the ferment for change. At the core of
the changing paradigm is a new emerging purpose for American companies.

Although global competitive pressures have intensified the need for a
changing view of corporate purpose in American companies, the reality is
that a customer-focused purpose also leads to outstanding performance for
companies facing primarily domestic competition. As we shall see in subsequent chapters, such a purpose provides (1) the product-market focus essential to the formulation of more competitive strategies; (2) a constellation of
goals reflecting key measures of marketplace performance that differ significantly from the capital-market–focused goals flowing from a purpose of
maximizing shareholder wealth; (3) an increased willingness to deploy capital; and (4) ends that bring greater meaning to the work of organizational
members, that act to merge their narrowly defined self-interests with corporate ends, and that enhance their abilities to create knowledge. It also
enables leaders to manage by granting greater autonomy to subunits and with

less restrictive management control systems. People can more readily be entrusted to do what they believe is right when a clear shared purpose and the strategy, goals, and policies into which the purpose is translated guide them. The result is the unleashing of human creativity and initiative—and the new knowledge that these forces are capable of developing—in the service of common purpose.

Failure to adapt to these realities of tomorrow's competition will extract heavy penalties. Those enterprises with leaders who recognize and act in anticipation of these changes will achieve a competitive edge over those that do not. History has shown that those companies that anticipated major social change at the beginning of the significant social movements of our day—be they civil rights, women's rights, environmental protection, or product safety—have generally fared much better than those who have been reluctantly dragged into accepting the legitimacy of these movements. The same will be true for the purposes driving competitors in the global marketplace of tomorrow. The victors will be those companies that proactively clearly define and consistently reinforce an ultimate purpose that promotes more competitive strategies and embodies values their members share.

A number of outstanding American companies have shown the way. Among their number are Hewlett-Packard, Johnson & Johnson, and Wal-Mart. Each of these industry leaders has a corporate purpose that focuses on serving customers' needs coupled with a commitment to create an environment of personal growth and development for the people who make up the company. These ends combine to create highly effective organizations with outstanding long-term competitive and financial performance.

Conclusion

The formulation and defense of corporate purpose is a central function of leadership. The "visible hand" of management[16] must harmonize the self-interests of employees, customers, and society so that they reinforce one another. Under a shareholder-focused purpose, all too often these interests conflict, dissipating energy into the friction of adversarial relationships. The leader is responsible for defining a purpose that has a significant positive effect on corporate performance, on employees, on the satisfaction of human needs, and thus on society. Considerable power is unleashed when the purpose of corporate activity is in harmony with the higher aspirations of employees. When corporate purpose unites these higher aspirations with collective organizational efforts, it takes on a moral quality and becomes a force that enables individuals to achieve their own higher purposes. The human spirit is lifted and human potential expanded. When this occurs, individuals exhibit intense loyalty and commitment to the source of this meaning—the company.

I   *Influences on Meaning, Strategy,*
Managing, and Performance

1   Purpose and Performance

Leveraging the Essence of a Corporation

Profit is not the proper end and aim of management—it is what makes all
of the proper ends and aims possible.
    —*David Packard*[1]

Purpose affects the soul of the corporation: its rationale for existing,
its strategy, its goals, its way of managing, and the motivation and commitment of its people. Because of these pervasive effects, when firms with different purposes collide in the marketplace, the one with the competitively
superior purpose will prevail, other things being equal.

The assault by international competitors with different purposes,
which has threatened many American companies, demonstrates this Darwinian truth. These global pressures are a macrocosm of the potential competitive power of purpose. Although intensifying international competition places
the issue of corporate purpose in high relief, it is an equally pressing domestic issue as well. Despite the prevailing ideology, in practice American firms
espouse a spectrum of purposes. Evidence shows that American companies
with corporate purposes that place the customer first significantly outperform
their domestic competitors that seek primarily to serve their shareholders or
to balance the interests of multiple constituents. Ironically, in the long run,
customer-focused companies create considerably more value for shareholders
than do their shareholder-focused competitors.

Today, the future purpose of American corporations is being actively
debated in boardrooms, company hallways, government offices, and MBA
classrooms across America. Some argue a corporation's ultimate responsibility is to balance the interests of all stakeholders (usually meaning shareholders, customers, employees, and the communities in which the company

does business), whereas others contend one or another of these constituents' interests should be given priority over the shareholders' interests. Most argue for the primacy of the shareholders' interests. Controversies over the appropriate roles of institutional investors and boards of directors in corporate governance and over the wisdom of hostile takeovers and corporate downsizing accent the debate. Takeovers and downsizing have cost hundreds of thousands of people their jobs—often diminishing the long-term competitiveness of these companies and thus their wealth-producing capacity. Nevertheless, their advocates often justify these actions by the immediate increase in shareholder wealth they can generate.

The resolution of this debate over purpose takes on added importance as corporate influence within society grows. Indications of this expanding power abound. Corporations are the main creators of wealth in society. As their own global scope and wealth grow, they gain greater independence from the political control of any single nation-state.[2] Their dominant objective threatens to become increasing the firm's power and independence. Service to the corporate self imperils service to society. What was originally a creation of society now challenges its control. Yet corporations are increasingly being relied on to solve many of the world's most pressing problems—from raising the worldwide standard of living, to solving America's urban crisis, to integrating welfare recipients into the workforce, to improving education and health care, and to developing technology for protecting the earth's environment. By custom and law, companies have also assumed expanded obligations for the welfare of their employees—from medical care to retirement funding, from training that enhances an individual's sense of self-worth and economic value to providing job security, or if that is not possible, adequate severance benefits.

If large publicly owned corporations are to retain their legitimacy in the twenty-first century, their expanding power must be accompanied by a commensurate increase in responsibility in exercising the power. The conflict between these broader societal responsibilities and the duty to shareholders generates much of the current debate over corporate purpose. This conflict is unlikely to be resolved until responsibility to a broader segment of society supplants the duty to shareholders as the dominant reason for the corporation to exist.

But this debate, while confronting important moral and economic issues, fails to address a central issue: the connection between purpose and competitive performance. Without strong competitive performance, a company cannot serve society or any specific constituent well.

A Customer-Focused Purpose Generates the Best Performance

To understand the linkage of purpose to performance, twenty-three companies with clear expressions of corporate purpose and strong corporate cultures were studied. The companies were drawn from the 202 firms investigated by Kotter and Heskett in *Culture and Performance*.[3] The results indicate that a corporate purpose focused on providing value to customers not only is competitively superior to a purpose of maximizing shareholder wealth, but also typically produces greater long-term returns to shareholders, and thus best serves society.

For our research, companies ranking in the top quartile in cultural strength were selected for study. These strong-culture companies were chosen because the values embodied in their corporate purpose were more likely to have permeated the organization. Thus, purpose in these companies can be assumed to have a greater influence on decisions throughout the company. Of this group of companies, the nature of their purpose was determined based on statements received from the companies. Companies in the upper quartile for which the formal statements were not available or were too ambiguous to identify a clear purpose were eliminated from the study. Of the remaining group of twenty-three strong-culture companies, eleven had a customer-focused purpose, six had a shareholder-focused purpose, and six had a purpose that called for balancing the interests of two or more stakeholders. The twenty-three companies represented 45 percent of the companies in this top tier of cultural strength in the Kotter and Heskett study.

The total return to shareholders (measured by stock price appreciation and dividends received) of these companies was then examined over a ten-year period of time (1983–1993). Each company's total return was then divided by the median performance of its industry to develop an industry-adjusted level of performance. Table 1.1 summarizes the results of the study.

Tellingly, the customer-focused companies' total return to shareholders performance outstripped the shareholder-focused ones. Customer-focused companies exceeded their industries' median performance by 36 percent, whereas shareholder-focused companies beat their industries by 17 percent.

Interestingly, the companies focused on balancing stakeholder inter-

TABLE 1.1   Total Return to Shareholders of Strong-Culture
             Companies with Differing Corporate Purposes
             (Percentage of Their Industry's Median Performance,
             1983–1993)

Corporate Purpose	Average Total Return to Shareholders Relative to Companies' Industries
Customer-Focused (n = 11)	136%
Shareholder-Focused (n = 6)	117%
Balancing Stakeholders (n = 6)	84%

ests provided the lowest total return to investors—lower than their industry medians. This purpose's inadequate focus and the resulting lack of cohesion and coherence in the strategy and decisions of these companies undoubtedly contribute to these results. Too often the proclamation of such a purpose is simply mediocre management hiding behind fashionable rhetoric.

The primary reasons for these differences in performance are three-fold: the impact the definition of purpose has on the motivation and commitment of employees, on corporate strategy, and on the way of managing. The influences of purpose on each of these are explored more fully in the next three chapters.

As corporate purpose is elaborated and internalized in a strategy, it leads to goals and functional policies that reflect that purpose. Strategy predicated on differing concepts of corporate purpose influence the patterns and nature of the allocation of corporate resources and the commitment of employees to the firm's objectives that in turn affect a company's performance. For example, goals reflecting a purpose of maximizing shareholder wealth focus on maximizing returns on investment and growth in profits, whereas goals attuned to serving the customer focus on value, as measured by market share, growth, product quality, cost, and so forth.

By providing a clear sense of fundamental priorities, purpose also influences a company's way of managing. It provides the bedrock for shared values and gives direction to decisions. A significant degree of control is achieved through purpose embodied in strategy, goals, and values. When employees find these ends worthy and share the values, this form of control—although powerful—does not feel restrictive to the individual. The result is more empowerment of the individual within the organization. Absent common purpose and shared values, other forms of management—such as those associated with authoritarian influence and strong, often bureaucratic management systems—must be used more to control decisions. Unfortunately, these ways of managing tend to be oppressive of the human spirit.

Corporate Purpose: A Problem of Priorities

Corporate purpose has such a substantial effect on performance because it answers the most fundamental question of corporate life—"Why does the company exist?" The answer has the power to touch the lives of the individuals who serve the firm, giving direction to action and bringing harmony to goals and values.

At one level, the answer to this central question is easy. Corporations the world over are creations of their societies, designed to serve people's needs. The first corporations were formed in England in the seventeenth century to do the work of the Crown. The corporation came into common use in early-nineteenth-century America to serve society's need to amass capital to build canals and toll roads. In America's early years, the rights to incorporation were closely guarded by the states. However, before long the states began to compete aggressively for the fees associated with corporations domiciled in a particular state. In their fervor to attract corporations, the states soon made the right to incorporation readily available.[4] Today the state charter of corporations is a vestige of the recognition that all corporations exist to serve societal needs. Nevertheless, the moral justification of corporate ends, as well as the corporation's legitimacy to act, continues to rest in its benefits to society. Fundamentally, corporations exist to satisfy human needs by providing useful goods and services and meaningful, fulfilling work—and to do so while adding to society's wealth.

At this level, purpose is consistent with metaphysical justifications for the existence of corporate organizations. For most major religions, the purpose of collective human activity is to serve mankind for the glory of God or to seek unity and harmony with the cosmos. Since these represent the highest aspirations of humanity, a secular corporate purpose that is consistent with these aspirations will generate a greater harmony of individual spiritual aims and organizational purpose. In this sense, a purpose grounded in the service of others, such as serving customers, and vigorously promoted by the company's leaders, can act to raise the moral level of the individual members of the organization. When this happens, the organization becomes an expression of the members' higher values. By appealing to people's highest nature—rather than the pursuit of narrow-minded self-interest—organizational work becomes a vehicle for people to enhance the moral integrity of their lives. Consequently, working for the company becomes a source of increased personal fulfillment and enrichment. The natural response is greater individual commitment to the organization.

At the next level, the answer becomes more controversial and is burdened with greater ideological baggage. What purpose best serves these social ends? In this context, defining a corporation's purpose becomes an exercise in establishing priorities among its constituents' needs. This raises the central dilemma of corporate purpose: what priority should be placed on different constituents' needs in defining the fundamental ends of corporate existence?

Corporate Purpose and the Betterment of Society

As society's principal wealth-producing institutions, corporations are central to the material advancement of humankind. From the perspective of society, this wealth is not measured by profits or shareholder wealth alone, although profits are critically important to a firm's wealth-producing capabilities. Society benefits even more from the value of the corporation's goods and services to customers (better products and services at lower prices increase the customers' satisfaction, buying power, and consequently their standard of living), the firm's efficiency in converting resources into worthwhile products and services, the compensation and quality of life employees derive from serving the company, and the taxes a firm pays to support the institutions of government. Each company is also part of a chain of activities within an industry and affects the wealth-producing capabilities of suppliers and distributors as well. The sum of these factors measures the company's total contribution to humanity's material welfare. This total activity can be called "value creation"—the creation of material wealth and a better quality of life for all people affected by a company's actions—to distinguish it from "shareholder wealth creation."[5]

Value Creation Versus Shareholder Wealth Creation. Much of the conflict between competitiveness and shareholder wealth maximization rests in this distinction between the creation of value—the central responsibility of business organizations—and the creation of shareholder wealth. At the core of the distinction are differences in how value is defined, how value is to be created, over what time period it is to be created, and how it is to be distributed.

Measuring performance by the wealth allocated to only one constituent—shareholders—is myopic. Dividends and stock price appreciation are only one aspect of value creation. Conventional accounting methods treat many of the other sources of societal value as current-period costs or reductions in revenues. For example, increased employee compensation, actions to improve the work environment, enhanced customer service, increased investments in R&D and equipment to improve the functionality and quality or lower the cost of a product or service, and reduced prices all can reduce near-term profitability. Profits represent the residual wealth produced by the company after accounting for its other value-producing and allocating activities. Shareholder wealth is predicated on the stream of dividends paid from these profits—in essence, it is a derivative of a derivative of a residual. Therefore, profits and return on investment—the common surrogate measures of shareholder wealth creation—are partial, indirect, and inadequate reflections of a company's ability to create value.

Competitiveness and the Creation and Allocation of Value. Management's decisions determine the aggregate amount of value created. Once created, management must decide how the value is shared among the company's various constituents. Do customers receive a larger share of the created value through lower prices or improvements in products and services without price increases? Do the employees receive a larger share in the form of increased pay, personal professional development, perks, job security, and improved working conditions? Or do shareholders receive a greater portion through higher returns? A simple example is the pricing decision. The reduction of prices can be viewed as allocating part of the company-created value to customers. Price reductions can also increase the absolute level of value produced by the company by increasing sales volume and thus lowering costs through the effects of learning and economies of scale. As market share increases, jobs become more secure and opportunities for personal advancement within the firm expand. Other allocations of created value, such as larger product development expenditures and improvements to the work environment, can have similar win-win benefits. A central management challenge is finding the pattern of allocation that creates the greatest aggregate value for society.

This is an awesome and difficult responsibility, but one corporate leaders cannot avoid. It is inherent in the job. Critical executive decisions—setting prices, investing in R&D, plant and equipment, hiring, developing and firing personnel, and determining employee compensation and work environment—are in essence decisions affecting the creation and allocation of value.

Competitiveness, the pattern of value allocation, and a firm's value-producing capacity are inextricably linked. In fact the definition of value creation and competitiveness are identical: the sustained ability to attract and convert resources efficiently into products and services preferred by customers over competing offerings. How managers' decisions distribute the created value among the company's key constituents will determine the sustainability of its competitive advantage. Competitiveness, in turn, determines the magnitude of value a firm is capable of creating over time. For example, if dividends are too large, wages too high, or prices too low, the value-producing capacity will be starved for resources and will atrophy. Similarly, if the pressure for near-term returns causes the quality of work life to erode, prices to be set too high, or investments in product improvements and plant to be too low, the company's competitiveness will be sapped.

Differences in the allocation of created value will be driven by management's concept of corporate purpose, whether it is explicit or implicit. A purpose focused solely on the residual value—shareholder wealth—is unlikely to maximize value creation, largely because managers become too ready to sacrifice critical determinants of long-term competitiveness in order to maximize the wealth of today's shareholders.

Sam Walton's creation of Wal-Mart provides a stark example of the competitive power of a purpose focused on service to customers. Service to customers and societal benefits were closely allied in Walton's mind. Wal-Mart's purpose was simple and clear. Walton talked about it in terms of a "philosophy," one "of putting the customer ahead of everything else."[6] He unrelentingly preached this philosophy, using a variety of means to do so. For example, whenever he visited a Wal-Mart store, he began by leading all of the employees (called associates) in the Wal-Mart cheer—a typical college or high school spell out. It begins "Give me a W! Give me an A!" and ends, "What does that spell? Wal-Mart! Who's number one? The customer!" The purpose was clear. "We are agents for our customers," Walton would constantly emphasize.[7]

Wal-Mart's customer-focused purpose was founded on a powerful premise—business can and should be a source of moral good in society. Shortly before his death, Walton reflected back on his career, saying,

> I am absolutely convinced that the only way we can improve one another's quality of life, which is something very real to those of us who grew up in the Depression, is through what we call free enterprise—practiced correctly and morally. And I really believe there haven't been many companies that have done the things we've done at Wal-Mart. We've improved the standard of living of our customers, whom we've saved billions of dollars, and of our associates, who have been able to share profits. Many of both groups have invested in our stock and profited all through the years.[8]

Wal-Mart's associates were always in the forefront of Walton's mind, and he seemed constantly aware that corporate activities must be a positive force in their lives. He knew that without motivated employees at all levels, the services delivered to customers would suffer. He considered the company's holistic effect on the associates' well-being one of Wal-Mart's most important contributions. For many associates, working for Wal-Mart has been their first meaningful job. He reflected,

> I think those associates in our company who believe in our ideals and our goals and get with the program have felt some spiritual satisfaction—in the psychological rather than religious sense—out of the whole experience. They learn to stand up tall and look people in the eye and speak to them, and they feel better about themselves, and once they start gaining confidence there's no reason they can't keep on improving themselves. Many of them decide they want to go to college, or to manage a store, or take what they've learned and start their own business, or do a good job and take pride in that. Wal-Mart has helped their pocketbooks and their self-esteem. There are certainly some union folks and some middlemen out there who won't agree with me, but I believe that millions of people are better off today than they would have been if Wal-Mart had never existed. So I am just awfully proud of the whole deal, and I feel good about how I chose to expend my energies in this life.[9]

Walton's consistent and simple message of purpose made it clear that these associates' benefits were possible only by a wholehearted commitment to serving the customers. The associates' "spiritual satisfaction" had its origin in this sense of service. The company's incredible competitive success and the accompanying growth and profitability were consequences of this focus.

Wal-Mart's purpose permeates its strategy, giving it clarity, focus, and consistency. The customer focus rings clear in Sam Walton's concise explanation of the strategy:

> Almost from the beginning, our objective has been to charge just as little as possible for our merchandise, and to try and use what muscle we've had to work out deals with our suppliers so we can offer the very best quality we can. Many people in this business are still trying to charge whatever the traffic will bear, and they're simply on the wrong track. I'll tell you this: those companies out there who aren't thinking about the customer and focusing on the customers' interests are just going to get lost in the shuffle—if they haven't already. Those who get greedy are going to be left in the dust.[10]

The Role of Profits

Profits play an important, but quite different role, depending on the corporate purpose. Nothing said above should be construed as meaning customer-focused competitors do not aggressively seek to make a profit—they do. Profits are critical to a firm's ability to provide any benefits to society and are a measure of its effectiveness and efficiency in doing so. Profits provide a discipline on management's decisions and act as a guide to value creation. Because profits are indicative of the value being created for customers, they are an important criterion in selecting which customers to serve. The critical issues are the *level* of profitability companies seek, whether profits are viewed as *ends* in themselves or as a *means* to achieving other ends (and therefore must be adequate to achieve these ends, rather than to be maximized), and how managers trade profitability off against concerns of growth, employment, or expanded relationships with principal creditors. These concerns directly affect competitiveness.

When the corporation's purpose is the maximization of shareholder wealth, profits are often treated as the internal measure of this end. The level and growth of profitability over time are closely correlated with the creation of shareholder wealth. The importance of profits is accentuated because they are measurable with some precision, provide seemingly objective measures of performance, and are to a degree under the direct control of the organization. Measurability, objectivity, and control are of critical importance to formal management systems. Unlike the company's stock price, which is influenced by the vagaries of the capital markets, the results of decisions can be measured in terms of a common denominator: the profits and returns on investment they generate.

When the corporation's purpose is serving customer needs, profits become a means. They are an important source of funds to finance actions that serve the organization's ultimate purpose and fuel its growth.[11] For U.S. non-financial corporations in aggregate, 83 percent of their total sources of funds came from their own cash flow from 1985 through 2000. Profits are also measures of the firm's success in achieving its purpose. They reflect the value customers place on the company's goods or services. They also measure the organization's efficiency in using its resources in the pursuit of its aims. They are the result of—and an effective measure of—people's ingenuity in increasing the company's productivity and innovativeness. When a company is providing greater perceived value to its customers in a more efficient manner than its competitors, it will be rewarded with greater operating profitability. However, in the pursuit of advancing the level of customer satisfaction, the company may choose to expend these "profits" on price reductions, additional research and development, entry into new markets, greater customer service, and enhanced product quality, performance, and features—actions that reduce accounting profits but can increase competitiveness and total value creation.

Profits also provide insurance for mistakes, which allows leaders throughout the organization to take more risk, thus enabling greater innovation and longer-term thinking. High levels of profitability shield the company from adverse capital-market pressures. Consequently, managers are able to take a long-term view in their decisions.

Without adequate levels of profitability, the company is more vulnerable to the consequences of an economic downturn, a competitive attack, or making a strategic mistake. The margin for error becomes thinner. Managers, responding rationally to this increased operating risk, typically become more risk averse in their decision making. Because the higher risk makes jobs more insecure, personal concerns can make decisions even more conservative. Higher profits ensure against these risks and can be conducive to bolder, more innovative strategic moves.

As profits become means to achieving valued ends, their role in the organization is transformed. They are no longer seen as a frustrating constraint on creativity and individual initiative—restricting a manager's freedom to do what he or she thinks is right. Instead, they become valued by virtue of their connection with worthy ends. As we shall see in the next three chapters, this transformation affects morale, decisions, and the effectiveness of measurement and control systems.

Hewlett-Packard (HP) has long held this view of profits. HP's first stated objective is "to achieve *sufficient* profit to finance our company growth and to provide the resources we need to achieve our other corporate objectives. In our economic system, the profit we generate from our operations is the ultimate source of the funds we need to prosper and grow" (emphasis added). Profits are means to more important ends. They provide the necessary financial resources that, as David Packard said, "make all of the proper ends and aims possible."[12]

Similarly, Johnson & Johnson's "Credo" places customers' interests first and shareholders' last among four priorities. It states, "Our final responsibility is to our stockholders. Business must make a *sound* profit. We must experiment with new ideas. Research must be carried on, innovative programs developed and mistakes paid for. New equipment must be purchased, new facilities provided and new products launched. Reserves must be created to provide for adverse times. When we operate according to these principles, the stockholders should realize a *fair* return" (emphasis added).

Both companies realize profits are critical to being able to finance the pursuit of more fundamental objectives, and both have high performance standards. But profit clearly remains a means, not an end.

An even stronger position is taken by the founder of Lincoln Electric, an arc-welder manufacturer with one of the most impressive records of sustained productivity growth in America. Convincingly, in growing to become the market leader, Lincoln Electric forced much larger competitors, such as General Electric and Westinghouse, out of the industry. Many observers attribute Lincoln Electric's success to its unique reward system made up of piece work, guaranteed employment, and large bonuses based on company and individual performance. But the reality is much more complicated and subtle. James Lincoln created a philosophy of management grounded in a strong sense of purpose, a belief that "man has limitless latent abilities,"[13] and a strong set of values predicated on merit, individual freedom, and responsibility in the workplace. To Lincoln, strong leaders focus on the creation of value, not the personal accumulation of wealth. He believed that the first question management should ask is "What is the reason for the operation of this company?" To him, the answer was "to make a more and more useful product to be sold at a lower and lower price; profit is to be a by-product of this effort."[14] Lincoln's incentive management system plays an important role, but it is this broader purpose that gives it power. The system is "like a religious conversion," James Lincoln said. "It is a plan for making industry and all its parts more useful to mankind." James Lincoln's purpose was clear and simple: to serve the customers through better and less expensive products.

Lincoln outspokenly attacked the concept of a corporate purpose predicated on the maximization of profits for the benefit of shareholders:

> This end is completely and narrowly selfish. It rivets the attention in the wrong place. It will not prove very profitable in most cases. If we are thinking solely of how much profit can be made, there will be little thought on how good and efficiently the product can be made. If the mind is on, "How much do I get?" it will not be on, "How do I make this better, cheaper, and more useful?" The difference is fundamental and decisive.
>
> No great amount of enthusiasm can be engendered if the only end in view is the making of greater profit for some absentee stockholder. As a matter of fact, most of those in the operation would be glad if the stockholders never got a cent. Human nature does not cherish the thought of working for some absentee whom they already think of as being rich. In general, we can get much more enthusiasm in a project to stop such profit, if we feel that the stockholder does no useful work himself.
>
> If, instead of that viewpoint for the activity, we concentrate on the making of a better and better product to be sold at a lower and lower price, we have an entirely different reaction. Here is a project that is worthwhile. Here is a job that can capture the imagination of all. This same reaction will be present even when the workers still know that a profit, and a large one, is made, if they feel that it is secondary and that it is properly divided. It is extremely doubtful if much enthusiasm can be engendered in any organization unless the results of efficiency are properly divided with those who have been the producers of it.
>
> There is no doubt that the added income has its attraction to the worker, but that is not the real point. The source of the enthusiastic cooperation found in proper incentive management stems from the feeling that all have of uniting their efforts in one activity which they regard as worthwhile and to which their contribution is recognized and real. It is the playing of the game that is most important in developing cooperation.[15]

> The present policy of operating industry for stockholders is unreasonable. The rewards now given to him are far too much. He gets income that should really go to the worker and the management. The usual absentee stockholder contributes nothing to efficiency. He buys a stock today and sells it tomorrow. He often doesn't even know what the company makes. Why should he be rewarded by large dividends?[16]

Echoing the beliefs of Sam Walton, David Packard, General Robert Johnson, and James Lincoln, some of the most influential management scholars have described the role of profits—and the misconceptions about this role—well. Chester Barnard, in his classic *The Functions of the Executive*, argued that the purpose of a business is to produce goods and services, not profit. Profit is an essential means to attract the necessary capital and to have sufficient surplus to provide incentives to employees and suppliers to cooperate with the organization.[17]

Similarly, Peter Drucker sees profits as a means—often a limiting factor—not an end. But he goes further, warning of the danger of misunderstanding the role of profits:

> A business cannot be defined or explained in terms of profit. Asked what a business is, the typical businessman is likely to answer, "An organization to make a profit." The typical economist is likely to give the same answer. This answer is not only false, it is irrelevant. . . . The concept of profit maximization is, in fact, meaningless. . . .
>
> In fact, the concept is worse than irrelevant: it does harm. It is a major cause for the misunderstanding of the nature of profit in our society and for the deep-seated hostility to profit which are among the most dangerous diseases of an industrial society. And it is in large part responsible for the prevailing belief that there is an inherent contradiction between profit and a company's ability to make a social contribution. Actually, a company can make a social contribution only if it is highly profitable. . . .
>
> Profitability is not the purpose of but a limiting factor on business enterprise and business activity. Profit is not the explanation, cause, or rationale of business behavior and business decisions, but the test of their validity.[18]

Corporate leaders' view of profits will determine how well their actions serve the interests of the corporation and society in the twenty-first century. Clearly, maximizing corporate competitiveness over time (or what is equivalent, maximizing the total value created by the firm) best serves the combined interests of customers, employees, and long-term shareholders. The objectives that best equate to competitiveness are growth in revenues and in market share, and improvements in the performance, quality, and cost of the products and services from which growth is derived. Profitability becomes a means to these more important ends. Profits must be adequate to fuel competitive advantage and growth. But, except for the shareholder, maximization of profitability is of secondary concern to each of the other principal constituents.

Purpose and Conflicting Constituents' Interests

Corporate leaders cannot escape their responsibility to resolve the often conflicting claims among a company's constituents. In fact, the development of a competitively sound conception of corporate purpose is a process of delineating means and ends. Since the ultimate end of serving society does not provide sufficient direction to decisions, an operational corporate purpose must be sought at the next level of ends. Which constituents is the company primarily in business to serve? Which constituents' interests are means to this end? Is serving the customers' or employees' needs a means to the maximization of shareholder wealth or are fair returns to shareholders a means of generating the capital necessary to serve the customer, the employees, or the community well? These distinctions are not trivial. The answers to these questions have significant societal, competitive, managerial, and human implications. Leadership fails when corporate purpose is not clearly articulated and embodied in word, action, policy, and management processes and systems.

But confusion of purpose in senior management's words and actions abound. Consider the words of one CEO in a letter to shareholders. He states, "Simply, we are in business to meet the needs of consumers and will do everything possible to maintain and enhance their trust by supplying products with outstanding performance that is consistently valued over the competition." This sounds like customers are the company's reason for being. But read on. Three paragraphs later he says, "Our stockholders own the company and are the final beneficiaries if we serve our other constituencies well. Our ultimate objective is to generate a superior return for our stockholders."[19] This confusion of purpose is not uncommon in even the best-managed companies. Too often the purpose espoused in public relations slogans (designed for both internal and external consumption) conflicts with messages sent internally by the words and actions of senior managers. Unfortunately, sometimes the words are inconsistent with the actions. The result is often a collective belief in nothing, or worse, a cynicism among employees toward the loftiest of their leaders' proclamations.

Balancing Stakeholders' Interests Is a Vacuous Purpose. Some managers purport to resolve the problem of priorities by stating, "Our purpose is to balance the interests of all stakeholders." But the problem cannot be wished away by such facile and vague proclamations. This solution is simply not practical. The interests of shareholders do often conflict with those of customers and employees. In fact, some of the most perplexing and critical decisions senior managers face involve conflicts among these constituents' interests. Someone has to resolve these conflicts.

A purpose that calls for the balancing of all constituents' interests has a practical yet fatal fault. It provides no organizational focus. The definition of the ultimate purpose of each particular action is left up to the individual decision makers. Since there is no objective way of measuring the conflicting claims, managers must apply their own sense of the appropriate balance among the vying interests. A powerful strategy requires coherence and consistency—both internally among its parts and externally with the marketplace. A call to balance interests provides neither coherence nor consistency.

If corporate leaders do not clearly define and consistently reinforce a set of priorities, middle managers will. And they will do so often driven by self-interest, which flourishes in the absence of clear priorities, and under the pressure of reward systems usually dominated by measures of short-term financial performance. Even when senior management's rhetoric—and often its sincere commitment—stresses balancing constituent interests, the middle manager's reality comprises pressure to meet the budgeted financial performance and the need to resolve very tangible conflicts among the constituents' interests. In such circumstances, absent a clear purpose, decisions are most likely to be ultimately influenced by the pressure for performance imposed by the measurement and reward system. The result is decisions designed to meet budget targets rather than serve customer needs. Concern for customers becomes subordinated to short-term financial objectives. This tendency is especially strong when a manager's compensation is tied to these financial measures. These middle-management decisions often dismay senior managers, running counter to their desire to make the organization more customer-driven. But absent strong, clear priorities, consistently reinforced by management systems, middle-management decisions are destined to take a shorter-term, financially driven focus.

An Effective Purpose Establishes Priorities Among Constituents' Interests. In practice, corporate leaders confront the problem of reconciling conflicting interests with great regularity. Many of their most important dilemmas involve conflicts among their constituents' interests. This is particularly true of the conflict between the actions that serve shareholder interests, on the one hand, and customers and employees, on the other. When interests clash, managers must decide which should take precedence.

Consider the decision of whether to invest in research and development for a product that is clearly desired by customers but that requires investments with returns estimated to be below the expectations of shareholders. Development of the product would serve multiple needs. The customers benefit from the availability of the new product. The firm's competencies expand as a consequence of the knowledge created during the development process. The product champions, researchers, and marketers experience the exhilaration of witnessing the tangible expression of their creativity and initiative in the birth of the new product. The new product might also promise to increase the firm's market share, thus strengthening its competitive position and eventually its returns. But these benefits would be at the expense of satisfying short-term shareholder expectations, and thus theoretically would incrementally lower the firm's stock price. What should the manager decide to do?

Similarly, should the decisions of a CEO coping with an economic downturn give profitability precedence over job security, pay, increased personal development, or improved working conditions? Layoffs might enhance current shareholder wealth (for example, in 1996 AT&T's market value increased $6 billion on the two days following its announcement of a forty-thousand-person layoff), but they risk alienating the remaining organization members, increasing self-interested behavior, and breaking up groups that were repositories of embedded knowledge. These risks can have critical long-term competitive implications. AT&T's difficulties since the layoffs bear witness to these consequences, and by 2002 the company was teetering on the brink of dissolution.

Setting priorities does not mean a lack of attention to the interests of those constituents not given top priority. As most executives appreciate, corporate ends are more complex and diverse than solely the maximization of any one constituent's interests. It is undeniably important that all constituents receive *fair* compensation for their contributions to the corporation's operations. Otherwise, their willingness to contribute to the ends of the organization will diminish. The result would be reduction in resources and human commitment, and a subsequent decline in corporate performance. But fair treatment does not negate the need for priorities among conflicting interests.

The practical need for priorities is simple. When interests conflict, someone must decide how the conflict is to be resolved. Corporate purpose and the priorities it embodies provide guidance in these critical circumstances—acting as the ultimate tiebreaker for resolving conflicts. Even when this priority is implicit, it influences managers' deliberations. Ultimately, over time, decisions form a pattern that reflects, and reinforces, the dominance of one interest. The priorities expressed by this pattern become the guide to decision making throughout the organization. Making this priority explicit is a key executive function.

Determining the Priorities of Corporate Purpose

Three questions help define the appropriate priority among the interests of different constituents that should be embodied in the corporate purpose. First, as discussed above, what priority among these constituents' interests best serves society? Second, which constituents have the strongest claims on the firm's wealth-producing capacity? Corporate purpose, if it is to be the foundation upon which competitive strategies rest, should realistically reflect the priority among these claims. Third, what purpose creates the best competitive performance? As we have seen, a customer-oriented purpose typically produces long-term results superior to companies that are focused either on serving the shareholder or on balancing their constituents' interests.

The Strength of Different Constituents' Claims on the Corporation. The strength and legitimacy of a constituent group's claims on a corporation are determined by two factors: (1) the importance of the group's contributions to the company and (2) the extent to which the group's well-being is affected by the firm's actions. In essence, these claims can be thought of in terms of the constituents' risk-adjusted contributions to the organization.

Although many segments of society are affected by corporate actions, three constituent groups have the greatest claim on the corporation: shareholders, employees, and customers. Each group has legitimate claims. They make significant contributions to the corporation and are heavily affected by corporate actions. Shareholders have committed their capital (although some for only minutes or days, and usually with little direct benefit to the company since they are buying the shares on the secondary market). Employees have committed their expertise, effort, time, and usually emotions. Customers expend their resources to buy a company's product or service with the expectation of enhancing their lives or businesses in some way. Which is the more important claim and how should one be offset against the other?

Contribution has three principal dimensions: direct contributions to performance, responsibility for performance, and accountability for performance. Asked which of these constituent groups make the greatest contribution to their company, most executives answer it is the employees followed by customers. A company's people have sole responsibility and accountability for its performance. Most CEOs will agree that the major constraint on the successful implementation of their strategies is people, not capital. In an age when competitive advantage is derived from knowledge-based core competencies embedded in the social fabric of organizations, employees clearly make the most valuable contributions to performance. Their creativity, initiative, and hard work produce results. As Peter Drucker observes, "The 'resources' capable of enlargement can only be human resources. All other resources stand under the laws of mechanics. They can be better or worse utilized, but they can never have an output greater than the sum of inputs. Man, alone of all resources available to man, can grow and develop."[20] Employees' contributions also come at the greatest personal cost—the commitment of a major portion of their waking lives and the psychological identity they have with their work.

Employees also bear the greatest risk. When performance lags, they risk the loss of jobs, income, work-related opportunities that stimulate personal growth, and the social relationships tied to the workplace. Unlike shareholders, they cannot diversify their "work portfolio" to reduce this risk. Their eggs are clearly in one basket.

Most corporate activity focuses on satisfying the needs of customers. In return, through their buying decisions, customers give firms the bulk of the resources they need to grow and prosper. Their decisions, which reflect what they value, are the ultimate determinants of competitive advantage. They are the supreme judges of the value of the company's products and services. Without their contributions there could be no corporation. When substitute products are available from other competitors, the customers' risk is low. When alternatives are not available, the customers' risk is determined by the importance of the product or service to their lives. In some cases, such as medical products and services, the customers' risk can be quite high indeed.

What about shareholders? In established publicly owned companies, the risk and contribution of individual shareholders are actually quite low. For financial institutions with widely diversified portfolios, the risk is even lower. If a shareholder does not like the actions of a corporation, the stock can be sold in seconds. Also the contributions of shareholders are less important than they might initially appear. True, their trading establishes the company's market value. However, market value tangibly affects corporate performance only when a firm seeks to raise capital through the sale of new common stock or to use stock to finance acquisitions. But few major American companies issue new shares of equity to finance their growth. Their growth is financed predominantly by internal cash flow and additional debt. Consequently, shareholders finance a very small portion of the incremental capital needs of established corporate enterprises. Shareholders largely buy and sell shares among themselves in the secondary market with little direct benefit or cost to the company.

From the standpoint of contribution, risk, and accountability for performance, employees clearly have the greatest claim. Therefore, it would seem that corporate purpose should give priority to employees' needs. But a purpose with the ultimate priority on serving employees' interests carries within itself the potential seeds of its own destruction. Such a purpose has four major disadvantages.

First, given human nature, there is no compelling force to ensure that an employee-focused purpose does not degenerate into self-serving complacency. Guided by such a purpose, the company becomes a tool to benefit current employees, not to create enduring competitive positions for the benefit of society, customers, investors, and future employees.

Second, the purpose threatens to create an excessively internal focus that diverts attention and resources from the product markets. Over time, neglect of the intense competitive discipline of the marketplace can threaten an organization's very survival. The measure of success becomes whether the quality of life within the organization has increased incrementally from last year. The organization can become quite content with its performance even when competitors are drubbing it in the marketplace. Being satisfied with 6 percent growth when the market is growing at 10 percent is a formula for competitive extinction.

The problems of an employee-focused purpose are highlighted by the difficulties many Japanese companies had in adapting to the rapid changes and intensified competition of the 1990s. Tied to a purpose of maintaining employment for the benefit of Japan, they were slow in adopting the innovations necessary to retain their world-class cost competitiveness. Not only did these policies reduce the ability to cut payroll costs, but the lack of workforce mobility hampered the placement of the right person in the right job at the right time, thus constraining productivity increases.

Third, the purpose potentially encourages politicization of the organization as individuals and groups compete among themselves for a larger share of the corporate pie. There is nothing inherent in the employee-focused purpose to counteract such motivations. In fact, the purpose, when applied parochially, can be used to justify self-interested behavior on the part of employees.

Fourth—and this is a subtle, counterintuitive, yet critically important distinction—an environment that places paramount emphasis on the employees' interests does *not* best serve an individual's self-interest. By appealing to the employees' narrow self-interest, not to their service of others, an employee-focused purpose fails to provide a morally uplifting cause to which their work is dedicated.

In contrast, making the customer's well-being the purpose of work and stressing the dignity of the individual employee in the pursuit of this end creates an environment conducive to the greatest potential individual fulfillment. Meaning and self-actualization are realized in large part through the accomplishment of tasks that beneficially link the individual to the larger community. When this occurs, work embodies the intrinsic values individuals hold most dear. Because they are dedicated to the service of others, these strivings have a moral quality. They see their efforts contributing to socially worthwhile ends larger than themselves. Work takes on greater meaning. They are making a difference with their lives!

High-performance companies that espouse employees' welfare as a primary purpose (such as Hewlett-Packard and Herman Miller in the United States and a plethora of companies in Japan and continental Europe, including industry leaders like Toyota and Kyocera) invariably couple it with service to the customer. Intuitively, they understand that the employees' interests are not best served by a unilateral focus on these interests. The focus on the customer provides meaning and creates the value from which the employees gain greater potential benefit over the long term.

In addition, because the interests of customers and employees are usually in harmony, a customer-focused purpose does not require significant sacrifices of employee interests. To the contrary, work environments that foster creativity, initiative, and a high degree of commitment and motivation among employees generally produce superior products and services at lower costs for customers. This is why outstanding companies place such a significant emphasis on their employees' welfare and development.

Given the mutual interests of customers and employees, why should not the purpose be to serve both? For the same reasons that a solely employee-focused purpose is unsatisfactory, so is a purpose calling for a balance among customer and employee interests. A charge to balance the interests of customers and employees can easily be translated into a self-serving, imbalanced employee focus as individuals make decisions reflecting their self-interests—a process they consider to have been institutionally condoned. Although having the CEO and other corporate executives place nearly equal emphases on the customer and the employees can be beneficial, it is clearly dysfunctional when first-level employees and midlevel supervisors come to believe the company's primary purpose is to serve their own and their colleagues' personal interests. Human nature being what it is, the "balance" is quickly lost in favor of actions that disproportionately emphasize employees' own interests and those of fellow employees. These concerns are the most immediate, most tangible, and most personal. The result can be an inward-looking, politicized, and complacent organization—characteristics that threaten the very employee welfare the actions set out to enhance.

Outstanding corporate leaders have a visceral philosophical understanding—often not articulated—that they have a moral responsibility to the people whose lives are touched by their actions. They recognize what is needed is a purpose that is consistent with employees' needs, but provides an external product-market focus, embodies ends beneficial to society, and has the potential to be morally inspiring. A customer-oriented purpose does just that.

These leaders have a deep intuitive appreciation that this purpose not only creates the greatest value for society, but also produces the greatest benefit to their fellow employees. It provides greater opportunities for personal growth, for satisfaction from their achievements, for the gratification of winning as a team, and ultimately for obtaining greater meaning from work through serving a worthwhile cause beyond their own selves. In this way, the interests of society, customers, and employees—and in the long run, shareholders—converge at a high level. But only if the clearly dominant purpose is serving the customer.

A Purpose with Global Reach. There is another important reason to have a customer-focused purpose. With the growing globalization of companies, corporate purpose must be capable of retaining its meaning and power while spanning national and cultural boundaries. To motivate and direct a culturally diverse workforce, the purpose must relate to the work of individuals regardless of their national origin. Clearly, purposes rooted in nationalism or shareholder wealth (shareholders largely tend to be from the home country and therefore alien to managers from elsewhere) do not travel well. Only three purposes can be readily transported: service to society worldwide, service to employees, and service to customers. Only the latter relates directly to the firm's product-market activities and therefore to the work of all organizational members. Through serving customer needs well, a firm also benefits society and the employees, as well as long-term shareholders.

Purpose and Competitiveness

Competitiveness and the maximization of current shareholder wealth are not synonymous. Although competitiveness and shareholders' returns tend to converge in the long term, the critical issue is what enables them to converge at a high rather than low level. It is a fallacy to believe that future competitiveness can be equated to achieving a high discounted rate of return on capital today. Often the opposite is true. The pursuit of high returns can curtail investment, consume commitment, and thus undermine competitiveness. The fact is that some economic value may need to be sacrificed today to ensure tomorrow's competitiveness.

While this difference between high returns on investment and competitiveness is not sufficiently recognized today, it was well understood by Adam Smith. In reflecting on the tendency of businessmen to attribute their poor performance to external causes, rather than to look at their own behavior, he said, "Our merchants and master-manufacturers complain much of the bad effects of high wages in raising the price, and thereby lessening the sale of their goods both at home and abroad. They say nothing concerning the bad effects of high profits. They are silent with regard to the pernicious effects of their own gains. They complain only of those of other people."[21]

Stock-price appreciation and dividends determine shareholder wealth. Stock price is a function (at least in theory) of the discounted present value of the expected future stream of dividends. Thus shareholder wealth is a result of the return shareholders expect—or the discount factor applied to future dividends—and the timing and magnitude of the dividend stream. The higher the expected return, the lower is the present value of a future dollar of dividends. Therefore, other things being equal, companies pursuing higher expected returns will not only be more selective in their investments, but will also place less value on future profitability than will companies with lower return objectives. The result is a reduced proclivity to make investments that enhance long-term competitiveness, even though they are expected to generate significant returns in the more distant future. This is particularly true of higher-risk, long-term investments such as entry into new markets or developing new products.

Competitiveness is a long-term game that cannot be scored solely by current or discounted future financial returns. Competitiveness is determined by the customers' perception of the value of a company's products and services relative to competitors. This value, which is defined by the price, quality, and performance of the company's offerings, results from years of sustained investment to develop core competencies. Although enhanced competitiveness should pay off in increased earning capability five or ten years hence, the investments necessary to achieve this competitiveness can potentially reduce today's stock price. This is because the net present value of future dividends upon which stock prices are theoretically based places considerably more value on near-term cash flow—the years in which the investments that decrease cash flow are made—than cash flow reaped in the distant future from the firm's increased competitive strength. An investment dollar spent today is worth a dollar. But, if the shareholders expect a return of 15 percent, a dollar returned ten years from now is worth only twenty-five cents today. Consequently, investments with long-term competitive benefits often are at a disadvantage in competing for funds in the "internal" capital market. At the same time, investments that promise future competitiveness are of little solace to today's short-term shareholders, who may see the value of their holdings not appreciate as rapidly as they expected.

When the competing firms play by different rules—in that they judge their performance against different ends and evaluate investments on dissimilar criteria—the conflict between returns and competitiveness becomes even more marked. This reality is accentuated in the global marketplace, where firms, seeking to serve the interest of employees or their nation, have historically outinvested competitors seeking to maximize their return on investment.

In this competitive environment, companies with lower standards for acceptable returns and access to capital at least equivalent to their competitors achieve a competitive advantage by pursuing a broader array of investments, reducing prices, or increasing service. Of course, these companies must generate returns sufficient to provide the cash flow required to fuel their growth and protect against risk. But sufficient returns are quite different from maximum returns. Hamel and Prahalad have shown that many companies—particularly Japanese and Korean ones—have consciously pursued strategies to gain the investment initiative from their competitors. By outinvesting competitors in areas such as plant expansion, equipment, and product development, they gain the advantages of scale, productivity, and the learning that hones core competencies. Often this begins by serving as a low-cost source of product on an OEM basis. As competitors lose their economic advantages, they are likely to retreat from manufacturing the product all together. Without manufacturing, product development and marketing capabilities can atrophy. When this occurs, competitors lose both a vital link in their ability to create the new knowledge on which their core competencies rest and the ability to respond rapidly to market needs. This strategy is made possible by the asymmetry of the corporate purposes. Many American businesses are caught between the need to provide returns to shareholders that meet the capital markets' conventional norms and the need to compete against companies (many of which are foreign) that are willing and able to invest capital at lower returns.

Unable to resolve the dilemma, but anxious to meet stock market expectations, many of these U.S. businesses have elected to curtail investment in projects that provide "substandard" returns. But as their level of investment declines, so does competitive vitality. Strategies designed to shore up short-term returns to shareholders have actually eroded these companies' competitiveness and thus their ability to provide long-term returns to all constituents: shareholders, employees, customers, suppliers, and society.

To deal effectively with this predicament, managers will have to make fundamental and difficult choices that go beyond tactical and strategic product-market maneuvers. If executives don't make these tough choices now and instead take actions that maximize near-term returns but sap long-term competitive strength, superior competitors will eventually force lower returns on them. But this will occur only after the company's competitive position has so deteriorated that its strategic options have narrowed and its growth has stopped. Or managers can decide to make proactive investments to strengthen their company's competitive position and maintain its growth over the long term, even if that means lowering the rate of return.

The consequence is a gradual—almost imperceptible—pressure on companies to put less emphasis on shareholder returns and more on building long-term competitive strengths. The issue strikes at the corporation's heart. Managers must reassess their basic purpose. In the simplest form, the question is this: to what extent must we compromise today's shareholder wealth to improve our competitive position in the world marketplace and thus enhance the prospect of achieving acceptable levels of future shareholder wealth? To remain competitive, many companies will need to undertake projects that may bring returns below their current standards. The inevitable result is anathema to many U.S. managers: the conscious destruction of shareholder value in the short term. Yet the alternative is lower returns at a later date caused by a deteriorated market position—from which the company might never recover.[22]

In a world of knowledge-based competition, lean production, and rapid diffusion of technology, the future rests with those businesses that focus resources, decisions, and efforts on securing greater competitiveness, not necessarily the highest current returns. In such a world, an emphasis on committing capital and marshaling human abilities to serve customer needs is the only purpose compatible with American beliefs that will yield a durable competitive edge. This is consistent with a basic economic truth: customers are the source of a company's growth and income, and they are the ultimate judges of its competitiveness. The customers' determination of what is value results in buying decisions that provide resources to one company and not another. In a very basic sense, serving the customer well creates the wealth from which the ability to achieve other corporate aims is derived. Thus, the key to success rests in unleashing human potential in the service of the needs of other people—the consumers of the firm's products and services.

Harmony Among Competitiveness and the Interests of Customers and Employees. Because knowledge is increasingly the key to competitive advantage, the impact of purpose on organizational members takes on greater importance. At all levels of the organization, the application of the individual's full capabilities and potential—more intellectual than physical—is necessary to achieve outstanding competitive performance. Knowledge is required to create state-of-the-art manufacturing operations and product technology. It is also required in marketing and customer service, as well as in the management skills necessary to integrate increasingly complex operations in order to respond quickly to intensely competitive environments characterized by accelerating rates of change. Consequently, employee loyalty, commitment, and motivation are becoming ever more critical to achieving competitive advantage.

Fortunately, when properly communicated and implemented, a customer-oriented purpose is in many—if not most—ways in harmony with the employees' interest. People desire secure jobs, fair compensation, and a healthy social environment. They want opportunities for achievement, the expression of their creativity, personal growth and development, and the self-transcending sense that their work is serving worthy ends. Increased competitiveness directly serves each of these needs by providing greater corporate growth, opportunity, and security. Customer-oriented purpose broadens managers' investment horizons and places less restrictions on their creative thinking. The result can be greater innovation, flexibility, and speed in responding to changing competitive conditions. Personal and corporate growth are closely aligned. In this truth rests the harmony of interests between the customer and employees.

Importantly, an externally focused, worthwhile purpose prevents an employee-centered way of managing from deteriorating into self-serving decadence. When organizational purpose encompasses values people share, individual self-interest can be merged with—and appear to be subordinated to—the corporate interest. But this behavior, which seems from a distance to be self-sacrifice in the service of company goals, in reality benefits individuals by enabling them to realize more fully their potential and to establish their identity and worth relative to the external world.

A Crisis of Ideology:
Shareholder Wealth's Dominance of Purpose

The debate over corporate purpose reflects a crisis of ideology—the set of commonly accepted ideas and beliefs that underlie the way corporate purposes are defined. There are several reasons the maximization of shareholder wealth is so deeply ingrained in American business. In part, it is an ideology that has gone largely unchallenged by those within the business community until recent years. It has been simply accepted as the starting point in thinking about management.

The preeminence of the shareholders' interest in the United States originates with the American view of property rights as applied to common stock. The argument is simple and familiar. It is based on two principal beliefs. First, since common stock is private property, the shareholders own the corporate assets and have the right to expect that this property and the people employed by the firm will be managed to serve their interests—as long as doing so hurts no one else. Flatly stated, managers do not have the right, much less a responsibility, to subordinate the interests of shareholders to the interest of any other constituent. Second, it is argued that such a purpose leads to other desirable ends. By seeking to maximize the rate of return on the shareholders' investment, capital is allocated most efficiently throughout the economy to its highest and best use based on the collective utility of the populace. This efficient allocation of capital by the market's "invisible hand" betters the well-being of society by giving people what they want as determined by what they choose to buy. This thinking has become deeply embedded in the ideology of American business.

The great moral philosopher and economist Adam Smith originally proposed the moral foundation for the shareholders' rights of ownership. His argument was based on three factors: the union of interest between ownership and production, the belief that this union would "promote the general welfare," and the assumption that the owner would behave frugally, investing heavily to increase output. In other words, the owner-manager had an implied responsibility to expand the business by reducing costs and increasing the value and quantity of its output. This can mean compromising today's economic value in order to make investments that enhance long-term competitiveness—something that potentially conflicts with shareholder wealth maximization as measured by the current stock price.

Adam Smith's first factor is no longer true for corporate America. Ownership and control of productive corporate assets are now divorced. Managers control the corporate property. As Adolph Berle and Gardiner Means observed in their 1932 classic, *The Modern Corporation and Private Property*, this "new form of economic organization of society"[23] raises fundamental questions:

> Must we not, therefore, recognize that we are no longer dealing with property in the old sense? Does the traditional logic of property still apply? Because an owner who also exercises control over his wealth is protected in the full receipt of the advantages derived from it, must it necessarily follow that an owner who has surrendered control of his wealth should likewise be protected to the full? May not this surrender have so essentially changed his relation to his wealth as to have changed the logic applicable to his interest in that wealth?[24]

For a fundamental idea with such profound consequences, most managers have a rather vague and elementary understanding of the philosophical concepts underlying property rights. They generally recognize there is a link between these rights and personal freedom—and as an extension of this freedom, individualism. Property can become closely identified with one's persona. It can aid in the realization of one's full personality and can act as an expression of that personality. The right to benefit from one's own industry in using and amassing personal property is also seen as a powerful positive motivation for individuals to exert efforts to create wealth that will benefit society in general. Freedom, individual fulfillment, and the right to the fruits of one's own efforts are basic human values. Consequently, the beliefs and assumptions associated with them, such as the beliefs related to shareholder wealth maximization as the primary purpose of corporations, are usually highly emotionally charged, if simplistic.

Too often managers fail to understand the full relationship between property rights and the individual. Ironically, in the name of individual rights of shareholders to their property, they often squash the individuality of employees. People are asked to subordinate their creativity, judgment, and too often their moral conscience to ensure decisions are made to maximize shareholder wealth.

Many managers also tend to neglect the responsibilities that accompany these rights. Furthermore, the extent to which the ownership of common stock gives the owner claims to the underlying assets similar to owner-ship of personal property is rarely questioned. Is the ownership of a hundred shares of IBM as vital to the development and expression of an individual's personality as is one's home, clothing, or personal computer? Should the ownership of stock in a large, publicly owned corporation carry with it the same rights *and* responsibilities as the shares of an entrepreneur who owns and runs her own company? Today's shareholders are distant and uninvolved in the management of the firms they "own." Their motivations are normally exclusively financial gain on their securities. Do these facts—coupled with the substantial evidence that wealth and happiness are not highly corre-lated—cast doubt on whether the promotion of the shareholders' interests "promotes the general welfare?" Without such a foundation, is the legitimacy of shareholders' near-absolute rights over corporate assets morally defensi-ble? What makes common stock more than a financial claim to the residual cash flow of a company (a claim different only from debt in its priority and upside potential)? Does the shareholders' almost total lack of personal responsibility for the company's actions lessen their claim to property rights to the underlying corporate assets? These questions challenge the legitimacy of the shareholders' rights to dictate the use of corporate assets (people and capital) for their benefit. Suffice it to say, the combination of emotionally charged beliefs and the shallow—almost knee-jerk—understanding of the nature of the property rights associated with stock ownership cause our soci-ety to tenaciously cling to the ideology of shareholder wealth maximization.

The ideology is also perpetuated and reinforced by what MBAs are commonly taught in the United States. Maximization of shareholder wealth—or its surrogates, return on investment and the net present value of investments discounted at the risk-adjusted cost of capital—remains the accepted basic objective of business with which most of our 130,000 annu-ally graduating MBAs are indoctrinated. The objective provides a simple, clear, and quantifiable end on which management theory can target. It allows students to ignore the real-world complexity of multiple responsibil-ities that many of them find difficult to comprehend, much less fully appre-ciate. When academics and students study managerial decision making, it allows them to avoid the necessity of developing conceptual ways of trading one corporate responsibility off against another—the shareholders' interests are dominant. For academics it simplifies the world sufficiently to allow ele-gant, tightly reasoned quantitative theories to be developed. The moral justification of these theories is in essence that "greed is good"—the individual pursuit of wealth is assumed to lead to decisions that allocate financial capital to its highest and best use throughout society. This belief is predicated in part on the outdated assumption that financial capital, not human capital, is the primary source of competitive advantage. The problem goes beyond courses in finance and financial accounting. Other courses (such as strategy, organizational behavior, operations, and marketing), which should challenge this orthodoxy, do not. The objective of the activity under study is assumed to be the maximization of the firm's net present value. The result is a bifurcation of people and economic issues. People become means to financial ends. The consequence of all of this is that students graduate indoctrinated in a narrow, mostly unchallenged set of beliefs about what the purpose of corporations is and should be.

Yet the tenacious power of this end goes beyond the fact that it is a convenient, widely accepted conventional wisdom. It simplifies the complex job of managing today's multimillion dollar corporation; it provides a basis for justifying and defending many of management's controversial actions; and it can be used to provide management with increased independence from accountability to any constituency.

Providing one clear, and to some extent quantifiable, priority against which actions can be measured, simplifies the many conflicting claims placed on corporations in today's society. Managers can justify most of their actions on moral grounds by invoking the utilitarian argument that the pursuit of greater shareholder wealth (which many of these managers presumably equate to personal happiness) will create the greatest happiness for society.

Also, the ideology of shareholder wealth enhances the independence of senior managers from all constituencies. By arguing that their overriding allegiance is and should be (both legally and morally) to the shareholders, senior managers can align themselves with one of their most docile major constituencies and thus increase their professional freedom. In large part this is because shareholders do not have strong means of controlling managers. Management-selected directors dominate boards of directors, and shareholders are increasingly composed of financial institutions that would rather sell their shares than spend the time and energy necessary to gain the knowledge and power needed to influence management's actions. Consequently, managers can use their responsibilities to shareholders to keep other constituents at bay.

The potential adverse consequences for America's competitive fabric of continued adherence to this outdated ideology are staggering. Time is short. The major economic and social trends that will shape competition in the twenty-first century are taking form. The danger is that many American managers will not change their espoused beliefs in sufficient time to prevent irreversible harm to their companies' competitiveness.

2 Corporations and Individuals
Creating Meaning and Competitiveness

The purpose of life is a life of purpose.
—*Robert Burns*

This is the true joy in life, the being used for a purpose recognized by yourself as a mighty one; the being thoroughly worn out before you are thrown
on the scrap heap; the being a force of Nature instead of a feverish selfish
little clod of ailments and grievances complaining that the world will not
devote itself to making you happy. And also the only real tragedy in life is
the being used by personally minded men for purposes which you recognize
to be base. All the rest is at worst mere misfortune and mortality.
—*George Bernard Shaw*[1]

Without work all life goes rotten. But when work is soulless, life stifles
and dies.
—*Albert Camus*

People are increasingly adrift in their search to find meaning for their
own personal existence. Profound social changes have decreased the influence
of families, organized religion, and communities in many Americans' lives—
institutions that have traditionally been sources of meaning, a sense of belonging, and identity for individuals. Significantly, these events have increased the
importance of corporations to the lives of individuals—particularly for the
people who work in them. Jean Riboud, the extraordinary former CEO of
Schlumberger Ltd., believed that to be successful in the future, corporations
must learn that they "have the responsibility that religion used to have."[2] By
this he meant that people "need to believe in something greater than themselves."[3] Work—particularly when dedicated to the service of worthwhile purposes—has long been recognized as critical to the ability to craft a meaning-

ful life. In an age of estrangement, finding added meaning for one's life in work becomes an increasingly difficult and urgent need.

Initially, the talk of meaning and work may sound academic or abstract to the pragmatic manager who believes that while these issues may have consumed philosophers and theologians over the centuries, they have little to do with the daily realities of management. But the historical battle between work as a source of drudgery and alienation and work as a creative, fulfilling experience continues today. It is within senior management's power to shape the outcome of this conflict. Indeed, one of management's principal responsibilities is to create an environment that enables their associates to satisfy deep inner needs through work—an environment in which people can serve worthwhile purposes, exercise creativity, experience a sense of accomplishment, and achieve personal growth. Such a climate generates the commitment and individual initiative that are the wellsprings of competitively critical knowledge. Clearly, the company with a committed, creative, ever-improving workforce capable of rapidly generating valuable knowledge has an advantage over one with cynical, indifferent—even alienated—employees. In this way, corporate purpose, meaningful work, and corporate success are inextricably linked.

Purpose performs two profoundly important, but often unrecognized, roles in this process. First, it helps people transcend the boundary between the self and the other. As individuals experience a sense of being united with a valued cause and with the colleagues with whom they work to serve it, the boundaries of the self become enlarged to encompass these relationships of people and ends. The self is expanded—opened to new realities and aspirations. Life draws greater meaning from these relationships.

Second, self-transcendence and the personal identification with the corporate purpose have consequences that benefit the company's performance. These forces further the creation of knowledge by increasing loyalty and enhancing the exchange of new insights and existing knowledge. Because people value an organization that provides them with opportunities to transcend the boundaries of self in life-enriching ways, their loyalty to the company is increased. Loyalty brings with it lower turnover, more stable relationships, and the subordination of narrow self-interest to the common interest. The firm's knowledge is less likely to walk out the door, and knowledge-creating networks remain intact. Trust is enhanced. People are more aware of to whom among their colleagues they can go to receive useful insight and knowledge applicable to solving a particular problem. As the boundaries surrounding the self become more permeable, the barriers between people fall. Consequently, individuals are more open to the ideas of others and exchange ideas more freely. In addition, being more in harmony with the corporate cause and those around them increases people's confidence and motivation to go beyond the old self in addressing challenges. The result is greater personal growth, enhanced competency, and increased initiative to take action on new ideas.

An understanding of the human search for meaning in work can deepen one's understanding of the effect different constructs of purpose and ways of managing have on the commitment, motivation, creativity, and initiative of employees. What do most people seek from their work? Are they primarily driven to further their self-interest through enhanced security, material well-being, power, and prestige? Or do people also seek greater meaning for their lives by working in community with other human beings to serve worthy causes larger than themselves? Are the most powerful sources of motivation at work found in activities that bring meaning to one's life— opportunities to use and expand one's creative powers and to serve worthwhile ends? Understanding the answers to these fundamental questions will enhance the appreciation of the importance of meaningful work to the art of leadership.

This chapter examines how corporate purpose and constructive work interact to bring added meaning to people's lives and value to the organizations they serve. It begins by looking at a symptom of the failure of many American corporations to provide an environment in which meaning can become a constructive force: the current wave of alienation and cynicism that is eroding the loyalty of many people to their companies. We will then explore the long and rich tradition of thought about the meaning of work and its impact on the human spirit. The chapter concludes with the implications of these ideas for twenty-first-century leaders.

The Erosion of Loyalty

The enhanced responsibilities and power of corporations come at a time when market pressures have forced many companies to take actions that bring hardships to employees and communities. Competitive demands and threats of hostile takeovers and mergers have combined to put severe pressures on managers to increase productivity, rationalize the use of assets, and create responsive, lean organizations. The result has been continuing waves of corporate restructuring, outsourcing, and accompanying layoffs. From 1991 through 2000, corporate America laid off an average of 550,000 people per year.[4] The peak year was not during the 1990 recession, but at the economy's strongest point, in 1998, when the announced layoffs totaled 675,000 people. Then in 2001 alone, a massive wave of layoffs resulted in 1,957,000 people losing their jobs. Troubled behemoths, such as General Motors, AT&T, and IBM, and highly successful companies, such as GE, have been affected alike. These actions have eroded the sense of job security and have undermined the traditional views of loyalty.

For professional managers, the thinning of the middle ranks proved particularly traumatic. The assumed contract of job security in return for loyalty, hard work, and solid performance was torn asunder. In its place a new contract has emerged. This new contract reads, "There is no job security here. You will have a job as long as you find ways to add value. In return for your value added, the company will provide the experience and training needed to enhance your skills and, if necessary, to enable you to be employable elsewhere. Also, you will receive compensation that reflects your contribution." Jack Welch, a leading advocate of the new contract, argues:

> Like many other large companies in the United States, Europe and Japan, GE has had an implicit psychological contract based on perceived lifetime employment. This produced a paternal, feudal, fuzzy kind of loyalty. You put in your time, worked hard, and the company took care of you for life.
> That kind of loyalty tends to focus people inward. But given today's environment, people's emotional energy must be focused outward on a competitive world where no business is a safe haven for employment unless it is winning in the marketplace. The psychological contract has to change.
> The new psychological contract, if there is such a thing, is that jobs at GE are the best in the world for people who are willing to compete. We have the best training and development resources and an environment committed to providing opportunities for personal and professional growth.[5]

This contract is predicated on two principal assumptions. First, competitive realities necessitate the renegotiation. Second, the revised contract forces people to be more oriented to the product market, less inward focused, harder working, and more creative. But the validity of these assumptions is questionable. Competitive realities are demanding greater loyalty and organizational cohesion, not less. Knowledge-based core competencies require it. In addition, if people are encouraged by senior managers to place their primary focus on their own careers, they are unlikely to be more outward looking. Gone are the counterbalances to self-interest that can be found in shared purpose and end values—forces that act to unite self-interest with common objectives. Career, not vocation, reigns supreme. Knowledge creation atrophies, as even the most talented people hesitate to push innovative ideas that may put themselves or their friends out of a job.

In fact, in many circles this new contract has given rise to a new view of professional managers. They are seen not as members of a team committed to common purposes, but as hired guns whose professional skills are their principal security as they move from job to job. In this view, the self-interested honing of marketable skills, rather than devotion to a common purpose, is the hallmark of the day. Improving one's career has eclipsed the pursuit of one's vocation. Certainly, in today's highly competitive product marketplace, skill development and organizational learning are critical to success. But there is a major difference in people's commitment to corporate goals when they view skills development as serving valued organizational purposes rather than primarily serving their own career interests.

Managers subjected to this unilaterally renegotiated contract feel jilted. Traditionally they viewed their loyalty to their companies as a two-way street. But these individuals now believe that when tested their companies did not hold up their end of the bargain. Exacerbating the problem is the fact that many people do not find corporate ends worthy of loyalty. Rightly or wrongly, many employees feel that under pressure, profits matter more to the company than people, customers, or long-term competitiveness. (Granted, in some cases this is a narrow view reflecting the immediate personal consequences and ignoring the company's need to be cost-competitive in order to survive and to be able to provide future benefits to customers and employees alike.) Consequently, the alienation from work, which often has been associated with the blue-collar worker, has spread to the ranks of middle management.

In the 1990s, *Business Week* and *Fortune* each carried multiple cover stories regarding this phenomenon. One *Business Week* article, subtitled

"The only security for today's migrant managers and professionals is in the portfolio of skills they can sell," observes:

> Every day, thousands of managers, bankers, sales executives, lawyers, accountants, and other professionals are driven to anger and despair by the hard realities of the changing world of work. The once-solid foundation for millions of middle-class families—the corporate career—is in shambles. The Organization Man of the 1950s and 1960s is being replaced by the migrant manager and free-lance professional of the 1990s. . . .
>
> White-collar workers at [companies recently announcing layoffs] will join the growing ranks of once-secure employees who are finding themselves on the outside—alone, afraid, and angry.[6]

Business Week then asks, "But is this breakdown in the bonds of employment good for Corporate America? Can U.S. corporations compete against Japanese and European rivals that often retain the lifelong loyalty and commitment of their employees?"[7] The central strategic question is whether it is possible to have the level of collaborative effort necessary to compete successfully in the world marketplace of tomorrow if employees are essentially working for themselves and increasingly alienated from their employers.

The implications of managing a group of "migrant managers and free-lance professionals" are manifold and of great significance to performance. If this condition is accepted as an inevitable reality, then the managerial focus becomes one of motivating people through inducements that enhance their career. Career betterment becomes the principal end of individual effort. Meaning is found extrinsically *through* work in personal advancement, financial rewards, and increased status and prestige. When this happens, the concept of vocation becomes lost. No longer is meaning found intrinsically *in* the work and serving organizational purposes greater than oneself. The enhancement of narrowly defined self-interest, not the service of ends outside of self, dominates. Gone is the gratification of serving a bigger cause that can bring a fuller meaning to one's life; and the value of teamwork and the joy of team victories are seriously eroded.

Of course, the consequence of the competitive pressures necessitating restructuring and layoffs has not been all negative. Many senior executives have recognized that past managerial practices are no longer sufficient to achieve outstanding performance. They increasingly understand that the organization needs the intellectual help of people at all levels of the organization to bring innovation, efficiency, and responsiveness to world-class levels. Using these lessons, often learned at a great cost from competitors, managers have turned to increased employee participation in problem solving. For example, teams of manufacturing workers have been created to identify quality, productivity, and product-design problems and to recommend solutions. Cross-functional teams of marketers, design engineers, and production managers have been used to speed new products to market. Much of the power of these efforts is derived from returning to workers, at all organizational levels, the dignity of being creators—of leaving a distinct mark on their work in which they can take pride. In most companies where teams have taken hold, they have unleashed considerable creative thought and effort. The increased sense of empowerment felt by the worker has led to increased satisfaction and enthusiasm. Consequently, people have become more committed to their jobs and the purposes their jobs serve.

However, attempts to implement the team concept often meet considerable skepticism, if not outright resistance, from workers. Reflecting years of experience, they see these efforts as simply business as usual—camouflaged attempts to get people to work harder and faster under the guise of increasing quality or other slogans. There exists in many organizations considerable skepticism that senior managers have any motives other than improving the bottom line and enhancing their own and the shareholders' financial self-interests.

Middle managers' cynicism toward senior managers has grown rapidly. A survey of 750,000 middle managers by the Hay Group found that between 1987 and 1990 these managers' most common appraisal of their bosses' overall abilities fell from "generally high" to "frankly awful." The percentage of middle managers who viewed the ability of their senior managers favorably fell from 54 percent to 38 percent over this same period.[8] Furthermore, the proportion of employees who often do not believe what their managers say rose from a third in 1988 to 40 percent in 1996.[9]

Also in recent years there has been a substantial decline in the sense of job security among management and nonmanagement employees alike. According to surveys conducted since 1980, in the 1980–82 period 79 percent of management and 75 percent of nonmanagement employees rated their job security as "good" or "very good." By 1992–94, the percentages had fallen to 55 percent and 51 percent, respectively.[10] This erosion of sense of security is well founded. A 1998 survey conducted by Shell Oil Company found that over half of the American workforce have either been downsized,

work for a company that has been merged or acquired, or have been transferred to another city because of their job.[11]

The erosion of job security has been accompanied by a significant
decline in employee satisfaction and commitment to the company. Numerous
studies document that this decline began in the early 1980s and continued
through the 1990s.[12] Understandably, the erosion was greater for those firms
that had downsized than for those that had not. The shredding of the traditional implied employment contract has increased the concentration of employees on their narrowly defined self-interest, as people shift their focus from commitment to the corporation to looking out for their own career. In a survey of
managers, only 2 percent felt that commitment to the company was a key to
success, whereas 56 percent considered personal ambition as key.[13]

Although the rise in careerism might be prompted by the hard realities of experience, this does not mean that the resulting arm's-length contractual relationship with the firm is what people desire. Even though many
people might not expect or want to work for the same organization for most
of their work life, during their time at a particular company most people
desire reciprocal respect and commitment and a sense of being part of an
endeavor in which they can justifiably take pride.

The morale and motivational consequences of the "new employment
contract" is causing it to fail. This can be seen in the financial results of many
companies that have downsized. For a majority of these firms, despite the
reduced payroll, the near-term costs have exceeded the benefits. The longer-
term costs from the damage to employee loyalty and morale promise to be even
greater. Studies have shown that of the companies that downsized in the 1990
recession less than 33 percent reported an increase in competitive advantage,
only 34 percent reported increases in productivity, and less than 50 percent met
their operating profit goals after the layoffs.[14] But 80 percent of downsizing
companies admit employee moral has "been mugged."[15] Despite these dismal
results, nearly 40 percent of senior executives surveyed by Bain & Co. in 2001
said layoffs remained their first response to a downturn.[16]

This change in employee sentiment has profound implications for senior managers' abilities to lead. When the competency of these managers is
suspect and the morale of their people is low, their strategies, policies, and
initiatives are more readily questioned and resisted. Middle managers are
motivated to oppose these initiatives either for the good of the company (if
they believe top management is increasingly out of touch with the real prob-

lems of the organization) or to protect their own self-interest (if they no longer believe senior management has their best interests at heart). Increasingly, middle managers believe top management is not listening to their problems and complaints. According to the Hay Group's survey, in 1990 only 35 percent of middle managers felt positive about the extent to which top management listened to them.[17]

Thus, although the influence of businesses on the lives of employees is growing, the corporation's impact on these lives is mixed. Some people have experienced increasing alienation from their work and a growing cynicism toward senior management; for others it has been a time of greater participation in decision making and greater commitment to their company's ends. For companies that are becoming estranged from their employees, the long-term competitive consequences are dire.

Loyalty, Commitment, and Achieving Competitive Advantage through Knowledge Creation

Ironically, just at the time when loyalty is in rapid decline, the changing nature of competition and the accelerating importance of knowledge to performance have placed greater emphasis on loyalty, commitment, and the fuller realization of the employees' potential.

The advance of technology has changed the character of work. At all organizational levels, the work with the greatest competitive value requires a high degree of skill and knowledge. Consequently, the quality of the workforce and how well it is managed are the keys to securing and sustaining a competitive advantage.

As Robert Reich argues, in a fundamental sense America must begin thinking about international competitiveness in terms of its workforce, not its corporations or "American industry."[18] Only the workforce is not readily transferable across national borders. Capital and technology can flow rather freely. In a world where knowledge has become the coin of international competition, only a nation's or a firm's people develop the ideas that determine future competitive advantage.

Of increasing importance to *sustainable* competitive advantage is knowledge created by a network of complex social relationships. It forms the core competencies that are not readily transferable to competitors. As Joseph Badaracco Jr. has observed, specific individuals do not possess much of the most strategically critical knowledge. "In an age of rapidly proliferating knowledge, the [core of a firm] is a social network that absorbs, creates, stores, transforms, buys, sells, and communicates knowledge. Its stronghold is the knowledge embedded in a dense web of social, economic, contractual, and administrative relationships." He distinguishes between two kinds of knowledge—migratory and embedded.

Knowledge that can migrate quickly and simultaneously in multiple directions through licensing, reverse engineering, consultants, manuals, drawings, or the hiring of personnel from competitors provides fleeting advantages. Competitors are often able to duplicate the advantages at lower cost and with less risk by being a fast follower. Embedded knowledge is different. It is "sticky" and moves slowly.

> [Embedded knowledge] resides in relationships, usually complex social relationships, . . . and in particular norms, attitudes, information flows, and ways of making decisions that shape their dealings with each other. . . . A team, a department, or a company sometimes "knows" things that none of its individual members know, and some of its knowledge cannot be fully articulated. . . .
>
> Once a company has secured embedded knowledge—by dint of its own efforts, by learning from another organization, or both—it has capabilities, skills, know-how, and knowledge that are secure for a much longer period than migratory knowledge is, because embedded knowledge does not slip away so easily.[19]

As knowledge—and particularly embedded knowledge—becomes ever more critical to performance, the motivation and stability of the workforce will be increasingly important. Today, the source of competitive advantage can walk out the door—or at a minimum can opt not to devote the effort necessary to be a world-class competitor. Enron learned this lesson just days before its collapse, when its trading screens went dark because the energy traders simply did not show up for work.

Loyalty is essential to maximizing the willingness of organizational members to think for themselves, to openly and candidly stand up for ideas, and to challenge conventional wisdom. Consequently, loyalty is inextricably intertwined with individual initiative, the expression of creativity, and openness and candor in the decision-making process. These traits are essential to the innovation, rapid response, and decisiveness that are so critical to success in today's rapidly changing marketplace.

Albert Hirschman, in the insightful *Exit, Voice, and Loyalty*, draws a distinction between a member's motivation to leave an organization—or at least to stand by passively while the firm's performance suffers—and to stay engaged and fight in "an attempt at changing the practices, policies and outputs of the firm" in order to transform "an objectionable state of affairs." The "hallmark of loyalist behavior" is "the reluctance to exit in spite of disagreement with the organization. . . . In deciding whether the time has come to leave an organization, members, *especially the more influential ones*, will sometimes be held back not so much by the moral and material sufferings they would themselves have to go through as a result of exit, but by the anticipation that the *organization to which they belong would go from bad to worse if they left.*"[20] They are bound to the organization by a deep sense of caring for its purposes.

In many ways, these competitive realities have placed us at a turning point—a point that calls for senior managers to reevaluate their companies' internal environment that determines people's relationship to their work. A critical management question is how to regain and maintain the loyalty and commitment of the members of the organization. The answer to the question rests in an understanding of the source of loyalty and commitment. Loyalty by definition is directed to an object. Josiah Royce, in *The Philosophy of Loyalty*, defines loyalty as "The willing and practical and thoroughgoing devotion of a person to a cause . . . beyond your private self, greater than you are."[21] In corporations, this loyalty is tied to purpose, for loyalty springs from a deep attachment to the *cause* of the organization. True loyalty can be achieved only if the cause represented by the organization's purpose is deemed worthy of attachment and devotion.

The issue is not one of blind loyalty to the corporation. The days of the "organization man," which never were very uplifting for the human spirit, are long gone. However, the desire for a personal cause worthy of loyalty is very much alive in people's hearts.

Commitment to benefiting the customer transcends the corporation. When work's purpose focuses on serving the customer, it becomes embodied in the product or service. This is a more direct and tangible object of individual loyalty than is attachment to the abstract notion of the corporation itself. The resulting loyalty can be threefold: first, to fellow team members who have often prevailed over outsider attacks—including management—on their ideas to increase the customers' benefits; second, to the product or service the individual helps create; and third, to the company that makes this possible. Each object of loyalty reinforces the others, and as the corporation takes on increased personal value, the motivational and directional power of purpose is enhanced.

Work and the Search for Meaning

Mentally healthy people, regardless of their organizational position, take their lives—and consequently their work—very seriously. They struggle in their own ways to find meaning for their lives.

Some, in despair of finding meaning and happiness, pursue hedonistic impulses and turn to materialism and consumption. Work becomes a means for seeking fulfillment through wealth and possessions. As a result, work's value is primarily extrinsic. But this has proved to be a largely hollow pursuit. Studies have shown that, above the poverty level, differences in the level of wealth and income level make a "very meager difference" in the sense of well-being.[22]

The reality is that much of people's waking time is spent on the job. Consequently, the intrinsic rewards derived from work provide some of the best potential sources of meaning. Companies can fill some of the void created by the eroding influence of other institutions by providing meaningful work—work that offers the opportunity for the exercise of creativity and initiative in the service of worthwhile ends. In fact, an essential aspect of executive leadership is the assumption of the responsibility to create a work environment that makes the realization of meaning possible.

Unfortunately, through ineptitude, managers can quite readily create an environment in which work becomes demeaning. People are treated impersonally—as inputs into the productive process rather than as individual human beings, and as means to ends they do not value. Too often, they are not given opportunities to participate in decisions that affect them and their work, and therefore they have a sense of powerlessness. In such cases, individuals must strive mightily on their own to find meaning in their work. And many do. But these situations are simply bad management—and they will threaten an organization's survival in the twenty-first century.

To understand the interrelationship of work and meaning, one must first understand the human quest for meaning, the ways in which meaning has traditionally been found, and how the work ethic has evolved in our society. Many have offered insights, including philosophers, psychologists, and theologians. What can be distilled from their teachings are five sources of meaning: (1) the affirmation of one's being, (2) the expression of one's creativity, (3) serving worthwhile purposes, (4) achieving a closer relationship to the divine, and (5) gaining knowledge of self through one's relationship to other humans and to creation—a knowledge that can result in a transcendence of self. Writers have related each of these sources of meaning to work in a variety of ways.

Evolution of the Western Work Ethic[23]

In primitive societies, work was directly related to fulfilling biological needs. The satisfaction derived from work was immediate and direct. Work was something that humans naturally did. Still today, in many primitive societies little distinction is made between work and play.

As civilizations formed, a growing division of labor characterized work. Increasing specialization reduced the diversity and skill inherent in most people's tasks. Work was no longer directly related to the satisfaction of biological needs. Instead, the craftsmen found fulfillment in the creation of the end products of their work. For them, work began to take on value in itself.

Before the Reformation, most Western philosophers and theologians believed that people were trapped by the necessity to work. Plato and Aristotle thought that a life of leisure and reflection, embodied in the concept of the philosopher-king, was the only fit life. The purpose of work was to enable leisure. Work had no inherent dignity or value, and toil was nearly equated with slavery.

In the Middle Ages, in accord with ancient Judeo-Christian belief, work was considered a necessity of life—a wearisome and painful task that helped humans atone for their sinfulness. To the early Christians, work had two additional purposes: to provide the means for extending charity to their needy fellow human beings and to improve one's character by muzzling "the evil and disobedient flesh."[24] As Saint Augustine taught, the superior life remained one of cloistered contemplation and passive meditation on divine matters, not actively changing the world. The acquisitive desires of man beyond his needs of sustenance were anathema to him and the other early church fathers. Accumulated wealth should be given to one's needy brothers.

Not all of Christendom took such a dim view of work. For example, the Benedictines viewed work more positively, arguing that laziness was "the enemy of the soul" and "to work is to pray." Work not only kept people out of mischief, but also fulfilled their duty to God.

Interestingly, part of the early Hebrew tradition also saw work differently. Work provided an avenue for bringing the world back to the cosmic harmony that existed before the original sin. The Rabbinical literature teaches that "to work is to cooperate with God in the great purpose of the world's salvation. The labor of man continues and prolongs the divine energy which overflowed in the act of creation."[25] Work involves man in the mystery of creation. This view was also to dominate Christendom after the Reformation.

The ideas of the Reformation dramatically changed the Western concept of work. Martin Luther—who placed greater value on the active life than on Saint Augustine's cloistered, contemplative one—gave birth to the doctrine of the "calling." He believed that God called everyone to a productive vocation that served the common good and increased God's glory. A person's occupation was a direct result of God's will. To persevere in this assigned work was a religious duty. It was carrying out God's will. Thus, a new idea came into the world: the fulfillment of one's worldly duty is the highest form of moral activity.[26] This meant that all forms of legitimate work done in obedience to God and in the spirit of love for one's neighbors were given equal spiritual dignity.[27] Furthermore, Luther's principle of justification by faith alone, not by good works, liberated man to focus his work on the material world, unfettered by ecclesiastical restraints.

John Calvin augmented the idea of the calling with the concept of predestination. He believed that God in His unfathomable wisdom elected only a part of humanity to have everlasting life. God channeled His activity on earth through these elect. In doing so, God put His mark on them and their actions. To Calvin, the only evidence of one's election was to be found in one's actions. The elect lived to glorify God, not for themselves. Good works would not bring salvation (to believe so would mean that God's will could be changed by human intervention), but they were signs of God's favor. Understandably, individual believers, filled with doubt as to whether they were among the saved, had a great need to try to live as the elect would live. Did one's works reflect the deeper, fuller religious life that a saved person would naturally be drawn to follow? To dislike work was a clear sign of not being elected. These ideas, when combined with the natural human psychological need to prove one's own salvation, led to prodigious effort devoted to work.

Calvin, like Luther, saw work as the expression of God's will—God's way to establish His kingdom on earth. Therefore, like his predecessors, Calvin taught that people should renounce the fruits of their own labor. Any profits beyond that needed to provide the necessities for one's family should not be hoarded or expended on luxuries. Instead, profits should be reinvested in new works that further God's will or given to the needy. Unlike Luther, this view of work led Calvin to believe that man's duty is to pursue the vocation that provided the greatest return to him and thus to society. No virtue is to be found in staying in the class or profession into which one is born, as Luther had argued. In *The Protestant Ethic and the Spirit of Capitalism*, Max Weber documents the special significance Calvin's doctrine of the calling held for the American Puritans: "This calling is not, as it was for the Lutheran, a fate to which he must submit and which he must make the best of, but God's commandment to the individual to work for the divine glory."[28]

Soon, the idea of work as vehicle for fulfilling God's will was generalized. Work began to be viewed as an act of creation by which man subjugated nature to his needs. Swiss Reformation leader Huldrych Zwingli captured this idea in a sentence, "There is nothing in the universe so like God as the worker." After all, in Genesis, God gave man dominion over the earth and charged him to subdue it.[29] Through his work, man was to be God's agent on earth, carrying out the divine plan.

These were revolutionary ideas with profound consequences. They sanctified work as part of God's will for humankind, unleashed considerable initiative to better one's lot in life, and provided impetus to the emergent system of capitalism. Work was no longer a burden carried in the atonement for sin but "the core of a moral life."[30] Wasting time was a sin. Extracting the greatest returns from work in order to glorify God on earth and to enable maximum charity to one's needy neighbors became a human duty.

Released from the strict ecclesiastical constraints, man set about developing a worldly justification of work. By the late eighteenth century, the belief in a calling gradually became secularized, especially in the United States. The idea that individuals could improve their lot through persistence, frugality, and diligent hard work became widely accepted.

The notion of social duty also took on a more secular form. Work was seen not so much as a source of human dignity, but as being useful in securing other ends.[31] Work represented a creative act that enabled people to make a difference in the world. Origins of this idea can be found in the mid-eighteenth century in Adam Smith's *The Theory of Moral Sentiments*. Smith believed, "Man was made for action and to promote by the exertion of his faculties such changes in the external circumstances both of himself and others, as may seem most favourable to the happiness of all."[32] Instead of work being considered the end for which man was created (as most theologians of his day believed), Smith thought of work as a means of serving society—a means of "bettering our condition" and achieving the "happiness of all." Achieving this happiness meant working to provide more desired goods. "Consumption is the sole end and purpose of all production; and the interest of the producer ought to be attended to, only so far as it may be necessary for promoting that of the consumer."[33] In essence, Adam Smith argues that happiness results from a purpose tied to the customer, not to the owner.

As the Industrial Revolution progressed, the Protestant work ethic underwent a worldly transformation, and the concept of usefulness became more widely accepted. To produce was a social duty to help build the country, tame the frontier, and improve the lot of humankind. This conviction was helpful in surmounting the challenges of the American frontier.

However, the harsh realities accompanying industrialization challenged the traditional values associated with work. Many people were trapped in monotonous factory jobs with little or no room for creativity, working for wages at the pleasure of other people. By the mid-nineteenth century, there was considerable concern regarding the degrading effect machines had on workers. The specialization of work weakened the link between hard work and success and distanced workers from the products of their efforts. To view one's efforts as a mastery of nature became increasingly difficult.

Karl Marx predicted these forces would result in the alienation of workers. For Marx, man's alienation from himself, from nature, and from other people originated with the separation of the individual from the product of his work. The more of his life that he contributed to routine industrial work, the more he was demeaned:

> The worker relates to the product of his labour as to an alien object. . . .
> The more the worker externalizes himself in his work, the more powerful

becomes the alien, objective world that he creates opposite himself, the poorer he becomes himself in his inner life and the less he can call his own. . . . The worker puts his life into the object and this means that it no longer belongs to him but to the object. . . . So the greater this product the less he is himself. . . . The life that he has lent to the object affronts him, hostile and alien.[34]

Marx held this view, in part, because he viewed work in capitalist societies narrowly. He saw only two purposes for work under capitalism: to earn the wages needed to sustain life and to help capitalists accumulate capital. Marx believed this need not be. In what he considered to be a properly organized society, work had value beyond merely sustaining existence. The mastery of work was a means to self-fulfillment and the creation of a better world. Work was man's "life-expression."[35] Indeed, the human task is to attain "the full development of the mastery . . . over the forces of nature, those of so-called nature as well as of humanity's own nature."[36]

Most mainline Western thinkers, although they shared Marx's concerns, proposed fundamentally different solutions to cope with the rapid changes brought on by industrialization. These solutions shared a common belief in the value of individual initiative and creativity. The ideas underlying individualism—ideas of self-improvement, creative expression through work, and usefulness—became more fully developed by the mid-nineteenth century. The result was a continued secularization of the traditional values. This secularization took several forms.

For moralists, such as Thomas Carlyle, work was an antidote to the destructive human passions, "the grand cure for all the maladies and miseries that beset mankind." Hard work built character and assisted in the development of moral discipline. Historian Daniel Rodgers describes the essence of this school of thought:

In what Carlyle called the "purifying fire" of regular labor, mid-nineteenth-century moralists hoped to consume the sexual passions that seemed increasingly to threaten them. But they hoped for more as well. Work cleared away doubts and vanquished despair; it curbed the animal instincts to violence; it distracted the laborer from the siren call of radicalism; it redeemed the convict prisoner. It did all this in part by character building, by ingraining habits of fortitude, self-control, and perseverance, and in part by systematic exhaustion.[37]

Some individualists adhered to the belief that work provided a means for the creative expression of self through placing one's personal imprint on the world. Ralph Waldo Emerson's thoughts capture this secular idea: "A man coins himself into his labor; turns his day, his strength, his thoughts, his affection into some product which remains a visible sign of his power." Work was important as an extension of oneself. Its product provided a living legacy of one's mastery.

For many others, the most important aspect of work was that it held the promise of upward mobility. The American response to the potential degrading effect of working for wages was to view work itself as a means to improve oneself, to achieve greater independence, to raise one's social status, and eventually to acquire wealth. The promise of upward mobility, characterized in popular tales such as those of Horatio Alger, was widely accepted in American culture.[38] The ideal of the self-made man became a widely shared belief. Initially, upward mobility meant becoming self-employed. Abraham Lincoln, who personified the promise of upward mobility, articulated well the beliefs of his day when he observed:

> There is no permanent class of hired laborers among us. The prudent, penniless beginner in the world labors for wages awhile, saves a surplus with which to buy tools or land for himself, then labors on his own account another while, and at length hires another new beginner to help him. . . . If any continue through life in the condition of the hired laborer; it is not the fault of the system, but because of either a dependent nature which prefers it, or improvidence, folly, or singular misfortune.[39]

At the turn of the century, even John D. Rockefeller reflected the sentiment that the promise of success from hard work was still alive, saying that the rise from wage earner to corporate leader was a "constant procession. . . . No boy, howsoever lowly—the barefoot country boy, the humble newsboy, the child of the tenement—need despair. . . . They have but to master the knack of economy, thrift, honesty, and perseverance, and success is theirs."[40] Rockefeller's words are not substantially different from Benjamin Franklin's, nearly one and a half centuries earlier, regarding the belief that success flows directly from virtues of hard work and sound character.

By the early twentieth century, the goal began to shift from self-employment to climbing the organizational ladder. The scale and scope of industry were expanding at a rapid rate, increasing the capital required to start a new venture. Small proprietorships in many industries became obsolete. The prospect of eventually working in one's own business diminished. However, opportunities in corporate America were rapidly expanding. The exploitation of these opportunities required skills of knowledge and judgment, not just the willingness to do hard physical work. As a consequence, factory workers found it increasingly difficult to envision significant upward mobility for themselves. They seemed trapped in their jobs. As they began to transfer the promise for mobility from themselves to their children, education became a critical factor of success.

These different, but compatible, ideas converged "to reaffirm the central premise of the work ethic: that work was the core of the moral life. Work made men useful in a world of economic scarcity; it staved off the doubts and temptations that preyed on idleness; it opened the way to deserved wealth and status; it allowed one to put the impress of mind and skill on the material world."[41]

But a new threat to this moral code arose in the late nineteenth century and early twentieth century. The advocates of scientific management challenged the moralists for the attention of the public and of managers. Over the objections of unionists, these management gurus of their day called for increasing standardization and systematic measurement of work. Ironically, Frederick Taylor argued that his efforts to regiment activity and tie pay to output would restore individuality to the worker. Each job, and thus each worker, would be defined separately. The worker, Taylor reasoned, could determine how hard he would work and thus could control his wages and, consequently, his social position. Individuality was to be found through the distinct requirements placed on each job and through piecework compensation. However, in practice, the regimentation and control of work robbed the worker of much of his freedom on the job and, consequently, of his ability to identify with the product of his work and to control his own destiny. The realization of the traditional ideals in factory work was threatened with extinction.

Following World War I, a very different movement erupted—industrial democracy. The movement was born of the war's production experience. During the war, cooperation between labor and management and a high degree of worker input through "work committees" were widespread.[42] Woodrow Wilson declared the labor problem to be the nation's most important postwar issue. The solution to the problem, he said, required "a new form and spirit to industrial organization," one that resulted in a "genuine democratization of industry." Wilson envisioned giving workers the right "to participate in some organic way in every decision which directly affects their welfare or the part they are to play in industry."[43]

Although churches swiftly endorsed the concept of industrial democracy, managers were slow to adopt what many saw as a radical new idea. The American Federation of Labor, seeing a threat to its power and concluding that the weak work committees were too susceptible to management manipulation, vigorously opposed the fledgling movement through widespread strikes. Thus the movement, which had so many parallels to the trend to teams and empowerment in today's workplace, quickly died.

Subsequently, the Depression, with its consolidation of collective bargaining, led to a formal recognition of the gulf of interest that separated labor and management. They now faced each other as antagonists—each with considerable power.

The industrial democracy movement was a microcosm of the tensions that shaped the nature of work in America throughout the twentieth century. There has been a constant struggle between the ideals of work and its reality. A central question has been how to bring the reality more in line with the ideals.

One response to this dilemma was to give up on work as a source of fulfillment and turn instead to leisure. The deprivation of creativity in work, the rise of the culture of the "organization man," and the physical and psychological dangers from overwork led people to focus on activity outside of work. Creative expression and fulfillment was increasingly sought in leisure-time activity. By midcentury, leisure time was expected to expand and to be an important source of satisfaction. But the promise of leisure proved both hollow and fleeting. Time spent at work has actually increased since the 1960s. The average American in 1987 worked 1,949 hours, 163 more hours (or twenty more eight-hour workdays) than in 1969.[44] Although the 1987 workload is substantially lower than the peak of feverish work activity in the mid-nineteenth century (when the average American worked from 3,150 to 3,650 hours), it is considerably higher than the 1,440 to 1,620 hours worked by peasants and casual laborers in thirteenth- and fourteenth-century medieval England.[45] By 1994, Americans were working longer than their Japanese, British, and German counterparts.[46]

Meaning Through Work: The Current Realities

With the failure of the promise of leisure, the focus has once again turned to work as a source of meaning. Today's beliefs are truly an amalgam of the beliefs of the last five hundred years. Work in today's world has many facets. It is viewed as a creative act through which people can express their individuality and leave an imprint on something beyond themselves. It is a means to making a useful contribution to society, and many Americans see their work as their meager contribution to fulfilling God's will for His creation. In our society, which values meritocracy, hard work is still closely linked to success and personal improvement. For most people, work remains the core of a moral life. We feel guilty when we slack off—sensing we are cheating ourselves of a fulfilling, self-actualizing experience and others of our fullest contribution to their welfare.

A Contemporary Theological View of Work. Sociologist Peter Berger, giving voice to the living legacy of Zwingli's thoughts from an earlier era, describes the spiritual power of the belief that work is a creative act with social—even religious—purpose: "If work means to build a world, then it entails, in a religious perspective, a repetition or imitation of the divine acts by which the world was originally built—and perhaps even a competition with these divine acts, as the myth of Prometheus suggests. To work is no light matter. To work is to mime creation itself."[47]

John Paul II, reflecting the contemporary theological view of work, sees work serving multiple human needs. It has the "power to build a community" in part by uniting people socially in the shared endeavor to achieve common good; it can lead to individual expression and fulfillment as a human being; and it embodies a responsibility shared by everyone to leave the world a better place.[48] "In the final analysis it is always man who is the purpose of the work, whatever work it is that is done by man. . . . Work is not only good in the sense that it is useful or something to enjoy; it is also good as being something worthy, that is to say, something that corresponds to man's dignity, that expresses this dignity and increases it."[49]

The words of Peter Berger and John Paul II could have been spoken at any time over the last four hundred years. They reflect beliefs that have stood the test of time. These are beliefs that have been handed down over the ages. Work derives meaning from its impact on the worker and from the benefit of its output for other human beings.

A *Psychological Perspective of Work.* In the twentieth century, a new group of people struggled to unlock the secrets of human happiness and motivation—psychologists and psychiatrists. The debate within this community over differing views of the human motivation to work provides insight into the individual needs that people seek to fulfill through their work today.

Freud, although he wrote sparingly on the subject of work, concluded that mentally healthy people do two things well: "Love and work." He considered work, which was "created by external necessity," and the power of love to be the foundations of civilized communal life.[50] He attributed to work the potential for self-actualization and for integrating the self with the reality of the external world. "No other technique for the conduct of life," he said, "attaches the individual so firmly to reality as laying emphasis on work; for his work at least gives him a secure place in a portion of reality, in the human community."[51] More important to Freud, however, work was seen as a means to dissipate energies and aggressions that otherwise might cause social or psychological problems for the individual. "The possibility it offers of displacing a large amount of libidinal components, whether narcissistic, aggressive or even erotic, on to professional work and on to the human relations connected with it lends it a value by no means second to what it enjoys as something indispensable to the preservation and justification of existence in society."[52]

But in the end, to Freud, the pleasure principle remained the dominant motivation of humans. "As a path to happiness, work is not highly prized by men. They do not strive after it as they do after other possibilities of satisfaction. The great majority of people only work under the stress of necessity, and this natural human aversion to work raises most difficult social problems."[53] Work is not seen as pleasurable in itself. Rather, it represents a socially acceptable way in which people can satisfy their natural sexual and aggressive impulses (a process Freud termed "sublimation").

Karl Menninger later added that work sublimates the basic instincts of love and aggression to achieve constructive outcomes: "Of all the methods available for absorbing the aggressive energies of mankind, work takes first place. . . . The essential point is that in work, as contrasted with purposeless destruction, the aggressive impulses are molded and guided in a constructive direction by the influence of the creative (erotic) instinct."[54]

For Carl Jung, work is a potential source of creativity that can result in greater levels of self-actualization. "The supreme ideal of man is to fulfill himself as a unique creative individual according to his own innate potentialities and within the limits of reality. . . . The best liberation is ensured by regular work. Work, nevertheless, is only salutary when it is a free act and has nothing of infantile constraint about it."[55] Jung believed that without freedom and creativity, work becomes a source of frustration, not fulfillment. A person diverted from the goal of realizing his or her innate potential as a unique individual becomes a "crippled animal."

When the individual values the corporation's purpose, work becomes more a "free act," moving closer to the ideals of creative expression and the fulfillment of one's potential. When the purpose is not valued by the individual, behavior needs to be manipulated by other means, such as by management systems (planning and budgeting systems that set goals, and compensation systems that evaluate and reward performance), to motivate behavior consistent with the corporate ends. If this must be done, personal fulfillment more readily eludes the individual and frustration sets in.

Much of the psychoanalytical literature seems to argue that ideals are not what motivate people to work. In fact, to Freud and many of the others, ideals seem to be alien to what is natural to human beings. However, psychoanalyst Viktor Frankl's studies of Nazi prisoners during World War II provide a different answer.

In Frankl's moving account of his internment in Nazi concentration camps, he concluded, "man's search for meaning is the primary motivation in his life." He contradicts the beliefs of Freud that people are primarily driven by the pleasure principle and of Adler that people are centrally motivated by "striving for superiority" and power. He criticized them for believing that ideals and values are "nothing but defense mechanisms, reaction formations and sublimations." Frankl observed that he would not be willing to live by or die for these motivations, but that "man, however, is able to live and even die for the sake of his ideals and values!"[56] For Frankl,

The true meaning of life is to be discovered in the world rather than within man or his own psyche, as though it were a closed system. . . . Being human always points, and is directed, to something, or someone, other

than oneself—be it a meaning to fulfill or another human being to en-
counter. The more one forgets himself—by giving himself to a cause to
serve or another person to love—the more human he is and the more he
actualizes himself. What is called self-actualization is not an attainable aim
at all, for the simple reason that the more one would strive for it, the more
he would miss it. In other words, self-actualization is possible only as a
side-effect of self-transcendence.[57]

The world's great religions, with their common emphasis on finding
meaning for life through self-transcendence—as well as the willingness
of men to die in religious wars over the ages—gives credence to Frankl's
arguments.

More recently, Abraham Maslow furthered the development of the
concept of self-actualization and work—in particular the power of work
to link individuals to valued purposes outside themselves. Maslow sees
work as a potential source of satisfaction of a hierarchy of needs beginning
with physiological and safety needs, extending through needs for love, the
respect of others, self-esteem, and culminating in self-actualization or self-
fulfillment. Capturing the essence of self-actualization, Maslow asserted,
"What a man *can* be, he *must* be." In his later writings, he attributes this
fulfillment to a vocation that enables individuals to become devoted to
ends beyond self—to a "beloved job outside themselves." When this
occurs, work takes on intrinsic value. Thus his thinking about self-actualization merged with and became part of self-transcendence—in essence, a
secular version of Martin Luther's concept of a "calling." Maslow sum-
marized the findings of his thirty years of research since the development
of his hierarchy:

> Self-actualizing people are, without one single exception, involved in a
> cause outside their own skin, in something outside of themselves. They
> are devoted, working at something, something that is very precious to
> them—some calling or vocation in the old sense, the priestly sense. They
> are working at something which fate has called them to somehow and
> which they work at and which they love, so that the work-joy dichotomy
> in them disappears. . . .
> Generally the devotion and dedication is so marked that one can fairly
> use the old world vocation, calling, or mission to describe their passionate,
> selfless, and profound feelings for their "work." We could even use the
> words destiny or fate. I have sometimes gone so far as to speak of oblation
> in the religious sense, in the sense of offering oneself or dedicating oneself

upon some altar for some particular task, some cause outside oneself and bigger than oneself, something not merely selfish, something impersonal. . . .

Such vocation-loving individuals tend to identify with their "work" and to make it into a defining-characteristic of the self. It becomes part of the self. . . .

All, in one way or another, devote their lives to the search for . . . the ultimate values which are intrinsic, which cannot be reduced to anything more ultimate. . . . The tasks to which [self-actualizing individuals] are dedicated seem to be interpretable as embodiments or incarnations of intrinsic values (rather than as a means to ends outside the work itself, and rather than as functionally autonomous). The tasks are loved (and introjected[58]) BECAUSE they embody these values. That is, ultimately it is the values that are loved rather than the job as such. . . . This introjection means that the self has enlarged to include aspects of the world and that therefore the distinction between self and not-self (outside, other) has been transcended. . . . [59]

Although self-actualization may sound like the person becomes outer-directed, with goals determined by social needs external to the self, the reality is quite the opposite. Meaningful self-actualization comes from actions that serve inner-directed goals that are in harmony with the essence of the self, and that challenge and stretch one's abilities.

These ideas have profound implications for corporate leadership. It is the *company* that must align its ends with those valued by its individual members. When the ends of the company and the individual are harmonious, an environment is created in which the individual has greater opportunity to enrich his life though work experiences. When this occurs, work and the organization that makes the experience possible take on intrinsic value.

In his book *Flow: The Psychology of Optimal Experience*, psychologist Mihaly Csikszentmihalyi concludes that the actions of people who enjoy optimal experiences are dominated by goals that "originate within the self"—"a strongly directed purpose that is not self-seeking."[60] Driven by these goals to higher levels of performance, the individual undertakes actions that challenge his or her abilities. The person experiences a "sense of discovery" as new competencies are acquired. The result is a growth of the self—a "new [elevated] state of consciousness."

This harmonious, purposive activity gives one's life greater meaning. "People who find their lives meaningful usually have a goal that is challenging enough to take up all their energies, a goal that can give significance to their lives. . . . When an important goal is pursued with resolution, and all [of] one's varied activities fit together into a unified flow experience, the result is that *harmony* is brought to consciousness. Someone who knows his desires and works with purpose to achieve them is a person whose feelings, thoughts, and actions are congruent with one another, and is therefore a person who has achieved inner harmony."[61]

Fulfillment in work—and the happiness derived from this fulfillment—comes from values intrinsic to the task, from achievement and possibilities for personal growth. Underlying each of these ideas is the perceived quality of the ends the work serves. But when managers create work environments that require individuals to compromise their high ideals and values in order to achieve success, work is drained of the power to provide this fulfillment.

Three Sociological Concepts of Work. Clearly, work has many facets and is viewed differently by different people. Sociologist Robert Bellah describes three concepts of work:

1. A "job" that is "a way of making money and making a living; it supports a self defined by economic success, security and all that money can buy."
2. A "career" that "traces one's progress through life by achievement and advancement in an occupation" and defines self in terms of social standing, prestige, and an "expanding power and competency that renders work itself a source of self-esteem."
3. A "calling" that makes work morally inseparable from one's life and "subsumes the self into a community of disciplined practice and sound judgment whose activity has meaning and value in itself, not just in the output or profit that results from it," and "links a person to a larger community, a whole in which the calling of each is a contribution to the good of all."[62]

The first two concepts view work as an exchange. In a "job" or "career," physical and mental efforts are exchanged for tangible financial rewards and security and for intangibles such as power, prestige, and self-esteem. Work is a *means* to these desired ends—devoid of meaning outside of self-gratification. Erich Fromm argues that this view of work can lead to boredom, dissatisfaction, apathy, and alienation. The worker comes to "hate himself, because he sees his life passing by, without making any sense beyond the momentary intoxication of success."[63] However, this is not inevitable. When work becomes a "calling" that energizes the moral aspirations of individuals by relating them to broader purposes, work becomes valued for itself. Work and the self-transcendent ends become united. Such is the power of a corporate purpose that unites the hearts of members of an organization with its mission.

Work and the Higher Human Aspirations

Common to much of the writing about work and motivation is a fundamental truth. Beyond financial reward, status, security, and the prospect of career advancement, people value work that provides meaning to their existence. In each case this meaning is derived from work's role in relating the individual to nature, to other human beings, and to the realities of the external world. Work touches people's deepest motivations when it *affirms their existence and dignity*, enables them to contribute to *worthwhile purposes*, challenges their *creativity*, and gives them a sense of *pride and accomplishment*. Belonging to a financially successful team is important but not enough. Work can be much more than a means of gaining money, power, and prestige.

Work and the Affirmation of Being. One's need to affirm one's existence is captured in the often-expressed desire to "make a difference." It is also exhibited in the strong drive to control nature—to prove one's unique powers. The need to affirm one's existence by the exercise of power over things is also often extended to power and influence over other individuals. While the exercise of creative power over things is usually a constructive motivation, craving power over other human beings can be corrosive of character and can undermine true leadership. However, leaders who respect their "followers" create environments that confer dignity on their organizations' members and provide opportunities for them to "leave a mark." As a result these leaders are able to attract high-quality people and unlock more of their potential, and enable them to harmonize their personal goals with service to the organization's objectives.

One's being is affirmed through work in three principal ways: first, by the exercise of creativity; second, by an ability to see and understand the value of the consequences of one's work—to confirm that one is truly making a meaningful difference in other people's lives; and third, by working in an environment that respects the dignity of individuals. Dignity comes from being treated as an end, not an animate cog in a production process. It is conveyed through respect for individuals—by soliciting, listening to, and responding to the ideas of employees regarding decisions affecting them and their work; by consistently reinforcing the importance of their welfare to the collective mission of the organization; and by defining the mission in terms that they value. Respect for individuals requires that people be treated with honesty and fairness; that their rights be respected; that independent thinking and openness and candor in decision making be valued; that decisions be made on the merit of the ideas presented; and that individual contributions of all members be recognized. By conveying dignity to individuals, these characteristics form the cornerstones of healthy, high-performing organizations.

Meaning Derived from Serving Worthwhile Purposes. Meaning in life comes from the satisfaction of personal ideals—ideals such as courage, truth, beauty, creativity, justice, honesty, self-fulfillment, and compassion. John Stuart Mill believed that people can achieve personal happiness only if they "have their minds fixed on some object other than their own happiness: on the happiness of others, on the improvement of mankind, even on some art or pursuit, followed not as a means, but as itself an ideal end."[64] In this sense, meaning as well as happiness, originates with purposive behavior. Philosopher Irving Singer describes this relationship:

> For most people there is virtually no experience—not even a highly pleasurable one—that will seem meaningful unless it can be justified in terms of an ideal one has chosen. . . . Ideals awaken the spirit to burgeoning possibilities for self-realization. Different ideals will be geared to different consummations, and even in the healthiest person ideals can always conflict with one another. But such constraints belong to a dynamic process that does not throttle human nature. On the contrary, it affords the maximum opportunity for creating new and more satisfying patterns of meaning.
>
> A meaningful life results from this intermeshing of means and ends, purposeful efforts to satisfy ideals leading to gratifications that matter not only in themselves but also in their ability to awaken new desires and new pursuits.[65]

Human ideals relate the individual to the world—to other human beings and to nature. Finding significance for our lives by responsibly relating to a system of purposes, ideas, and values larger than ourselves is critical to the essence of human well-being. This relatedness usually carries with it a sense of obligation—to other people and as a steward of nature. As John Gardner observes:

> Humans are in their nature seekers of meaning. . . . We have throughout history shown a compelling need to arrive at conceptions of the universe *in terms of which we could regard our own lives as meaningful.* We want to know where *we* fit into the scheme of things. We want to understand how the great facts of the objective world relate to *us* and what they imply for our behavior. We want to know what significance may be found in our own existence, the succeeding generations of our kind and the vivid events of our inner life. We seek some kind of meaningful framework in which to understand (or at least to reconcile ourselves to) the indignities of chance and circumstance and the fact of death. . . .
>
> The meanings in any life are multiple and varied. . . . But each kind of meaning implies a relationship between the person and some larger system of ideas or values, a relationship involving obligations as well as rewards. In the individual life, meaning, purpose and commitment are inseparable.[66]

When worthy corporate aims act to place individual efforts in a broader context, serving these ends can enhance the meaningfulness of one's life. This occurs when the company's purpose is defined in terms of the wider economic and social benefits of its products or services. Bertrand Russell captured the essence of the relationship of work, purpose, and meaning when he said, "Continuity of purpose is one of the most essential ingredients in happiness in the long run, and for most men this comes chiefly through their work. . . . Something is built up which remains as a monument when the work is completed. . . . The satisfaction to be derived from success in a great constructive enterprise is one of the most massive life has to offer."[67] To Russell, the constancy of purpose was important. "The most satisfactory purposes are those that lead on indefinitely from one success to another without ever coming to a dead end."[68] Ideally, this is true of corporate purpose and the purposiveness of individual efforts that serve it.

When quality of corporate ends generates a desire to better serve the cause, which in turn motivates individuals to expend greater effort to more fully realize their human potential, self-interest at its highest level begins to merge with corporate interest. Work in the service of others and in community with fellow workers, in E. F. Schumacher's words, "liberates ourselves from our inborn egocentricity."[69] He adds, "In the process of doing good work the ego of the worker disappears. He frees himself from his ego, so that the divine element in him can become active."[70]

John Gardner similarly argues that individuals must strive "toward meaningful goals—goals that relate the individual to a larger context of purposes. . . . [Leaders] must help the individual reestablish a meaningful relationship with a larger context of purposes."[71] This relationship can transform egocentric, selfish behavior into actions that serve common purpose. Gardner continues, "Humans are complex and contradictory beings, egocentric but inescapably involved with their fellow beings, selfish but capable of superb selflessness. We are preoccupied with our own needs, yet find no meaning in life unless we relate ourselves to something more comprehensive than those needs."[72]

One thoughtful executive related these ideas to the potential for deriving meaning from corporate purpose: "Business does not exist merely to produce more goods and services, or better goods and services for more people, though that is no small part of its task. Business also, particularly in these days, affords the principal or the only means whereby individual men and women may gain the satisfaction of accomplishing something more than merely sustaining their own lives."[73]

In some small way, an individual's contribution benefits customers and leaves a legacy on which the company's future service of worthwhile ends depends. Through the individual's impact on the less mortal company, he can achieve some added sense of immortality.

For some, the purpose of work is serving ends that transcend the corporation itself and encompass serving spiritual ends embodied in the concept of the calling. Work provides a closer connection with the divine and a unity with the whole of creation. In some of these cases, the corporation becomes the vehicle that enables the individual to serve these higher purposes. For example, ServiceMaster's corporate objectives begin "To honor God in all we do." Outside the entrance to its headquarters stands an eleven-foot white marble statue. Chairman Bill Pollard explains its significance. "It is a free-flowing representation of Jesus washing the feet of a disciple. This illustration from history is a great reminder for all of us that we have the potential to grow as we contribute and serve others."[74]

Regardless of the level on which purpose is defined, placing one's life in the context of broader meanings allows the individual to say, "My life has some importance. I have made a difference!" Leaders who infuse corporate purpose with a quality that appeals to these higher human motivations create organizations of greater vitality and cohesion.

Creativity and Meaning. Work is an act of creation in which people develop otherwise latent abilities and apply them with imagination and originality to produce something new. Creativity is essentially a very personal act—an expression of self that demonstrates one's mastery of nature, reminds one of human supremacy among living things, and, for some, joins them with God's creative force. Yet the act of transforming nature also unites human beings with nature, making them feel more one with the wholeness of creation. Productive work is "an extension of human personality into nature."[75] Erich Fromm explains this phenomenon:

> Work is not only an inescapable necessity for man. Work is also his liberator from nature, his creator as a social and independent being. In the process of work, that is, the molding and changing of nature outside of himself, man molds and changes himself. He emerges from nature by mastering her; he develops his powers of cooperation, of reason, his sense of beauty. He separates himself from nature, from the original unity with her, but at the same time unites himself with her again as her master and builder. The more his work develops, the more his individuality develops. In molding nature and re-creating her, he learns to make use of his powers, increasing his skill and his creativeness.[76]

By putting their personal stamp on events outside themselves, people give part of what is uniquely themselves to their work—and thus become even more committed to the purpose of their work. From this comes a sense of pride and ownership.

But there is a dichotomy in applying one's creative talents in business organizations. On the one hand, people widely recognize that collective cooperation enables the creative powers of each individual to achieve more than any one of them could otherwise achieve alone. On the other hand, bureaucratic and routinized organizational activity can stifle creativity. They bring with them the threat of dulling, repetitive human work that saps individual initiative. Meaningful work requires not only the freedom to create, but also the freedom from bureaucratic barriers to self-expression.

When individuals are asked to perform work that is inconsistent with their own purposes, Csikszentmihalyi observes, "it is as if [their] psychic energy is being wasted." The job becomes a necessary "burden imposed from the outside, an effort that takes life away from the ledger of their existence."[77] As a result they are blocked from realizing optimal experiences through work, even though the tasks may be enjoyable on occasion. The result is that creative energies are drained and initiative inhibited.

On the other hand, harmony of individual and corporate purpose can unleash innovative impulses. When people are "intrinsically motivated in their actions, they are not easily disturbed by external threats," Csikszentmihalyi finds. The result is a personal constancy of purpose and courage to act, which are the foundations of creativity and initiative. "With enough psychic energy free to observe and analyze their surroundings objectively," he concludes, individuals "have a better chance of discovering in [their environment] new opportunities for action."[78] The result is increased creativity.

The reality of these forces means that for creative expression to thrive in the workplace, leaders must align corporate purposes with the common purposes of their people and must diligently prevent the all-too-common incessant creep of bureaucracy and the glorification of process over substance. When these efforts are successful, the benefits are twofold: an increase in creativity and a simplification of decision-making processes, both of which lead to better decisions and more committed people.

Meaning and Performance

For those companies that create an environment in which individuals can derive meaning from their work, the benefits are great. Commitment increases; work becomes more focused; greater collaboration and cohesion are fostered among the organization's members; actions throughout the firm are more coherent with the corporate ends; people work harder and more thoughtfully; and people take more responsibility for their own development. Individuals become more purposive, and their interests are more closely aligned with the organization's competitive ends. As the commitment to a meaningful common purpose increases, the barriers to sharing ideas fall and innovation is significantly enhanced. The alternative is continued drift toward greater alienation, growing cynicism, and an intensified pursuit of narrow self-interest.

The latent human potential in most organizations is great. A Daniel Yankelovich poll asked people which of the following statements they most agreed with:

1. I have an inner need to do the very best job I can regardless of pay.
2. Work is a mere business transaction, I work only as much as I get paid.
3. Working for a living is one of life's necessities. I would not do it if I didn't have to.

Of those asked, 78 percent identified with the first view, 7 percent identified with the second view, and 15 percent identified with the third. When asked how much control respondents felt they had over the effort they gave their jobs, 88 percent said they had a great deal of control. However, when asked whether they used this freedom to fulfill their "inner need to do the very best job," only 16 percent said that they did.[79]

In polls conducted by the Gallup Organization and the National Opinion Research Center, fully 67 percent of those polled said they would not welcome less emphasis on working hard, and 90 percent agreed or strongly agreed with the statement "I am willing to work harder than I have to in order to help this organization succeed." But only 52 percent were satisfied with Americans' "willingness to work hard to better themselves," indicating that nearly half of those polled believed that there was considerable room for harder work.[80]

These findings suggest that managers have failed to draw upon the deep reservoir of energy and commitment of their organizations' members, particularly the energy embodied in the widespread need to do the very best job possible. Corporate leadership that focuses primarily on the returns generated for shareholders, rather than on broader purposes or shared values, offers only a limited sense of purpose to the organization's members. Outstanding performance comes from the "hearts and minds" of employees who are attracted to and motivated by higher values and purposes. The leader's job is to harness people's deep needs and aspirations.

Furthermore, an understanding of these most basic yearnings can deepen the leader's faith in his or her fellow human beings. The degree of faith in coworkers' intentions is an essential determinant of how one manages. A belief that people strive to find meaning in their lives through work critically influences managers' actions. It determines the degree of autonomy granted subordinates, the honesty and openness with which they are treated, the rigidity and comprehensiveness of control systems, the extent to which opportunities for self-expression are created, how firmly corporate purpose is grounded in important human ends, how much attention is given to how well the quality of corporate purpose is reflected in daily actions, and how well each individual's contribution to this purpose is recognized. These organizational attributes not only enable work to be a source of personal development, self-realization, and increased dignity, which increase motivation and commitment, but also are characteristics that create high-performance organizations.

Corporate purpose of a particular character is critical to infusing work with meaning. Purpose answers the question "What ultimate ends are served by the contribution of my personal energies and abilities at work?" The moral quality of the answer—one that links corporate activities to serving other human beings in worthwhile ways—enables individuals to ground the reason for their existence in the pursuit of ideals outside themselves. When the purpose of one's work touches the essence of one's being, it becomes a powerful stimulus to commitment. The company becomes a valued instrument for relating the individual to a broader reality. Because of this personal value, individuals are quick to defend it. The result is a constancy of purpose that provides coherence to decisions and cohesion to values. This coherence and cohesiveness makes possible greater openness, candor, and constructive conflict regarding how to achieve the collective purpose. The result is more effective and efficient decisions.

The Responsibilities of Leadership

The profound effect corporate leaders can have on the lives of those in their organizations carries with it heavy responsibility, as any thoughtful executive can attest. But do corporate leaders have a real responsibility to create environments that provide employees an opportunity to find greater meaning for their lives? The answer is clearly yes.

The responsibility to create environments conducive to greater meaning has its origin in two fundamental duties of management. The first is to ensure that employees are treated with respect and dignity, not as tools to corporate ends. In the pragmatic reality of daily competitive life, this is possible only if there is a harmony of individual and corporate purposes related to work. When the corporate end is one the individual finds of personal value and worthy of service, then actions to achieve this end become, in essence, acts to encourage the achievement of personal aims. From the employees' viewpoint, the company becomes an instrument for realizing some of their highest aspirations through their work. Only when the corporation truly becomes a path to meaning and fulfillment for the people who work there is it possible to treat people as ends in themselves.

The second source of this responsibility is grounded in duties to customers, employees, shareholders, and society—the leader's responsibility for corporate performance. The company's contribution to each of these constituents can be measured by its ability to create value (recall the distinction made earlier between creating value and shareholder wealth maximization). Value creation is solely determined by the contributions of the firm's people and their ingenuity in using the capital at their disposal. People who find meaning and opportunities for personal growth and achievement through work perform at higher levels, with more commitment, intensity, cohesion, and creativity; thus they enhance corporate performance to the benefit of all major constituents. This collective performance is the ultimate responsibility of management.

Conclusion

In the final analysis, organizational purpose, meaning, commitment, and knowledge creation are truly inseparable. Considerable human potential and commitment is unleashed when leaders identify purposes worth serving, nurture environments conducive to creative self-expression and self-actualization, and infuse the workplace with a sense of dignity and respect for the individual. This is not an easy task. It requires *consistent hard work* on the part of the leader. But the reward is a more competitive organization—one that more fully utilizes the knowledge of its members.

At its core, outstanding performance comes from the inspired human spirit. People need to imagine a future worth striving to achieve. This is a key function of corporate purpose. A purpose of inspirational quality can raise the spirit and focus commitment and effort. Properly constructed, it provides confidence that at the end of the day our efforts will not have been in vain. Work that enables us to contribute in creative ways to worthwhile ends can touch the depths of our being. It can satisfy our need for creativity and a sense of usefulness. It makes our efforts at one with society rather than in conflict with it. It encourages us to put our soul into our work. Common sense dictates that when the ends of corporate activity—and how people are encouraged to relate to one another—appeal to people's highest instincts, performance will increase. In this rests senior management's responsibility to create work environments and purposes that enable people to find fulfillment and meaning in working for the company.

3 Strategy

*Defining Corporate Mission,
Priorities, and Direction*

Corporate purpose is the central unifying concept of strategy—the core guiding principle to which all aspects of a company's strategy should relate.[1] It provides the reason why the company's strategy is important and defines the ultimate ends the strategy is designed to achieve. It brings significance to the corporate mission and direction to critical decisions. Corporate purpose shapes the content of strategy, the process by which strategy is formulated, the goals that flow from the strategy, and the decisions through which strategy becomes reality. When purpose is vague or weakly ingrained in an organization, strategy can lose the power of coherence and internal consistency. The right corporate purpose infuses a company's strategy with the power of meaning and basic intent.

Ironically, given the importance of purpose, many leading contemporary strategy scholars grant it scarce attention. They focus on better ways to understand the firm's environment and to achieve competitive advantage, but they typically ignore the ends that give competitive advantage its importance. Competitive advantage is accepted as an end in itself. The potential conflict between competitiveness and financial returns is conveniently disregarded. Implicitly, however, most of these thought-leaders give primacy to competitiveness over returns, assuming correctly that in the long run increased competitiveness will result in more attractive returns.

Just as it is fallacious to begin developing a strategy with predetermined financial objectives as the target and then asking how the business can achieve them, it is equally misguided to create a strategic mission statement without an understanding of the fundamental purpose it is to serve. Strategy exists to achieve the purpose of the corporation.

Purpose: The Source of Strategic Coherence and Consistency

As Benjamin Disraeli once observed, "The secret of success is constancy of purpose." In business as in diplomacy, the constancy of purpose and strategy provides coherence to policy and action. How management defines the corporation's purpose determines the consistency between product-market strategy and purpose. Different purposes yield different degrees of strategic coherence and consistency. Purpose, no matter how clearly articulated, does not bring coherence and consistency to strategy unless it fits with the competitive environment and defines ends with which the organization's members can identify.

Purpose brings meaning to the external environment. It provides individuals with the assumptions and beliefs that form the lenses through which they view external circumstances. Similar situations can appear quite different to individuals in a company with a purpose of maximizing shareholder wealth than to those in one with a purpose of serving customer needs. The differing actions resulting from these contrasting views can have significant strategic consequences.

The essence of strategy is serving customer needs in ways valued by the customer and not readily duplicated by competitors. However, when its purpose is shareholder wealth maximization, an organization becomes schizophrenic—aiming for capital-market ends while living with the daily realities of a product-market world. The aims and the realities often conflict. When capital-market aims dominate strategy, the motivational power of the aspirations of the organization is diminished, and financial results are placed ahead of product-market concerns. As attention is diverted from the competitive marketplace, the firm's ability to develop needed core competencies erodes and the development and execution of a sound strategy is frustrated.

Even more important than an intellectual understanding of corporate purpose is a belief in the cause it represents.[2] A purpose that represents ends employees consider admirable and worthy acts to unite strategy and values. When purpose embodies values held by the individual contributors, it—along with the strategy to achieve it—becomes a source of commitment and focus. The resulting coherence of action and motivation can become a powerful strategic weapon.

Conversely, a lack of a shared understanding of purpose throughout an organization makes coordination difficult and effective cooperation less likely. Different individuals make decisions based on different underlying objectives. As a consequence, their actions do not form a cohesive, coherent, and mutually reinforcing whole. These conflicting, fragmented decisions dissipate resources and diffuse the firm's strategic focus.

Influencing the Components of Strategy Through Corporate Purpose

Purpose's effects on strategy are ubiquitous. Strategy provides a conceptual understanding of what a firm is to be and how it is to realize its purpose. The various components of a firm's strategy—vision, the competitive concept for realizing the vision, and functional policies—represent increasingly specific expressions of the firm's ends and how they are to be achieved. Each level provides the contextual framework for thinking about the lower levels. Thus the corporate purpose influences a given level both directly and by its effect on the other higher levels.

At the highest level of generality is the company's purpose for existing, followed by an expression of the organization's loftiest aspirations. The *aspiration level*, which reflects the purpose, has been defined variously in terms such as *"vision"* and *"strategic intent"*[3] (or its close cousin, "Big Hairy Audacious Goals"[4]).

At the next level, the *competitive concept of the business* gives shape to the firm's purpose and aspirations. The concept of the business makes explicit (1) the customer needs to be served by the firm's products and services, (2) the market segments the firm will target, and (3) the competitive advantage the firm seeks in these markets. An effective strategy focuses on the customers' needs to be served, not on the product or service per se. It segments the market in meaningful ways and specifically identifies the targeted segment and what these customers consider value. Then the company establishes how it will deliver the highest possible perceived value to its customers at the lowest possible delivered cost. To achieve this, the firm must either (1) differentiate its products or services from its competitors in unique ways that increase customer satisfaction, or (2) become the low-cost producer so it can provide a similar product or service at a lower price. By targeting an identifiable niche in the marketplace, the firm can further focus its unique skills and resources to its competitive advantage. Success in implementing these strategies requires the development of distinctive core competencies—a set of unique skills and technologies that enable the firm to provide value to its customers.[5] The competitive concept of the business should identify the core competencies sought. A clearly defined concept of the business captures the essence of the organization's mission and focuses activities by delineating the businesses the firm will be in, the needs to be served, and the competitive advantages sought.

The company's purpose, as refined by the business concept, translates into strategy's third level, the company's *economic objectives* (targets for growth, market share, new product development, quality, cost reduction, profit margins, return on investment, etc.). These economic measures can take on strategic meaning only within the context of the company's purpose and concept of the business. Thus they are *not* the starting point in thinking about strategy, but rather they are guideposts for making decisions and evaluating success in implementing strategy.

Finally, the fourth level of a strategy consists of the major *functional policies* (R&D, operations, marketing, sales, finance, human resources, etc.) that guide the actions through which the firm pursues its purpose, business concept, and economic objectives. Although the collection of policies in a given functional area is often referred to as a functional strategy, such as a "marketing strategy" or "financial strategy," it lacks the holistic nature of a business strategy. Rather, it represents the building blocks from which an effective strategy is built. The foundation for this edifice is corporate purpose.

Purpose and Strategic Aspirations

Purpose and Vision. A company's vision should infuse strategy with meaning and value. Unfortunately, however, in recent years "vision" has taken the form of a management fad, and the term has become so widely used as to lose the essence of its meaning. Derisively, it has degenerated into "the vision thing." For many CEOs, having a vision is a prerequisite to being considered an enlightened, modern leader. Consequently, vision statements have blossomed. Company after company has drafted statements to hang on walls and to place in public relations materials disseminated to employees, shareholders, and the public. The terms vision, purpose, mission, shared values, and strategy are often used indiscriminately and even interchangeably.

This debasement of the concept notwithstanding, vision remains a critical characteristic of outstanding leadership. But what is vision? Vision is not something separate from purpose, mission, strategy, and shared values. It is the quality that is ingrained in each of these that defines a desired future state of the organization resulting from the fulfillment of the purpose and the strategy to get there. As John Young, Hewlett-Packard's former CEO, observes, "Vision is simply mission and purpose made tangible in people's minds." It "refers to a vivid description or picture of what it will be like when the mission is accomplished or the purpose fulfilled."[6] Vision combines an unusual discernment of the competitive future with foresight and wisdom as to how the company can make a valued social contribution in tomorrow's marketplace. This discernment and foresight are woven into the substance of the company's purpose, mission, strategy, and values and are not separate from these concepts.

An effective vision is emotionally shared by the people of the organization. It describes the possible future in a way that that touches people's hearts, lifts them to a higher level of moral aspiration, and moves them to act. Vision captures the essence of the organization's aspirations and long-term end values. Thus, when expressed in a formal statement, it can be an inspirational summary of the firm's purpose and mission.[7] However, if the purpose itself is not inspirational, the envisioned future certainly cannot be either. The vision cannot rise above the quality of ultimate ends it is designed to achieve. The power of the vision rests in its ability to define a future that connects individuals within the organization with the service of noble ends beyond themselves. The vision defines something worth contributing to, something that brings meaning to the individual life. This aspiration begins with the firm's purpose.

By describing the desired future for the organization—capturing the essence of the contributions it seeks to make to tomorrow's stakeholders and how it will make these contributions—the vision provides people with a clear sense of not only why the company exists, but why its existence is important. Purpose defines the cause. The mission gives it depth and richness. Strategy gives it life. All three combine to give meaning to corporate activity by defining ends that inspire people to commitment and action.

Hewlett-Packard exemplifies the power that flows when purpose and values are integrated to create a stable consistent vision. Hewlett-Packard's clarity of purpose and related values help explain its long-term success. Ever since Dave Packard and Bill Hewlett first published HP's "Corporate Objectives" in 1957, this ingeniously crafted sixteen-page pamphlet has provided the guiding focus to the "HP Way." These objectives state in part, "We believe the central purpose of our business—the reason HP exists—is to satisfy real customer needs." Thus, HP's mission is "to provide products and services of the highest quality and the greatest possible value to our customers, thereby gaining and holding their respect and loyalty." The statement continues, "HP's basic purpose is to improve our customers' competitiveness and operational performance by providing innovative products and services that help them develop and manage their information environment."

In 1993, Lew Platt, HP's CEO, recognizing a need for a more concise expression of HP's purpose, crafted a statement asserting that HP's mission is "to create information products that accelerate the advancement of knowledge and fundamentally improve the effectiveness of people and organizations." In less than twenty words, HP defines its business ("information products") and provides an inspirational aim that captures both the company's reason for existing and the source of the company's competitive advantage ("accelerate the advancement of knowledge and fundamentally improve the effectiveness of people and organizations"). Platt believes this statement of purpose provides an "anchor for our people" and serves to "keep us sane in this time of very, very rapid change."[8] The company elaborates on the key words and phrases in the statement:

> "Create" means that we make a technological contribution valued by customers in our fields of interest; we're *not* a clone company.
>
> To "fundamentally improve" means that what we do makes a real and positive difference.
>
> "The effectiveness of people and organizations" means that we improve the way people live and work. We focus our efforts on the world of work, but the benefits we provide go beyond the workplace to encompass people's lives—e.g., cleaner environment, better health, information access from the home, etc.[9]

HP exists to make a difference in people's lives. It seeks its competitive advantage by providing *unique* products that contribute in significant ways to the advancement of knowledge and by improving the effectiveness of individuals. Clearly these aims demand a strategy of differentiation with rapid development of innovative new products that "make a contribution" by providing real value to customers beyond that available from competitors. The statement is easy to understand; its aims are admirable; and it stimulates commitment and brings meaning to HP employees' work. Consequently, it links purpose, strategy, and work in a way that fosters organizational cohesion and coherence.

These fundamental beliefs are woven into the company's shared values and provide the foundation for the "HP Way." The means and ends are clearly delineated in the statement of "Corporate Objectives" and consistently reinforced by senior management's words and actions. As John Young, former CEO of Hewlett-Packard, explains:

> Our basic principles have endured intact since our founders conceived them. We distinguish between core values and practices; the core values don't change, but the practices might. We've also remained clear that profit—as important as it is—is not *why* the Hewlett-Packard Company exists; it exists for more fundamental reasons. . . . The HP way basically means respect and concern for the individual; it says "Do unto others as you would have them do unto you." That's what it's all about. . . .
>
> Maximizing shareholder wealth has always been way down the list. Yes, profit is a cornerstone of what we do—it is a measure of our contribution and a means of self-financed growth—but it has never been the *point* in and of itself. The point, in fact, is to *win*, and winning is judged in the eyes of the customer and by doing something you can be proud of. There is symmetry of logic in this. If we provide real satisfaction to real customers—we will be profitable.[10]

The stability of these values within the company over time is remarkable. In 1960, David Packard addressed the people responsible for executing HP's newly initiated management development program and selected HP's corporate purpose as the central focus of his talk. He began:

> I want to discuss *why* a company exists in the first place. In other words, why are we here? I think many people assume, wrongly, that a company exists simply to make money. While this is an important result of a company's existence, we have to go deeper and find the real reasons for our being. As we investigate this, we inevitably come to the conclusion that a group of people get together and exist as an institution that we call a company so they are able to accomplish something collectively that they could not accomplish separately—they make a contribution to society, a phrase

which sounds trite but is fundamental. . . . You can look around and still see people who are interested in money and nothing else, but the underlying drives come largely from a desire to do something else—to make a product—to give a service—generally to do something which is of value. So with that in mind, let us discuss why the Hewlett-Packard Company exists. . . . The real reason for our existence is that we provide something which is unique [that makes a contribution].[11]

Purpose and mission—and the vision they manifest—need to be compelling enough to be shared by people throughout the organization. Hewlett-Packard has provided such a purpose and mission for most of its employees. The power of vision embodied in purpose and mission rests with the commitment of individuals. The strength of truly common aspirations that bind people together is realized only if the organization's individual members value the purpose, mission, and vision. People must deeply care for what these ideas represent. There is a vast difference when the attitude within a company is that the vision is "the company's vision" (where the vision has been handed down from above and has not been internalized by individual employees), or "my vision" (where the vision can differ by individual), or "our vision" (where people share common aspirations for the future).

A "company's vision" has limited motivational and directive power. It may be accepted; but more often it is subjected to cynicism either because people do not consider it a future worth striving to achieve or because senior managers' actions are seen to be inconsistent with their professed vision. In either case, the vision is not heartfelt.

The "my vision" attitude leads to a balkanization of visions, as each individual's potentially idiosyncratic view of the desired future for the organization motivates different actions in similar situations.

However, when it is "our vision," the vision becomes a cohesive force that takes form in daily actions. In doing so, it brings forth creativity, initiative, and learning. As Peter Senge observes, "The loftiness of the target compels new ways of thinking and acting."[12]

Truly shared aspirations cannot be developed without people valuing the purpose of those aspirations. When the purpose is to maximize the shareholders' wealth and the vision addresses the firm's planned contributions to customers, there is a basic conflict. In such cases, the vision is not a consistent extension of the reason for the organization's existence. The result often is corrosive cynicism. Senior management professes commitment to making a valued social contribution through the firm's products and services, but the organization's real purpose is to be a moneymaking machine for the benefit of a specific group of constituents. Dissonance reigns. Even though the values of the organizational members may be consistent with the social aims of the vision, the conflicting purpose negates true commitment. The corporate purpose—and the goals and performance measures into which it is translated—are consistent with neither the expressed vision nor the people's values and daily activities. Only service to customers provides a purpose consistent with most vision statements.

Purpose and Strategic Intent. Gary Hamel and C. K. Prahalad, in their important work on strategy, argue that a strategic vision, or what they call "strategic intent," is the key distinguishing element of companies that have risen to global leadership in the past two decades. At the center of the strategic intent concept are competitive objectives that are "out of all proportions to their resources and capabilities" and result in "an obsession with winning at all levels of the organization."[13]

Closely related to the concept of strategic intent are the bold missions that James Collins and Jerry Porras, in their study of visionary companies, call "Big Hairy Audacious Goals" or "BHAGs."[14] They observe:

> Like the moon mission, a true BHAG is clear and compelling and serves as a unifying focal point of effort—often creating immense team spirit. It has a clear finish line, so the organization can know when it has achieved the goal. . . . A BHAG engages people—it reaches out and grabs them in the gut. It is tangible, energizing, highly focused. People "get it" right away: it takes little or no explanation.[15]

Collins and Porras conclude that the judicious use of BHAGs by visionary companies have "stimulated progress" and enabled the companies to "blast past the comparison companies at critical points in history."[16] All of the bold missions the authors cite as examples of visionary companies are oriented to the product market. None talk about shareholder returns.

Classic examples of slogans that capture the essence of strategic intent are Komatsu's ambition to "Encircle Caterpillar," Canon's goal to "Catch Xerox through technological differentiation," and Toyota's slogan, "Beat GM." Each of these objectives calls for outpacing the recognized industry leader in providing value to customers. When first established, these "seemingly unattainable goals" identified "an extreme misfit between resources and ambitions."[17] This misfit motivated these companies to systematically set out to develop the competencies necessary to achieve their ambitions. They became organizations dedicated to learning new skills. In this way, the concept of strategic intent affects means as well as ends. It defines a goal that is "stable over time," "provides consistency to short-term action," sets "a target that deserves personal effort and commitment" and can be used "consistently to guide resource allocations," and brings strategic consistency to actions at both the corporate and business-unit levels of the organization.[18]

These effects are quite similar to those attributed to corporate purpose. Is corporate purpose simply different terminology for strategic intent? The answer is no. Strategic intent flows from corporate purpose. The obsession with winning that is central to strategic intent begs the question "Win for what purpose?" Is it merely to win for winning's sake in order to gratify humankind's aggressive instincts? In outstanding organizations, the answer can be found in a purpose that ties winning to serving targeted customers better than could be done by anyone in the world. Winning is for a noble cause. This quality of purpose gives strategic intent its power and constancy. The development of strategic intent is hollow without a clarity of purpose that defines ends that are valued throughout the organization. Only when there is a clear corporate purpose focused on the product markets (i.e., serving the customers) can strategic intent be sustained over the long periods of time needed to develop core competencies.

Winning, although satisfying collective needs for achievement and helping build a spirit of team cohesiveness, is not in itself morally uplifting. The moral quality comes from winning in the pursuit of a worthwhile cause. A primary responsibility of executive leadership is to give common meaning to corporate purpose and to instill it with a moral quality. This can be done only through consistent communication, policy, and action.

The words of the leaders of Toyota are instructive as to the line between purpose and strategic intent. At Toyota the goals associated with strategic intent are manifestations of deeper, more fundamental purposes. Winning is the means to a greater fulfillment of these purposes. It also represents a tangible measure of this achievement. The core ends of Toyota, like those of many other highly respected Japanese companies, are purposes tied to serving society—and in these cases, often primarily Japanese society and company employees.

Toyota Motor Company has had a statement of purpose since its founding. The guiding principle of the original statement issued in 1935 was to serve the national "development and welfare" of Japan.[19] This purpose remained unaltered until the company's international competitive success and increasing globalization gave rise to protectionist pressures and some foreign-customer backlash. These circumstances caused a change of rhetoric. In the mid-1980s, the expressed focus began to shift from benefiting Japan to benefiting the world society. Slogans explicitly aimed at surpassing General Motors as the world's leading automobile manufacturer became less direct, such as "Global 10." This slogan was shorthand for the objective of achieving 10 percent of the world market—GM's approximate market share.

The common thread throughout Toyota's existence has been serving society—and for most of its history, explicitly Japanese society—through providing value to customers through "quality products at affordable prices." It is a short step from this purpose to aspirations of world leadership in the automobile industry—thus, the slogans "Beat GM" and "Global 10." Only global leadership will represent fulfillment of the purpose and the fullest satisfaction of the aspirations of Toyota employees. Consequently, growth has consistently dominated profitability as a corporate goal.

This "strategic intent" clearly represents an "audacious goal," particularly when it was first proclaimed. Unlike a goal (which can be accomplished, has an end, and is finite), corporate purpose is never satisfied and, like strategic intent and BHAGs, is the stimulus to constant, obsessive striving. Similarly, the inspirational power of bold missions exists only when the goals remain unfulfilled. The value of the ends embodied in corporate purpose gives the force, constancy, and motivational power to both strategic intent and BHAGs, as they evolve to meet changing market and geopolitical realities. Purpose—to have meaning and effect—must be translated into action through strategy and a consistent set of shared values that define the organization's character.

Leading Japanese companies provide some of the best examples of strategic intent and the development of core competencies, because they tend to have a strong sense of purpose—purposes grounded in service to a group or company and to society, usually Japanese society. This purpose is facilitated by institutionalized relationships with the providers of capital, particularly shareholders, that lessen the pressure for short-term returns on capital and enable an overriding focus on product-market performance. It is hard to imagine "maximization of shareholder wealth" providing the personal motivation for strategic intent or the foundation for inspirational bold missions.

Purpose: Bringing Strategic Discipline to the Concept of the Business

A clear customer-focused purpose brings strategic discipline to all aspects of a firm's business concept. It orients the strategy to the product market. Managers are directed to define the scope of their businesses and strategies for achieving a competitive advantage in terms of providing real value to customers. It highlights the importance of the people in the organization whose capabilities, efforts, and commitment are the sources of the firm's competencies on which the strategic advantage depends. The litmus test of a sound policy or decision is whether it serves the purpose of providing long-term value to customers.

In the final analysis, the dynamics of the competitive marketplace—the changing needs of customers and the actions of competitors—determines corporate performance and provides the discipline for managers' actions. The product market's punishment for ineffective or inefficient decisions that produce mediocre results can be swift and sure. Competitors attack areas of weakness and customers defect to providers of greater value. The capital market has no means to exact such discipline. Only when performance seriously erodes—which can take years—does the market normally move to cut off the flow of capital or threaten a hostile takeover.

Purpose and Strategic Orientation. A corporation's purpose directs the fundamental orientation of its strategy. Does the purpose focus internally on the organization, does it concentrate on external realities, or is it rudderless? If its focus is external, is it directed toward the capital markets or the product markets?

An internal focus can result from lack of clear purpose or a purpose primarily focused on serving employees' interests. The concern with pay, perks, prestige, and security can lead to an emphasis on incremental improvements over last year's performance. The company tends to measure its performance against itself, not against competition. The result can be a distancing of the organization from the realities of the competitive marketplace.

An externally oriented purpose focuses the organization on either the product markets or capital markets, depending on the substance of the purpose. Serving shareholder interests directs the organization's attention to the capital markets. In essence, the dominant financial goals of the organization (such as return on investment, profit margins, and consistent earnings growth) are simply an internalization of the objectives of the capital market.

Serving customers highlights the product markets. The result is substantially different strategies—one attuned to the capital market's needs and objectives, the other to the product market.

Manifestly, a sound strategy requires an external focus on the competitive realities of the marketplace. Regardless of its corporate purpose, a company's stated strategy is by its very nature aimed at a product market. It defines the businesses and market segments in which the company plans to compete, the competitive advantage to be attained, and the specific functional policies that will enable the company to achieve this advantage. Because a customer-oriented purpose reinforces strategy by placing the emphasis on the product market, it promises to be the most competitive.

For companies with a purpose of shareholder wealth maximization, however, the product-market strategy may conflict with its orientation to the capital market. This high-level conflict is reflected throughout the organization in functional policies, subunit strategies (product development, procurement, operations, marketing, finance, human resources, and such), and the substance of increasingly specific goals.

When purpose and strategy conflict, individual managers become uncertain about which ends they should serve. While the company espouses a capital-market purpose, the daily decisions that constitute the execution of strategy must deal with specific realities of the product market. The purpose establishes one set of priorities and the strategy another. The ultimate reference points that provide policy with meaning are ambiguous, and therefore policy becomes confused in people's eyes. Operating management must rationalize a strategy driven by the capital market (and the related goals) with the needs of customers and the threat of competitors. These basic needs and objectives conflict, giving rise to organizational schizophrenia. Typically, the result is either a lack of coherence between the strategy and the operating decisions that implement the strategy or operating decisions that are inconsistent at times with the competitive needs of the product markets. In either case, the organization begins to lose the close, harmonious contact it needs with its market environment. Consequently, the power of an internally consistent, coherent strategy made up of mutually reinforcing operating policies is dissipated. Management's ability to build purpose and strategic thinking into the social structure of the organization is undermined. With a less ingrained purpose and strategy, organizational commitment and cohesion atrophies. Inconsistent action is an inherent result.

This conflict arises in part because the needs, objectives, and preoccupations of the two worlds of the product markets and the capital markets are quite different. The company's contact with the financial world consists of investment bankers, institutional investors, security analysts, lenders, and bond-rating agencies. A few corporate managers—usually only the CEO, the CFO, and the treasurer—handle the relationships with these financial institutions. The frequency and force of these outside capital-market contacts often result in the company's adoption of a financially oriented external perspective, causing its performance to be evaluated primarily against abstract quantitative measures (quarterly increases in earnings per share, return on equity, price-earnings ratios, dividend payouts, and credit ratings).

When the managers' attention is on the capital markets, less attention is paid to the dynamic competitive realities of the product markets. Less also is the inclination to take often costly proactive actions to increase competitiveness or to confront attacking competitors.

Ironically, as capital-market needs are internalized within the firm through measures such as return on investment and budgeted earnings growth, the organization risks converting the external capital-market focus into an internal focus. Results become evaluated in terms of these internal financial measures. The product markets become secondary to the driving forces *within* the company. Attention is directed to incremental improvement over past financial performance. As with a purpose of serving employees, the company compares itself to itself, not to competition. Too often the focus is on "making the budget" rather than on outpacing competitors or satisfying changing customer needs.

The financial world of the capital markets is alien to the competitive one that operating managers face. They must be concerned with the actions of customers, competitors, suppliers, and distributors, as well as ensuring that their own internal operations meet customer needs better than the competition does. The real work of the corporation is these product-market activities—the design, production, and delivery of goods and services. Success in this work is judged by concrete measures such as market share and the performance, quality, cost, and timeliness of products and services.

In contrast to a purpose oriented to the capital market, a purpose of serving customers forms the foundation for a consistent and coherent product-market strategy. Attention is placed on the actions required to create and sustain a competitive advantage—those actions that develop corporate capabilities and efficiently create more value for the customers than do competitors. The customer focus helps ensure that decisions are driven by what the customer actually considers value, not by some internal conception of what the customer should have.

With a customer-focused purpose, the competitive marketplace provides a strong impetus to decisions that are consistent throughout the management ranks. As the strategy and goals become increasingly specific as they descend the organization, action remains focused on one central aim—to serve customers efficiently and effectively. Service to customers provides the common denominator to all decisions. External capital and retained earnings are critical resources for competitive performance, but they are means to serving the customer competitively, not ends in themselves. Profitable operations provide the resources required to serve customers better.

Purpose and the Definition of the Business. Corporate purpose guides—and often constrains—managers' choices of the scope and diversity of the businesses in which their firm competes, the breadth of market segments it serves, and the needs of these specific customers it aims to satisfy. A customer-focused purpose (and the mission reflecting the purpose) keeps the spotlight on the essence of any business—anticipating and satisfying customer needs. Pursuit of this purpose demands that the company define who its customers are and think deeply about what these customers value. Measuring success in terms of market share and the quality, cost, and functionality of products and services motivates employees to extend their individual and collective competencies in ways that naturally and beneficially expand the business. The simplicity of this fundamental verity of business is often lost in the increasing complexity of our world. Conflicting messages emanate from different constituents. Seeking to maximize shareholder wealth can blur the definition of a company's business, and the choice of businesses in which to compete can be based more on financial considerations than product-market competitiveness. One consequence can be unfocused diversification.

The best examples of constructive, organic expansion of the business concept can be found in the outstanding companies that tie the importance of employees closely to their customer-oriented purpose. Employees are seen as the most valuable contributors to corporate success. When corporate leaders take their responsibilities to employees seriously, the customer-focused purpose and the priority placed on employees converge to create an unquenchable drive to develop the capabilities required to meet the anticipated future needs of customers. The result is a concerted effort to constantly upgrade core competencies in existing businesses and to search continually for opportunities to extend these competencies to new businesses. In precisely this way, Canon developed competencies in precision mechanics, fine optics, microelectronics, and electronic imaging and used these capabilities to take the company from 35mm cameras into a wide variety of businesses, including video and still cameras, copiers, bubble jet and laser printers, fax machines, cell analyzers, and semiconductor-manufacturing equipment.[20] Each of these businesses typically uses three or more of Canon's four core competencies.

Frequently, corporate leaders fail to see these potential new applications of a firm's capabilities. Whether it is 3M's Post-its or Intel's microprocessors, midlevel managers often are first to identify new opportunities or the need for revised strategies. Andrew Grove attributes middle managers with anticipating Intel's decision to move from a dual emphasis on memory chips and microprocessors to a focus solely on microprocessors—the most important decision in the company's history. They began shifting resources from memory chips to microprocessors a full two years before corporate management saw the strategic need to do so. By the time corporate management made the "strategic" decision to get out of the memory chip business, Intel was producing these chips in only one of its eight silicon fabrication plants. Grove explains that although top management might have been "fooled by our strategic rhetoric, those on the front lines could see that we had to retreat from memory chips. . . . People formulate strategy with their fingertips. Our most significant strategic decision was made not in response to some clear-sighted corporate vision but by the marketing and investment decisions of front-line managers who really knew what was going on."[21]

A focus on customer needs and organizational competencies brings clarity to the definition of the businesses in which the company competes. This contrasts sharply with blurred corporate boundaries that can result from a shareholder-focused purpose. The pursuit of higher shareholder returns can stimulate desires to diversify into unrelated businesses. Returns, rather than customer needs and core competencies, dominate the choice of the businesses in which to compete. However, many companies that have sought increased value through diversification have produced disappointing results. As studies have shown, successful unrelated diversification is rare and difficult to achieve.[22] Too often diversification diffuses the company's human and financial resources and diverts management's attention from the competitive battle in its existing businesses. The promised increase in earnings per share owing to the financial benefits of acquisitions or the hoped-for increase in the price/earnings ratio (because of the appeal of the "story line" to Wall Street) are often used to justify the diversion of resources from existing businesses. Competencies go fallow. The future competitiveness of the core business is put at risk. The conglomerate craze of the 1960s was a prime example—a chain letter phenomenon that over a period of several years reaped considerable benefits for these companies' investment bankers and for their shareholders (if they were wise enough to sell before the bubble burst), but created little real value. Many of the megamergers of the 1990s produced the same disappointing results.

Kazuo Inamori, founder and chairman of Kyocera, one of Japan's most respected and innovative companies, emphasizes the importance of never forgetting "the essence" of one's business. In the early 1970s, many Japanese companies were rushing to make real estate investments to take advantage of the Japanese land boom. A chief executive seeking to maximize shareholder returns would most likely have followed this rush. But Kyocera refused to be distracted. Inamori recounts, "Our banker, in fact, came to plead with us. He said he was delighted that we were depositing our profits with him—yet as our banker, he felt compelled to advise us that we could be making a fortune by investing in real estate! I politely replied that our business was to make profit in the traditional way—by manufacturing products and adding value, not by speculating in land prices."[23] When the oil crisis hit, Kyocera was able to invest heavily in plant and equipment, while its competitors' capital was tied up in real estate. The result was a significant competitive advantage for Kyocera at a critical stage in its development.

Purpose and Competitive Advantage. The content of the corporate purpose determines the cohesiveness of strategic decisions and directly affects an organization's ability to develop the core competencies on which competitive advantage is predicated. The aspirations that flow from purpose can stimulate the development of these competencies and increase the willingness of the company to make the necessary investment in people, plant, and technologies.

Viewing competitiveness through the lenses of competencies highlights the importance of purpose to competitive advantage. Core competencies result from organizational capabilities that integrate technologies and processes in unique, fast, highly effective, and efficient ways. The resulting technologies and processes are sources of perceived value to the customer. Often these capabilities are applicable to a variety of markets, and they are always difficult for competitors to duplicate.[24] An emphasis on the customer places high priority on bringing the fruits of these competencies quickly to market through intense development of new products and services. As competition intensifies and product life cycles shrink dramatically, this ability becomes critical.

Outstanding value-creating companies usually have an emphasis on employees that comes right after the customers. The priority given to employees makes a company more ready to invest in their development and to create a work environment that respects the dignity and contribution of each individual. The result is increased creative input and commitment from employees and a heightened individual emphasis on the development of personal abilities that enrich the company's collective core competencies. The commitment translates into harder work that is focused more on corporate goals than narrow self-interest. Because employees share the purpose-related goals, decisions are made more quickly. They are not conflicted between customer-oriented and shareholder-oriented goals. People are simply doing what they think is right.

The coupling of a customer-oriented purpose and an emphasis on developing core-competency-based competitive advantages can enable a firm to "capture the investment initiative" from competitors.[25] When people have priority and competitive advantage rests in sustaining the lead in core competencies, the investment in people development, research, plant, and equipment becomes greater. The investment includes the retention of employees in whom the capabilities reside. Lowering employee turnover enables a firm to reap the benefits of large employee-development investments in deeper, more sophisticated ways and over a longer period of time.[26] Also, knowledge-creating social networks are maintained. Loyalty becomes an important competitive weapon.

Hewlett-Packard has long eschewed long-term borrowing, in part because it viewed its commitment to employees as a fixed cost. The company wanted to be able to avoid laying off its most valuable asset during economic downturns. The sole reliance on internal cash flow for investment has had two other strategic benefits. To increase capital available for growth, employees throughout the company have become very cost-conscious and focused on the rapid development of unique, high-value-added, high-margin products. As a consequence, HP's focus on the customer and employees has paid off in a dramatic pace of new product introductions. For example, in 1992, over half of the company's sales came from products introduced in 1992 or 1991. In the Computer Systems Organization, an outstanding 98 percent of 1992 sales were from products introduced in 1991 or 1992.[27]

For companies focused on the objective of maximizing shareholder wealth, the results are likely to be quite different. When faced with a tough competitive market, the managers are more likely to be willing to opt to divest, milk, or gradually withdraw from the business rather than make the commitments necessary to enhance competitive posture. In existing businesses, the single-minded pursuit of higher returns can also motivate firms to serve the increasingly narrow market niches in which higher returns can be maintained. These firms often concede the lower-return, more competitive mass segments of the market to rivals. As a consequence, the competitors reap increasing benefits of scale, scope, wider brand recognition, and the continual competitive pressure to hone their skills further. The long-term effect of such actions on a firm's competitiveness is obvious. By choice many American manufacturers, such as those in consumer electronics, memory chips, and machine tools, have withdrawn from defensible business positions when challenged by foreign competitors with different priorities of purpose.

Increasing Institutional Integrity and Customer Trust. The determination of a company's competitive advantage ultimately rests with the decisions of customers. Their perception of the company's trustworthiness influences their buying choices. The priority given to constituent interests can affect customers' responses—and often of society's as a whole—to a company's products and services and to its actions. When customers believe the company is striving to serve their best interests in a morally responsible way, they can respond with considerable loyalty.

A classic example of this is the Tylenol poisoning crisis Johnson & Johnson faced in the early 1980s. Guided by the company's "Credo," which places customers' interests first, Johnson & Johnson's managers took rapid action to protect the customer. Within hours of receiving information of the poisoning, they recalled the ninety-three thousand bottles from the poisoned batch and warned 450,000 retailers, doctors, and hospitals of the threat. By the end of the week, Tylenol was removed from store shelves throughout the country, and a customer refund program was instituted that did not require proof of purchase. Industry experts and Wall Street pundits concluded that the incident had killed the Tylenol brand. The immediate before-tax loss to Johnson & Johnson from the recall was estimated at nearly $200 million. But these experts were proved wrong. Tylenol was reintroduced with a marketing campaign based on trust in Johnson & Johnson. The consumer responded with considerable goodwill, and within two months Tylenol had regained 95 percent of the market share it enjoyed prior to the poisonings.[28]

James Burke, Johnson & Johnson's CEO at the time of the crisis, attributes the speed and quality of his company's response to the values embodied in the Credo, Johnson & Johnson's expression of purpose. Reflecting on the incident, he says,

> We had dozens of people making hundreds of decisions, and all on the fly. They had to make them as wisely as they knew how. And the reason they made them as well as they did is they knew what the set of beliefs of the institution they worked for were. So they made them based on that set of beliefs and we made very, very few mistakes.
>
> It was a worldwide story. Every one of our employees in the world knew the Credo was being tested. And a lot of them weren't sure that the company could live up to those so-called high flowing principles. But we did live up to them. And what did we get out of it? They [the consumers] gave us our product back—something everybody said couldn't happen. To me that is dramatic evidence of the validity of the morality inherent in the Credo. The public said, "They are doing all of this for us. I've got to believe them. And not only do I have to believe them, I want to help them in the process." And that is exactly what happened. And we have research that will demonstrate it.[29]

This episode reinforced Johnson & Johnson's institutional integrity—the coherence and wholeness that comes from a unity of purpose, strategy, values, and action. Institutional integrity affects all constituents. The pride employees derive from their work as a member of a highly respected organization increases. This organizational integrity fosters an increased sense of personal dignity and mutual respect. Customers and suppliers are treated with respect and fairness. Shareholders can take satisfaction in the moral behavior of their company and reap the long-term benefits of increased employee and customer loyalty.

A Confusion of Ideology

The ambivalence many CEOs have regarding the tension between capital-market and product-market orientations reflects a confusion of ideology that is common in Anglo-American business society. On the one hand, most managers believe in the efficacy of the free market for goods and services. In fact, Americans take pride in the nation's vibrant free-market economy and the sovereignty of the customer. On the other hand, there is a common allegiance to the maximization of shareholder wealth, an end that is (often vaguely) connected with the value of private property rights. Managers frequently find the strategic decisions they must make embody conflicts between these two ideals. The maximization of today's shareholder wealth may well require taking actions that have detrimental effects on the firm's competitive performance in the free product markets.

In essence, this tension highlights an important issue—the conflict between the importance of the free product market and the rights of *one* source of capital. How managers resolve this tension will influence the substance of the firm's strategy and its competitive performance. Only a primary focus on the customer allows the forces of the free-market economy to work uncompromised. Furthermore, in the final analysis, the product market exercises a more swift and effective discipline over corporate managers than does the capital market.

4 Managing
Transforming Purpose into Action

The effectiveness of the traditional sources of managerial control has been in decline for some time—and they probably never were as powerful an influence as their advocates believed. In the past, managers heavily relied upon the formal authority vested in their position, formal management systems (planning, information, control, reward, resource allocation systems, and the like), and changes in organizational structure. However, confronted by the dizzying pace of change in technology and the competitive environment and by the increasing complexity of the knowledge needed for success, exemplary corporate leaders recognize they have neither the wit, detailed knowledge, nor vision to ably direct all strategic decisions from on high. Key decisions must be made where the pertinent knowledge resides and rapid response is possible. Consequently, company after company is flattening its hierarchies, streamlining formal bureaucratic systems, and dramatically reducing the role of the corporate headquarters. This new structure presents corporate management with a problem of how best to guide decisions in the business units and functional divisions.

This decline in traditional sources of influence—although annoying and frustrating to senior managers—has its advantages. Managers are being required to lessen their dependence on sources of influence that have varied, and often unintended, consequences. People chafe under pressures exerted by both authority and formal systems. People do not like to be told what to do. Neither do they like to work constrained by systems considered bureaucratic, inflexible, and even oppressive—systems that create barriers to doing what they believe is right. Nowhere is this truer than with budgetary controls. The reality is that smart people can find ways to overcome systems they dislike, rendering them ineffective. As Walter Wriston, the former CEO of Citicorp, observes, "People with the ingenuity to build the Hoover Dam can figure out ways to beat the Hay System [of compensation rewards]." Consequently, influence exerted by systems has severe limits. This reality reflects the fundamental truth that the right to manage comes from the managed, not from position or the capital markets.

In the place of formal systems and positional authority, individual managers are beginning to focus on the two most positive forms of influence they have: (1) the appeal to shared values and (2) a commonly agreed-upon strategy and the operational goals into which the strategy is translated. By their very nature, common strategic goals and shared values provide the advantages of strong direction without the disadvantage of feeling unnecessarily restrictive to people. Because they are shared, people are acting in accordance with goals and values they themselves hold. These are powerful motivators without the taint of hierarchical constraints and authority. As Robert Haas, chairman and former CEO of Levi Strauss, asserts, "A company's values—what it stands for and what it believes in— are crucial to its competitive success. Indeed, values drive the business. . . . It's the *ideas* of a business that are controlling, not some manager with authority. Values provide a common language for aligning a company's leadership and its people."[1]

This is not a new phenomenon. IBM's leaders built one of the world's leading institutions based on three fundamental beliefs: (1) a respect for the dignity and rights of the individual, (2) a commitment to excellence in all endeavors, and (3) superior customer service. These beliefs define not only how IBM employees should relate to each other, but also how they should relate to the product market. Thomas Watson Jr. emphasizes the fundamental importance of these values, which encapsulate IBM's purpose:

> I firmly believe that any organization, in order to survive and achieve success, must have a sound set of beliefs on which it premises all its policies and actions.
>
> Next, I believe that the most important factor in corporate success is faithful adherence to those beliefs.
>
> And finally, I believe that if an organization is to meet the challenges of

a changing world, it must be prepared to change everything about itself except those beliefs as it moves through corporate life.

In other words, the basic philosophy, spirit, and drive of an organization have far more to do with its relative achievements than do technological or economic resources, organizational structure, innovation, and timing. All these things weigh heavily in success. But they are, I think, transcended by how strongly the people in the organization believe in its basic precepts and how faithfully they carry them out.[2]

Corporate purpose is central to this way of managing. Ultimately purpose is transformed into action. As purpose is internalized in the company's management systems and informal processes, its influence on decisions affecting strategy and shared values, and thus on competitive performance, increases. When purpose, values, strategy, and management systems are consistent and mutually reinforcing, the power of each to direct actions is enhanced. As we have seen, a customer-focused purpose provides this internal consistency in ways other formulations of purpose do not.

In the most fundamental sense, without a common purpose, an organization would not exist. An organization is predicated on the cooperation of individual contributors, and the willingness to cooperate requires a purpose of cooperation.[3] No effective leader would think of running a company without clear goals. But many managers give little attention to the most important end of all: the organization's purpose. When they accept the prevailing conventional wisdom that a firm's purpose is to maximize shareholder wealth (or some derivative of this purpose, such as maximizing profits or return on investment), corporate purpose can become divorced from strategy, operational goals, management systems, and the real work of the organization. Without clarity of purpose, the character-defining decisions, which are the essential building blocks of strategy and strong cultures, become diffuse at best and more often are conflicting and misguided.

For purpose to have meaning and significance, it must be infused into the way managers manage—into the way the company's strategy is formulated, and into the formal management systems (for example, performance measurement, compensation, control, and resource allocation systems) and organizational structures. It must also be reflected in the informal assumptions, beliefs, and values that form the company's culture. When this occurs, corporate purpose significantly influences the deployment of people and capital, the investment returns deemed acceptable for these commitments, the time horizon incorporated into managers' decisions, and the measures used to judge performance. In each of these decisions, a clearly articulated customer-focused corporate purpose can be a powerful counterbalance to short-term financial pressures.

Purpose and Managing by Strategic Thinking

The decline of traditional sources of managerial influences and the increased speed and complexity of business mean that corporate leaders need to shift from relying on top-down strategic planning processes to ensuring that strategic thinking permeates decision making at all organizational levels at all times. Christopher Bartlett and Sumantra Ghoshal challenge the assumption that CEOs of global companies should be the formulators of strategy at all. Instead, they argue that the CEOs should focus on "purpose, process and people" to guide their firms to competitive success. They maintain that "in an environment where the fast-changing knowledge and expertise required to make such decisions are usually found on the front lines, [the assumption] that the CEO *should* be the corporation's chief strategist is untenable." They conclude, "Purpose—not strategy—is the reason an organization exists. Its definition and articulation must be top management's first priority."[4] They cite the efforts of the CEOs they studied "to embed a clearly articulated, well-defined ambition in the thinking of every individual while giving each person the freedom to interpret the company's broad objectives creatively." These executives "articulated the corporate ambition in terms designed to capture employees' attention and interest rather than in terms related to strategic or financial goals."[5] Their study raises important unanswered questions as to the specific role of purpose in guiding an organization and whether any corporate purpose can achieve the desired results. In seeking answers to these questions, one thing is clear: not any purpose will do.

Some of America's most successful companies, such as Hewlett-Packard and Johnson & Johnson, have ingrained a sense of strategic thinking in their people. The leaders of these companies recognize that individuals throughout the organizational hierarchy need a shared understanding of the strategy, need to know how their operations relate to the strategy, need an appreciation of the specific actions they must take to fulfill the strategic mission, and need to measure key decisions and daily actions by how well they serve the strategy. To achieve this, a central element of the interactions in the chain of command between general manager and general manager and between general manager and functional manager is the strategic implications of specific decisions. These leaders work hard to develop a shared understanding of the few critical things that need to be achieved—and when—to implement a unit's strategy. Then the senior manager's responsibility is to continually question and probe to ensure that the junior manager's decisions are consistent with the strategy—in other words, that the junior manager is thinking strategically and long term. The result is a continual adaptation of strategy to external events and to the firm's growing capabilities.

Not only does this process of strategic thinking maintain senior management's control over the critical aspects of decision making, but also it increases the force of strategy within the company. The processes by which strategy is formulated become less ritualistic. Strategy formulation becomes a real-time event, not a once-a-year bureaucratic process with substantial time delays between the business unit's proposal of a strategy, subsequent corporate-management approval, and its ultimate execution. Each decision potentially shapes an evolving strategy. Strategy is truly being formulated "with their fingertips."

Unfortunately, as planning processes become formalized and elaborated, they threaten to drive out substantive strategic thinking. Corporate leaders must be vigilant to ensure that this does not happen.

Johnson & Johnson provides a good example of how strategic thinking can work. Although the strategic plans are forged from very active debates both within the businesses and between business-unit and corporate managers, the plans themselves are kept simple. In fact, the CEO receives only a two-page summary with only four numbers (dollar and unit sales, dollar profits, and return on investment) for the current year and five and ten years out.[6] The plans submitted to the CEO define the strategic mission, the business-unit management's convictions about the future, and how they are going to achieve their objectives. The plans are used to set aspirations, to clarify mission, and to find and correct problems. They are not used as a form of negative control or to punish. Management is held accountable for the strategic mission statement, not for making the numbers. The objective of the interactive process is to force in-depth thinking about strategy, to stretch the imagination of business-unit managers, to encourage expansive thinking, and to develop action plans. There are no penalties for inaccuracies in the plans.

Corporate management rarely forces revisions in the strategy and does not issue top-down performance targets at start of the process. Business-unit managers' bonuses are determined by subjective criteria and are not tied to a profit formula. To lessen the tyranny of the budget, the budgeting process includes contingencies, three revisions throughout the year, and close monitoring of performance. The result is a process that encourages accountability and solving the problems that vex performance, but in the service of long-term strategic aspirations and the values embodied in the company's Credo.

One highly admired former CEO observes that directness, simplicity, and focus are essential to creating a sound strategy—themes that resonate at Johnson & Johnson and Hewlett-Packard:

> The greatest purpose of planning is not to create the plan but to tell the manager what he should be doing with his time. The plan is not important. What is important is that the people who make the plan know what they must do. Every time we make a plan, each divisional chief executive must report to the group president the five most important things he must do to make the plan happen.
>
> It's most important that a person and his boss are together on what they should be doing. A boss has the obligation to use his experience to help. If someone is about to put his foot in a bucket and the boss doesn't see it, they are making a co-mistake. When it comes time to lay the lash, the boss is going to be more tolerant and fair.
>
> The general manager's [whether divisional or corporate] prime obligation is to "feel" his business—to have a sensitivity to the market trends and geopolitical forces that will impact his market. If you don't sense where the market is going, then all else can be lost. This sense needs to be a very personal one, and it is difficult to achieve working through a staff.[7]

This observation captures the essence of creating strategic thinking in an organization. Managers up and down the line have the responsibility to reach agreement on key issues, to identify these issues clearly, and to keep in close communication over the progress of planned actions to address the issues. The thought process and resulting understandings are more important than a formal document. Responsibility is mutual. Decisions are made within the context of and with reference to the purpose-driven strategy.

The strategy-formulation process can differ significantly depending on the content of the corporate purpose. When the purpose is focused on the shareholder, strategy is often shaped to conform to top-down financial goals such as return on investment and earnings growth. Short-term financial concerns disproportionately influence decisions, creating a middle-management perception that strategic concerns are not critically important. As a result, financial targets drive decisions that form the *real* strategy, which might be fundamentally different from the company's stated strategy. Measures of competitiveness (such as market share, efficiency, speed of new product development, and product functionality and quality) take on their significance as means to producing the required returns.

In contrast, a customer-focused purpose directs the organization's attention to changing customer needs, competitors' actions, and the company's long-term competitiveness. Consequently, there is no inherent conflict between purpose-derived corporate goals and business-unit strategies. Both are product-market driven. This consistency enables an ongoing, interactive, and cooperative strategy-formulation process involving multiple levels of management. Ideally, the strategy results from a marketplace for ideas, where openness, candor, and constructive conflict characterize the debate over competing strategic visions. In this environment, substance dominates the process. What matters is the quality of ideas, not elaborate presentations or voluminous forms. A collectively understood, marketplace-focused purpose provides a clear common denominator, helps concentrate the debate on ideas not personalities, and maintains cohesion even at times of heated differences. The ultimate test of an idea becomes how well it serves the corporate purpose. From this environment emerge strong competitive strategies. The strategy drives the development of goals, some of which are financial measures of success. When managers must make difficult decisions, in a customer-focused company the central issue guiding their deliberations is whether the action will enable the firm to serve customers better and more efficiently than competitors over time. Financial considerations are an important part of the discussion, but unlike shareholder-focused companies, customer-focused companies do not allow financial considerations to drive the discussion.

At Johnson & Johnson (J&J), a company that prides itself on decentralized creativity, purpose provides strategic cohesion and direction. "How do we keep them all together?" James Burke, J&J's former chairman and CEO, rhetorically asks. "We try to do it by an overall set of principles and the fundamental moral precepts of the Credo, which everyone buys into and responds to," he explains. "At some level, everybody is a moral creature, whether they want to admit it or not."[8] For Burke, J&J's Credo, which places customers first, employees second, and shareholders last, provides both the moral and strategic compass:

> I believe in the Credo with a passion because I believe in the long run every institution in society has to serve all of its constituencies or it doesn't survive.
>
> What the Credo says is that the first thing you have to do is be totally involved with the people who use your products and services. If you don't, it is a simple fact of life you will die, because someone else will.
>
> The second thing it says is that the most important raw material you have is the employees. It is their creative energies that do it, after all. Everybody has money and the other things required for success. What's really required is the creative ability of people.[9]

Burke firmly believes that if the company serves the customers and employees well and is sensitive to the needs of the communities in which it does business, then it will serve the long-term shareholder well also.

Reflecting Purpose in Operational Goals

The specific goals that guide decisions throughout an organization have their genesis in corporate purpose. In essence, goals internalize the preferences of the markets the company has chosen to serve. A principal task of management is to embed corporate purpose in a set of ever more precise and specific goals and performance measures as they cascade down the organization and, as Peter Drucker has observed, "degenerate into work." Throughout the organization the direction of work is fundamentally shaped by the embodiment of purpose in more specific goals that act as targets of aspiration as well as measures of achievement. Formal management systems rely on a pattern of performance measures to evaluate alternatives, to guide choice, and to appraise individual performance. The substance of these measures is critical. As Bill Hewlett was fond of saying, "You cannot manage what you cannot measure," to which he added, "What gets measured gets done."[10] The wrong measures will lead to the wrong outcomes.

Purposes of increasing shareholder wealth and serving customers' needs are manifested in fundamentally different priorities in goals. One set of goals reflects the capital market, the other the product market. One set emphasizes financial returns, the other growth and innovation. For the long-term health of the company, financial goals should be the results of—not the drivers of—product-market strategies. They should act as guideposts for measuring progress in achieving desired competitive results and in generating the necessary internal funds to finance the chosen strategy.

This distinction between shareholder-driven and customer-driven goals is continually refined through the goal-setting and decision-making processes at all organizational levels. This process of refinement determines the relative emphasis people place on financial results versus competitive market position. The varying patterns of decisions, which result from this difference in emphasis, affect the development of core competencies and the deployment of key resources. The result can be fundamentally different strategies. One might produce higher returns today (on a net present value basis), but the other will generate greater competitiveness and *future* returns.

Infusing operational goals with a higher purpose enhances their power to direct decision making. When individuals understand and accept the corporate purpose, they have a deeper comprehension of the intent of the specific goals that apply to their tasks. A clear, readily grasped central purpose helps explain the reasons for the specific, fragmented goals and brings coherence to these goals. The goals of organizational subunits (such as marketing, operations, and research) and of individuals are placed in the context of the higher, externally oriented aims, thus providing the core value that guides decisions and infuses actions with a higher level of meaning. With this understanding comes a greater acceptance of and, if they are consistent with the person's values, commitment to the individual goals.

Without a clear sense of corporate purpose, people cannot fully know what is expected of them. True, they might have specific performance targets to guide their actions. However, absent an understanding of the corporation's purpose, they will be unable to relate these targets, orders by their superiors, or their own actions to the organization's reason for being. Individuals are left to decipher the corporate purpose from the mosaic of senior management actions and the messages conveyed by the formal systems, such as the measurement and control systems and the resource allocation system. Prejudicially, these professional tools of management tend to be dominated by financial measures that are surrogates for the enhancement of shareholder wealth. The message from these systems is clear: people's careers are advanced or retarded by the ability to contribute consistently to the achievement of increased returns and growth in earnings on an annual, quarterly, or monthly basis. A clear, customer-focused corporate purpose can provide a counterbalance to the tyranny of these short-term financial pressures.

When purpose is ambiguous, individuals are often free to project their own values onto corporate purpose, redefining it to be consistent with their own assumptions and beliefs. They then use this self-constructed sense of corporate purpose to test the validity of superiors' orders and alternative actions. As Nobel Prize winner Herbert Simon has observed, if the value premises that guide decisions are left to individual discretion, the correctness of any decision will depend upon the value premises the individual has selected, and there is no criterion for right or wrong that can be applied to this selection.[11] Individuals may resist orders and reject the validity of certain goals—or pay them lip service—when they believe the directives and goals conflict with their version of the central purpose of the organization. The consequence can be actions that serve neither senior management's sense of purpose nor the resulting strategy.

Measuring Performance

Because performance measurement systems often produce results contrary to their intended purpose, they are the bane of many managers. For example, ROI-based systems intended to increase income (ROI's numerator) instead can lead to a reduction in investment (the denominator) and slower long-term earnings growth. Since incentive compensation schemes are based largely on historical financial results, they can motivate an emphasis on the short run rather than the intended long-term competitive benefits. Even stock option plans can lead to a short-term emphasis on maximizing the number of shares under option (e.g., the size of this year's grant, which is normally tied to near-term historical financial performance) rather than on the long-term performance of the stock. Short vesting periods can compound the problem of excessive stress on short-term financial performance.

These unintended consequences can result when performance measurement and compensation systems are too narrowly focused on financial results and there is a lack of understanding of the role of profits in value creation. Conventional accounting measures are limited by their focus on non-human physical assets and their neglect of the assets most related to competitiveness and value creation—human capital and customer loyalty. Activities critical to competitiveness (such as investments in research and people development to produce knowledge-based core competencies, strong brand loyalty, and close relationships with customers) are treated as period costs, not investments. The value of the expanding skills, initiative, and creativity of the organization's people appear nowhere in the financial statements.

However, financial performance need not be seen as a constraint on competitiveness and value creation. This false dichotomy can exist only if financial returns are allowed to eclipse competitive value creation in importance. The leader must dispel this misunderstanding. What should emerge is a shared understanding of profits as critical means to the creation of a highly competitive enterprise—a firm capable of outpacing competitors in providing value to customers and of providing an enriching environment in which employees can work. A proper understanding of the role of profits and of conventional performance measures prevents financial goals from tyrannizing efforts to increase customer and employee value—and thus long-term competitiveness.

In the pursuit of a customer-focused purpose, leaders need not apologize for the importance of profits to their company. Rather they should make the relationship of profits to the achievement of the organization's purpose and mission clear. This understanding will pay considerable dividends in terms of decision making, motivation, and the effectiveness of the budgeting and planning processes. Factual information regarding the company's reliance on profits to fund its growth and make strategic investments should be provided so people at all levels can understand the practical function of profits.

Profits often take on a negative connotation because the pressure to increase near-term profitability is seen as coming from the capital markets to serve the shareholders' interests. In most companies, the majority of employees feel that this pressure forces them to curtail some initiatives and to modify decisions, all to the detriment of the firm's long-term welfare—and the welfare of customers. In many companies, this is actually the case. Ironically, however, attractive levels of profitability can act to insulate managers from capital-market pressures, and senior managers should be aware of this.

Given a proper understanding of profits, what is needed is what Norton and Kaplan call a "balanced scorecard," but one driven by a clear sense of purpose-centered priorities.[12] The leader must take responsibility to develop a set of performance measures aligned with the customer-focused corporate purpose—measures that emphasize the primary determinants of value creation: satisfied, loyal customers and innovative, committed employees.

Although developing the appropriate array of performance measures is important, even more critical is the weight given to the various measures. Too many companies have an adequate set of measures but place the vast majority of the weight on the financial measures, causing them to swamp the other more strategic goals. Logically, a customer-focused purpose, coupled with recognition of the employees' key role in creating value, should result in more weight being given to customer and employee goals than to the financial ones.

Measuring the Value Created for Customers. Obviously, a customer-oriented purpose translates first and foremost into goals measuring the value received by customers. The strongest measure of customer benefit is market share. If the company's revenues in its chosen market segments are growing faster than its competitors', customers have voted with their purchasing dollars to indicate the company is providing superior value. Related measures include the company's share of each key customer's total spending on the product or service, customer satisfaction (determined by surveys), and customer loyalty (measured by the percentage of the company's customers defecting to competitors and the company's success in attracting new customers within its targeted segments). Direct measures of the value received by customers include price, functionality, quality, reliability, and timeliness of the product or service—each of which need to be benchmarked against competitors for specific market segments.

To ensure that the company is creating value and not merely transferring value from employees and shareholders to the customers, the profitability of key customer groups needs to be determined. Activity-based accounting can be used to make these estimates. Frederick Reichheld recommends that the measures go beyond current period costs to reflect the estimated net present value (net profit less the cost to acquire the customer) of the customer over the expected lifetime of the relationship.[13]

Measuring the Value Created by and for Employees. The key to creating value for the customer rests with the employees—their ingenuity, initiative, and commitment. Consequently, the realization of the corporate purpose depends on their caliber, skills, and character. The measures of the performance of the firm relative to its employees can be divided into two areas—the productivity of the firm's human capital and the value received by the employees from their association with the company.

The efficiency and effectiveness of the firm's people can be measured by revenue per employee or even more precisely by value-added (revenue less purchased materials and services) per employee. The value-added measure has the collateral benefit of encouraging the development and growth of higher value-added products and services.

The magnitude, speed, and cost of innovation are also critical aspects of people's performance. Innovation can be measured by the percentage of total revenues represented by new products introduced in each of the last two to five years (the length depending on the product life cycle typical for the business). The gross margins realized by new products are indicative of the value and magnitude of innovations. Some companies might also appropriately measure the percentage of revenues from proprietary products.

Speed is measured by time-to-market—the time period between when a new customer need is identified and when the product or service to meet the need is introduced to the market.

The effectiveness of the company's development activities in creating value can be captured by the ratio of operating profit to total development costs (as is done at Analog Devices) and the product's break-even time (the time from the beginning of product development until the product generates cumulative profits sufficient to pay back the development cost, a measure used by Hewlett-Packard).[14] When practical, these measures should be benchmarked against the performance of key competitors.

The extrinsic and intrinsic value received by employees is critical to their commitment, loyalty, and motivation. A customer-focused purpose can forge an alignment of personal and corporate goals that forms a constructive bond between the individual and the corporation. As seen in Chapter 2, meaningful work is the source of immense value to the individual. It costs the company nothing. To the contrary, the commitment to shared goals reduces internal friction and facilitates delegation of responsibility. Similarly, when the firm provides its people opportunities for personal growth and significant achievement, their job satisfaction increases.

Job security spawned by a recognized real commitment on the part of the company to its employees can be a source of a reciprocal employee commitment to the company. Employees evaluate the company's commitment not on its words, but on its actions. When financial results fall below expectations, who bears the consequences: the employees in layoffs or the shareholders in reduced returns? The leader should make clear the nature of the company's commitment to employees and the implicit priority placed on employees in difficult times. Hewlett-Packard has historically had an abiding commitment to its employees. HP's "Corporate Objectives" state in part that its objective is

> To help HP people share in the company's success, which they make possible; to provide employment security based on their performance; to ensure them a safe and pleasant work environment; to recognize their individual achievements; and to help them gain a sense of satisfaction and accomplishment from their work.
>
> The company has been built around the individual, the personal dignity of each, and the recognition of personal achievements.
>
> HP selects and manages it businesses with a goal of providing long-term employment for its people and opportunities for personal growth and development. In return, HP people are expected to meet certain standards of performance on the job, to adjust to changes in work assignments and schedules when necessary, and to be willing to learn new skills and to apply them where most critically needed. This flexibility is particularly important in our industry where rapid technological change and intensifying worldwide competition compel us all to continually seek better ways to do our jobs.

HP's Objectives also stress the importance of managers developing their people and providing each individual with "the recognition he or she needs and deserves." This is particularly important because of HP's commitment to promote from within whenever possible. "In the final analysis," the Objectives conclude, "people at all levels determine the character and strength of our company."

These objectives make the commitment of the company to its people clear and define values that guide behavior. Even so, during the tumultuous downsizing that swept America in the 1990s, Lou Platt felt the need to clarify the nature of the commitment. While the objectives do not guarantee permanent employment, conventional wisdom among many HP employees was that it did. This belief was reinforced by the fact that HP had never, except as a result of mergers, had layoffs in the past.

When faced with the downturn of its business in 1998, Hewlett-Packard implemented phased responses similar to ones used in prior economics dips. The company began with more symbolic cuts, such as eliminating company picnics. As the downturn lengthened, managers took a three-month 5 percent pay cut. Ultimately the company offered a voluntary separation plan to twenty-five hundred people.

Specific measures of the full value employees receive from the company (except for job satisfaction, goal alignment, and fair compensation) are difficult to develop. Goal alignment across organizational levels—particularly as it relates to corporate purpose—and job satisfaction can be measured as part of employee satisfaction surveys. These surveys should be routinely made and employee turnover rates closely followed. They can be vital guides to decisions regarding how to increase the value received by employees and should be an integral part of a manager's performance evaluation process.

Specific values that define the firm's character—values of meritocracy, the dignity of each individual, mutual respect, recognition for personal achievement, and flexibility—are also sources of value to employees. Consequently, the leaders must promote and defend these values through highly consistent words and actions and work diligently to instill an appreciation of their importance in each individual. Care should be taken to ensure that personnel who share these critical values are promoted. Those who repeatedly violate the values at the core of the organization's integrity—such as honesty and respect for others—must be culled from the organization, regardless of their performance.

Subjective goals in each of these critical areas should be agreed upon between leaders and their direct reports. Each person should prepare an annual report on achievements relative to these goals and a meaningful portion of the overall performance evaluation should be linked to progress in these areas.

Measuring the Value Created for Shareholders. Shareholders receive value through stock price appreciation and dividends. To measure these sources of value, the capital market is internalized in the form of metrics regarding return on investment (asset turnover and operating margins) and earnings growth. A central issue for corporate leaders is defining what constitutes a fair return to shareholders and the priority to be placed on pursuing this return when such action erodes the value received by customers, or employees, or both. The corporate purpose defines the desired priority.

When a company's purpose is to create value for customers and the second priority is the employees who create the value, in times of competitive or cyclical pressure on financial performance, leaders must act accordingly. They need to have the courage to require a greater sacrifice from the short-term interests of shareholders than from employees in order to maintain the flow of value to customers. Of course, in the long term, the more permanent shareholders will benefit as well from this priority. Only the interests of those shareholders contemplating the sale of their shares in the near term are sacrificed.

A central conundrum of performance measurement is that the most readily calculated and by far the most visible of all performance measures are those related to *historical* shareholder wealth creation; yet the most important measures relate to the future—those that define the firm's competitive position and ability to create long-term value—and are difficult to gauge and dependent on the future actions of employees, customers, and competitors. Corporate leaders have a responsibility to ensure that the management processes achieve a balance among the goals that reflects the priorities embodied in the corporate purpose and counteracts the tendency of short-term financial goals to dominate longer-term strategic ones. This is the true essence of a balanced scorecard.

Bringing Purpose to Traditional Budgetary Control

As corporate managers radically decentralize their operations in response to the forces of increasing change, complexity, and competition, the temptation is to rely more heavily on two financially dominated processes to maintain control over the autonomous units: (1) formal capital budgeting processes that use net present value as a common denominator in choosing among investment alternatives, and (2) the annual budget, which controls operating expenditures. These processes represent the most "objective," "rational," and facile way to manage a set of diverse units. When the firm's purpose is the financially oriented maximization of shareholder wealth, this temptation is accentuated. The value of hard-to-measure, more intangible assets—such as employee skills and morale, the organization's technological competencies, and its ability to learn and adapt quickly—is often neglected, even though these are critical to success. The budget threatens to become the medium for planning. Short-term financial concerns begin to dominate strategic concerns. Each expenditure decision tends to become discrete, ignoring holistic strategic concerns. Numbers begin to substitute for corporate management's understanding of the business, masquerading as strategic thinking. A tyranny of the budgets—capital and operating—is established.

Clearly, managerial influence gained through strategic thinking and shared values is much different from control exerted through budgets. Financial objectives are blunt instruments, providing little strategic direction. Budgets do not discriminate among the multitude of line items according to their importance. Each line item is a candidate for cutting in order to "make the budget." Although the budget process provides important information and discipline, it is not sufficient for making key resource allocation decisions. In the best case, budgets are now-oriented, focusing on *today's* profitability. In the worst case, they are historically oriented, preoccupied with what accounting conventions say happened last month or last quarter. This orientation can stifle the investment needed to enhance a firm's future competitiveness.

Unfortunately, when budgets, performance measures, and resource allocation decisions continually reinforce the message that shareholders' interests are paramount, the employees' inclination to be responsive to customer needs is undermined. The budget becomes an embodiment of the disharmony of purposes between the individual and the company.

But this need not be the case. A remarkable change in mind-set occurs when profit pressures represented by the budget are internalized as vital *means* to serving the customer and as measures of the firm's success in doing so. When this occurs, the budget becomes a tool to valued ends. It is no longer seen as an unwanted financial constraint on a manager's activities imposed from above. Of course, the tension between profit and customer interests remains, but two important transformations take place.

First, profits are regarded not as ends in themselves, but as a necessary source of funds for investing in the future and as a valid measure of current performance in serving customers. The budget also represents a standard of excellence, both in terms of the efficiency by which the firm creates value for the customer (the cost portion of the budget) and the magnitude of the value being created (the revenue portion of the budget in terms of growth in sales and the price relative to costs). Therefore the budget—rather than relating to profit pressures in a discrete, short-term time period—manifests long-term interests tied to worthwhile ends.

Second, managers at all organizational levels assume greater ownership of the responsibility to resolve the tension between current profits and the interests of the customers. This is because profitability is understood to relate directly to those aspects of the managers' jobs that deal with creating value for the customer over time. During the year, actual performance relative to the budget may present difficult choices—for example, whether to "make the budget" or to overrun the budget in order to maintain a given level of service and product development expenditures. But the trade-off is made based on what will best serve present and *future* customers. Generally speaking, profits are resources to make investments in the future, whereas the budget revenues and expenditures represent current-period customer benefits, such as prices and service. The conflict is less between the interests of shareholders and customers than between the interests of present and future customers. In many ways this is a more difficult conflict to resolve than the decision of how to meet the profit targets in the budget. But it is one that unifies profitability with the customers' interests. The issue is, on the one hand, the availability of funds to invest in enhancing future service to the customer (i.e., making the budget), and thus future competitiveness, and on the other hand, expending funds now for the benefit of today's customers and current competitiveness (i.e., overrunning the budget). The hard decisions do not go away, but they are made with an eye to the future.

One result of this transformation in thinking is that the tyranny of short-term financial pressures is broken. Conflict across organizational levels over budget issues—a commonplace managerial barrier to strategic thinking—is also overcome. The purpose of the annual operating budget and capital budgeting processes is not to control managers, but to aid them in making decisions that will ensure adequate profits to fund their strategies. Budgets also facilitate decentralized decision making. They represent "contracts" between levels of managers. Abiding by the contract provides the junior manager with considerable discretion, but also considerable responsibility. The budgets become tools for achieving their most fundamental objectives. This can be a remarkable transformation in psychological orientation to budgeting—the budget is helpful in generating funds rather than constraining funds, and it is a vehicle for increased freedom instead of a bureaucratic form of top-down control. But it will occur only if senior managers are committed to a customer-focused purpose, share the understanding of the role of profits, are willing to delegate, are vigilant in eliminating unnecessary bureaucratic processes, and yet are vigorous in holding subordinates accountable for fulfilling their responsibilities. Moreover, senior managers must assume the constant responsibility to educate their people in the real role of profits and the budget. When the company espouses a shareholder-focused purpose, these lessons will ring hollow to most people in the organization.

In companies like Hewlett-Packard and Johnson & Johnson, which have strong operational control systems, operating managers generally do not see the systems as burdensome. Senior managers, reflecting the purpose of their companies, make it clear that these systems serve ends beyond profit and are part of a broader strategic perspective. In both companies, profits are clearly important means to other, higher ends. Both have a strong strategic orientation to the competitive markets with a focus on satisfying customer needs.

At one highly regarded, technology-driven company, corporate managers became disenchanted with the consequences of its textbook capital-budgeting system. Their principal concern was that the system was stifling value-creating investments and innovation. Although the firm's hurdle rate was 12 percent, (2 percent above the company's estimated cost of capital), 98 percent of the 139 projects submitted to corporate management for approval projected returns of 15 percent or more, and 59 percent of the projects projected returns above 30 percent.[15] These high rates of return meant many lower-return, value-increasing projects were left on the shelf. The company was not realizing its potential. To address the adverse motivations resulting from this process, corporate management decided to eliminate the requirement for divisions to provide capital-budgeting analyses to corporate for review. Furthermore, division managers were given the discretion to decide whether or not to use capital-budgeting techniques to aid their decision making.

In a world where senior managers know less and less about the specific product-market situations, and where most ideas with strategic implications originate with highly knowledgeable specialists lower in the organization, senior managers must delegate more. Consequently, they are less able to use direct action to counteract the negative influence short-term financial objectives can have on an organization. Strategy and values form the new counterbalance to the potential tyranny of short-term financial measures. Financial objectives are still necessary and important, but they are an integral part of strategy and exist to serve the purpose.

Ensuring That Management Systems Do Not Undermine Strategic Priorities. A principal executive responsibility is to ensure that management systems, such as the performance measurement, reward, planning, and budgeting systems, result in goals, directions, and incentives compatible with the firm's purpose and strategic priorities. Too often they do not.

At one of the nation's largest corporations—a company with a purpose of maximizing shareholder wealth—a new strategy was conceived to move its core business from its traditional commodity products to specialized products. This move would enable the business to differentiate its products more, escape the intense competitive pressure in its current product line, and grow more rapidly. The president of the core business unit had a formal compensation agreement containing twelve measures. Eight of these measures related to strategic objectives. They consisted of objectives such as "Develop a strategy, program, and milestones and achieve better balance in the company's portfolio of business through redeployment of assets, commercial development, and acquisition," and "Develop, communicate, and implement a specialty [product] strategy, including at least one significant acquisition." Each of these eight objectives had significant competitive implications. The other four measures consisted of financial objectives: a pretax profit target, generating a target level of free cash flow, achieving a target return on assets, and reducing current assets. The problem was not the content of the listed goals but rather in the weights. No single strategic objective accounted for more than 6 percent of total performance and all eight strategic objectives totaled only 30 percent of the overall evaluation; 70 percent was allocated the financial objectives (30 percent each to the profit and free cash flow objectives). The talk was of a strategic shift with significant growth in specialized products, but the incentives were tied overwhelmingly to milking the business. It is not surprising that the new strategy was very slow in evolving.

At Sears, a company that has spent over a century building a brand reputation founded on consumer trust, this brand was dealt a severe and costly blow by an ill-conceived incentive system. Under pressure for improved financial results, in the early 1990s Sears's senior management implemented a change in the way the performance of mechanics and service advisors was measured and compensated. Under the new system, the service advisors' performance and commissions were judged on *specific product* sales quotas and dollar volume quotas. Consequently, on a slow day, they had the financial incentive to find more repairs on each customer's car. If the mix of repair needs was not right to meet the specific quotas—say brakes or shock absorbers—the compensation system financially benefited those advisors who "found" more of these repairs on the cars brought to their shops. Similarly, part of the mechanics' compensation was shifted to piece rates. In California, to receive the same compensation as before the change, the mechanics' quotas effectively increased from approximately thirty-five dollars to fifty-five dollars per hour. Between pressure from the service managers and the new compensation system, some mechanics felt coerced to increase the number of service jobs they performed per hour. This meant finding more things wrong with the cars on the rack.[16]

Within months, Sears was embroiled in a very public controversy over performing unnecessary repairs. First as a result of a state investigation in California and eventually in forty-four states the attorneys general filed suits against Sears. A century of brand building was severely tarnished.

In designing and implementing the revised compensation plan, the Sears executives failed in fulfilling their responsibilities to customers, who were overbilled; to employees, who were coerced to act unethically; and also to shareholders, who saw Sears's automobile-service profits decline. In pursuit of short-term profit, Sears's managers seemingly lost sight of their tradition of putting the customers' interests first. In this business, where most customers are at the mercy of the honesty of the service advisors and mechanics, the potential for adverse consequences from such a compensation system should be clear.

Managers at Sears—as elsewhere—have a responsibility to ensure that the measurement and reward systems they design do not have unintended consequences. This is often, as it was at Sears, a moral responsibility to prevent the systems from placing undue pressure on people that leads them to take unethical actions. It is not sufficient to rationalize that individuals have the responsibility to do the right thing (which of course they do) and then turn up the heat under them by implementing a high-powered performance measurement system that potentially threatens their jobs and incomes. In imposing such a system, managers have a responsibility also to implement effective counterbalances to the undesired consequences.

When a customer-focused purpose permeates the company's value system, such errors in judgment are less likely to occur. In these companies, one test of a system's effectiveness is whether or not it will enhance the value created for customers. If it does not, then people are more likely to speak out against the system and be heard, because a personal and corporate core value is at stake.

TABLE **4.1** **Percentage Distribution of Companies by Different Corporate Purposes and Strength of Culture**

Strength of Culture	Focus of Corporate Purpose		
	Customers (n = 17)	Balanced (n = 47)	Shareholders (n = 24)
Strongest 20%	41.2%	17.0%	12.5%
61% to 80%	23.5%	17.0%	25.0%
41% to 60%	11.8%	27.7%	12.5%
21% to 40%	11.8%	21.3%	25.0%
Weakest 20%	11.8%	17.0%	25.0%

Managerial Influence Through Culture and Shared Values Grounded in Purpose

Corporate purpose is *the* core end value of the organization. The values, beliefs, and assumptions embedded in corporate purpose shape corporate character and are the bedrock of the corporate value system. The values that cluster around alternative conceptions of purpose have a decidedly different quality, and consequently generate cultures of disparate strength. The company can be viewed as either a moneymaking machine or a vehicle for meeting human needs. By definition, if the central end value is not shared—if employees do not believe in its intrinsic worth—then this foundation and the resulting corporate culture are weakened and corporate values lose much of their power to influence and direct actions.

Companies with customer-oriented purposes tend to have the strongest cultures. This tendency is demonstrated by analyzing the correlation between the strength of culture and different corporate purposes. When eighty-eight companies were ranked in descending order by their strength of culture, 41 percent of the companies with a customer-focused purpose were in the top 20 percent in terms of cultural strength.[17] This compares with only 17 percent of companies that seek to balance priorities among constituents and 12 percent for shareholder-focused companies that were in this top tier group of strong culture companies. Fully 50 percent of shareholder-focused companies were among the 40 percent of companies with the weakest cultures. (The summary of this analysis is shown in Table 4.1)

Although the cause-and-effect linkages cannot be clearly determined from the data presented in Table 4.1, it seems reasonable to deduce that the substance of corporate purpose affects the strength of corporate culture. The conclusion that customer-oriented companies have stronger cultures has profound implications for management. As values and informal systems become increasingly important in directing corporate activity, a purpose that strengthens the positive influence of values and beliefs can significantly improve management effectiveness.

Achieving Harmony Among Constituent Interests

Purpose can act either to bring the interests of the company's constituents into greater harmony with one another or to exacerbate conflicts among these interests. A shareholder-focused purpose with its return-oriented goals leads to conflicts among constituents' interests. In contrast, a harmony of interests can be found in a customer-focused purpose with its direct relationship to the essence of people's work and its growth-oriented goals. Growth can serve the interests of shareholders, customers, employees, suppliers, communities, and the nation alike. Since market-share growth is normally accompanied by a stronger competitive position, it reduces the risk to all constituents. The increased sales volume—and the related cost advantages derived from increases in scale, scope, and learning—better enable the firm to withstand cyclical swings and competitive attack.

Customers' interests and growth—particularly growth in market share—are practically synonymous, because a company's existing businesses can grow only if customers buy more of its products and services. To grow faster than the market, the perceived value of a firm's products and services to the customer must be superior to that offered by competitors.

Growth provides employees increased opportunities for advancement and personal growth, more challenging and interesting work, the satisfaction of being on a winning team, and the affirmation that their efforts are producing goods and services valued by customers. Except for the benefits derived from incentive compensation plans, most employees receive few benefits from higher returns unassociated with growth. In fact, attempts to achieve higher returns through downsizing are a direct threat to employees.

Creating an environment of challenge, accomplishment, personal growth, and meaning for employees requires strong marketplace performance. The challenge is to provide an improved product or service at low cost. A sense of accomplishment comes from achieving more than individuals thought themselves capable of and from beating the competition. Recognition and autonomy to make decisions—so employees can see their own tracks in the sand and know that others recognize them as well—accentuate the power of accomplishment and personal expression. For these opportunities to be combined with job security and highly competitive levels of compensation, the company must generate adequate profits and growth. Only serving the customer well can do this. From this reality comes the harmony of customer and employee interests.

When individuals are asked to work harder or to endure some personal sacrifice in order to enrich the financial wealth for one set of constituents (the shareholders), the consequences are considerably different from when they are asked to do the same to better serve other people with whom they can identify—customers and fellow employees. Many employees have daily contact with customers. As one automobile assembly line worker said in explaining his commitment to quality work, "One of my family members may be the buyer of a car I help make." But rarely do employees know shareholders, who are distant from the reality of the their day-to-day activities, and many employees do not consider them particularly deserving of commitment.

Of course it is not always evident that the interests of customers and employees are in concert. To serve customers' needs better than competitors do, corporate leaders often need to be tough taskmasters. They set high standards for performance and demand accountability. Leaders motivate and stretch people to do things that employees often initially believe themselves incapable of achieving. In the short run, people can feel that their interests are being sacrificed to the corporate ends. Furthermore, at times of severe competitive pressure or rapid technological change, management may need to lay off some employees to attain competitive levels of cost. Clearly, for the individuals who lose their jobs, the customers' interests conflicted strongly with theirs. But as competitive success is realized, the sense of personal achievement and the satisfaction of being on a winning team while serving worthy purposes can bring considerable personal reward. When the organizational members internalize the quality of the corporate ends, the sacrifices can become justified. Of course, some people (usually those with a less competitive drive, a lower tolerance for hard work, or a cynical view of all corporate activity) will not consider these rewards worth the personal price.

Growth and the accompanying competitive strength provide the potential for expanded (although not necessarily maximum) profits to shareholders. For shareholders the issue is twofold. First, whether the benefits of growth more than offset the costs of achieving the growth—do profits expand more rapidly than they would under a less aggressive product-market strategy? Second, will the benefits be realized while the individual or institution is still a shareholder? Or in other words, does the delayed benefit mean the shareholders' capital can generate higher returns in another stock in the near term? In the long term, the increased competitiveness derived from a customer-oriented purpose and strategy should increase the share price beyond that achieved by a purpose consistently focused on maximizing returns. This result was demonstrated earlier by the greater returns to shareholders for the customer-focused companies.

Suppliers of material, services, and new capital benefit from increased business with the company as it grows. The providers of capital also benefit from the reduced risk that usually accompanies increased competitiveness. The nation and host communities enjoy enhanced economic vitality, growth in employment, and usually an improved balance of payments.

The greater harmony of interests for companies with growth-oriented purposes helps explain the dominance of such purposes in countries like Japan, Korea, and Germany. In the Asian countries, the Confucian belief in social harmony and duty to society is deeply embedded in their cultures, often taking a nationalistic or familial form. Growth-oriented purposes are consistent with these cultural values. In Germany, growth-oriented purposes reflect welfare-state values and a strong dose of nationalism. Government-imposed corporate-governance structures and regulations cause German companies to be concerned with the stability of employment and with corporate growth—both of which serve the interests of German society.

Managing Change with Purpose

Beyond directing decisions, corporate purpose can be critically important in redirecting them—in managing organizational change. The substance of an organization's purpose can affect its ability to anticipate the need to change, to gain broad acceptance of proposed changes, and to effectively implement the changes.

When a firm focuses its primary attention on its long-run ability to provide greater perceived value to customers than do competitors, the organization's sensitivity to the future requirements of the marketplace is heightened. The organization becomes attuned to the necessity of anticipating customer needs, competitors' moves, and the evolution of the firm's valued core competencies—and then taking action. Change is more likely to become proactive than reactive. For example, to develop the competencies critical to meeting anticipated future needs, employee development and organizational learning are emphasized. As a result, the change can produce benefits for individual employees, such as increased opportunities for personal growth and greater exercise of individual initiative and creativity.

A customer-focused purpose can also help gain the acceptance of the needed change. In a company centered on the marketplace and accustomed to putting the customer first, people are more likely to understand the importance of proactive change that provides more value to the customer. Change might not be comfortable, but it is seen as necessary. In fact, change can even be valued when it is seen as a means to better serving the customer—the firm's most valued and highest end.

A customer-focused purpose provides the ultimate test of whether proposed changes move the organization toward its professed ends. These ends are integral to the required changes, giving product-market direction to goals and to individuals making decisions. Consequently, decentralized decisions are more consistent with the needed changes. This coherence in decision making, coupled with the organization's acceptance of the need to change, significantly aids the effective implementation of change.

A shareholder focus, on the other hand, places the primary focus on financial returns, or more specifically on numbers. Good numbers can mask the seeds of future competitive problems. As a consequence, management can delay undertaking needed changes. Unfortunately, by allowing the need for change to fester, when change is finally undertaken, it often is after the company has come under menacing competitive attack. Not only does the change need to be larger because the problems have grown more severe, but the alternative actions are fewer. The natural tendency is for management to work first on the one area in which it assumes it can get financial results the fastest—on costs. This syndrome commonly results in the employees bearing the brunt of the burden of change through layoffs, pay freezes (or give-backs), and a poorer work environment. These actions can be corrosive to the firm's core competencies and can eat away at other factors critical to the firm's competitiveness such as service, the timeliness of new product development, and people's commitment.

Typically, change in a shareholder-focused company is perceived to be motivated by the need to serve shareholders' financial interests—an end not valued by most employees. At best, in this environment change appeals to the self-interest of managers who own stock or have bonuses tied to short-term financial performance. But self-interest is not a high or inspiring motivation. There is little satisfaction in seeing others laid off to further one's own financial welfare. At worse, change threatens one's job and can make one's skills obsolete—in the employees' eyes, all without a valued purpose. The overall result is organizational resistance to change.

Conclusion

In this age of rapid change and discontinuity, one prediction is certain: the American corporation of tomorrow will be different from that of today. It is encouraging that in recent years more U.S. companies have begun to establish goals that go beyond single-minded considerations of shareholder wealth to reflect the composite objectives and stakeholders that companies like Hewlett-Packard, Johnson & Johnson, and Wal-Mart have long taken into account, with a primary focus on the customer.

In summary, all corporate activity does—or at least should—relate to the purpose of the business. This truth must be translated into action through people acting in concert with their conception of the purpose. Without a clear understanding of the ends and fundamental priorities, organizational activities are unlikely to be coherent, cohesive, and purposive. How this central purpose is defined molds goals, shapes the allocation of resources, stimulates personal commitment to corporate ends, and determines competitive performance.

The purposes of corporations vary across societies and even across companies in America. They have become embedded in contrasting ideologies that lead to different goals, different patterns of investment, and different levels of employee commitment, which pose a central competitive dilemma. A global Darwinian struggle is under way that will determine the nature of capitalism in the twenty-first century and, consequently, which companies will be the survivors. The prevailing view of corporate purpose in America is under competitive attack, both from companies within the country and from without. A break from the past is needed. How U.S. business leaders respond will determine the future vitality of their organizations and the nation.

5 Capital-Market Relationships
The Myths of Shareholder Wealth Maximization

In this time of great paradox, the allegiance to the maximization of shareholder wealth is stronger than ever before; yet the importance of the shareholder's contribution to competitive advantage has never been smaller. Capital is readily available and has given way to knowledge—to the ingenuity and dedication of people—as the key to competitive advantage and wealth creation. Furthermore, our preoccupation with equity market performance belies the fact that most American companies rely primarily on retained earnings for financing their investment needs, and the credit markets, not the equity markets, provide the vast majority—if not all—of their external funds.

Corporations are the world's main wealth-producing institutions. Their essential purpose is to use this capacity to better society. On these points there is little disagreement. However, there is strong divergence of belief—both in the United States and across countries—regarding the corporate purpose that best achieves this desired end. In the United States and the United Kingdom, most managers—and even more academics and business journalists—argue that firms seeking to maximize the return to shareholders best serve this end. They tie corporate purpose directly to the capital markets.

However, many leading American companies—and even more Asian and continental European companies—believe society is best served by some other operative purpose: serving customers, employees, the nation, family, or some combination of specific constituents. In doing so, they relegate direct shareholder financial returns to a secondary priority. Returns must be sufficient to achieve the firm's higher purposes, but they are clearly means, not ends.

These fundamentally different definitions of corporate purpose influence and are influenced by the nature of the linkage between firms and capital-market institutions. Corporate purpose determines not only the priority managers place on the interests of capital-market institutions relative to other constituents' interests, but also the priority among different segments of the capital markets, such as stockholders, lenders, and investment bankers. For example, a purpose of maximizing shareholder's wealth expressly places the interests of equity-market participants ahead of those of the credit market.

The Capital Market's Effect on Corporate Competitiveness

Capital markets affect competitiveness in many ways. They influence the availability of capital, the distribution of capital among competing needs, the cost of capital (in terms of required returns, levels of acceptable risk, and the "transaction costs" associated with securing capital), and the time horizon in which investors expect to receive their returns. They also can require more transparent reporting of corporate results, which aids not only in allocating capital but also in holding management accountable for performance.

Cost and Availability of Capital

Although capital-market institutions are potential allies in forging competitiveness, they can also be powerful obstacles to the execution of effective strategies. The effects depend on how corporate managers use and respond to the markets. For example, a firm's relationships with capital-market institutions affect the willingness of its managers to invest capital. This willingness is influenced by the managers' *perceptions* of the cost and future availability of capital, the importance they give to these perceived costs in their investment decisions, the goals that drive the investment decision, and the degree to which they adhere to capital-market conventions governing corporate financial policies (such as the acceptable amount of debt in the capital structure, limits on issuing new equity, and the target dividend payout).

These policies in combination with retained cash flow determine the amount of capital available to a company.

With a vibrant equities market, an active commercial paper market, a strong banking system and a variety of long-term investors (including pension funds, insurance companies, mutual funds, and individuals), the U.S. capital market has no equal in any other country. Its depth, breadth, and efficiency should provide more abundant amounts of low-cost capital and thus be a source of competitive advantage. However, for this to benefit a company's long-term competitiveness, corporate leaders must have the wisdom to develop financial policies and form relationships with capital-market institutions that enhance the firm's ability to finance strategic initiatives. Unfortunately, the widespread use of conventional rules of thumb to determine capital structure and managers' prevalent reluctance to issue common stock for internal financing purposes negates these potential advantages. When capital-market conventions regarding performance expectations, dividend-payout ratios, debt-equity ratios, bond ratings, and the stigma associated with the issuance of common stock are internalized in corporate policies, they can starve strategies for lack of funds. By setting specific debt-equity targets and by refusing to issue equity for fear of diluting earnings per share, management arbitrarily limits its available capital. Consequently, the capital potentially available becomes an irrelevant, unused "asset."[1] The unchallenged acceptance of these conventions gives the capital market undue influence over a crucial determinant of strategy—the availability of capital.

Transparency

The capital markets' demand for transparency and effective professional accounting practices facilitates the evaluation of corporate performance by investors, managers, and the press alike. The availability of reliable financial information improves investment decisions both in the capital markets and inside the firm.

The risk of opaque financial reporting is evident in the collapse of the Asian capital markets in the late 1990s, where loans were extended often under government direction and without a clear understanding of the underlying creditworthiness of the assets and operations. An important lesson was learned regarding the value of government's role in ensuring thorough and timely disclosure of corporate information, such as performed by the U.S. Securities and Exchange Commission. The government's role should include requiring adherence to a recognized international accounting standard (such as the International Accounting Standards or the United States' Generally Accepted Accounting Principles) and adequate enforcement to ensure compliance.

Yet transparent corporate reporting is not sufficient to guarantee the effective allocation of capital by the markets, as evidenced by repeated American debacles such as the savings and loan, Long-Term Capital Management, the dot-com bubble, Enron, and other fiascoes of recent times. Without objective governmental oversight and skilled inspection of financial institutions, grave and pervasive errors in judgment can be made by the people responsible for the capital markets' resource allocation decisions. Greater transparency in corporate reporting is just the first step in the effective regulation of banks and other financial institutions.

Capital-Market Discipline

Capital markets exert pressure on managers—often euphemistically called "capital-market discipline." In the most egregious cases of poor managerial performance, the discipline can be quite direct, ranging from the withdrawal of debt capital from the company to shareholder pressure on the board of directors to change the chief executive, or even a hostile takeover. Indirect pressure can take the form of reductions in the company's stock price.

The capital market's ability to discipline industrial companies raises three additional paradoxes. First, although the discipline of the *equity* market gets the most attention, the *credit* market's discipline has the greatest and most direct impact on most firms' performance. Second, "capital-market discipline," although usually talked about in general terms, is not monolithic. The credit market's discipline takes quite a different form from that of the equity market. These differences must be understood to properly evaluate the costs and benefits of the discipline. Third, the benefits of capital-market discipline—more particularly, equity-market discipline—differ widely across companies. Although it serves a useful function when applied to companies with weak management and poor performance, it can be a counterproductive force in most other firms.

The credit markets provide the bulk of the external capital raised by American companies. From 1984 to 2000, the credit markets provided $3.2 trillion in net new loans to nonfinancial corporations. Simultaneously, these same companies were experiencing a massive withdrawal of equity capital through mergers, acquisitions, leveraged buyouts, and corporate restructuring involving equity buybacks. During this period $1.4 trillion of equity (net of new issues) was removed from nonfinancial corporations. These equity repurchases were largely financed by debt. Including the borrowing capacity that could have been supported by the repurchased equity, over $2 trillion was sapped from corporate America's potential to finance productive investments. In essence, the investment banking community has proved more adept in removing equity than in providing it.

The importance of the credit market as a source of funds pales when compared with the internal cash flow retained by corporate America. Cash flow generated $8.8 trillion, nearly three times more new funds than did the credit market during this period and almost five times more than the credit and equity markets combined.

Because of their reliance on internal cash flow and avoidance of new equity issues, corporate managers are able to significantly—and often consciously—reduce their reliance on the equity markets for funds. This enables managers to distance themselves from the direct discipline of the capital markets. Ironically, however, even though the equity markets in recent years have actually reduced the availability of funds for internal financing, the stock market attracts the bulk of corporate managers' attention and thus has the greatest influence on their behavior.

Another significant difference between the equity and credit markets is that the credit market's discipline focuses more on risk and the availability of future cash flow, while the equity market emphasizes returns. This distinction is a logical result of the fact that lenders receive a contractually fixed return whereas the stockholders participate fully in a company's upside return potential. From the standpoint of the credit market, returns need to provide an acceptable margin of debt service coverage and liquidity, but this can be far short of the returns necessary to maximize shareholder returns. The debt market can contractually restrict a company's behavior through loan covenants and ultimately can refuse to renew existing loans or extend new loans. These differences can pit equity and credit market institutions against one another in their policy positions toward corporations, particularly during times of adversity.

While the equity markets can reject new equity issues, shareholders cannot withdraw their funds once invested. Even the equity market's potential threat to prevent the company from issuing new equity is somewhat hollow, since few companies over their mature life actually make primary issues of common stock. The equity market's principal threats are to lower the price of the stock through normal market trading and for institutional investors to make specific demands directly of boards of directors and chief executives. In some cases, there may be the potential threat of a hostile takeover. However, in practice, the ability, as well as the motivation, for institutional investors to communicate directly with management or directors to affect change is limited. A Korn/Ferry survey of over a thousand CEOs and directors found that only 18.5 percent of the companies surveyed had been contacted by institutional investors for explanations of corporate performance or governance issues. Only 10.8 percent of the companies reported that the contact had any influence on the company. The resulting actions of these companies ranged from directors becoming more aggressive in evaluating management's performance to consultation with the institutional investors regarding board nominees.[2]

When institutional investors become displeased with management's performance, the normal remedy is to sell the stock. This leaves the impact on stock price as the most powerful consequence of equity-market discipline. When a firm's quarterly earnings fall below expectations, its stock price can fall precipitously, and management is subjected to second-guessing not only in the markets, but even more powerfully in the press.

Much of the argument regarding the benefit of capital-market discipline focuses on the benefits derived from its effect on poorly managed, bottom-dwelling companies. However, this neglects the consequences of these same pressures on firms with sound performance and decent management. The equity markets' pressure on companies for short-term financial performance can have pernicious effects. Equity-market discipline directs managers' attention to financial returns and current shareholder value at the possible expense of future shareholder returns and competitiveness. Investment and innovation can be curtailed and long-term strategic initiatives shelved. Corporate leaders must have the courage and vision to withstand these pressures, to chart a strategic direction toward meaningful ends and stay the course.

Product-Market Discipline

By contrast, the discipline of the product market is usually swift, sure, and direct. Although for companies with poorly performing managers, capital-market discipline can precipitate a change in management, the competitive product markets provide more effective, more constructive, and stronger discipline for most corporate managers. Product-market discipline powerfully and directly affects a company's competitive advantage and financial performance. Customers increase or decrease their buying of the company's products based on the perceived value delivered. Competitors consistently innovate to render former competitive advantages obsolete. Managers have no choice but to respond to this "discipline."

When a company is focused on responding quickly, effectively, and efficiently to this product-market discipline, its ability to create value for society is almost assured. The perceived value delivered to the customer increases, costs are contained, and competitors' thrusts are parried. Innovation and speed become central to the firm's activities. However, when concern with capital-market discipline dominates managers' thinking, the perceived pressures for short-term financial performance can cause innovation—and consequently, long-term competitive advantage—to languish.

The Internalization of Capital-Market Influences

To properly understand the capital markets' influence on corporate strategy, one must distinguish between the two channels through which the influence manifests itself. The first is the institutionalized differences across nations in the relationship between industrial corporations and capital-market firms. The second is the way in which corporate leaders choose to internalize these relationships into their companies through their decisions, the selection of operational goals, and the formulation of specific corporate financial policies. Particularly in the United States, managers have considerable latitude in choosing how to reflect capital-market pressures in their decisions. The market's influence is greatest—but indirect—when corporate managers internalize capital-market objectives in the form of performance measures (such as EVA, ROI, profit margins, and earnings growth) and design control systems that emphasize performance against near-term financial targets. Because the capital market's controls are indirect, they often lead to undesirable and unintended consequences, such as the sacrifice of long-term value creation for short-term financial benefit.

Courageous leaders devise a strategy they deem best and use the services of capital-market institutions to further this strategy. They avoid the temptation to subordinate the firm's strategic interests to those of capital-market institutions, regardless of the pressures (real or imagined) flowing from the capital markets. The courage to subordinate the interests of the capital market to product-market strategies is a sign of true leadership. This courage is particularly needed in an age when the popular press tends to glorify short-term financial success and vilify short-term financial disappointments, and when short-term financial sacrifices are required to achieve long-term competitive advantage and superior long-term financial performance.

Relationships Between Industrial Corporations and Capital-Market Institutions

Different corporate relationships with capital-market institutions have divergent influences on strategy. Some institutional relationships support effective corporate strategies, whereas others constrain them. Historically, as American firms faced increasing competition from other nations, the structural differences between nations in these relationships took on new and greater importance. These new competitors had different domestic capital-market relationships, different ownership structures, and different managerial beliefs about their firms' relationships with the financial community and with society. These differences, which reflect the institutionalization of different corporate purposes, soon began to show signs of being a source of competitive disadvantage for American industry.

These structural differences in corporate relationships with capital-market institutions have become increasingly critical to a company's competitiveness, in part because of capital's increased importance to competitive advantage and also because of the globalization of markets, which has squeezed returns on investment. Increases in productivity and in capital intensity throughout the industrialized world have heightened the relative importance of capital to the value added by manufacturers and reduced the importance of direct labor. In addition, differentials in wages have been, or are rapidly being, reduced in the most competitive industrialized countries of the world. Germany has long had a higher unit-labor cost than the United States,

Japan's unit-labor cost surpassed that of the United States in 1987, and Korea's unit-labor cost is rising rapidly. As a result, in most advanced industries the relative competitive advantage in value added gained from lower cost labor is no longer decisive. Consequently, know-how and the ability to manage well are increasingly the sources of competitive advantage.

The capital and knowledge advantages interact, particularly in the high-value-added industries of tomorrow. The increasing technological sophistication of today's capital investments requires greater knowledge on the part of equipment operators and managers alike. As a consequence of this shift, the willingness to commit capital to new investment, the cost of that capital, the efficiency of the investment, and management's target returns on capital all strongly affect competitiveness.

However, neither management's willingness to commit capital to state-of-the-art facilities nor the cost of capital appears to be as evenly allocated throughout the industrial world as does labor costs. Since the 1970s, Germany, Japan, and other Asian countries from Korea to China have outinvested the United States in terms of fixed assets relative to gross domestic product (GDP). In 1996, investment accounted for over 35 percent of GDP in most Asian countries, nearly twice the U.S. level. This is due in part to the willingness of corporate managers and financial institutions in these countries to accept lower returns on their investments in order to pursue objectives of growth and market share, and in part to the structure of their capital markets, which results in a greater use of debt and consequently a lower cost of capital.

Shareholder Wealth Maximization as the Dominant American Corporate Purpose

The roots of the dominant Anglo-American economic ideology of shareholder wealth maximization can be found in Adam Smith, from whom it draws somewhat selectively. The ideology is predicated on two central beliefs. First, if each individual (and by extension, the corporations that individuals collectively own) pursues his or her own economic self-interest, society as a whole benefits. In the world of corporations, this pursuit is translated as the maximization of the wealth of those individuals who are shareholders. Seeking the greatest return, capital flows to its highest and best uses as determined by the "vote" of customers in free markets. This produces the greatest wealth for society.

These beliefs embody a set of assumptions about how capital is allocated in the American system. In essence, stock market investors and lenders are thought to be able to make better capital-allocation decisions than corporate managers are. This assumes that the investors have better information, more admirable motivations, greater objectivity, and, possibly, greater wisdom than corporate managers have. Capital-market allocation decisions are also assumed to create the most competitive companies—placing a discipline on corporate managers' decisions to ensure that return on investment, not personal self-interest, guides decisions. Most important, shareholder wealth is assumed to accurately reflect the total wealth created by the firm.

The second belief is that since the shareholders are owners of the corporation, the only legitimate corporate purpose is to create wealth for them. This view emanates from deeply ingrained beliefs about property rights and individualism, ideas that originated with the thoughts of philosophers Thomas Hobbes and John Locke in the seventeenth century. Because an understanding of the arguments for individual property rights is so critical to evaluating shareholder-focused corporate purpose, the next chapter will be devoted to this issue. Suffice it to say here, the way in which historical thought regarding property rights is currently applied to share ownership ignores the individual responsibility upon which the moral justification for property rights is predicated. Ideas developed in a largely agrarian world, when management and owners were one, are applied today under very different circumstances. The separation of management from ownership and the subsequent institutionalization of that ownership through pension funds, mutual funds, and other financial intermediaries have dissolved the remnants of individual shareholders' responsibility in exercising their rights. The resulting imbalance of rights without responsibilities generates a serious tension in society. Thinking in America regarding how this tension should be resolved is still evolving.

Defining corporate purpose in terms of shareholder wealth maximization has proved to be quite analytically seductive. The return to shareholders in the form of dividends and stock price appreciation is readily measurable and highly visible and can be internalized by management in such seemingly objective metrics as return on investment, profit margins, and capital turnover. Consequently, total return to shareholders—particularly stock price—is seized upon by the business press as a convenient—and often daily—measure of corporate and CEO performance. This continued repetition in the press reinforces the ideology of shareholder wealth maximization.

Shareholder-Value-Based Management

Under banners of "value-based management" and "economic value added" (EVA[3]) the internalization of shareholder value creation as the principal corporate performance measure has become *the* American management fad of the early 2000s. However, it leads to unintended adverse consequences that affect employee morale and motivation and erode expected benefits. The focus on historical financial returns is seen by many employees as myopic—if not mindless—and as a barrier to "doing the right thing" for the company's long-term competitive performance. The result is frustration, a sense of powerlessness, and ultimately cynicism. These shortcomings are compounded by the questionable underlying logic of shareholder-value-based management (SVBM).

If management seeks to maximize *current* shareholder value, then the logic of shareholder-value-based management is sound. The flaws are in arguments that it also creates the maximum wealth for society, that it maximizes *future* shareholder wealth, and that it is consistent with increased corporate competitiveness. In reality, SVBM fails to deliver on each of these objectives.

Shareholder-value-based management and other ways managers internalize shareholder value maximization in their firms can have pernicious unintended effects on investment. To ensure that return on investment targets are met, managers often demand returns higher than their company's cost of capital. In 1997 J. P. Morgan & Company found that 70 percent of two hundred companies they studied required new investments to return more than the firm's cost of capital. Typically the margin was two percentage points.[4] These companies are leaving behind investments that promise both to increase wealth and to enhance competitiveness. The way is opened for competitors to make these investments unchallenged, increasing their competitive advantages. The long-term effect of a continued differential in investment can be quite significant.

The shareholder-value-based management concept is not a new one. It is based on the assumption that the current market value of a firm's common stock is an unbiased measure of the value of all future cash flows accruing to the shareholders (discounted to their present value by the shareholders' expected rate of return). In essence, the discounted net present value techniques commonly used in capital budgeting are extended to overall performance measurement. The prescription is that managers should undertake only those investments that increase *today's* shareholder value. In other words, the present value of future cash flow (discounted at the company's cost of capital) should exceed the value of the capital employed. The amount of shareholder wealth created is simply the difference between the *current* market value of its common stock and the total capital shareholders have invested over time in the company (the sum of primary stock issues and retained earnings). This difference is often called "market value added."

To create an internal measure of the shareholder value created by ongoing operations, the company's or business unit's current operating profit (after some adjustments) is reduced by a risk-adjusted charge for the cost of the capital employed in the business.[5] If the result is positive, then shareholder value is being created; if it is negative, shareholder value is being destroyed.

This preoccupation with developing an unbiased quantifiable measure of performance confuses causes with effects. Stock market performance is often argued to be a source of competitive performance rather than simply the result of sound competitive strategies. However, for reasons that will be discussed later, a firm's current stock price is often a flawed barometer of a firm's future competitiveness and provides only limited direct financial benefit to the company.

The emphasis American CEOs place on their company's stock price attests to the pervasiveness of the ideology underlying shareholder value-based management. Most CEOs receive current stock price quotations throughout the day, either real time by computer or periodically in writing from a staff member. The preoccupation of security analysts, institutional investors, and the business press with near-term earnings performance results in public commitments by senior company executives to short-term financial targets. Their reputations as corporate leaders are on the line. Failure to produce the expected results risks their being savaged in the press and the stock market. With their reputations at stake, other competing interests can become subordinate.

This phenomenon is analogous to the psychological concept of operant conditioning. Immediate positive feedback or punishment conditions subjects—often rats or pigeons—to behave in prescribed ways. The press's and stock market's rewards and punishments can be swift and can elicit strong emotional responses from senior managers. Consequently, many executives have become conditioned to run the short-term capital-market maze.

Logical Flaws in the Shareholder Value Ideology

The arguments for maximizing shareholder wealth contain several serious flaws of logic. First, and this might be their biggest flaw, they ignore the impact of shareholder-value-based management on the members of the organization—on their commitment, motivation, and decisions. Since this influence was evaluated at length in earlier chapters, it will not be discussed here. The other principal logical flaws flow from the following five erroneous assumptions: (1) a company's wealth-producing capacity can be captured by a single measure—the wealth accruing only to the shareholders; (2) current (or historical) shareholder value creation equates to a firm's future competitiveness; (3) a company's stock price directly and significantly affects competitive performance; (4) managers of Wall Street institutions can make better resource allocation decisions than can the managers of the industrial firms in which the resources are actually deployed; and (5) the shareholders are a monolithic body with a single objective and one time horizon.

Shareholder Wealth Maximization Measures a Company's
Wealth-Producing Capacity Too Narrowly

The legitimacy of shareholder wealth maximization as the dominant corporate purpose rests on the assumption that the pursuit of this end produces the greatest good for society. The logic is that by maximizing returns on investment, capital will be allocated to its highest and best use, and the material wealth of society will grow at the fastest possible rate. Too often we lose sight of the central fact that shareholder wealth maximization is justified as a *means* to a more fundamental end—the welfare of society. Thoughtful shareholder-wealth advocates agree that maximization of shareholder wealth cannot be justified in and of itself as the purpose of a corporation. It can be justified only if it improves society's welfare more than does any other alternative concept of purpose.

The wealth-producing capacities of the modern corporation are truly awesome and something to be highly valued. But a single measure that narrowly circumscribes corporate contributions is inadequate to capture the multiplicity of ways a corporation generates value for society. Wealth for shareholders is a relatively small portion of the total value created by corporations. A much broader view is necessary if society's interests are to be fully served.

Corporations can directly improve the material well-being of investors, customers, employees, suppliers, distributors, and communities; and indirectly they benefit society through tax payments. The wealth created is not all material. By offering employees work serving worthwhile ends in an enriching environment, they can enable individuals to achieve a greater sense of personal dignity, self-worth, and meaning for their lives. One might ask, in terms of human benefit, is the quality of individual lives more influenced by growth in their net worth from investment income on common stocks than by the sum of the other benefits produced by corporate activity? These other benefits include the income, psychological and social benefits individuals receive from working for a firm, the satisfaction received from the products and services they consume, and the impact corporations have on their communities. In terms of personal happiness, for most people incremental changes in their net worth pales in comparison to these other benefits.

Wealth Capture Is Not Wealth Creation. Focusing on shareholder wealth creation threatens to be transformed into a focus on "wealth capture" rather than "wealth creation." Most advocates of internalized measures of shareholder wealth, such as EVA and shareholder value added, agree that beyond a certain point customer satisfaction and employee welfare potentially conflict with creating the maximum value for the shareholder. Consequently, shareholder value added measures encourage the development of strategies to capture wealth from customers, employees, governments, and suppliers for the benefit of shareholders. Strategies producing the maximum increase in shareholder wealth are considered good, even if the wealth of these other constituents has been diminished by an amount greater than the increase in the shareholders' wealth. Clearly, society as a whole does not benefit from such a strategy.

What is needed is a strategy that focuses on "wealth creation." To understand the essential difference between wealth capture and wealth creation, think of a pie. Expanding its total size is wealth creation. Increasing the size of one particular slice of the pie at the expense of the remaining slices is wealth capture. Society's material wealth, which increases only when real output increases (when nominal output increases faster than inflation), is determined solely by the size of the pie, whereas shareholder wealth often can be enhanced more by the capture of wealth than by the growth in the size of the pie. Financial restructuring, in which the company incurs additional debt to buy back its stock, provides a simple example of this distinction. The value of the common stock increases in the short run because of the temporary increase in the demand for the shares during the buyback. Stock price is raised in the long run because the tax deduction provided by the interest on the increased debt lowers its cost of capital and because fewer shares participate in the company's upside potential. However, no net wealth is created for society—wealth is merely captured by the corporation from the government through lower taxes and possibly from the pre-restructuring lenders who may see the credit quality of their loans decline. We may viscerally applaud the results—but not because it creates wealth. Furthermore, if the risks associated with the increased financial leverage reduce the company's willingness to make investments, total wealth created in the future will decline. Examples of wealth capture from employees include layoffs, lower compensation, and less attractive work environments. Wealth can be captured from customers by increasing prices or cutting back expenditures that promise to create customer value (for example, spending on product development and customer service). The short-term result is likely to be an increase in the shareholders' current wealth, but it leads to reduced customer satisfaction and ultimately to reduced competitiveness.

There is no economic law that states that the wealth captured by the shareholder will exceed the wealth (existing or prospective) lost by other individuals in society. There is, however, abundant evidence that total wealth creation often does not equate to maximizing shareholder wealth creation. Consequently, using shareholder returns as the dominant governor of the allocation of capital throughout an economy is difficult to justify.

Many continental European and Asian companies are criticized in the United States for making investments at low returns, and thus eroding their potential to create shareholder wealth. However, there is little question that these companies have created substantial wealth for their domestic societies and for consumers throughout the world. The term "economic miracle" has been successively applied to Germany, Japan, and Korea to capture their stunning pace of industrial development and the accompanying improvement in personal incomes. The economic adjustments that began in the late 1990s notwithstanding, the long-term results have been impressive. For example, Germany has been the world's leader in per capita exports for the last twenty years and has rivaled the United States in absolute dollar volume of exports. It has achieved this position while paying the highest wages in the world. In less than thirty years Korea went from a war-torn agrarian society to the eleventh largest industrial producer in the world. The increase in the Korean standard of living has been remarkable. And it has progressed to the front edge of technology in some very sophisticated industries, including becoming the world's largest producer of memory chips. The competitive accomplishments of Japan have been well chronicled.

Ask yourself, has the material welfare of humans across the globe been improved by the below cost-of-capital investments made by Asian firms? The answer is undoubtedly yes. Consider two of the most economically salient industries in the world: semiconductors and automobiles. In memory chips, Japan—and later Korea—drove the world's price/performance ratio rapidly lower. This required massive investments and innovations in manufacturing processes. The result was the creation of substantial wealth for consumers and companies throughout the world. But the returns throughout the industry since the mid-1970s have been meager. In 1985 and 1986 alone, aggregate worldwide losses in the semiconductor industry were $6 billion.[6] In the automobile industry, Toyota's innovations in total quality management and just-in-time inventory systems ushered in a new era of quality and low costs. Consumers, Toyota employees, and the Japanese economy benefited handsomely, but Toyota's pretax returns on total capital were low, averaging only 9.5 percent from 1989 to 1993 and falling to 8.4 percent from 2000 to 2001.[7] These stories repeat themselves in industry after industry—from shipbuilding to steelmaking, and from industrial robots to semiconductor-manufacturing equipment. The aggressive pricing of Asian companies also helps explain how low inflation was able to coexist with low unemployment in the United States in the late 1990s.

Measuring a Firm's Wealth Production. Managers need to evaluate their company's performance using measures that reflect the firm's material contributions to society—what Peter Drucker calls "the wealth-producing capacity of the enterprise . . . the objective on which all constituencies depend for the satisfaction of their expectations and objectives, whether shareholders, customers, or employees."[8] A firm's long-term ability to create value for society is dependent on its competitiveness—its ability in a fair and open market to provide customers with products and services having greater perceived value (functionality and quality) at a lower cost than competitors, while making the necessary investments to ensure the firm's future ability to do so. Declining competitiveness eventually leads to declining wealth production, and vice versa. Therefore, measures of wealth-producing capacity need to capture both the firm's competitive trajectory and its economic efficiency in using the human and financial resources at its disposal. A single measure, such as net present value or economic value added, is insufficient to capture the essence of sustained wealth creation.

Just as a pilot requires multiple gauges on an airplane's instrument panel for safe, efficient, and effective flight, corporate leaders need several dials to successfully guide the firm's wealth creation.[9] Most good companies already use many of these measures. Managers simply need to become accustomed to applying them all in tandem and to weight them appropriately. One set of dials measures the firm's current performance in providing greater value to customers than competitors do (air speed). These dials measure revenue growth, market share, customer satisfaction, brand value, and the timeliness (time-to-market) and quality of product innovations relative to competitors. Another set of dials measures the firm's progress in developing competency-based competitive advantages that strategically position the firm for the future (the compass and the altimeter). Success in the development of people (and measures of their satisfaction) and progress in creating proprietary knowledge are essential measures of the firm's development of the core competencies that will yield the core products of the future. A third set of dials measures the firm's efficiency in converting its resources (the fuel gauge). Return on investment (operating margins and asset turnover) and the costs of key activities benchmarked against competitors' costs and best practices are key measures of this efficiency.

All of these gauges are important, and none can directly substitute for the others. The essence of corporate wealth-producing capacity is captured by growth in revenues accompanied by levels of profitability sufficient to fund the necessary investments needed to achieve the growth, to insure against the risks of the business, and to make the necessary investments to ensure future competitiveness. The determination of competitiveness *ends* with financial measures, whereas shareholder value maximization typically *begins* with financial measures. For a company that is focused on enhancing its competitiveness, financial measures are not important in and of themselves. Their importance is derived from their ability to reflect the value placed on the company's products and services by customers, the company's efficiency in using its resources, and the magnitude of resources available to fuel the company's strategy.

Current Shareholder Value Does Not Equate to Future Competitiveness

While it is true that in the long term shareholder wealth and corporate competitiveness should converge, there is no reason to believe that actions to secure long-term competitiveness will maximize shareholder value in the short term. Even in the long term, competitiveness and returns can meet at either a high or low level. This raises a critical question for corporate performance. Will focusing on the customer or on the shareholder—on the product market or the capital market—be more likely to cause a higher-level convergence of competitiveness and shareholder wealth in the long term?

A drive to maximize shareholder wealth potentially constrains expenditures on people, plant, research, and development, creating a cycle in which eroding competitiveness causes returns to decline, which motivates managers to bolster returns with further reductions in investment, disintegrating competitiveness further. Returns and competitiveness converge, but in a downward spiral. The result is the destruction of the firm's value-producing capacity.

Nevertheless, advocates of shareholder-value-based management assert that adopting their techniques will increase a company's competitiveness. They also candidly admit that the interests of shareholders can conflict with actions to increase the value provided to customers. They assume decisions that increase customer satisfaction, but reduce shareholder value, will erode competitiveness, as the authors of *The Value Imperative* explain:

> Whenever shareholders subsidize customers in a significant way, the financial health of the company is diminished, ultimately to the detriment of all stakeholders. Not only is the company's cash flow lower than it would be otherwise, but its long-term competitiveness is also eroded by the increase in its cost structure and investment base. Over time, any company that pursues this type of uneconomic investment will undoubtedly face competitors.[10]

Assertions such as this rest on faulty logic. If a company lowers its return-on-investment hurdle rate, it will be able to undertake more investments or simply lower prices. Increasing investments in product and process improvements should increase the value delivered to customers and should improve the cost structure, not erode it. These improvements are the foundation for increased long-term competitiveness, not reduced competitiveness. Instead of attracting competitors, companies that price and invest aggressively decrease the financial attractiveness of their markets, thus discouraging new competitors. To the contrary, economic logic dictates that high-return companies invite competitors. Just consider the numerous industries, such as automobiles, consumer electronics, flat panel displays, and semiconductors, that the Japanese entered in the United States with great success, in part because they were willing to accept much lower returns and consequently outinvested and underpriced their American competitors.

The belief that competitiveness and current shareholder wealth are necessarily equivalent is based on several other false assumptions. A common thread running through these assumptions is the implicit belief that competitiveness is more closely linked to the capital markets than to the product markets and can be measured best by current financial results. Subordinating the need to respond to competitors' actions and the interests of customers and employees to financial results turns a company's strategy on its head. Financial strength is a result of fundamental competitive advantages in the product market. Financial returns reflect these advantages, but they do not cause them. Therefore, the principal strategic focus must be on activities that provide a similar product or service at a lower price than competitors and/or provide greater value to the customer in terms of the functionality and quality of the product or service. These activities take place in the product markets. Capital markets—particularly the credit markets—are important sources of financial resources, but the product market determines long-term competitiveness. From the standpoint of competitiveness, returns on capital must be sufficient to fund the necessary investments, to insure against business risks, and to pay for mistakes. This means managers must be attentive to returns, but they do not need to subordinate competitiveness to the maximization of current returns.

Shareholder-value-based management falsely assumes that all competitors play by the same rules. Clearly, in the global marketplace, not all firms do. For reasons discussed in Chapter 9, many firms give preference to growth over return on investment, and to customers, employees, or the nation over shareholders. The same is true in the domestic economy as well. Not all managers seek to maximize their company's *current* market value. Many corporate leaders seek to expand their firms' market power and long-term competitive position (even if it must be at the expense of today's potential shareholder value) in the knowledge that doing so will increase *future* shareholder wealth. Because they undertake a broader range of investments, these firms have distinct strategic advantages in competing with companies that first seek to maximize shareholder wealth.

Another false assumption is the assertion that shareholder value and the market value of the firm's common stock are direct and reliable measures of future competitiveness. In fact, instead of being leading indicators of competitiveness, they are often lagging indicators. Since shareholder-value-based management measures (such as EVA) are based on historical results, using them to guide decision making is much like looking in the rearview mirror to judge the competitive road ahead. In today's rapidly changing, complex world, yesterday is often a poor reflection of tomorrow's competitive realities. Similarly, for reasons explained later in this chapter, today's market value of a company's common stock—although it is theoretically assumed to be the discounted present value of the company's future cash flow—is often biased to the short term.

In the world of shareholder-value-based management, today's valuation is what counts. Strategic moves that promise to significantly improve future competitiveness (and future shareholder value) are not acceptable if they do not increase shareholder value *today*. This is the essence of the net present value concept. Consequently, future shareholder value can be jeopardized by actions intended to create shareholder wealth today. Ignoring the potential conflict between future competitiveness and current market value is the Achilles' heel of shareholder value analysis and can cause it to become the enemy of sound strategy.

The third erroneous assumption is that if a company does not earn returns at least equal to its cost of capital, it will eventually not be able to raise as much capital as its shareholder-value-creating competitors. This is a cornerstone of the belief that the capital markets—not corporate managers—are the most effective allocators of capital in society. However, in a world awash in capital this assumption is simply not justified. As witnessed by the Asian investment debacles leading to the market adjustments in 1997 and 1998, by the dot-com craze of the late 1990s, and by Enron's bankruptcy in 2001, capital can flow rather freely to finance low-return projects. Loans to these Asian firms came not only from domestic financial institutions but also from American, European, and Japanese institutions. The reality is that throughout the developed world, large firms earning substantially below their cost of capital are consistently able to attract large amounts of new capital and to generate considerable internal cash flow that can be retained for investment. In 1999, although availability of capital was not a concern, half of the *Fortune* 500 companies had a return on total assets under 3.8 percent, and fully one-third of the companies for which data are available regarding ten-year total return to shareholders (from stock price appreciation and reinvested dividends) had total returns below 9.5 percent even in the record bull market of the 1990s. Yet capital flowed freely to these companies.

The fourth false assumption is that all actions creating shareholder wealth are assumed not to harm competitiveness. However, because shareholder-value added (SVA) is typically calculated by reducing current earnings by a risk-adjusted charge for the capital employed, two of the quickest and least risky ways to enhance SVA—reducing investments and financial restructuring (issuing debt to buy back stock)—can negatively affect competitiveness. SVA improves right away if investments are cut and the business milked. Reducing the investment base is immediate, but the returns on the forgone investment are usually several years in the future and thus do not adversely affect the current SVA calculation. The larger the investment forgone, the more today's SVA benefits. Also, financial restructuring can increase shareholder value by capturing value from the government (in lower taxes because of the higher interest expenses) and possibly from pre-existing debt holders (as the riskiness of debt increases, its value declines). But the increased debt/equity ratio carries with it greater financial risk. If the company wants to prevent its overall risk from rising above the level existing prior to the restructuring, managers must reduce business risk by changing the company's pattern of investment. Riskier investments are rejected. Unfortunately, some of the most innovative strategic investments are characterized by greater uncertainty, and these investments are the ones most likely to be cut. SVA becomes a barrier to the pathfinding strategies that stretch a firm's aspirations beyond its current capabilities and resources.[11]

Not only do large investments to create future competitive advantage (investments that increase market share and breakthrough innovations in product and processes) reduce SVA *today*, but also some might not produce a positive net present value over their life. In part, this is because the financial benefits may be too far in the future for their current discounted value to exceed the amount invested. The further in the future the positive cash flows generated by these investments are received, the less they are worth today. Nevertheless, future competitiveness would be improved and *future* shareholder value increased. Most innovative strategies for outpacing competition do not pay off for several years. Should a company undertake such investments? The advocates of shareholder-value-based management would often answer no. To understand the long-term implications of such a decision, consider the following example.

Two companies—Shareholder Returns Inc. (SRI) and Growth and Competitiveness Corporation (GCC)—compete in the same industry and possess identical management skills, technology, and resources. Both have a cost of capital of 14 percent. As long as either firm earns at least 10 percent on its capital, the availability of external capital from the credit and equity markets is unlimited. In 2002, both companies receive new CEOs who have clear views of the strategic objectives of their respective companies. The CEO at SRI is dedicated to the principles of shareholder-value-based management and will undertake only those investments with returns greater than or equal to the cost of capital (14 percent). GCC's CEO is committed to maximizing the company's long-term competitiveness and is willing to sacrifice current shareholder value in order to achieve it. The company is willing to make investments that return 11 percent or more.

In the early years of these CEOs' tenure, SRI's shareholder value is greater than GCC's. Because of its lower investment level and higher rate of return, SRI also has more cash flow available to pay dividends or repurchase stock.

GCC meanwhile is consistently outinvesting SRI because of its willingness to undertake investment opportunities with returns of 11 percent to 14 percent—investments that SRI rejects because of their "inadequate" return. These incremental investments are in a number of areas. To gain market share, GCC undercuts SRI's prices. Also, GCC more aggressively invests in entering new markets, in R&D to improve the value of its products and services and to create more efficient manufacturing and logistical processes, and in the development of its people's capabilities. As a result of these investments, GCC's core competencies develop at a faster pace than SRI's. In essence, GCC has "captured the investment initiative" from SRI.[12] Over time, these additional investments give GCC lower operating costs than SRI has (both because of the process improvements and because of the scale economies and learning advantages associated with the larger share of market). GCC's products provide the customer greater value because of the increased research and development activities, and its competencies are being extended more rapidly into new markets and new products, which result in additional scale and scope economies. Of course, because its growth is more rapid and its returns lower, GCC will probably need to either borrow more heavily than SRI or issue equity to finance its strategy.

Initially, to respond to GCC's competitive assault and to maintain shareholder value, SRI retreats to market niches where the higher returns are possible. Its growth atrophies. Eventually, GCC's competitive strength becomes overwhelming. GCC has both better products and lower costs. It attacks SRI's market niches one by one. To survive, SRI must now compete head-to-head with GCC. But to do so, it must undercut GCC's prices in order to sell its inferior products. Because SRI's cost structure is higher, its returns—and shareholder value—plummet to levels substantially below GCC's.

Even in hindsight, SRI's strategy could well have been the right one to achieve the CEO's expressed purpose of maximizing *current* shareholder value. Although in the long term the company's survival became threatened, in each year in the early period of their competition the net present value of SRI's future cash flows exceeded that of GCC. Obviously, at some point GCC's net present value will exceed SRI's. However, the logic of shareholder-value-based management is predicated on value today, not tomorrow. As this example clearly demonstrates, the maximization of *today's* shareholder wealth is not equivalent to competitiveness (or to future shareholder wealth).

In a hypercompetitive world, the pace of strategic innovation is unrelenting. A key premise of economic theory is that intensifying competition reduces returns. Thus, the competitive pressure to undertake new strategic commitments that erode *present* shareholder value is intense. This is the "creative destruction" of the twenty-first century. If these investments are not made, the current value of the firm will benefit, but its future value will be reduced. Managers lacking the courage to make these investments are most likely—although unintentionally—presiding over the competitive decline of their companies.

Stock Price Does Not Directly Affect Most Corporations' Competitiveness

Although today's stock price may reflect a firm's historical competitiveness and expectations for future cash flow generation, for most large established companies stock price rarely affects future competitiveness *directly*. To have an effect, stock price must influence the investment patterns of the firm, primarily by affecting the availability or cost of funds. Yet most managers are reluctant to issue equity to finance existing businesses. For these companies, common stock becomes a somewhat irrelevant vehicle for financing their strategies or entering into alliances other than acquisitions. Therefore, the cost of this source of capital also loses much of its competitive relevance.

There are three exceptions to the strategic irrelevance of the stock price. First, for companies pursuing a strategy that entails the acquisition of other companies, the stock price can affect the cost of these acquisitions. However, even for acquisitions, alternative forms of financing (debt and internal cash flow) have lower capital costs than common stock. Paradoxically, many senior American managers are willing to use common stock to finance acquisitions of businesses about which they often know relatively little, but they are reluctant to issue common stock to finance investments that promise to enhance the company's strategy in its existing businesses—businesses they know well. Second, for those few managers who are willing to issue equity to finance their strategies, the stock price can influence their willingness to do so, as well as the cost of the capital raised and the extent the existing shareholders' ownership is diluted. Finally, for start-up and smaller rapid-growth companies, initial public offerings and subsequent equity issues can be essential to the realization of their growth potential. But each of these cases requires a proactive intent on the part of managers to use equity financing as an important part of their strategy.

This raises a rather odd paradox that plagues the competitiveness of many American companies. The United States has the most efficient equity market in the world, yet it has proved to be a peripheral tool for increasing the competitiveness of most large publicly owned companies in the United States. In fact, in recent years some American managers and leading strategic thinkers, such as Lester Thurow and Michael Porter, have argued that the equity markets have exerted negative influence on U.S. competitiveness.[13]

The evidence regarding the reluctance of American managers to use equity issues to finance internal needs is clear. From 1960 to 1987, only 35 percent of a sample of 250 *Fortune* 500 companies *ever* issued equity to finance internal capital needs, as shown in Table 5.1. With the exception of 1983, in no year did more than 4 percent of the companies issue common

TABLE **5.1**   **Equity Offerings for Internal Use of Funds by** *Fortune* **500 Companies**

	1940–1978	1960–1987
Companies issuing equity *at least once*	21%	35%
Companies issuing equity *more than once*	8%	13%

Note: The two periods are based on separate samples of 250 companies, each taken from the *Fortune* 500 listing for the ending year. Where data were available for a company over the entire period, companies were selected on an every-other-company basis to obtain as even a dispersion based on company size as possible. An equity offering was counted if any of the proceeds were used for internal financing purposes, including the retirement of debt.

stock for internal investment purposes. Only 13 percent of the companies issued equity more than once for internal financing purposes over this twenty-seven-year period—only 6 percent more than twice. The proclivity to use equity for internal financing is essentially the same across companies of different size, although smaller firms that issue equity do so more frequently. Of the companies ranking below 250, 19 percent issued equity more than once during these twenty-seven years, whereas less than 10 percent of the companies ranking 250 or larger did so.

In most instances, the stock issues were relatively small and infrequent. Therefore, they did not make a significant difference in the company's overall source of capital. For the 164 common stock issues by these companies for which there is public information regarding the issues' dollar value, 73 percent had a value of less than 15 percent of the market value of the company's common stock at the time of the issuance. (Presumably those issues for which data are not available are less material and thus considerably smaller in size.)

When the reluctance to issue equity is combined with capital-structure policies that impose voluntary limits on the amount the company chooses to borrow, the capital available for investments can be arbitrarily constrained. This problem has many causes. In part it is the result of conventional wisdom regarding the adverse effect primary stock issues have on stock price—at least in the short term—and the "last resort" image of equity financing because of its high cost. New equity issues are often viewed with disdain because they dilute near-term earnings per share and/or because they are perceived to be a failure of management to attract low-cost funds in other forms. Given these widely held views regarding equity financing and the intense pressure for short-term increases in shareholder value (from both institutional shareholders and the specter of hostile takeovers), the reluctance to issue common stock is understandable.

The leveraged buyout (LBO) and financial restructuring phenomena have compounded the problem. The corporate ability to raise capital has been consumed to acquire financial assets, not productive assets. The competitive problem with LBOs goes beyond the increased risk that results from the increased financial leverage. It is their impact on investment. Companies mortgage their future ability to make productive investments. LBOs and corporate financial restructuring absorb substantial amounts of debt capacity that otherwise could be used constructively for investment in product development, productivity improvements, and battles for market share. To ward off potential raiders, many corporate managers believe they must make investment decisions that enhance short-term financial results at the expense of long-term performance. Even the perceived threat of hostile takeovers can have a deleterious effect. The motivation for many corporate financial restructurings has been to consume available debt capacity, making this capacity unavailable to finance a hostile takeover and, therefore, making the firm less attractive to raiders. The net result of these activities is that companies are buying back nearly 2 percent of their outstanding equity every year.

The causal linkage of stock appreciation to increased industrial output is tenuous. The link assumes that the higher evaluation of shares will make more and lower-cost equity financing available to firms. The underlying assumption is that firms will use the equity financing alternative. However, the evidence is that few do. In fact, in 1996–2000, a period of high price/earnings ratios, stock repurchases by nonfinancial corporations exceeded new equity issues by $760 billion. By comparison, during the same five years, these companies raised a net $1.7 trillion of new capital from credit markets in the form of debt.

To understand the weakness of this link, consider the following hypothetical example. Assume that no company financed with equity, and that no investors withdrew funds from the capital markets, but solely traded debt and equity securities among themselves in an attempt to secure more advantageous returns and increase their net worth. Although these assumptions are somewhat rigid, they largely reflect reality for large publicly owned companies. Under these conditions, increasing the prices of common stocks does not directly affect corporate investment. The trading of stocks by investors in the secondary market—what John Maynard Keynes called "the froth on the stream of competitive enterprise"—simply increases or decreases their personal net worth and generates capital-gains tax payments. Economists estimate between 1 percent to 5 percent of all increases in net worth find their way into the economy through increased consumer spending with increases in wealth from shareholdings having an effect on consumption nearer the lower end of these estimates.[14] During the unprecedented bull market of the late 1990s consumption of luxuries such as expensive cars, jewelry, and boats did soar; however, in more normal times, the net result of secondary stock trading for society is often little more than a wash.

Managers of Financial Institutions Are at a Disadvantage in Making Resource Allocation Decisions

Implicit in the ideology of shareholder wealth maximization is the belief that employees of capital-market institutions generally make better resource allocation decisions than do managers of corporate enterprises. At a time of active debate regarding whether CEOs of complex firms can effectively design their company's strategy or whether this responsibility should be delegated to business-unit managers, it seems odd that so many people still argue that employees of capital-market institutions—who are much further removed from the product-market realities than are corporate CEOs—can best make these strategic resource allocation decisions for the economy.

Certainly capital-market managers—be they investment bankers, professional fund managers, or security traders—see a wider array of investment alternatives and may possess a distance from the more parochial company-specific concerns of corporate managers. However, serious limitations prevent them from making optimal resource allocation decisions. Primary among these barriers are insufficient access to information, motivations that are not aligned with value-maximizing decisions, a lack of commitment to the long-term health of individual firms, and little control over the decisions of the corporate managers who ultimately invest the funds provided by the capital markets.

Information is critical to making wise investment decisions. In their quest for an information advantage over competitors, investment bankers and industrial companies spend billions of dollars each year. Particularly important is information regarding the firm's present competitive position, its current and prospective competencies, the future needs of customers, the strategic options available to it, the potential moves and countermoves of competitors, and the possible future changes in the structure of the industry. Good predictions of the future competitive environment and the potential consequences of alternative strategies require a detailed, in-depth, and intuitive understanding of the industry and the capabilities of the firm's human capital. For chief executive officers and senior executives, this more-than-full-time job requires the processing and synthesis of information from a multitude of sources. Managers of financial institutions have insufficient time and more limited access to information than do their corporate counterparts.

Of course, for the large and increasing amount of capital invested in index funds, company-specific information becomes extraneous. Arguments regarding conscious resource-allocation decision making simply do not apply to index fund managers.

To compensate for this information gap, capital-market decision makers become highly dependent on those with the best information—corporate managers. Most corporate managers, knowing the importance of their communications with the investment community, carefully shape and often sanitize the information they transfer. Their objective is to manage expectations and to put the most favorable face on the company's prospects, without being overtly misleading. Aware that their competitors are likely to gain access to the information given security analysts, corporate managers must exercise care in divulging aspects of the company's strategy. In addition, corporate managers must abide by Security and Exchange Commission (SEC) dictates regarding the nature of information that can be communicated. The SEC wants to ensure that corporate managers do not use their information to unduly manipulate the price of the company's stock. This further limits managers' communications to financial institutions regarding their strategies and predicted financial results. Furthermore, to avoid being considered "insiders" by the SEC and subject to trading restrictions, institutional investors must limit the information to which they are privy.

Dependent on corporate managers for information and with inadequate time, access, and resources to develop information of comparable quality on their own, managers of financial institutions are at an information dis-advantage relative to corporate managers in making resource allocation decisions.

In addition, the basic motivations of capital-market managers can divert them from making optimal investment decisions. Security analysts, the source of much of the data analysis upon which investment decisions are based, are increasingly motivated by the need to generate trading commissions and investment banking business for their firms.

Analysts' bonuses are typically one to three times their salary and are based on measures not directly related to the quality of their earnings forecasts. Their performance measurements tend to be dominated by success in generating stock trading and investment banking fees from clients, and by their standing in the polls conducted by *Institutional Investors* and Greenwich Associates. The importance of trading to an analyst's success gives rise to a bias for buy recommendations and, since brokerages earn most of their commissions from speculative traders, to the short term.

Success in "client services" is usually measured by the sales force and includes speaking at meetings, traveling to meet clients, and commissions generated by "buy" or "sell" recommendations. It is not unusual for security analysts to be required to make sixty to two hundred calls a month to large institutional clients. This pressure significantly reduces the amount of time available to do penetrating research. As one analyst complained, "I do my research between 10 P.M. and 4 A.M."[15] With severe constraints on the time available for research and with incentives based on the generation of commissions and fees, it is only natural that the emphasis is placed on getting the short term right. Consequently, long-term fundamental research, which is difficult and time-consuming, is sacrificed.

The pressure on security analysts to scout for initial public offerings (IPOs) and merger deals intensified in the 1990s. As a result, the line between being an objective analyst and an investment banker who advocates for clients has blurred. As Alan Johnson, an investment banking compensation consultant, observes, "Of all the jobs on Wall Street, the company analyst's role has changed the most in the last five years. The analyst today is an investment banker in sheep's clothing."[16]

The analyst's lifeblood is access to corporate managers for information. Therefore, they walk a fine line between objectivity and not offending managers with negative reports, which could threaten their access. This fear is well founded. A Tempest Consultants Inc. survey found that about a third of U.S. companies' response to an analyst's sell recommendation would be to exclude the analyst's firm from its investment banking business and to "reduce communications and reduce access [for the analyst]."[17] In addition, the analyst's own firm can take action against him or her. One analyst, ranked by *Institutional Investor* as the leading regional bank analyst for eight out of nine years, was sacked by his firm because, he claims, his criticism of banking industry mergers interfered with the firm's attempts to build its merger business. He says, "I believed many of the acquisitions are destroying shareholder value. I heard from my colleagues that the new investment bankers wanted me out. I was viewed as being negative on mergers and acquisitions."[18]

One consequence of these pressures is a marked change in the ratio of buy and sell recommendations. In the early 1980s about a quarter of security analysts' recommendations were "buys" and a quarter "sells"—a balance one would expect if the market were assumed to effectively price stocks. By 1999 only 0.3 percent of 33,169 recommendations were sells, and fully 71 percent were buys.[19] Compounding this bias is the fact that many analysts own the stock of the companies they cover. In 2001, against a backdrop of congressional hearings and a SEC probe of conflicts of interest regarding research, Merrill Lynch became the first major investment banker to institute a policy prohibiting analysts from buying stock in the companies they research.

These facts call into question the validity of the information on which investors rely to make their decisions. Biased and short-term-focused information undermines the market's ability to allocate capital effectively.

Exacerbating this information problem, investment bankers are motivated to complete "the deal" to generate fees, and traders seek short-term pricing imperfections based on new information. None of these motivations necessarily align with making investments that maximize shareholder wealth in either the near or long term. The investment banking emphasis on immediate, deal-based compensation furthers the short-term bias in decisions. This bias also lessens the prospect that financial-institution managers will conduct their due diligence responsibilities with great care and make highly objective decisions. As a consequence, few large industrial companies, if they are not in financial distress, have their financing capacity restricted by the capital markets because of concerns that the funds will be invested in projects with substandard returns. What is important is that the deal be consummated, the fees collected, relationships maintained, and the industrial firm not embarrass the investment banker by failing to meet its financial obligations. These criteria are far removed from concerns regarding value-enhancing investments. The dot-com IPO bubble of the late 1990s is a prime example of these forces. Investment banks brought to market many companies with insufficient future earnings potential to justify the initial offering price.

This seemingly compromised commitment to the industrial firm's long-term welfare is facilitated by the ease with which institutional investors can sell their holdings in a company when they are concerned about the wisdom of corporate managers' decisions. The alternative to selling is to become involved in a long and time-consuming dialogue with company managers and directors in anticipation of creating change in either the senior executives or their decisions. Even if capital-market managers desire to remedy faulty managerial decision making, their means of doing so are limited. They lack any effective direct control over managers. Only in the most egregious and high-profile cases of mismanagement can they generate support from fellow institutional shareholders (usually in the form of voting their proxies against management) and from the business press, which is often decisive in creating change. Even when institutional investors choose to target specific companies to ferment change, they can do so only with a handful of underperforming, usually high-profile companies. Therefore, most firms are immune to threats of institutional-investor intervention. Ironically, the legal covenants in loan agreements often give lenders (bondholders and banks) more control than shareholders over the decisions of managers.

Boards of directors sit between management and the institutional shareholders. Board members, while having a fiduciary responsibility to shareholders, operate under the "business judgment doctrine." Legally, this doctrine means that as long as directors are acting in accordance with their twin duties of "loyalty" and "care" (loyalty to the firm's shareholders by avoiding conflicts of interest and care to exercise due diligence in making decisions), the courts will not challenge their decisions. Therefore, directors have no legal imperative to ensure that shareholder value is maximized in the short term. In essence, if directors avoid negligence and self-dealing in their decisions, they have the legal freedom to make decisions that subordinate current shareholder value to the creation of long-term benefits. Furthermore, over time, most board members forge close relationships with the chairperson and CEO and cannot be counted on to be close allies of disgruntled institutional shareholders.

Because of these factors, corporate managers are in a better position than financial-institution managers to allocate resources in a manner that generates the greatest wealth for society and, in the long run, for shareholders. The board of directors' responsibility is to ensure that they do so and to have the courage to replace CEOs who fail to maintain their companies' competitive vitality.

Shareholders Are Not a Monolithic Body

Too often discussions regarding shareholder wealth maximization are conducted at a theoretical level, ignoring the realities of the shareholders' widely varying motivations. The investments of all shareholders are motivated by the desire to increase their net worth—or the net worth of their clients. But shareholders are a diverse group made up of individuals (a group that spans from the proverbial "widows and orphans" to short-term speculators), traders and institutional money managers at pension funds, mutual funds, and insurance companies, and a range of active investors such as Warren Buffett at Berkshire Hathaway, Mitt Romney at Bain Capital, and Henry Kravis at KKR.[20] The time horizons of these shareholders vary greatly—from literally minutes to a decade or more. Buffett's preferred holding period is "forever." Some are deeply concerned that "their" companies conduct themselves in a socially responsible manner. Active investors, such as Buffett and Romney, act like true owners and bear a responsibility for the performance of "their" companies—Buffett for the long term and Romney until the company is resold. For others, it is purely a financial transaction with no sense of responsibility for the firm's behavior. For some, they own "a stock" not a company, and they view their market transactions as "a trade" not an investment. Most individual investors do not even vote their proxies.

Warren Buffett declares, "We simply don't care what earnings we report quarterly."[21] He explained his philosophy of ownership in "An Owner's Manual," distributed to all shareholders since 1996:

> [My partner] Charlie and I hope that you do not think of yourself as merely owning a piece of paper whose price wiggles around daily and that is a candidate for sale when some economic or political event makes you nervous. We hope you instead visualize yourself as part owner of a business that you expect to stay with indefinitely, much as you might if you owned a farm or apartment house in partnership with members of your family.

For our part, we do not view Berkshire shareholders as faceless members of an ever-shifting crowd, but rather as co-venturers who have entrusted their funds to us for what may well turn out to be the remainder of their lives. . . .

You should be fully aware of one attitude Charlie and I share that hurts our financial performance: Regardless of price, we have no interest at all in selling any good businesses that Berkshire owns. We are also very reluctant to sell sub-par businesses as long as we expect them to generate at least some cash and as long as we feel good about their managers and labor relations. We hope not to repeat the capital-allocation mistakes that led us into such sub-par businesses. And we react with great caution to suggestions that our poor businesses can be restored to satisfactory profitability by major capital expenditures. (The projections will be dazzling and the advocates sincere, but, in the end, major additional investment in a terrible industry usually is about as rewarding as struggling in quicksand.) Nevertheless, gin rummy managerial behavior (discard your least promising business at each turn) is not our style. We would rather have our overall results penalized a bit than engage in that kind of behavior.[22]

A weakness of America's financial structure is the shortage of dedicated, patient capital. The commitment of Warren Buffett—a real owner with close, trust-based relationships with the managers of "his" companies—results in mutual responsibility and respect, and better information. In fact, he is an exemplar of the very positive influence engaged long-term owners can have on companies. This constructive interaction between owner and manager requires a significant ownership position, a sincere long-term commitment to a company, and a track record of shared experiences that reinforce the essence of the relationship.

Buffett is leery of providing too much advice to the managers. He sees his principal role as attending "to capital allocation and the care and feeding of our key managers. Most of these managers are happiest when they are left alone to run their businesses, and that is customarily just how we leave them."[23] Buffett and Berkshire's twelve-person headquarters acts as an internal capital market. Buffett explains that by sending their excess cash to headquarters, managers "don't get diverted by the various enticements that would come their way were they responsible for deploying the cash their businesses throw off. Furthermore, Charlie and I are exposed to a much wider range of possibilities for investing these funds than any of our managers could find in his or her own industry."[24] If Berkshire Hathaway were in fact a microcosm of the entire capital market, the tension between corporate competitiveness and long-term shareholder wealth would dissipate.

For most institutional investors, no matter how noble their intentions, the factors underlying such a relationship unfortunately are missing. Only when the investment is sizable and carries with it a commitment to the company's long-term welfare are such relationships likely to be created.

This diversity among shareholders raises a fundamental question confronting managers seeking to maximize their firm's shareholders' wealth, "For which shareholders?" The answer determines the desired strategic action.

An appreciation of the evolving ownership structure of American companies is helpful to understanding the implications this diversity of shareholder objectives has for management practice. The last quarter of the twentieth century witnessed a dramatic revolution in the ownership of public companies. The percentage of shares directly owned by individuals fell sharply, whereas the institutional ownership of stock, led by pension funds and mutual funds, increased significantly. In 2000, less than 40 percent of the shares of American companies were owned directly by individuals, down from 86 percent in 1960 and 60 percent in 1980. Pension funds controlled 23 percent of the shares, followed by mutual funds with 19 percent.

The shift of ownership to financial institutions has been accompanied by a significant change in the time horizons and motivations of those making the investment decisions. The increased turnover of stock on America's exchanges is a reflection of this change. Because financial institutions are involved in the vast majority of securities transactions, the institutional ownership of stock in the United States has an effect on stock prices disproportional to its ownership percentage. Reflecting increased institutional trading and the intensification of pressure on financial intermediaries for short-term investment performance, the turnover on the New York Stock Exchange (NYSE) has climbed steadily since the early 1970s. Trading volume surged in the 1990s, with NYSE turnover reaching 88 percent in 2000 on an average daily volume of 1.04 billion shares, an amazing twenty-three-fold increase since 1980. The turnover on the more volatile NASDAQ was a staggering 387 percent in 2000. Reflecting on this high turnover, Steven Galbraith, chief investment strategist for Morgan Stanley, observes, "People are renting stocks, not owning them." NYSE large block trading (10,000 shares or more per trade) was over 50 percent of total volume in 2000, and 21.2

percent of the volume was the result of computer-driven program trading. In the 1970s, large block trading never represented more than 26 percent of total NYSE volume and was in the teens for most of the decade.[25] Approximately 80 percent of all volume on the NYSE currently involves trades by institutional investors. In 1993 the average portfolio turnover rate for the seven hundred largest U.S. institutional money managers was 62 percent. Of these managers 80 percent had an average annual holding period of less than thirty-three months.[26] In 2000, the average turnover rate for equity mutual funds was 87 percent according to Lipper Analytics.

The heavy influence of institutional investors in the trading—and thus the pricing—of stocks and the increasingly short-term nature of their ownership has led some observers to conclude that the U.S. market has become "a casino." When he was executive vice president and managing director of institutional sales at Prudential-Bache, Greg A. Smith gave this assessment of the equity markets:

> The competition for business among money managers has gotten enormous. It leads to escalating promises, such as, "You can make them 20 percent to 30 percent a year" when a long-term investment gives them only 10 percent. . . . Investment opinions aren't being formed on traditional fundamental analysis anymore. The typical investment cycle was three to five years in the 1960s. The money managers looked for good results over a year. That became quarterly. Now it's weekly and daily. It used to be we had an investment policy committee. Now there's no restraint on decision-making. It's more a casino operation.[27]

Because of this environment and the shorter time frame in which competitive investment management performance is measured, traditionally long-term investors such as John Templeton, founder of the highly respected Templeton Funds, have been required to take a shorter-term focus. Templeton explains that now, "when a stock becomes a remarkably good value we don't say, 'Well, let's start buying it immediately.' We'll put it on a watch list, and when it begins to show that other people are taking an interest in it, then we'll buy it. In other words, we've introduced a way to be patient and not to rush in just because a stock's a real bargain."[28] Leon Cooperman, a Goldman, Sachs partner, described the consequence of these trends on corporate managers, saying, "I don't think any company can afford a long-term investment today unless its managers own 51 percent of it."[29]

These trends have generated complaints from corporate executives concerning the pressures placed on them for short-term financial performance that, they argue, make it increasingly difficult to manage for the long term. Many pension fund managers counter that the corporate managers themselves are the source of the pressure. For companies with defined-benefit pension plans, the gains and losses on the fund's portfolio affect the firm's reported net income. Consequently, most of the corporate managers measure their pension-fund managers' performance quarterly or more often and display a certain quickness in replacing inadequately performing portfolio managers. As a result, fund managers are under considerable pressure to make decisions that will ensure superior short-term investment performance. This entails buying and selling stocks more frequently than in the past. Consequently, in an ironic twist, the capital market's pressures on corporate managers for short-term financial performance originate in part with the pressures corporate managers themselves exert on their own companies' pension fund managers.

To avoid the negative consequences of these counterproductive short-term pressures, forward-looking corporate leaders have begun to engage in active campaigns to increase the amount of their stock in the hands of committed long-term shareholders. Concerned about these conditions, Coca-Cola management in the 1980s set out to attract shareholders with a true ownership mentality. This effort ended in the sizable purchase of Coke stock by Buffett's Berkshire Hathaway. Frederick Reichheld chronicles the development of a similar program at Nike to attract investors who would buy and hold their stock.[30] Both companies recognized the importance of committed owners to their ability to execute strategies that promise both enhanced competitiveness and exceptional wealth creation in the long term.

Conclusion

Structural relationships between firms, their owners, and sources of capital affect strategy in critical ways. They influence investment by their impact on the cost of capital and on the objectives held by the lenders and shareholders who provide the firm with capital. In a world of global competition, when these relationships differ, competitive advantage can be profoundly affected.

These market realities challenge the validity of the shareholder-value ideology's claim to superiority. In fact, a chain of events affecting information and investor motivation causes the U.S. stock market's myopia. The information on which investment decisions are made is biased toward the short term and to "what sells." The market pressures for shortsighted trading are not offset by quality security-analyst research that provides decision makers with long-term-oriented information. Professional fund managers are pressured to maintain a short-term focus in order to beat the monthly, quarterly, or annual market averages and the performance of competing managers. This occurs in part because of the short-term performance measures imposed on fund managers by their firms and indirectly by their firms' clients and is exacerbated by the short-term forces that dominate the market's pricing of securities.

A corporate purpose of maximizing shareholder wealth has been shown to be less effective than a customer-focused one in enhancing a firm's competitive advantage and in expanding its total wealth-producing capacity. Therefore only one major argument for the priority of shareholder wealth as corporate purpose remains: shareholders are the legal owners of the company, a status that gives them the right to expect managers will act as their agents to maximize their welfare. The merit of this argument is the focus of the next chapter.

6   Property Rights

The Shareholders' Rights and Responsibilities

Ask managers what the purpose of the typical American company is and their usual response is "to make a profit." Some will add—often after probing as to what ends the profits serve—"to enhance the shareholders' wealth." But to get to the core reason why this should be a firm's purpose usually requires considerable additional prodding. Eventually someone will say, "Because they are the owners," and a few will connect this to some vague conception of property rights associated with stock ownership.

These responses indicate that the ideas central to the American ideology of the maximization of shareholder wealth are so deeply ingrained in our beliefs that neither is the logic of the arguments underlying their origin widely understood nor is their current relevance questioned. The fundamental justification for this corporate purpose resides in the shareholders' rights as owners—in the principle of property rights. Our ideas of the rights and responsibilities of shareholders are rooted in the Western concept of property rights as it has evolved over the last twenty-four hundred years. Ideas that originated in a different age to cope with different realities have been selectively extended to the ownership of common stock in today's world. Clearly there is room for considerable misfit in this application.

Beliefs regarding the rights associated with the ownership of business assets were spawned in societies where businesses were either owner-managed proprietorships or chartered corporations doing the work of the state. For Saint Thomas Aquinas the commercial world revolved around the medieval manor; for Luther and Calvin it was the guild system; for John Locke and Adam Smith in the eighteenth century, large corporate enterprises consisted of state-sponsored monopolies such as the East India Company and the Hudson's Bay Company; for nineteenth-century utilitarians it was owner-managed proprietorships. In those days, labor, raw materials, and capital were considered to be the principal source of value. Ownership and management were united in the same person.

By the end of the twentieth century, the principal source of value shifted to knowledge creation. Similarly, during the century, the nature of the business owner evolved from a proprietor, to an owner-manager, then to individual shareholders unrelated to the firm's founders or managers, and finally to financial institutions. These new institutional owners have no role—and little practical say—in management and negligible responsibility for corporate performance. We are in an age when investors' average holding periods are so short that people are considered to be renting, not owning stocks, and when computer-driven program trading accounts for nearly a quarter of all trades on the NYSE, which raises serious questions regarding whether major investors are really "owners." Yet, although today's realities are quite different, the beliefs surrounding property rights associated with business ownership are much the same as they were two centuries ago.

Moreover, for the first time in our history as a nation, American companies are now faced with the necessity of competing with companies from Asia and Europe with capabilities and resources similar to ours but who have different philosophical heritages. The major industrial powers of these continents have significantly different beliefs regarding shareholders' property rights. Competing in the global marketplace with companies holding divergent beliefs has had significant competitive implications—implications that will continue to shape our relative competitive advantage in the twenty-first century.

We adhere to a set of beliefs rooted in the past. Property rights are correctly tied to the sanctity of individual human beings and their freedom. But these beliefs have been extended to apply to common stock—and the underlying corporate assets—just as they do to the most personal and prized of possessions. Consequently, owners of common stock are given rights to control the destiny of corporate organizations unrivaled by the holders of any other corporate security. These beliefs give corporations almost unbridled power to use their assets—within the law—to the benefit of the firm's shareholders. Yet, our government is putting ever-increasing restrictions on the exercise of this power. We are at a watershed. As a society, we are conflicted. We believe in the linkage of property rights and individual freedom—and its implications for the natural right of people to grow and realize their potential, to extend their powers, and to own the product of their own activity. Yet we also believe, if the legislation passed by our representatives and upheld by our judges is any indication, that the power of corporations should be controlled in significant ways for the common good. Invariably this implies an encroachment on the shareholders' property rights. Through the legislative and judicial processes, these rights are increasingly being subordinated to the broader needs of society.

The Ideas and Beliefs That Form the American Ideology

To understand today's ideas regarding shareholders' rights and how these ideas may evolve in the future, it is necessary to examine the historical flow of the ideas regarding private property and wealth.

Throughout time, human beings have grappled with the seemingly irresistible urge to accumulate wealth and possessions. For most of recorded history, this urge has been considered one of our most destructive impulses. These acquisitive instincts have been inextricably linked with the passions of avarice and lust for power that have fueled violence, wars, and a lack of compassion for others. However, over a period of two centuries—from the Middle Ages to the Enlightenment—acquisitive passions evolved from being considered a cardinal sin, to being seen as a pragmatic counterbalance to other more destructive human passions, to eventually becoming a virtue that furthers human welfare.[1] Hence, today a person can declare, "Greed is good!" and be taken seriously. Not until the Enlightenment, bolstered by the ideas emerging from the earlier Age of Reason and Reformation, did the view of property rights as an inalienable human right take full flower.

Over the ages five sets of questions have marked debates regarding property rights. First, what gives human beings dominion over things? What gives individuals the right to claim a thing as their own? Why should not most, if not all, things be held in common for the collective good? This debate focuses on the legitimacy of private property. It also encompasses differences of opinion as to whether property rights originate in natural law or in conventions made by people for their own benefit. These concerns have led philosophers, theologians, and political theorists to consider what limits, if any, should be placed on the accumulation of wealth—how much property can one individual legitimately possess?

Second, do the ends that private property serves make a difference in the legitimacy of the private ownership? Should a distinction be made between accumulating property for productive use—property necessary to meet needs for security, freedom, and the control of one's destiny—and property acquired solely to enhance one's pleasure or power over others? Are both aims equally legitimate?

The third set of questions addresses the origin and nature of the strong human drive to accumulate property. What gives rise to this passion? Is it a constructive drive or a sinful and corrupting one? Does the self-interested drive to accumulate wealth serve the common good or corrupt one's character and oppress the less fortunate of society? Is one's property an extension of one's own personality, and if so, is an attack on private property an attack on one's personality?

Fourth, can property rights be justified only if the possessor of the right assumes certain responsibilities in the exercise of the right? If so, what are the duties and responsibilities accompanying the right to possess private property? All rights impose responsibilities and duties on both the possessor of the right and on others who must respect the right. For example, your property rights imply a moral obligation on the part of others to allow you to enjoy those rights. It is often argued that all duties originate from the fundamental responsibilities to promote the general good of society and to respect the dignity of all human beings. Does this imply duties that restrict the use of private property? What is the appropriate balance of these rights and responsibilities?

The final set of ideas relates to the interrelationship of property and the conception of the state. Does the state exist to provide protection of private property or to achieve distributive justice? What limits can the state legitimately place on the individual's right to property?

As is evident from these questions, thinking about property involves multifaceted concerns that are important to an understanding of our present ideology. The idea of property rights is inextricably linked with fundamental issues of individual freedom, the extent to which nonconsensual power over other individuals is legitimate, distributive justice, the role of the state in resolving the conflicts inherent within and across each of these issues, and ultimately, how best to progress toward human perfection. Playing sotto voce in these debates is the question of whether human beings are basically good or evil—whether people can be trusted to use property in ways that benefit society or whether they will use it to further their own selfish ends, oppressing others in the process.

A Philosophical History of Property Rights

As we briefly examine the evolution of Western thought regarding these questions, it is important to keep in mind that each philosopher's view of property rights to some extent reflects the realities of his time. Some philosophers were more visionary than others were. Our task is to test these ideas relative to the human and institutional conditions of today. An appreciation for the evolving nature and enduring quality of these ideas, coupled with an understanding of the rapidly changing environment in which these ideas take life, will aid our understanding of the tenuous nature of our current beliefs.

The Lessons of Antiquity

The ancient prophets of the Old Testament and the classical Greek philosophers shared a disdain for the pursuit of wealth's corrupting influence on the individual and on society. They originated a long line of thought that was not to be challenged until the Reformation and the Age of Reason in the fifteenth and sixteenth centuries. They believed that knowledge of the good, or religious teachings regarding what is good in God's eyes, would lead people to do good. When people devote their lives to the pursuit of property—and the subsequent power and prestige it brings—they do so because they do not know what is good. People erroneously believe that possessions create happiness. Therefore, they place a greater emphasis on tending to their possessions than to their soul. To remedy this misdirected thinking, these prophets and philosophers set out to show humans the truth of what is good.

The Old Testament prophets, although recognizing the legitimacy of private property, proclaimed that a person's relationship to property should be one of stewardship. All earthly goods belong to God. Human beings are only stewards. The existence of some private property is necessary to the individual's fullest development. However, people hold private property in trust to do God's will for society as a whole. Consequently, the private right to the use of property carries with it the public responsibility to use the property in ways beneficial to humankind. In part this meant that a portion of the land's produce should be reserved for God directly through tithes and indirectly by making it available to the needy.[2]

In many ways the classical Greek philosophers took a more critical view of private property than did the Old Testament. Socrates (469–399 B.C.) and Plato (427–347 B.C.) argued that the pursuit of property interferes with the perfection of the soul. In Plato's "Apology," Socrates states he does "nothing but go about persuading you all, old and young alike, not to take thought for your persons or your properties, but first and chiefly to care about the greatest improvement of the soul. I tell you that virtue is not given by money, but that from virtue comes money and every other good of man, public as well as private."[3] At another time, he rebukes a friend for "undervaluing the greater and overvaluing the less," saying, "Are you not ashamed of heaping up the greatest amount of money and honor and reputation, and caring so little about wisdom and truth and the greatest improvement of the soul, which you never regard or heed at all?"[4]

Plato considered wealth to be "the parent of luxury, indolence and discontent"[5] and warned of the corrupting power of the pursuit of material goods—corrupting both the individual and society. He believed, "As [people] advance in the pursuit of wealth, the more they hold that in honor, the less they honor virtue. May not the opposition of wealth and virtue be conceived as if each lay in the scale of a balance inclining opposite ways."[6] For Plato, property and family are strong forces that can cause people to assert their individual interests to the detriment of social unity. Therefore, while the majority of the population (the "producers") was free to pursue "having and spending," in Plato's ideal republic the ruling class—the philosopher-kings— would be held to a higher standard. For the philosopher-king, "the motives which make another man desirous of having and spending, have no place in his character."[7] He should be "the reverse of covetous" and should not "have any private property whatsoever, except what is absolutely necessary."[8] Because of these concerns, Plato believed that much of private property should be held in common.

Aristotle (384–322 B.C.) rejected Plato's arguments for common property. Instead, Aristotle believed that private ownership promotes the smooth functioning of society and its economy. But he shared Plato's repudiation of the unlimited accumulation of wealth. In doing so, Aristotle distinguished between the desirability of private dominion over property and its use: "Clearly it is better for property to remain in private hands, but we should make the use of it communal."[9]

Acknowledging that "money and self [are] what all men love," he considered private property an expression of one's personality and a source of self-esteem and pleasure, and thus necessary for individuals to realize their full being. Because the possession of private property enables generosity, requires temperance in restraining one's use of others' property, and encourages industry—all noble virtues—it can stimulate the growth of character. Society directly benefits, since private property motivates greater personal effort, lessens conflicts, and increases social cohesion. Concerned that communal property would be considered no one's and therefore would be treated with indifference, Aristotle advocated private property to increase industry "as each person will labor to improve his own private property." Also, because common property often leads to conflicts over rights to use the property, private property reduces conflict and promotes a greater sense of unity in society.[10] Thus private property is a means to a more stable society and to the good life—a good life for all people.

Like Plato, Aristotle believed that the desire to accumulate property threatened to corrupt the state and the individual. He distinguished between accumulating wealth to invest in business ("for economy requires the possession of wealth, but not on its own account but with another view, to purchase things necessary therewith") and accumulating money for consumption or simply to increase one's wealth. The former is necessary for the economy. The latter is without limits—one can always consume more or hoard more money. A material appetite without bounds breeds corruption. "Such persons make everything subservient to money-getting, as if this was the only end; and to the end everything ought to refer."[11] If they cannot get money by honest endeavors, "they will endeavor to do it by other ways, and apply all their powers to a purpose they were not by nature intended for." Consequently, excessive wealth (as well as excessive poverty) has negative effects on the state as well as on individuals.

Similarly, later in Rome, Seneca, a leading Stoic thinker, warned that the pursuit of wealth produces an anxiety—the never-ending drive to accumulate more wealth that can cause individuals to forget its intended use and threatens to enslave them to their possessions. When this occurs, Seneca concluded, the individual "ceases to be a master and becomes a servant."[12]

The Early Christian Church

Jesus accepts private property as a condition of social life. His main concern is the effect of property on a person's spiritual life. In part, he echoes the teachings of the Old Testament: mammon threatens to become a personal god, preventing the realization of the life God intends; the pursuit of wealth threatens one's virtue; and the individual bears the responsibility to use wealth for the benefit of others. Jesus' warnings of the dangers and responsibilities of wealth dot the Gospels. Property should be considered only a means to a person's increasing perfection. Therefore the right to property is predicated on it serving—or at least not obstructing—the divine idea of men and women as being created in the spiritual likeness of God.[13] He reinforces the Old Testament teaching that all things come from God, and thus a person's position relative to property is as a steward.

For Jesus, the right to private property is accompanied by an overriding duty to administer the property for the benefit of humankind. Thus, property is never an end in itself, but when used in the way intended by God, it becomes a means for furthering God's will.[14] Private property could be a blessing if deployed in the service of brotherly love. The admonition to "love your neighbor as yourself" leads to the logical conclusion that people should share their wealth with their brothers and sisters. Thus begins the Christian ideal that goods should be treated not as one's own, but as being held in trust for one's fellow human beings in proportion to their need.

Saint Augustine (A.D. 354–430), the most influential of the early church fathers, developed a view of private property that combines the thoughts of Plato, Christianity, and the Roman society in which he lived. Augustine believed that nothing in itself is evil. Rather, evil is the corruption or misuse of what is good. The evil in private property lies not in the riches themselves, but in the avarice that often accompanies them.[15] Possessions are good when used as a means to the enjoyment of God and are to be used to this end; enjoying them for themselves breeds avarice and greed.

Augustine, like most other early church fathers, believed that human beings, in their natural state, lived together in peace and happiness. In this condition there was no need for the institution of private property. Property had been given by God to humans in common. After the Fall, human sinfulness created passions, which brought people into conflict with each other—usually over property. The human appetite for material possessions became endless, which meant that no happiness could be found in pursuing property—only frustration from an insatiable desire. Augustine believed this desire for wealth, not its possession, was what Jesus condemned. But nevertheless, great wealth posed a danger to the soul. People who do not use their property in the service of God lose their moral claim over it.[16]

Augustine believed that the state was created to suppress these conflicts and to establish and maintain order. Politically organized society, although not natural, was necessary to remedy the social disorder and disintegration that resulted from what he considered to be the three principal sins: avarice, lust for power, and sexual lust. The state, in turn, created the social convention of private property to protect people—weak and strong alike—from the greed and covetousness of their neighbors and to maintain order in society.[17] Since private property is a creation of the state, the state has the right to regulate it and retains final control over it. Because private property must serve the needs of society, an individual's property rights are limited by the demands of society.[18]

Christianity and the Middle Ages

Saint Thomas Aquinas (1224–1274) attempted to create a synthesis of Christian and Aristotelian thought—of faith and reason. Thomas accepted Aristotle's idea that the state was a natural institution ordained by the divine plan to order all human life and direct it toward its highest possible development.[19] Therefore, the state had the divine right to both create private property and limit its use to meet the just demands of society.[20]

Human reason naturally inclines people toward seeking universal goods such as wisdom and community. The moral good is that which furthers the perfecting of human beings in accordance with the eternal laws of God. Individuals' own good is achieved by governing their actions and feelings through rational reflection on what best serves this end. If a person's good is equal to perfection in accordance with the divine plan, then "we do not offend God, except by doing something contrary to our own good."[21] This sounds somewhat utilitarian, but it is best understood in the context of Aquinas's definition of an individual's good as being synonymous with the divine plan. Applying his concepts of the state and the moral good to property, he concludes that private property is devised "by human reason for the benefit of human life."

Although Aquinas defended private property on utilitarian grounds similar to those of Aristotle (it fosters industry and responsibility, causes less confusion and conflict than would ensue "if everyone had to look after any one thing indeterminately," and promotes peace because each person "is contented with his own"), he distinguished between the right of the individual "to procure and dispense" property and the right to use it "as his own."[22] Thus, he furthered the belief that property has a public and private nature and that property rights are limited by the just demands of society.

The right to use property "as his own" is restricted because "the temporal goods, which God grants us, are ours as to the ownership, but as to the use of them they belong not to us alone but also to such others as we are able to succor out of what we have over and above our needs." Individuals can possess property but should be guided by God's plan in its use. Consequently, "man ought to possess external things, not as his own, but as common, so that to wit, he is ready to communicate them to others in their need."[23]

Aquinas's views of property are consistent with the realities of the medieval guild system of his day. In concept, business was a cooperative enterprise for the betterment of the town's people, governed by moral principles toward a religious end. Of course, practice fell far short of the canonists' rules. Nevertheless, since business was essentially a small-scale local undertaking, it remained clear to all that the competitive practices, quality of products, pricing, and working conditions reflected directly on the craftsmen and the welfare of the whole town. As commerce increased after the Dark Ages, cooperation was essential to protect against thieves and the oppressive grasp of the local lord. Cooperative group control of, and when necessary interference in, the property rights of individual businesses was seen as justified since the right to property existed within the context of group well-being. There were no absolute property rights apart from the group's well-being. If an owner refused to exercise good stewardship, the group— with the support of the church's doctrine—enforced it.[24]

The medieval period left a legacy consistent with the centuries of Judeo-Christian thought that preceded it. Doing God's will was seen as the ultimate end of all human activity, and Christian principles permeated all phases of human activity: family, political, economic, and religious. These principles continued to command that wealth be used to social ends and placed limits on the individual enjoyment of possessions. But this legacy was soon to be challenged.

The evolution of the medieval craft society into an increasingly complex economic life spawned an expanding bourgeois class with its attendant wealth. The redistribution of wealth to the middle class shifted economic power. The reality of daily economic activities became increasingly estranged from the moral and philosophical beliefs of the Middle Ages.

Politically, the middle class's control over property and economic activity and the expansion of commerce rapidly eroded the state's power over the individual business owner. Since the bourgeois business proprietors now dealt with a large number of customers, they were no longer as dependent on the favors of the feudal lord. The bourgeoisie found increasing power in collective acts in defiance of the lord. With the increasing wealth of the cities, they could now afford their own militia, whose power grew to equal or exceed that of the neighboring lord.

In an attempt to reverse the erosion of its influence, the traditional power structure could have violently opposed the expansion of commerce and industry. Instead, as Albert Hirschman argues in *The Passions and the Interests*, many of those in power welcomed and promoted it. The kings and lords, and particularly their advisers, were searching for "a behavioral equivalent for religious precept, for new rules of conduct and devices that would impose much needed discipline and constraints on both rulers and ruled. . . . The expansion of commerce and industry was thought to hold much promise in this regard."[25] The intellectual and administrative elite, concerned with the increasing frequency of wars and internal strife, accepted the rational pursuit of capital accumulation "not because the money-making activities were approved in themselves, but because they were thought to have a most beneficial side effect: they kept the men who were engaged in them 'out of mischief,' as it were, and had, more specifically, the virtue of imposing restraints on princely caprice, arbitrary government, and adventurous foreign policies."[26] The accumulation of wealth served practical political ends as a means to achieving a more peaceful, ordered society.

Adam Smith gives a somewhat different account of the lords' decline in power—which in prior times had been tyrannical and in practice considerably greater than the kings' power. The rise in manufacturing and commerce produced goods that the lords desired to own. As they diverted funds from the maintenance of their armies and retainers to enlarge their material possessions, their ability to procure the loyalty of their vassals and to threaten the business owners in the towns steadily eroded. In Smith's words,

> What all the violence of the feudal institutions could never have effected, the silent and insensible operation of foreign commerce and manufactures gradually brought about. These gradually furnished the great proprietors [lords] with something for which they could exchange the whole surplus produce of their lands, and which they could consume themselves without sharing it either with tenants or retainers. All for ourselves, and nothing for other people, seems, in every age of the world, to have been the vile maxim of the masters of mankind. As soon, therefore, as they could find a method of consuming the whole value of their rents themselves, they had no disposition to share them with any other persons. For a pair of diamond buckles perhaps, or for something as frivolous and useless, they exchanged the maintenance, or what is the same thing, the price of the maintenance of a thousand men for a year, and with it the whole weight and authority which it could give them. . . . Thus, for the gratification of the most childish, the meanest and the most sordid of all vanities, they gradually bartered their whole power and authority.[27]

As their ability to maintain their retainers declined, retainers and tenants were dismissed. A consolidation of farming ensued as fewer tenants farmed larger parcels of land. To fuel his acquisitive desires, the lord raised rents on these larger tenants beyond what the land would bear. Unable to pay without further improvements to the land, the tenants demanded, and were generally granted, long-term leases to allow them to reap the benefit of their additional investments. Naturally, the long-term leases undermined the lord's control over the tenants. The old feudal system was finished.

At about the same time, the Renaissance was bringing a revolution of thought and practice to the arts and philosophy and a renewal of the sense of the dignity of human society that had not been present since antiquity. Western society was poised on the threshold of a significant rise in the value of individual freedom and conscience. The stage was set for a transformation of Western thinking about property and wealth.

Faced with these new social realities, two forces—one political and the other religious—converged to give birth to a new ethic of industry and thrift. The birth of the idea of a limited state, ruling at the will of its people and dedicated to the protection of individual rights, including the right to property, provided the political foundation for the development of new privately owned enterprises. Religiously, what this transformation needed was a release from the ecclesiastical restraints on the accumulation and use of property. The Reformation, with its overriding emphasis on the *individual's* relationship with God, provided that release and, unintentionally, even more.

The new ethic was to have a profound effect on human thinking and actions. Work became a divine calling. All walks of life came to be considered intrinsically good. Prosperity in business became a sign of God's grace. The pursuit of wealth through productive work and business investment was destined to be transformed from a vice into a virtue.

The Reformation and Its Aftermath

Both Luther and Calvin accepted the existence of private property and maintained the belief that it carried with it a social responsibility. However, Calvin's view of possessions was less strict. For him, like Augustine, economic activity was evil only if it obscured a person's relationship with God. Thus, contrary to Luther's beliefs, Calvin implied that private property could be held in excess of needs.

However, Luther's and Calvin's ideas regarding property were not what were to have the greatest impact on values and beliefs regarding wealth accumulation. Instead, it was the application in practice, by the middle class and rulers alike, of some of the fundamental theological concepts of the Reformation that related directly to the meaning of work and indirectly to the use of surplus wealth generated from work.

The first conceptual contribution to this change was Luther's idea of the "calling": a lifetime commitment to a definite field of work to which one was called by God, and which was to be pursued with a sense of religious responsibility to society.[28] This was not a new idea. The concept existed in religious and philosophical thought dating back to Greek antiquity and the New Testament. However, Luther, and subsequently Calvin, gave it renewed meaning and a central role in Protestant theology. Max Weber, in *The Protestant Ethic and the Spirit of Capitalism*, identified this new essence:

> The valuation of the fulfillment of duty in worldly affairs [is] the highest form which the moral activity could assume. . . . It . . . inevitably gave everyday worldly activity a religious significance. . . . The only way of living acceptably to God was not to surpass worldly morality in monastic

asceticism, but solely through the fulfillment of the obligations imposed upon the individual by his position in the world. . . . Labour in a calling [is] the outward expression of brotherly love. Every legitimate calling [since it represents the will of God] has exactly the same worth in the sight of God.[29]

Pursuing one's calling with religious responsibility meant one's work served society in a way that glorified God. Although amassing wealth as an end in itself was still condemned, accumulation of wealth by the fruit of one's own labor was a sign of God's favor.

As this idea was secularized over time, it had a major, unintended consequence. Working people, believing that the full and continuous commitment to work was a necessary and essential part of life, began to behave as if they existed "for the sake of [their] business, instead of the reverse."[30] Ironically, secular values of industry and thrift were well on the path to becoming prime virtues.

Calvin recognized that a new social class devoted largely to commercial endeavors had emerged. His theology, in part, strove to create a moral code that would address Christianity to this new order. Not surprisingly, then, his theology was most openly embraced in those industrial areas where capitalism was most prominent. It became the religion of the middle class.

A cornerstone of Calvin's theology was the concept of predestination: some, but not all, people are elected for salvation. This election was by God's grace, not as a result of good works. This belief had three important effects among Calvin's followers.

First, the belief in predestination sparked a quest for assurance that one was elected. The decisive mark of election was the individual's personal relationship to God in the act of faith. In faith the elected person would naturally live a moral life. Christian living was the fruit of salvation, not the means to it. But how would one know one had sufficient faith and was elected? There were two symptoms of salvation: the blessing of God and the high moral standing of a person. Paul Tillich observes that this "psychologically brought about a situation in which the individual could gain certainty [of salvation] only by producing the marks of election in terms of a moral life and an economic blessing. This means that he tried to become a good bourgeois industrial citizen."[31]

Second, the asceticism that flowed from Calvinism showed people how wealth should be used differently than it had been in the past. Calvin saw the new Christian life—not as a joyful personal reunion with God, as did Luther—but as a life filled with self-denial as one attempted to fulfill the law of God in one's life. Calvin advocated an inner-worldly asceticism characterized by "cleanliness" (by which Calvin meant sobriety, chastity, and temperance) and profit through work.[32] This asceticism served to stimulate investment. Prior to Calvinism, the wealthy flaunted their riches in ostentatious living. If wealth is not used for glorious living, then profits must be either benevolently given away or reinvested in means of production that served the community. It was now acceptable to accumulate wealth to serve God's ends and to prove one's election. The accumulation of wealth is evil only if it is a temptation to idleness and sinful living or a distraction from the pursuit of a righteous life. Thus, savings for reinvestment in one's calling—so necessary for capitalism to prosper—was given a strong impetus.[33]

Third, the belief that faith, not good works, was the source of salvation sent the implicit message that a person need be less concerned with the perfection of moral character than the church had demanded in earlier centuries. Since work was not the means to salvation, one could be less circumspect in one's business dealings and in one's attitude toward wealth.[34] This further weakened the Christian admonition that individual property was to be held in trust for God.

Many reformers feared that their new precepts, with the accompanying religious individualism, would undermine the Christian restrictions on the accumulation and use of wealth. Worse yet, in secular society, the church's sanction of personal commercial gain would allow the innate human acquisitive drive to dominate religious admonitions. Consequently, wealth would soon become an end in itself. John Wesley, the founder of Methodism, lamented:

> I fear, wherever riches have increased, the essence of religion has decreased in the same proportion. Therefore I do not see how it is possible, in the nature of things, for any revival of true religion to continue long. For religion must necessarily produce both industry and frugality, and these cannot but produce riches. But as riches increase, so will pride, anger, and love of the world in all its branches. . . . Is there no way to prevent this—this continual decay of pure religion? We ought not to prevent people from being diligent and frugal; we must exhort all Christians to gain all they can, and to save all they can; that is, in effect to grow rich.[35]

Wesley's principal argument was that those who grow rich should "give all you can" and in this way gain God's favor. He justified his other two directions for the use of money—"gain all you can" and "save all you can"—by the fact that they were the means to the end of giving. In fact, Wesley expected that people following his precepts would live on the edge of poverty. But he knew in practice this was unlikely to be so.

The resulting Protestant ethic had the unintended consequences of relaxing the ecclesiastical restrictions on economic activity and sanctifying property accumulation for personal use. In the course of reinterpreting humanity's relationship to God, the Reformation showed people the way to become increasingly independent in matters of religion and their personal salvation. People increasingly believed in their individual goodness and in their ability to provide for their own progress through reliance on their own reason. The consequence of this legitimized religious individualism was that the church no longer served as the unifying force in society. Rather, Christianity's principal sphere of influence receded to spiritual matters. Political and economic activity was increasingly beyond the domain of the church.

For Protestants, the ascetic, otherworldly ideal of Christianity—an ideal that led people to believe that their natural life with its passions and pleasures should be forsaken for moral perfection in this world and immortality in eternity—was gone. In its place, people were freed to devote their efforts to what attracted them most: material welfare and the fulfillment of acquisitive desires.

These events set the stage for the "possessive individualism" that was to come to full bloom in the philosophy of Hobbes and Locke in the late sixteenth and early seventeenth centuries, and the subsequent political revolutions in America and France.[36]

The Age of Reason and Enlightened Self-Interest

Until the Age of Reason in the seventeenth century, philosophers had focused on developing moral precepts that would further the perfection of humanity, or at least restrain humanity's destructive passions. However, the transformation of the Reformation's ideas into secular materialistic practice and the wars that threatened to tear Europe asunder convinced many thinkers that religious and moral precepts alone were insufficient to affect people's behavior. Similarly, the state seemed impotent in suppressing people's surging desires for personal material progress. The attempts by the state and the church to coerce and repress humanity's sinful nature had failed.

The Age of Reason and the subsequent Enlightenment spawned the idea that the application of science and the exercise of reason by individuals could create the ideal human society. Hobbes, Locke, Hume, Smith, and Bentham were among the principal thinkers who established the philosophical basis for this new dream of a future millennium.

For more than two millennia the idea of human progress had lain fallow but had now been awakened. The Renaissance, although captivated by the achievements of antiquity, harbored no ambitions of regaining such glory. The conditions of the Middle Ages were not conducive to thoughts of progress—daily events proved reality to be quite the opposite. Even the Greeks and Romans had looked back with envy on the Golden Age from which they felt they had degenerated. So it was that only three centuries ago the belief in progress—which we take so for granted—was rekindled in humankind.[37]

By the eighteenth century, most influential thinkers ardently believed in the perfectibility of the human race.[38] Human beings were no longer considered inherently evil, as posed by the doctrine of original sin. If people are naturally good, then logic dictates that the pursuit of individual self-interest, guided by reason to know what is good, holds the promise of bettering the human condition. If individuals could provide for their own progress, this meant they were less dependent on God. The idea of individualism predicated on enlightened self-interest was born. This idea energized the American and French Revolutions and shaped the U.S. Constitution.

Freed from the oppression of the feudal lord and from many of the ecclesiastical restrictions that prohibited people from leading the life they inwardly desired, attention was turned to developing moral precepts and justifications to guide a person's acquisitive nature. The passions of greed and avarice, which philosophers and theologians over the centuries had struggled to find ways to control, became transformed into society-serving interests that could be used to counterbalance other, more destructive passions and to motivate the industriousness that would improve humankind's material well-being.[39]

This change came about in part because of a more pragmatic view of humanity. Reinforced by the drive for a positive philosophy based on reason, the attention moved away from the idealized, utopian view of humanity that had dominated past philosophy and turned to examining the reality of human nature. In 1670, Spinoza became one of the first to attack philosophers who "conceive men not as they are but as they would like them to be."[40] Natural human motivations were to be used as the basis for designing the practical, positive moral and political philosophy that would guide humanity to the ideal society.

It had been recognized throughout the ages that material objects are an extension and expression of personality. Aristotle had argued this. Individuals use possessions to magnify their sense of self and to extend their influence over nature and other people. Through the ideas of Hobbes and Locke, these ideas were extended to create a practical view of humans as possessions-oriented and market-focused beings.

Since the beginning of recorded history, the philosophers' concern with the destructive effects of the drive for possessions and power had been focused primarily on the aristocracy. Aristocrats were the predominant mischief makers, since only they possessed the means to pursue wealth and power beyond their natural needs. Machiavelli's opinion that the Prince's "own passions . . . are much greater than those of the people" was widely shared.[41] However, society was rapidly changing. Now the bourgeoisie, with their increasing wealth, were also of concern. In response to this reality, the philosophers' focus shifted from the aristocracy to humanity in general.

The power of past authoritarian systems to suppress the destructive consequences of lust and greed had proved ineffective. A new concept of the state was needed that was in harmony with the new pragmatic view of humanity. Repression of the passions of greed and lust for power assumed that humans were inherently evil. However, now human beings were seen as basically good but driven by strong acquisitive instincts. Harnessing, rather than repressing, the passions was more in keeping with humankind's true nature. "Once again the state, or 'society,'" Hirschman observes, "is called upon to perform this feat, yet this time not merely as a repressive bulwark, but as a transformer, a civilizing medium."[42] Thomas Hobbes and John Locke responded to this call for a new political philosophy.

The renewed sense of the moral worth of the individual created a tension between the relative roles of the individual and the community. Were the individual's interests in harmony with society's interests? If not, which interest should govern? Was there a difference between the moral value of the individual and of the community? Two principles led to the individual becoming the primary end—and they were both principles of individual freedom. People should be free, first, from the will of others and, second, to realize their full potential. The human desire to possess private property plays a central role in this transformation in Western thought.

Both Hobbes's and Locke's logic started with similar assumptions about the real nature of humanity: human beings are acquisitive individuals with "market instincts" and are devoted to improving their own condition.[43] They also came to the similar conclusion that the rise of the state was prompted by the need to control the destructive aspects of human acquisitive passions. However, they differed in what they saw as the origin of private property. Hobbes thought property was a human convention with no basis in natural law. For Locke, when a person mixed labor with a thing, that person had the natural right to claim the modified thing as a personal possession.

In his greatest work, *Leviathan*, published in 1651, Thomas Hobbes argues that in their natural state (without social institutions to provide law and order), human beings are motivated to seek their own self-preservation in disregard for others. This is a particularly dangerous condition since all human beings are equal on a very fundamental level: each individual, no matter how feeble, has the ability through conspiracy, stealth, or overt attack, to kill another. This essential equality breeds diffidence: "From this equality of ability, ariseth equality of hope in attaining of our ends. And therefore if any two men desire the same thing which nevertheless they cannot both enjoy, they become enemies . . . and endeavor to destroy, or subdue one another." This results in a constant state of war of "every one against every one." And Hobbes recognizes that some, driven by the desire to expand their own power (Hobbes considered riches, knowledge, and honor as forms of power), will pursue violence beyond the extent necessary for personal security. This belief leads Hobbes to conclude, "In the nature of man, we find three principal causes of quarrel. First, competition; secondly, diffidence; thirdly, glory."[44]

From this view of humanity, Hobbes defined three laws of nature. First, "Every man has right to every thing." Since this leads to constant conflict, human beings, for their own self-preservation possess the right to self-defense by all means possible. But the desire for self-preservation also drives people "to seek peace, and to follow it." Second, people are free to contract with one another to limit their rights to all things in order to reduce conflict and to promote security and self-interest. Third, justice requires "that men perform their covenants made."

These laws—coupled with "the passions that incline men to peace:

fear of death; desire of such things as are necessary to commodious living; and a hope by their industry to obtain them"—were sufficient to motivate individuals to construct a covenant in which they yielded power to the state. In return, the state protected the individual's freedom and possessions from the will of others. The overriding human desire is to preserve one's essential nature and personal autonomy, which are bound to freedom from the will of others and the control over the product of one's own efforts.[45] This Hobbesian covenant is a presumed contract, the essence of which is that every person says to every other person, "I authorize and give up my right of governing myself to this man, or to this assembly of men, on this condition, that thou give up thy right to him, and authorize all his actions in like manner." The giving up of one's right over everything is a voluntary act, and as with all voluntary acts, "the object is some *good to himself.*" From this contractual transfer of the right to every thing arose the need to enforce it, since it would be in some people's interest to break the contract. "Covenants, without the sword, are but words, and of no strength to secure a man at all." Thus is created "that great LEVIATHAN [the state], or rather, to speak more reverently, of that mortal God, to which we owe under the immortal God, our peace and defence."[46]

John Locke begins with a view of natural man similar to Hobbes's. By nature humans are all in "a *State of perfect Freedom* to order their Actions, and dispose of their Possessions and Persons as they think fit, within the bounds of the Law of Nature, without asking leave, or depending upon the Will of any other Man."[47] Natural man is also in a state of equality, "wherein all the Power and Jurisdiction is reciprocal, no one having more than another."[48] Since human beings are God's property and "all equal and independent, no one ought to harm another in his Life, Health, Liberty, or Possessions."[49] For Locke, as for Hobbes, individual freedom from the will of others is the essence of being human. The only justifiable limitation on an individual's freedom is the protection of another person's freedom; the individual owes nothing to society.[50]

From these assumptions about humankind, Locke derives the natural right to private property. Individuals have an inviolate right to their own person and consequently to the product of their work. Therefore, when they apply their energies to remove property from its natural state, their right to this property arises.

> Though the Earth, and all inferior Creatures be common to all Men, yet every Man has a *Property* in his own *Person*. This no Body has a Right to but himself. The *Labour* of his Body, and the *Work* of his Hands, we may say, are properly his. Whatsoever then he removes out of the State that Nature hath provided, and left it in, he hath mixed his *Labour* with, and joyned to it something that is his own, and thereby makes it his *Property*.[51]

Locke argues that the right to property carried with it two principal responsibilities. First, individuals should not accumulate more property than they can enjoy:

> The same Law of Nature, that does by this means give us Property, does also *bound* that *Property* too. *God has given us all things richly*, 1 Tim. v. 17. is the Voice of Reason confirmed by Inspiration.[52] But how far has he given it us? *To enjoy*. As much as any one can make use of to any advantage of life before it spoils; so much he may by his labour fix a Property in. Whatever is beyond this, is more than his share, and belongs to others. Nothing was made by God for Man to spoil or destroy.[53]

Second, man has a duty to be charitable:

> As *justice* gives every Man a Title to the product of his honest Industry, and the fair Acquisitions of his Ancestors descended to him; so *Charity* give every Man a Title to so much out of another's Plenty, as will keep him from extreme want, where he has no means to subsist otherwise; and a Man can no more justly make use of another's necessity, to force him to become his Vassal by withholding that Relief God requires him to afford to the wants of his Brother, than he that has more strength can seize upon a weaker, master him to his Obedience, and with a Dagger at his Throat offer him Death or Slavery.[54]

Setting the stage for the utilitarians who were to follow him, Locke believes that the institution of private property improves the condition of mankind by making the property more productive. By taking possession and cultivating one acre of land, Locke argues, a person can produce "ten times more, than those, which are yielded by an acre of Land, of an equal richnesse, lyeing waste in common. And therefore he, that incloses Land and has a greater plenty of the conveniencys of life from ten acres, than he could have from an hundred left to Nature, may truly be said, to give ninety acres to Mankind."[55]

For Locke, the state arose as a contractual means to protect private property and regulate the relationships among individual proprietors. The uncertainty and fear of the ability in nature to enjoy one's property leads individuals to give up their absolute freedom to the state in return for law to settle controversies, authority to judge according to the law, and the power to implement the sentence of the judge. In so doing, Locke replaces Hobbes's self-perpetuating sovereign with a government selected by the people and responsible to them.

Locke's dictum that "The great and *chief end* therefore, of Men uniting into Commonwealths, and putting themselves under Government, *is the Preservation of their Property*"[56] became the political gospel of America's founding fathers. They enshrined Locke's work in the Declaration of Independence and enacted it into law in the Constitution. Interestingly, however, Thomas Jefferson, in writing the Declaration of Independence, modified Locke's trilogy of life, liberty, and property to read "life, liberty and the pursuit of happiness." It was left to the Fifth Amendment to the Constitution (which reads "No person shall . . . be deprived of life, liberty, or property, without due process of law; nor shall private property be taken for public use without just compensation") to specifically address property rights.

In *The Political Theory of Possessive Individualism*, C. B. Macpherson concludes that the leading thinkers of this period conceived of society consisting of a series of market relations among free people who owe nothing to society for their freedom or their God-given capabilities. People enter into relations with others only voluntarily in the pursuit of their own self-interest. At the core of this philosophy of "possessive individualism" is the belief that "freedom from dependence on the wills of others" is essential to being human. This freedom "means freedom from any relations with others except those relations which the individual enters voluntarily with a view to his own interest." The only justified limits on this freedom are "such obligations and rules as are necessary to secure the same freedom for others."[57]

What emerges from these propositions is a materialistic view of individuals, not as moral agents, but as owners of themselves and of what they have acquired through their efforts. Essential to human beings is their freedom to pursue their acquisitive desires. The state is a "human contrivance" that exists to protect the individual's person and property and to maintain order conducive to commercial exchanges and the accumulation of possessions.[58]

Many of Hobbes's and Locke's assumptions live on in the beliefs that underlie American society today. The consequences are profound. Their ideas generated a renewed sense of the individual's moral worth that conflicted with the moral value of community so prevalent in previous Christian and philosophical thought. Gone are the individual's moral responsibilities associated with the right to property. The individual simply must ensure that in the pursuit of property the rights of others are not infringed upon.

The Reformation and Enlightenment in America

The ideas of the Reformation (as modified by Puritanism) and of the Enlightenment—particularly those of John Locke—shaped the values of American society. They generated an increased sense of personal responsibility and a reliance on conscience to guide individual action free of the church and state. Combined with Calvinism's asceticism, these ideas led Puritans to view wealth and property as God's gift to be administered prudently with an austere personal responsibility. H. G. Wood summarizes the Puritan beliefs:

> Private property rests on the [Ten Commandments], and the right of this institution possesses an inviolable and divine sanction. Differences in wealth and in social status are of God's ordering, and belong to the permanent structure of society. Riches, being God's gift, are in their nature a blessing, and are not lightly to be abandoned by the individual, though they bring grave temptations and dangers with them. Since riches are God's gift, no man is absolute owner: all men are God's stewards and must render an account of their stewardship. Economic wastefulness is therefore necessarily sinful. Men must make the most of themselves and their resources. No one has any right to be idle or careless. It is likewise a duty to use and spend money profitably, not wasting it in dicing and worldly pleasures of that kind. In making money, a man must beware of oppression; in spending it, he must seek for works of lasting utility to mankind and the Commonwealth. It is sinful for any one to press to the full the economic and social advantages of his position, and it is the recognized duty of the public authority to fix a fair price for necessaries and to restrain monopolists.[59]

The Puritan legacy to American society is "a rooted trust in individual responsibility and self-help."[60]

With the new ideas and values of the Reformation and the Enlightenment's emphasis on the human ability to reason what is good, the conditions were ripe for the rise of deism.[61] Deism—with its God who gave the world its initial movement and now sat in heaven detached from worldly affairs—fit well with the needs of an industrializing society. It left the world to humanity. With God at a distance, business owners were not disturbed by ecclesiastical restrictions in the conduct of their affairs.

This was a significant departure from the concept of God held by Calvin and the other reformers, who saw God as actively governing the world. All things were instruments through which God worked in every moment. However, Calvin had the foresight to see that the Enlightenment's infatuation with natural law threatened to make God into something separate from reality.[62]

Disregarding the warnings of Calvin, Wesley, and other reformers, deism prospered in the eighteenth century. Nowhere did deism thrive in practical affairs as it did in America.

The resulting beliefs in the virtue of industry, frugality, and wealth accumulation are reflected in Benjamin Franklin's advice in *Poor Richard's Almanack*. He may not have been the father of modern financial concepts such as "opportunity cost" and "net present value," but he certainly understood their logic. For example,

> Remember, that *time* is money. He that can earn ten shillings a day by his labour, and goes abroad, or sits idle, one half of that day, though he spends but sixpence during his diversion or idleness, ought not to reckon *that* the only expense; he has really spent, or rather thrown away, five shillings besides.
>
> Remember, that *credit* is money. If a man lets his money lie in my hands after it is due, he gives me the interest, or so much as I can make of it during that time. This amounts to a considerable sum where a man has good and large credit, and makes good use of it.
>
> Remember, that money is of the prolific, generating nature. Money can beget money, and its offspring can beget more, and so on. . . . The more there is of it, the more it produces every turning, so that the profits rise quicker. He that kills a breeding-sow, destroys all her offspring to the thousandth generation. He that murders a crown, destroys all that it might have produced, even scores of pounds.
>
> The Way to Wealth, if you desire it, is as plain as the Way to Market. It depends chiefly on two Words, INDUSTRY and FRUGALITY: i.e. Waste neither Time nor Money, but make the best Use of Both. He that gets all he can honestly, and saves all he gets (necessary Expences excepted) will certainly become rich: If that Being who governs the World, to whom all

should look for a Blessing on their honest Endeavors, doth not in his wise Providence otherwise determine.[63]

Laziness travels so slowly, that Poverty soon overtakes him.

Industry need not wish, as Poor Richard says, and He that lives upon Hope will die fasting. There are no Gains without Pains; . . . He that hath a Trade hath an Estate, and He that hath a Calling, hath an Office of Profit and Honour.

If you would be wealthy think of Saving as well as of Getting. . . .

Women and Wine, Game and Deceit,
Make the Wealth small, and the Wants great.

And farther, What maintains one Vice, would bring up two Children.[64]

Commenting on Franklin's writings, Max Weber observed, "Truly what is here preached is not simply a means of making one's way in the world, but a peculiar ethic. The infraction of its rules is treated not as foolishness but as forgetfulness of duty. . . . It is not mere business astuteness, that sort of thing is common enough, it is an ethos."[65] If one doubts the influence of the thought of Franklin's day on ours, a cursory reading of his short "The Way to Wealth" will dispel the doubts. The eight pages are filled with sayings still in wide use and considered part of our conventional wisdom.

As with Franklin, the writings of Thomas Jefferson provide a view of religion as a utilitarian moral code. Jefferson considered private property necessary to the promotion of industry among the citizens and thus to the general welfare. However, this assumed the owner exercised good stewardship in the use of property:

Whenever there is in any country uncultivated lands and unemployed poor, it is clear that the laws of property have been so far extended as to violate natural right. The earth is given as a common stock for man to labour and live on. If for the encouragement of industry we allow it to be appropriated, we must take care that other employment be provided to those excluded from the appropriation. If we do not, the fundamental right to labour the earth returns to the unemployed.[66]

The focus of American society was now on the rights of the individuals to their person and property, not on the associated responsibilities. The only obligatory responsibilities were not to harm others and to respect the rights of fellow Americans. In keeping with individualism, all other responsibilities were voluntary. This rights-oriented focus provided considerable benefits to an agrarian society rich in natural resources and with a rapidly expanding frontier that required development.

The conditions were established for the warnings of the ancient Greeks, Jesus, the Church Fathers, and the reformers to become a reality. Wealth had become an end in itself. In the final analysis, humankind's religious conscience proved no equal to the temptations of the new economic order. Humanity was now serving mammon.

Adam Smith and the Economic Justification of Property Rights

Adam Smith (1723–1790) augmented the political and moral arguments of his day with an economic and utilitarian justification for the self-constrained pursuit of individual self-interest. Simply put, by creating value, market-directed economic activity promotes the interests of society.

Smith argues that although few business owners have the knowledge or skill necessary to identify what is in the public interest or to advance it directly, they can serve society by pursuing their own economic self-interest. Smith sees the self-interested pursuit of "bettering our condition" as the strongest and most enduring human motivation, one that "comes with us from the womb and never leaves us till we go into the grave. An augmentation of fortune is the means by which the greater part of men propose and wish to better their condition. It is the means the most vulgar and the most obvious."[67]

Interestingly, Smith believed that people are motivated primarily not by the accumulation of wealth itself, nor by the material pleasures wealth may bring, but rather by the favorable attention and respect of others that is often derived from possessions. He says, "To be observed, to be attended to, to be taken notice of with sympathy, complacency, and appreciation, are all the advantages which we can propose to derive from [bettering our condition]. It is the vanity, not the ease or the pleasure, which interests us."[68]

Smith sees this motivation being leveraged into improvements for society. The marketplace, which reflects the wants and needs of society, assures that the pursuit of self-interest also produces the greatest benefit for humankind:

> As every individual . . . endeavors as much as he can both to employ his capital in the support of domestic industry, and so to direct that industry that its produce may be of the greatest value; every individual necessarily

labours to render the annual revenue of the society as great as he can. He generally, indeed, neither intends to promote the public interest, nor knows how much he is promoting it. By preferring the support of domestic to that of foreign industry, he intends only his own security; and by directing that industry in such a manner *as its produce may be of the greatest value*, he intends only his own gain, and he is in this, as in many other cases, led by an invisible hand to promote an end which was no part of his intention. Nor is it always the worse for the society that it was no part of it. By pursuing his own interest he frequently promotes that of the society more effectually than when he really intends to promote it. I have never known much good done by those who affected to trade for the public good. It is an affectation, indeed, not very common among merchants, and very few words need be employed in dissuading them of it. . . . It is thus that the private interests and passion of individuals naturally dispose them to turn their stock towards the employments which in ordinary cases are most advantageous to society.[69]

Smith argued that the principal ends of business activity should be increased productivity and growth. The value of goods produced is what benefits society. Profitability is a means to this wealth creation. Profits provide the surplus necessary for reinvestment in product improvements, increased productivity, and growth to meet market demands. The self-interested pursuit of profits leads to an allocation of capital that is "as nearly as possible in the proportion which is most agreeable to the interest of the whole society."[70] However, Smith does not consider economic self-interest as synonymous with profit maximization. In fact he believes that "high profits" can adversely affect market share and thus the ability to generate wealth—although businesspersons rarely recognize these "bad effects."[71]

As strong, enduring, and beneficial as the motivation to improve oneself is, Smith does not advocate unbridled pursuit of immediate self-interest. The right to pursue self-interest carries with it a responsibility for self-control. Frugality, prudence, and fair and just cooperation with others in the conduct of business are essential to promoting both the common good and long-term self-interest. Frugality, which increases savings and reinvestment, is the path to the "wealth of nations," as well as to individual wealth: "The most likely way of augmenting their fortune, is to save and accumulate some part of what they acquire."[72] This requires discipline in furthering one's self-interest. To be able to save, the individual needs to exercise "self-command" in curtailing the desire to consume. While Smith recognizes that the passion to consume for "present enjoyment" is strong and difficult to restrain, he considers "every prodigal . . . a public enemy, and every frugal man a public benefactor."[73] Prodigal behavior reduces the wealth of the nation by squandering resources on idleness and enjoyable living.

In his advocacy of savings, Smith took a long-term view of wealth creation. In part this is because he believed that productive property belongs not only to the current owner and proprietor, but to future generations as well:

> By what a frugal man annually saves, he not only affords maintenance to an additional number of productive hands, . . . but, like the founder of a public workhouse, he establishes as it were a perpetual fund for the maintenance of an equal number in all times to come. The perpetual allotment and destination of this fund, indeed, is not always guarded by any positive law, by any trust-right or deed of mortmain. It is always guarded, however, by a very powerful principle, *the plain and evident interest of every individual to whom any share of it shall ever belong.* . . .
>
> The prodigal perverts [the use of the fund] in this manner. By not confining his expence within his income, he encroaches upon his capital. Like him who perverts the revenues of some pious foundation to profane purposes, he pays the wages of idleness with those funds which the frugality of his forefathers had, as it were, consecrated to the maintenance of industry.[74]

Furthermore, Smith believed that the unbridled pursuit of self-interest endangers individual freedom and can run counter to what it means to be a moral person. A person's pursuit of self-interest is constrained by his or her natural interest in the welfare of others, as Smith states at the beginning of The Theory of Moral Sentiments: "How selfish soever man may be supposed, there are evidently some principles in his nature which interest him in the fortune of others and render their happiness necessary to him, though he derives nothing from it except the pleasure of seeing it."[75]

Smith saw morality as being composed of four principal elements: justice, propriety (the proper control and direction of our affections), prudence (the judicious pursuit of our self-interest), and benevolence (undertaking acts designed to increase the happiness of others). One's moral and economic freedom is predicated on the self-disciplined ability to pursue one's moral sentiments and to "command" oneself to act according to the objective principles of these four virtues. "Self-command is not only itself a great virtue, but from it all the other virtues seem to derive their principal lustre."[76]

The need for justice in society, and therefore individual prudence and benevolence, played a central role in Smith's thinking. Society "cannot subsist among those who are at all times ready to hurt and injure another. . . . Society may subsist, though not in the most comfortable state, without beneficence; but the prevalence of injustice must utterly destroy it."[77] Justice therefore is an individual responsibility accompanying the right to economic freedom.

Similar to Locke's thinking, Smith's emphasis on the moral and economic freedom of the individual results in a minimal role for the state, which includes only those activities necessary to create an environment conducive to the individual's pursuit of self-interest without interference from or injury to others. This leads Smith to conclude that the state "has only three duties": national defense, the administration of justice to protect each citizen "from the injustice or oppression" of others, and "erecting and maintaining certain public works and certain public institutions, which it can never be for the interest of any individual . . . to erect and maintain."[78]

Thus Adam Smith can be seen as a qualified advocate of the benefits of the pursuit of economic self-interest. He sees advancing industrialization as having degenerative effects on human character. For example, he argues that commerce "sinks the courage of mankind, and tends to extinguish martial spirit. . . . By having their minds constantly employed on the arts of luxury, they grow effeminate and dastardly."[79] He asserts that the pursuit of self-interest, if it is to serve society, must be exercised with considerable self-control and with a focus on the long-term implications of specific actions. Self-interest must be tempered with frugality, prudence, and honesty. The result is a system in which profits are viewed primarily as a means for expanding the enterprise and as a guide for allocating resources. Smith's emphasis was on the expansion of productive resources, not on personal consumption. Although he did not directly state it, it can be concluded from his argument that the continued minimal role of the state is predicated on the exercise of responsible "self-command" by businesspeople in their pursuit of self-interest.

Utilitarianism: The Final Philosophical Component of Our Ideology

Utilitarianism provided the secular moral compass for rationalizing the industrialization of society and the disparate accumulation of wealth. It furthered the shift from a duty-based society to a rights-based society by, in essence, absolving ownership and economic activity of many of their moral responsibilities to society. As one consequence, the role of religion in secular affairs declined even further.

As was true for Adam Smith, for the utilitarian the right of property springs from its tendency to promote the public good. Although utilitarian arguments for property rights could be found as part of many philosophers' arguments for property rights, David Hume (1711–1776) was one of the first to make utility the sole justification. He began by arguing that all rules of justice are conventions proved by experience to promote the general happiness. He then asserted that property rights are not natural rights but are a convention that people choose to adhere to because it is in their self-interest to do so.[80] Although taking a very different logical path than Locke, Hume came much to the same conclusion:

> Who sees not . . . that whatever is produced or improved by a man's art or industry ought, for ever, to be secured to him, in order to give encouragement to such *useful* habits and accomplishments? . . . That it may be [transferred to others] by consent, in order to beget that commerce and intercourse which is so *beneficial* to human society? And that all contracts and promises ought carefully to be fulfilled, in order to secure mutual trust and confidence, by which the general *interest* of mankind is so much promoted?
>
> Examine the writers on the laws of nature; and you will always find, that, whatever principles they set out with, they are sure to terminate here at last, and to assign, as the ultimate reason for every rule which they establish, the convenience and necessities of mankind. . . . What other reason, indeed, could writers ever give, why this must be *mine* and that *yours*; since uninstructed nature, surely, never made any such distinction?[81]

Hume considered property rights "of all circumstances the most necessary to the establishment of human society." After establishing the rule of private property and assuring its observance "there remains little or nothing to be done towards settling a perfect harmony and concord."[82] This led him to conclude, as did Locke, that the protection of private property is the principal end of the state.

The utilitarian's overriding moral principle, as originally defined by Jeremy Bentham (1748–1832), is to seek the greatest happiness for the greatest number. Bentham believed that "nature has placed mankind under the governance of two sovereign masters, *pain* and *pleasure*. It is for them alone to point out what we ought to do, as well as to determine what we shall do.

On the one hand the standard of right and wrong, on the other the chain of causes and effects, are fastened to their throne."[83] Human beings seek their own pleasure and try to avoid pain. The interest of the society as a whole is equal to the sum total of the pleasures and pains of its members.

Responsibilities had a secondary place in Bentham's thinking. He believed that the conflict between desires and duty was false. The real contest is between conflicting desires. Gratification as such is always good. Desires need to be suppressed only in order that other desires may be gratified.

Property "is nothing but a basis of expectation; the expectation of deriving certain advantages from a thing which we are said to possess."[84] People experience pleasure when their expectations are fulfilled and pain when they are disappointed.

Bentham believed that generally an equal distribution of wealth would provide for the greatest happiness, since at the margin the one with the fewest possessions would receive greater utility from an additional increment of wealth than would a wealthier person. But of overriding importance is that there must be as much wealth as possible to pass around. The size of the pie is more important to general happiness than the distribution. Therefore, the state—being a human contrivance to enable individuals to realize as many of their desires as possible—should encourage people to work and produce. This necessitates laws that secure to each individual the fruits of his or her efforts.

John Stuart Mill (1806–1873), a strong advocate of individuality and individual freedom, believed, "The sole end for which mankind are warranted, individually and collectively, in interfering with liberty of action of any of their number, is self-protection."[85] In a society of individuals, cohesion is produced from agreement on moral beliefs that are founded on reason. Rules such as keeping promises and not lying are utilitarian-based, since they are the result of hundreds of years of experience with the consequences of certain actions in affecting the general welfare. He believed that reason, not intuition, should guide people's actions; and the application of reason naturally leads to a utilitarian justification for action.

Given these principles, Mill mixed elements of the natural rights argument with the utilitarian justification of property rights: "The institution of property, when limited to its essential elements consists in the recognition, in each person, of a right to the exclusive disposal of what he or she have produced by their own exertions, or received either by gift or fair agreement, without force or fraud, from those who produced it. The foundation of the whole is the right of producers to what they themselves have produced."[86]

But Mill was troubled by the increasing separation of ownership from labor present in nineteenth-century society. This raised issues of how to justify landed property received through inheritance or land that was worked by someone other than the owner. This difficulty attracted him to the possibility of abolishing private ownership of all means of production so that the laborers could receive the full fruits of their labor. This led him to conclude that sometime in the future capital would be collectively owned.[87]

Mill's uncertainty about private ownership of capital was not the principal way in which utilitarian thought was to be applied to the future. Utilitarianism actually became a powerful counterargument to Marxism by arguing that since capital promotes the general welfare, it is generally more useful to accumulate capital for productive purposes than to distribute the surplus to the workers who generated it.

The Classical Economist: Shifting the Focus from Happiness to Production

Classical economists of the nineteenth century seized upon the utilitarian argument to undermine the natural rights theory. In what approaches an intellectual slight of hand, they made two major assumptions that were to change the way Americans thought about property rights. First, they argued that the greater the wealth generated by the society, the greater the happiness. Thus wealth, not happiness, became the measure of utility—a highly arguable assumption given the empirical psychological and sociological research that indicates little correlation between wealth and happiness. Second, they assumed that maximization of production led to greater wealth. By combining these two theoretical assumptions, they developed a concept of utility based on the maximum of production rather than on happiness. In two theoretical leaps, the measure of the consequences of property rights had moved from happiness to wealth to production.

This shift led economists to abandon the theory that those who worked to produce property should own it. The realities of the growing systems of mass production, with its increasing complexity and productivity, demonstrated the value of privately owned capital. Besides, it was now impractical to identify how much any one individual contributed to output. Workers, instead of having a natural right to the produce of their efforts, should be rewarded based on their marginal contribution to society's welfare. The labor market determines the value of this contribution.

Our Heritage—What Does It Mean?

The transformation of our ideology was now complete. Mixing one's sweat with nature was no longer the grounds for ownership. Private ownership of capital could be justified solely by its utilitarian benefits to society as determined by the marketplace. Responsibilities were only weakly limited to not harming others in the pursuit of one's self-interest.

The Industrial Revolution, and the attendant change in political and philosophical thinking, shook the philosophical foundations upon which humanity had been standing since the beginning of recorded history. Yet even with the rapid and momentous changes, we still approach corporate ownership with a set of ideas developed to address the realities of the eighteenth and nineteenth centuries. Little has changed in our beliefs about shareholders' property rights since the turn of the twentieth century, even though the nature of corporations, their role in society, and the composition of stockholders have changed significantly. America is entering the twenty-first century with an ideology stuck in the nineteenth century. An ultimate corporate purpose of maximizing shareholder wealth may have merit for an owner-managed proprietorship in which the owner bears responsibility for the use of wealth and the consequences of the organization's actions; but it loses its relevance to the twenty-first-century corporation.

Our professed beliefs regarding property have evolved considerably from the Judeo-Christian doctrine that prevailed for most of recorded history. The sixteenth-century Reformation, which planted the seeds of this evolution, freed individuals from their ecclesiastical constraints and in human eyes provided divine incentives for the accumulation of wealth. This change enabled increased freedom of thought, which led to a secular explanation of the origin of property rights—they were a person's natural right. The acceptance of the natural right theory and individuals' increasing reliance on their own reason, allowed them to become even more expansive in their thinking. If human beings are good, then the pursuit of self-interest should promise human progress. Through the use of reason, people could create heaven on earth. These ideas lessened the sense of dependence on God. Reasoning backward from the results of given actions, the utilitarian view of property rights was developed. The general welfare takes care of itself with the help of laws to protect property rights and to limit abuses of those rights. Utilitarianism was the last step in absolving property ownership and economic activity of their social responsibilities.

With the ascension of reason, the duties attached to the rights of property slowly disappeared. Although one ancient belief that originated with Aristotle remains—that possessions are an external expression of the individual personality and are a possible means to the fulfillment of one's human potential—most of the religious foundations of our beliefs about property rights have been gradually dismantled. To a large extent, gone from our public dialogue about property rights is the belief that all things belong to God and people serve only as stewards. Gone is the responsibility to use possessions for the benefit of one's fellow human being and the strong commitment to benevolence as a responsibility of wealth. Gone is the belief that wealth in excess of one's needs is sinful because it deprives the poor of the necessities of life. The social concept of the use of wealth has been substantially diminished, and in its place stands a utilitarian justification. If each individual pursues his or her own self-interest and respects the rights of others to do likewise (with the reinforcement of laws to ensure that these rights are respected), the general welfare will be served. The moral anchor provided by the Protestant ethic has been lost, and Americans have been cast morally afloat. No longer do they have the moral justifications for their own action and the collective actions of society. Material well-being began forcing out spiritual well-being.

Yet even with this increasing secularization of the justification of property rights, Americans are conflicted. We still have the vestigial feeling that we ought somehow to conduct our human relationships by an ethical code consistent with Judeo-Christian values. Most believe that wealth carries with it responsibilities similar to those professed by our Judeo-Christian heritage. We also understand the essential truth of the admonition that the pursuit of wealth diverts people from the fuller life intended for them—both in the spiritual and secular worlds.

Part of what concerns us is undoubtedly the distinction drawn by Reinhold Niebuhr between property that is essential to the full realization of the individual's worth and property that exceeds the requirements of personality and represents unjustified accumulation of social power.[88] How much property is morally permissible and when does the ends of property become personal glorification or personal accumulation of power over others? As a society, we bestow considerable respect on those who use their wealth for the benefit of others or who forgo wealth to aid others. It is the Albert Schweitzers and Mother Teresas of this world that demand our respect and affection. The mention of the Morgans, Fords, or Rockefellers of our time stirs little noble sentiment in our hearts.

Our view of property rights has been heavily influenced by our view of progress. Probably nowhere was progress a more powerful force than in America, with its open frontier, expanding ownership of property, and Puritan ethic. The frontier made property ownership available to all. This was in stark contrast to Europe, where wealth was in the hands of a few aristocrats, and from the eighteenth century on, revolutions were waged to distribute property more evenly. The frontier, with its abundant property for the taking, eliminated the need for revolution in the United States. The Puritan tradition encouraged frugality and hard work—two of the essential ingredients of progress.

In America, European philosophy took on a very pragmatic nature. Truths about human nature did not need to be deduced by tortuous logic from natural law or the general will. Rather some things—such as progress, equality of rights, and individual freedom—were simply considered "self-evident." As Daniel Boorstin observes,

> In America what would liberate men was not the opportunity to combat ancient and erroneous philosophic systems by modern ones, but the opportunity to bring all philosophy into the skeptical and earthy arena of daily life. No philosophy would be too sacred for such a test. Americans saw less value in the full-dress intellectual tournaments of learned academies, in the passionate arguments of artists and prophets on the Left Banks of the world, than in the free competition of the marketplace. Such competition was hardly yet known to Europe, and it might never be known there in its crude American form.[89]

American ideology has selectively and pragmatically combined portions of natural right and utilitarian theory. The words of the Declaration of Independence—"We hold these truths to be self-evident, that all men are created equal, that they are endowed by the Creator with certain unalienable Rights, that among these are Life, Liberty and the pursuit of Happiness"— are etched in the minds of most Americans. Private property, with its links to liberty and happiness, is an inalienable right. The values embodied in the culture through the Protestant ethic provided the moral responsibilities that accompanied this right.

In the end, however, the power of the market to swamp these responsibilities proved overwhelming. Eighteenth- and nineteenth-century values of self-discipline, delayed gratification, restraint, frugality, and charity began to break down. The focus gradually became the rights of the individual exclusive of the associated responsibilities. However, the respect for rights is only a minimal moral condition. It fails to address the essence of the meaningful life. It says nothing of the ends one's life should serve or how one should proactively engage with other people, only that each individual should respect the rights of others. By ignoring higher-order moral responsibilities that reach beyond the self, American society has been left groping for a moral grounding.

Contemporary thinkers such as Daniel Bell and Irving Kristol have expressed their concern that American capitalism has torn loose from its moral moorings. Bell laments:

> American capitalism has lost its traditional legitimacy, which was based on a moral system of reward rooted in the Protestant sanctification of work. It has substituted a hedonism which promises material ease and luxury, yet shies away from all the historic implications of a "voluptuary system," with all its social permissiveness and libertinism. The culture has been dominated (in the serious realm) by a principle of modernism that has been subversive of bourgeois life, and the middle-class life-styles by a hedonism that has undercut the Protestant ethic which provided the moral foundation for the society.
>
> What this abandonment of Puritanism and the Protestant ethic does, of course, is to leave capitalism with no moral or transcendental ethic. . . . On the one hand, the business corporation wants an individual to work hard, pursue career, accept delayed gratification—to be, in the crude sense, an organization man. And yet, in its products and its advertisements, the corporation promotes pleasure, instant joy, relaxing and letting go. One is to be "straight" by day and a "swinger" by night. This is self-fulfillment and self-realization![90]

Kristol believes that "we are at a unique moment in Western culture, the collapse of secular, rational humanism. . . . People want more. They want community and they want transcendence."[91] A new moral foundation is "desperately needed by the spiritually impoverished civilization that we have constructed on what once seemed to be sturdy bourgeois foundations."[92]

By extension, these insights into the American character challenge the validity of a corporate purpose that focuses primarily on the maximization of shareholder wealth. A new, more transcendent ethic of purpose is needed, one that helps to address this spiritual impoverishment.

Common Stock as Property

Do the property rights of common-share ownership in corporations carry with them the same rights to the underlying corporate assets as does, say, the ownership of a home? What responsibilities accompany the rights to share ownership?

Entering a discussion of these value-laden issues is fraught with challenges and potential misunderstandings. It touches values of individualism, property rights, and the validity of the private enterprise system that are deeply held but often only shallowly understood. We relate these values to our ability to be free from the will of others, to better our families and ourselves, and to be rewarded directly for our knowledge, skill, and effort. The consequence can be knee-jerk reactions rather than reflective, engaging thought. But the critical question is this: Are these ends best served by an ideology predicated on maximizing shareholder wealth?

The rights associated with the ownership of shares of a company's common stock as a financial security is not questioned, nor is the right to a reasonable return on these securities to offset the risks taken. However, these rights are quite different from a claim to the underlying corporate assets and the right to have the company managed primarily for the shareholders' benefit.

The reasons for the obsolescence of current justifications of strong property rights for shareholders are essentially fourfold. First, the strong form of property rights, which our present ideology grants to shareholders, actually erodes individual fulfillment in our society. Corporate activity touches the lives of employees and customers much more directly than it does shareholders. As we have seen, a corporation, if it truly seeks above all else to maximize the present value of the company's common stock, threatens to oppress the individual expression and fulfillment of its employees by subordinating ends they value to the ends of shareholders. Such a purpose can also reduce the potential benefits received by customers from the company's products and services. Employees and customers become means to financial ends.

Second, for reasons explained in the earlier chapters, America's private-enterprise system is not being well served by the ideological purpose of maximizing shareholder wealth. This ideology leads to a strategy focus on the capital market rather than the product market, to goals that place greater importance on return on investment than on growth, to a higher priority on shareholder interests than on customer and employee interests. These priorities affect operational goals, investment decisions, and employee morale. When a firm embracing this ideology faces a customer-oriented competitor, it is at a competitive disadvantage. For the free enterprise system to flourish in the future, many American firms will need to modify their ideology tied to shareholder wealth.

Third, absent enforceable responsibilities, too many presumed rights over the use of a corporation's underlying assets have been granted to shareholders. Shareholders possess a claim on the residual cash flow of a company—after employees, suppliers, lenders, government agencies (taxes), and other claimants have been satisfied. They, along with the government taxing authorities, participate in the unlimited upside potential of this stream. Shareholders deserve to receive a fair return that compensates them for their risk and the time value of their money, just as do lenders. On these issues there is little debate. But their moral right to the absolute control of the use of corporate assets primarily for their own benefit is problematic.

Fourth, our prevalent ideology of corporate purpose does not adequately serve many of society's needs, such as jobs that provide financial security and the sense of community among fellow workers and work that serves ends that bring meaning to people's lives.

The Effects of Changing Patterns of Corporate Ownership

The rapid dispersion of the ownership of common stock of American corporations raises important questions regarding shareholder rights. Not only have workers not gained a significant share of ownership in their companies, but management and ownership also have become separated. In 2001 individuals directly owned less than 40 percent of the shares of New York Stock Exchange–listed companies. Financial institutions owned the rest.

Berle and Means were the first to recognize the profound implications of the widening gulf between the ownership and control of corporate assets. In 1932 they observed:

> This dissolution of the atom of property [into its component parts, control and beneficial ownership] destroys the very foundation on which the economic order of the past three centuries has rested. Private enterprise, which has molded economic life since the close of the Middle Ages, has been rooted in the institution of private property. Under the feudal system, its predecessor, economic organization grew out of mutual obligations and privileges derived by various individuals from their relation to property which no one of them owned. Private enterprise, on the other hand, has assumed an owner of the instruments of production with complete property rights over those instruments. Whereas the organization of feudal economic life rested upon an elaborate system of binding customs, the organization under the system of private enterprise has rested upon the self-interest of the property owner—a self-interest held in check only by competition and the conditions of supply and demand. Such self-interest has long been regarded as the best guarantee of economic efficiency. It has been assumed that, if the individual is protected in the right both to use his own property as he sees fit and to receive the full fruits of its use, his desire for personal gain, for profits, can be relied upon as an effective incentive to this efficient use of any industrial property he may possess.
>
> In the quasi-public corporation, such an assumption no longer holds. . . . Those who control the destinies of the typical modern corporation own so insignificant a fraction of the company's stock that the returns from running the corporation profitably accrue to them in only a very minor degree. The stockholders, on the other hand, to whom the profits of the corporation go, cannot be motivated by those profits to a more efficient use of the property, since they have surrendered all disposition of it to those in control of the enterprise. The explosion of the atom of property destroys the basis of the old assumption that the quest for profits will spur the owner of industrial property to its effective use. It consequently challenges the fundamental economic principle of individual initiative in industrial enterprise. It raises for reexamination the question of the motive force back of industry, and the ends for which the modern corporation can be or will be run.[93]

The changes in ownership and control documented by Berle and Means—and which have since intensified—raise important issues regarding managerial accountability, the nature of shareholder property rights, and the ultimate purpose of corporations that have remained largely unresolved to this day.

What Do Shareholders Really Own?

The central question raised by these new realities is, how well does our cultural view of private property transfer to shareholders' property—both the individual ownership of the security and the "ownership" of the corporation's underlying assets?

In our heritage of ideas about property rights, there is one issue none of the philosophers and economists whose thinking we have discussed would debate: the legitimacy of corporations to act rests in their benefits for society. Once they cease to serve society, their reason for being dies. The corporation acts as an intermediary between society as a whole and individuals in their various roles: shareholders, consumers, employees, and citizens. As an institution of society, the corporation's right to exist is granted by the state, yet it is owned by individuals and their financial intermediaries (pension funds, mutual funds, life insurance companies, etc.). When people are at work, individual self-interest must be filtered through the organization. The question, then, is what concept of shareholder property rights in large publicly owned corporations best advances individual freedom and the general welfare of society?

To answer these questions regarding the appropriate view of shareholder property rights, it is instructive first to compare shareholder rights to those of bondholders. Both are owners of highly mobile pieces of paper, not physical instruments of commerce. Both securities are a means to store and enlarge one's wealth. Neither one is the direct product of a person's work, which is a critical requirement for the natural law justification of property rights. What gives the shareholder a greater claim on the underlying assets in terms of property rights? Clearly, there are contractual differences in the claims on the corporation's cash flow and the resulting differences in risk and expected return. However, are there justifications for different rights regarding the underlying corporate assets and the company's employees?

Is it not passé to talk about most corporations' most valuable assets being working capital, plant, and equipment? If the core competence that gives a company a competitive advantage is primarily derived from the knowledge and industry of its employees, are not these individuals the core asset? Clearly, a shareholder does not own them!

There can be little disagreement that the shareholders should have the right to buy, sell, or give away their common stock certificates. Consistent with historical thought, this right encourages social harmony and lessens potential hostile conflict. I cannot take your stock certificates for my benefit without your consent. This right also fosters industry by enabling a means of investing the returns from hard work that are in excess of immediate consumption needs. Consequently, the individual can receive status from accumulated wealth and the delayed gratification from spending the accumulated savings. Individuals are also encouraged to be diligent in their investment decisions. The result is a market that more efficiently values financial securities and indirectly allocates capital more effectively. But all of this could be said for a bondholder as well. These benefits relate to the ownership of a financial security, not to rights to the underlying assets. What is important to these consequences are returns (their level, timing, and risk), not control over the underlying assets.

If shareholders are to have greater rights over underlying assets, the reason must rest in one of two areas. First, these rights generate greater happiness for a greater number of people than does any alternative distribution of rights. This means, in part, that these rights on balance enhance the individuality and fulfillment of more people than does an alternative allocation of rights. Second, the shareholders as individuals assume greater responsibility for the outcomes of corporate action and thus can be presumed to have greater rights.

The issue of shareholder property rights and individual fulfillment—which is so critically important to society and, within the company, to strategy, to the way of managing, and to the meaning employees derive from their work—was addressed in depth earlier. Suffice it here to say, when discussing shareholder property rights and individual fulfillment, one must consider the effect of the rights on individuals in their various roles: as shareholders, consumers, employees, and citizens. Humans are much more than just "economic animals." The existing ideology of shareholder wealth maximization has dampened the individual fulfillment of Americans. In part this is because their individuality and quality of life are much more influenced by their work and the possessions and services they purchase from corporations than by the ownership of a certain type of financial instrument.

In determining the contribution of shareholder property rights to the general happiness, it must be recognized that the wealth related to shares and the goods and services into which it can be converted are only means to the end of happiness.[94] Happiness is derived from a meaningful, fulfilled life. It can be measured by the individual's satisfaction with his or her life as a whole and with one's personal growth and development—the realization of one's potential. These measures go far beyond the economic welfare used by most economists. The question then is, what view of property rights creates corporate behavior that is conducive to maximizing happiness?

Robert Lane, in his exceptionally well documented book *The Market Experience*, concludes that the market's contribution to happiness and satisfaction "will be judged by what it produces and distributes and by the *processes* of production and distribution." He brings together numerous studies to show that "individual economic welfare (above a decent minimum) has only a minimal relationship to a sense of well-being. . . . The evidence shows that income does not contribute so much to life satisfaction as, for example, people's beliefs that they have met life's challenges (economic and otherwise) and their experience of work enjoyment."[95] Unfortunately, some acts to enhance shareholder welfare can diminish people's enjoyment of work.

If the market is a poor judge of happiness, if happiness is largely derived from other than consumption of goods and services, and if the processes by which corporations produce goods and services may be more important to happiness than the products themselves, then the traditional arguments supporting a strong form of shareholder property rights are no longer valid. Requiring corporate acts to primarily serve shareholder self-interest cannot be justified by the "greatest happiness for the greatest number." The corporation has many constituents who are affected by its actions, many of whom are more directly and significantly affected than are shareholders. Employees receive jobs that provide meaning to their lives, the opportunity to serve ends they find worthwhile, opportunities for personal growth, a sense of community, and nearly all of their income. Customers often receive goods or services that affect their lives in more important ways than do their shareholdings—everything from life-saving drugs to products such as houses, art, clothing, personal computers, and automobiles that become extensions of their personality, facilitate the expression of their creativity, entertain them, and enable more fulfilling leisure-time experiences.

The buying and selling of common stock—an act of trading financial assets—has marginal effect on the common good. Although this trading determines the evaluation of the corporate assets and the stock market represents a means to accumulate and store wealth, little of the money represented by these transactions goes into productive investment. Therefore society's productivity is scarcely affected. Instead money exchanges hands among investors (most of whom are financial institutions). The values of stocks go up or down, affecting aggregate levels of wealth. But, unless capital from primary equity issues finds its way into investments in plant and equipment, research, product development, or marketing, the financial trades do not significantly affect the productive capacity of the society. The bulk of the gains that leave the market find their way into consumption (predominantly after retirement) and into inheritance and income taxes. But, in a major change from the assumptions on which our ideology rests, the investment in common stock of publicly owned corporations results in neither significant increases in productivity nor a responsibility on the part of the investors to manage or oversee the management of the corporate assets. Ironically, more of the bondholders' investments find their way into productive assets than do shareholders' investments.

Responsibility for the consequences of corporate action should logically lead to the right to control the action. But in practice, shareholders of major corporations have very limited control over these actions, and therefore almost no influence over or responsibility for the actions' consequences. It is the employees (managers and workers) that have the responsibilities and bear the major consequences. Shareholders do not go to jail for extreme acts of corporate irresponsibility, but employees do.

The shareholders' responsibilities are to themselves—or if they are financial intermediaries, to the people for whom they are agents. Their typical reaction to dissatisfaction with corporate actions is to sell their stock. Most feel little compunction when investing in companies with questionable social consequences, such as tobacco or gaming companies. They are attracted by potential returns relative to risk, rather than to the social benefits of the firm. Does the shareholders' limited influence on and responsibility for outcomes of corporate action erode their moral right to control the use of a firm's human and physical assets?

Even those financial institutions that have taken up the banner of shareholder activism, such as CALPERS, are able to target only five or six companies a year out of a portfolio of possibly a thousand companies. For practical reasons, only the largest and most egregiously managed companies can be singled out. When they are successful in exerting their influence, the direct result is typically a new CEO rather than specific changes in strategy.

The common argument that managers are simply agents for the shareholders and that the shareholders' interests should dominate their decisions tends to be an ideological argument rather than a pragmatic one. In practice, most senior managers can and do go to considerable lengths to insulate their actions from capital-market influence. The reality is that managers have considerable latitude in their decisions, if the company's performance is satisfactory (but short of maximizing shareholder wealth) because the capital market lacks significant ways to directly control management. The absence of a need to go to the equity market for new capital adds to management's independence. Consequently, today's managers—as they respond to the demands of the competitive marketplace, employees, and society—are in the uncomfortable position of placing other concerns ahead of shareholder interests in a society that clings to an ideology that does not give them the legitimacy to do so. Yet this ideology has lost its moral grounding and is losing its practical relevance. What is naturally evolving is a state of affairs in which managers must trade off the priorities of different constituent interests. The question is, what moral force is there behind different sets of priorities?

Two constituents emerge with the greatest moral claim on the corporation: the employees (whose individuality, personal fulfillment, and family welfare are directly affected by the company), and the customers (who benefit from consuming the firm's goods and services and whose purchases provide the bulk of the corporation's capital). Until these moral claims are in harmony with the prevalent ideology of corporate purpose, American society will be deeply conflicted. The conflict will continue to influence the legitimacy of corporations to take actions on controversial situations and to affect the way we manage our companies, the sense of meaning people receive from their work, and the opportunities for individual growth and expression. The moral claims tend to be immutable, but the ideology can change. From the harmony of ideology and moral claims comes strength. The sooner we achieve greater harmony, the greater will be our competitive strength.

7 Individualism
America's Competitive Advantage

I wish my life and decisions to depend on myself, not on external forces of whatever kind. I wish to be the instrument of my own, not of other men's acts of will. I wish to be . . . moved by reasons, by conscious purposes, which are my own, not by causes which affect me, as it were, from outside. I wish to be a doer . . . deciding, not being decided for, self-directed, and not acted upon by external nature.
—*Isaiah Berlin*[1]

The values of individualism, which are deeply rooted in American culture, and the creativity and initiative they spawn, are potential key sources of competitive advantage. Yet throughout the twentieth century many publicly owned enterprises have unintentionally sapped the individuality of the people they touch most directly—their employees. These are the people on whom corporate performance directly depends. Their knowledge, creativity, and industry are the cornerstones of the firm's core competencies and America's ingenuity. Yet most American companies have failed to capitalize fully on this inherent competitive advantage.

Ironically, this failure has often been the result of conscious acts done in the name of individuality. The principal culprit has been a corporate purpose of maximizing the shareholders' welfare—a purpose often justified by its tie to individualism. It is the familiar argument of the link between individualism and shareholders' property rights examined in the last chapter.

But the shareholders' right to have corporations managed primarily for their benefit has little influence on their individuality. True, their material self-interests may be served in the short run, but this right has a negligible effect on their self-expression, personal dignity, and the meaning of their lives. Any positive impact this purpose has on the shareholders' individuality pales in comparison to the potential toll such a purpose can take on the individual fulfillment of the men and women who work for the corporation. Their efforts become subservient to financial ends—ends that are tangential to their real work. Precisely because shareholder wealth maximization is not highly valued as the purpose of work, forceful management systems and greater corporate oversight are required to ensure that shareholder interests are fully incorporated into decision making. These actions run counter to increasing individualism. They usually create more restrictive management systems and, almost by necessity, spawn increasing bureaucracy and less decentralization. Individuals are often restrained from doing what they believe is right for both customers and the company by the tyranny of financial controls designed to secure short-term shareholder value. As a result, their individual autonomy and ability to express themselves in their work are limited.

But this need not be so. Corporate purpose, properly defined, can have a salutary effect on individuality. It can enhance the sense of self that is gained from relating oneself to the world, serving others through work, and increasing the opportunities to exercise one's abilities fully. These effects come from serving a cause the individual deems as socially worthwhile and from the power of shared purpose to direct action, lessening the need for oppressive managerial control systems that smother creativity and initiative.

Individualism: What Is It?

Although individualism is widely regarded as a distinguishing characteristic of American culture, the term has different meanings to different people.

Individualism begins with a cognitive understanding of one's existence. As Descartes declared, "I think—hence I am." Beyond the awareness of one's unique existence, individualism can express itself in five distinct and potentially conflicting ways: (1) in the selfishness of utilitarian egoism, (2) in a doctrine of the supreme value of the dignity of the individual, in which society is seen as only the means to individual ends, (3) in equality of opportunity that enables people through hard work to rise to the level in society to which their native abilities and character entitle them, (4) in self-actualization and the cultivation of the deeper expression of self—the expression of creativity, love, and feelings—as advocated by romantic individualism, and (5) in the relationship of the individual to others and achieving increased meaning for one's life through serving a cause or high ideal beyond oneself.[2]

Utilitarian egoism is predicated on the belief that by pursuing one's own pleasure and happiness, the greatest happiness within society is

achieved. It focuses on acquisitive self-gratification: the garnering of possessions, power, and status. It also emphasizes individuals' rights: the right to
think for ourselves, to make our own decisions, and to live our lives as we
see fit. Its roots can be traced back to John Locke's individual in the "state
of nature," struggling to maximize individual self-interest (a struggle that was
to give rise to the state as a means to protect the rights of each individual),
to Adam Smith's invisible hand, and to Jeremy Bentham's utilitarian arguments. When carried to a doctrinaire extreme, utilitarian egoism implies that
a person can infringe on other people's opportunities to realize his or her own
full potential.

In the late eighteenth century, Immanuel Kant gave voice to the belief
that individualism is directly linked to the supremacy of the dignity of the
individual. He espoused the conviction that "every man is to be respected as
an absolute end in himself; and it is a crime against the dignity that belongs
to him as a human being to use him as a mere means for some external purpose."[3] Kant derived this belief from the "categorical imperative" that
flowed directly from the commands of one's rational conscience. This imperative required each individual always to act in accordance with maxims he
or she would will to be universal laws of nature. This reasoning led Kant to
conclude that a person should never be treated as a means to other ends. People should be granted equality of opportunity to realize their fullest potential, recognizing that individuals had different abilities. He consequently
rejected prerogatives of class or birth. In the United States, these ideals were
embodied in the Constitution, in Benjamin Franklin's writings extolling the
opportunity to get ahead based solely on one's initiative, in the tales of rugged
individualism from settling the American frontier, and in the promise of
upward mobility expressed in the Horatio Alger stories.

By the twentieth century, the importance of individual initiative,
equality of opportunity, and upward mobility were deeply embedded in
American culture. Capturing this spirit, Herbert Hoover defined American
individualism as embracing "these great ideals":

> that while we build our society upon the attainment of the individual, we
> shall safeguard to every individual an equality of opportunity to that posi-
> tion in the community to which his intelligence, character, ability, and
> ambition entitle him; that we keep the social solution free from frozen
> strata of classes; that we shall stimulate effort of each individual to achieve-

ment; that through an enlarging sense of responsibility and understanding we shall assist him to this attainment; while he in turn must stand up to the emery wheel of competition.[4]

Despite these ideals, by the mid-nineteenth century, the dignity of the individual American corporate employee—except for the owners of the means of production—was being usurped. Contrary to Kant's arguments, people came to be used as means to accumulate wealth for others. Instead of the supreme value being placed on the individual and material things being used to promote individual dignity, the reverse became reality. Things were treasured and people used. This result was justified by the logic underlying utilitarian egoism.

In objecting to this state of affairs, Emerson, Thoreau, Hawthorne, and Whitman argued that the search for wealth should be put aside in favor of the cultivation of the deeper self to be found in feelings, love, and creativity. It was an appeal to a romantic ideal. They believed that each person was irreplaceable and had "a unique core of feelings and intuitions that should unfold or be expressed if individuality is to be realized. This core, though unique, is not necessarily alien to other persons or to nature. Under certain conditions, the expressive individualist may find it possible through intuitive feelings to 'merge' with other persons, with nature, or with the cosmos as a whole."[5]

The ideas of the romantic individualists have credence for managing today. The expression of one's uniqueness in creative acts develops and reinforces a positive sense of self. Creativity and the initiative to put the new ideas into practice enable a person to leave a track in the sand, to produce something of value by one's efforts, and to be able to say "this is mine." Erich Fromm has related the drive to create to our need to transcend our animal nature—to become creators in our own right. "In the act of creation man transcends himself as a creature, raises himself beyond the passivity and accidentalness of his existence into the realm of purposefulness and freedom."[6] Through creative acts, one becomes active in shaping one's life and does not go through life as a passive bystander. This urge to create is driven in part by the age-old need for mastery over nature. Vibrant individuals strive to go beyond the mundane and routine in life (which stifle the sense of self) to be involved in experiences that fill their lives with quality and meaning. When these creative acts are dedicated to worthwhile—often spiritual—goals, they take on even greater significance.

Throughout the history of industrialized America, ideas of self-reliance and individual autonomy conflicted with aspects of our Judeo-Christian tradition. Although this tradition stresses the sacredness of the individual soul, it also commands a responsibility to others. The second great commandment, "to love your neighbor as yourself," is rooted deeply in the Western conscience. The tension in American values between one's connectedness and responsibility to others and the satisfaction of the private appetite for material possessions, power, and status remains unresolved today. Robert Bellah and his fellow researchers in *Habits of the Heart*, an extensive study of American individualism and commitment, concluded that Americans "find ourselves not independently of other people and institutions, but through them. We never get to the bottom of our selves on our own."[7] We know that our life has no meaning unless it is related to others and becomes empty without "sustaining social commitments."[8] In this sense, individuality is predicated on external commitment—to other people or to an ideal bigger than oneself. The tension between individual autonomy and relatedness to others produces a "profound ambivalence about individualism in America among its most articulate defenders." This ambivalence is embodied in the conflict between "the fear that society may overwhelm the individual and destroy any chance of autonomy unless he stands against it," and the "recognition that it is only in relation to society that the individual can fulfill himself and that if the break with society is too radical, life has no meaning at all."[9]

Individualism, in its various manifestations and in its inherent conflicts, both positively and negatively affects managers' abilities to foster effective cooperative efforts in the pursuit of common organizational purposes. The responsibility of management is to develop and leverage the beneficial aspects of individualism and minimize the negative ones. Importantly, outstanding corporate leaders recognize that the most constructive ideals of individualism are accomplished through freedom of action, creative work, and one's relationship to others. The acts of leaders who truly desire to further individualism are likely to enhance knowledge-based, long-term competitive advantages, but at times can be at odds with actions that would increase the firm's stock price in the short term.

Shareholder-Focused Corporate Purpose
and the Erosion of Individualism

In the late nineteenth century, when ownership and management were joined, the linkage of individualism to a shareholder-oriented purpose had more credibility and legitimacy. The credibility came more from the fact that owner-managers used their energy and ingenuity to put their unique stamp on the company than from their ownership per se. But in those days, the "robber barons" who dominated some businesses were despised by much of society for their often-ruthless manipulation of others to satisfy a personal lust for power and wealth. However, other corporate magnates, such as Andrew Carnegie and, later in life, John D. Rockefeller Jr., believed that business leaders had a responsibility to act, not as owners but as trustees of the corporate wealth entrusted into their care to ensure that the assets were managed for the nation's benefit. In 1889, Carnegie wrote in his "Gospel of Wealth" that "the problem of our age is the proper administration of wealth, that the ties of brotherhood may still bind together the rich and poor in harmonious relationship."[10] John D. Rockefeller Jr. had a similar view, saying, "I believe that every right implies a responsibility; every opportunity an obligation; every possession a duty." But as management became separate from ownership, as ownership gravitated into the hands of institutional intermediaries, and as management practice became increasingly bureaucratic, the individualism of those most touched by corporations—the people that work in them—was suppressed.

In contemporary corporations, the prevailing corporate purpose of maximizing shareholder wealth undermines individualism in two significant ways. First, employees are treated as means to this end. Second, the end is not one that most employees value. The end is distant from their work, their daily activity, and their business relationships. More often than not, the primary expression of this end is in budgets and financial targets. The financial goals are capital-market abstractions that do not relate to the employees' day-to-day reality. Thus employees chafe under these restraints that they see as externally imposed controls on their activities—controls that constrain individual creativity and initiative.

When corporate purpose defines an end for individuals' work activity that they do not value highly, the employees' opportunity to enhance the sense of self through work that links them with other humans in a positive way is diminished. Moreover, management's actions often reinforce the perception of being considered a means to shareholders' ends: downsizing decisions that erode any sense of mutual loyalty, the imposition of oppressive bureaucratic procedures that stifle new ideas (often dominated by budgetary pressures to compromise service to customers), and reward systems governed by financial goals rather than broader measures of product-market performance. These messages sap individual dignity. Individuals come to view themselves as mercenaries serving someone else's cause, not their own. In the service of this cause, they often feel they must do things that run counter to what they believe is right for customers and the company's competitiveness, and to what enables a fuller expression of self on the job. Consequently, life becomes less meaningful.

When the employees do not value the company's purpose and many of the goals into which it is translated, there is no strong intrinsic motivation to act in accordance with them. Self-centered ends tend to fill the void, generating behavior that is often in conflict with the organization's best interests. Consequently, incentive and control systems need to be strengthened to augment the motivational and directive power of the shareholder-focused purpose and the related financially oriented goals. As the control systems become more elaborate and the individuals' activities become more routine, the sense of autonomy, creative expression, and contribution that individuals experience in their work atrophy. As individuals respond to these incentives and controls, they are left with a sense of selling out their higher ideals for personal financial gain. The controls are seen at best as bureaucratic hindrances to doing what is needed to serve customers better, and at worst a restriction on the opportunity to apply one's abilities to the solution of the organization's problems.

Importantly, a sense arises that the corporation has made individuals sell out and behave counter to their own instincts and values, stifling their individual fulfillment. A lingering feeling of resentment, apathy, and even despair can often arise. In these cases, rather than being a vehicle to greater meaning and individual expression, the corporation becomes a force for resigned conformance with corporately desired actions that drains the sense of individual dignity and autonomy and detracts from the ability to find meaning in work. (Even when individuals' actions under a purpose and goals they share—such as serving customers' needs—are similar to those driven by a shareholder-wealth oriented purpose, they are pursued with greater emotion and commitment, and bring a fuller sense of personal autonomy.)

Consequently, people intensify their search for avenues of individual expression and meaningful relationships outside of work. Work becomes a means to fulfillment off the job—a way of earning money to enjoy these other satisfactions. The employee's preoccupation with pay and security intensifies, usually to the detriment of performance. Given this preoccupation, and without a personal affinity for the corporate cause, greater selfishly motivated political activity often occurs.

The measurement and reward systems through which a shareholder-oriented purpose is internalized most often appeal to the appetitive nature of employees—to individual monetary incentives, to organizational power, and to career advancement and achievement. Although there is nothing intrinsically wrong with these appeals to individual autonomy and self-aggrandizement, they do not address the individual as a whole person or invoke his or her highest ideals. The employees' cooperation in achieving corporate goals is often viewed as being given in exchange for salary, perks, and prestige. In fact, in return for these benefits, the implied employment contract too often asks employees to give up much of their individuality: to work in the service of purposes they do not find particularly worthwhile, to subordinate personal values to the achievement of organizational objectives, to conform to organizational norms, and consequently, to curtail personal creativity and other forms of self-expression.

No organizational level is immune from a gnawing sense of emptiness from work. At the most senior levels, often the most extensive sacrifice of individuality is demanded. The executive finds it difficult to have a persona separate from his or her corporate identity. In the past, this reality gave rise to characterizations such as "the organization man" and the "man in the gray flannel suit."

In its rawest negative form, a corporate appeal to utilitarian egoism degenerates into a selfishness that dominates other virtues. Personal pleasure and happiness become the overriding ends that guide behavior. Individuals are seen as "socially independent atoms without obligations to society or to others, except if such obligations suit them."[11] The consequences can be an undermining of meaningful relationships, the politicization of organizations, and a fragmentation of society. The individual's relationship to the company becomes contractual. Loyalty is lost. Organized activity becomes more politicized, as individuals jockey to improve their personal position, either directly, or indirectly through enhancing their subunit's position.

Achieving Competitive Advantage Through Constructive Corporate Individualism

The corrosive effects of a shareholder-oriented purpose need not occur. Nor are the negative organizational effects of individualism inevitable. A culture of constructive corporate individualism grounded in a worthwhile corporate purpose promises enhanced competitiveness through greater individual expression and commitment at all organizational levels.

The core of constructive corporate individualism is the belief in the dignity, sacredness, and autonomy of the individual. It encompasses the dual ideas of the development of a self with integrity and coherence, and the recognition that an individual is not apart from his or her external reality. Constructive individualism fosters a positive sense of self. This sense is derived from several sources—each of which reflects an individual's relationship with his or her organization. It is embodied in action and thoughts—in initiative and creativity.

Judeo-Christian beliefs and the Enlightenment's secular humanist beliefs both concur that authentic selfhood originates in one's relation with fellow humans, from the validation received from them, and in serving them in some valued way. A customer-focused corporate purpose can link a person's work to the service of others, drawing the individual beyond the self. Individual fulfillment is enhanced when a person's identity rises above that confined to the role within the organization—by position and nature of work—to that determined by relationships in the service of others. Working together to achieve a valued common aim can increase fellowship and sense of belonging similar to being a member of a functional family or of a winning athletic team. Not surprisingly, leaders often refer to their organizations in terms of "family" and "team." To achieve this sense of relatedness, outstanding corporate leaders devote considerable time and energy to infusing the organization with a purpose that brings people together to serve a valued cause—a cause that becomes the individual's cause and adds fullness and meaning to life.

When these efforts are successful, organizational performance is enhanced. Increased individual expression and fulfillment, born of shared purpose, create competitive advantages by increasing the employees' opportunities to use their imagination, originality, and enterprise without sacrificing organizational coherence. When individualism is applied to business activity, its essence is much like the drive behind Joseph Schumpeter's entrepreneur, who finds and executes "new combinations" that lead to "creative destruction" of capital.[12] In a fundamental sense, creativity and initiative are the wellsprings of entrepreneurial activity. Today's Herculean efforts to increase entrepreneurship in organizations are directed at increasing these two forces—two critical sources of self-identity as well as innovative ideas and more rapid responses to customer needs.

As knowledge increasingly becomes the coin of competitive advantage, creativity and initiative in organizations become critical determinants of performance. The importance of knowledge, the rapidity of technological and market change, and the rise of the lean enterprise each place greater demand on innovation at all levels of the organization.

The quality of knowledge is determined in part by the creativity applied to its development. But knowledge has little value if not applied. Thus the commercialization of knowledge requires initiative. People must be willing to articulate new ways of doing things and to champion the new ideas until they are put into practice. Personal enterprise demands the courage to put oneself on the line—to risk rejection or failure and to jeopardize one's self-interest—for the sake of creating something new that benefits customers and consequently furthers corporate ends.

The rapidity of technological change demands faster and more decentralized decision making. Senior management no longer has either the knowledge or the time to gain and process the necessary information to make many critical decisions. Consequently, they must rely on people lower in the organization to make these decisions, guided by goals, values, and judgment.

The rise of the lean enterprise with its intense pressure on product cost, quality, and performance also necessitates a greater decentralization of strategic decision making. More rapid and creative solutions to problems of cost, quality, product development, and customer service are needed. As organization structures become flatter, people at all levels of the organization must take on more responsibility for developing innovative solutions.

Constructive corporate individualism—and the creativity and initiative that are at its core—takes on even greater competitive significance in the global marketplace. Countries like Japan, Korea, and Germany have achieved their competitive successes despite highly bureaucratic organizational structures that often stifle creativity and discourage individual initiative. In addition, particularly in the case of Japan, their educational systems and management development processes are not conducive to the development of creativity. As knowledge creation becomes more important to competitive success, one of American businesses' greatest comparative advantages will be the individual expression of their people. Corporate leaders need to learn how to nurture it and channel it in constructive ways. There are significant cultural barriers to many of our strongest international competitors adopting America's creative advantages.

These human forces can be a powerful aid to managers seeking to build a vibrant, innovative organization. The drive for self-expression, the need to achieve, and the desire to leave a positive mark on the external world can significantly enhance organizational performance when they are properly embodied in strategy, culture, and way of managing. The opportunity to take initiative and to express one's creativity can result in harder, more careful work and more fruitful ideas. These are the wellsprings of a company's creativity and ability to innovate.

Contrary to what some pundits will argue, increased individual expression in an organization need not threaten cohesiveness or result in conflicting decisions that sap competitiveness. Just the opposite is true. Many of the values underlying constructive corporate individualism enhance cohesiveness and performance. They represent characteristics that are hallmarks of organizations that are able to attract and retain high-caliber people. For example,

- When the corporate ends and individuals' ends coincide, people naturally act in accordance with them, following their own instincts and values as to what actions are appropriate. When this occurs, people are quick to defend against attacks on the purpose. This congruence of company and individual ends results in a more cohesive organization and more coherent actions.
- When independent thinking becomes a valued part of company culture, it acts as an antidote to organizational groupthink, results in ready challenges to outmoded conventional wisdom, and promotes the identification and advocacy of needed change.
- Openness and candor, combined with a culture that encourages constructive conflict, lead to self-expression and better decisions

based on more information and a superior processing of information.

- Openness and constructive conflict also undermine the tendency to promote separate agendas through political maneuvering. Such activity is more quickly exposed for what it is. A leader who keeps the organization focused on the substance of its activities places a spotlight on political maneuvering to the detriment of the perpetrator.

- A meritocracy—in which equality of opportunity is real, individual initiative is emphasized, rewards are based on contributions to performance, and decisions are made on the merit of the conflicting arguments—attracts and retains high-caliber talent, encourages individual initiative, and enhances morale. (Morale suffers if chronic underperformers and political actors are treated the same way as high achievers.) A meritocracy reinforces an environment of openness and candor and also leads to decisions based on the quality of ideas, not on the political strength of the proponents or opponents of a particular position.

- Greater autonomy enables faster decision making closer to the market by people who generally have more information and decision-specific knowledge about an issue.

- Simplicity of organizational processes reduces the bureaucratic hurdles that so frustrate high-caliber people and often motivate greater politicization of decision-making processes. Furthermore, since creativity is nurtured by personal autonomy born of less restrictive oversight, organizational innovation increases when shared purpose enables a reduction in formal controls. People are more able to "do their own thing" (shared purpose) in their own way (with less oversight).

- High ethical standards—such as honesty, fairness, mutual respect and trust, and compassion and sensitivity in the exercise of power—by their very nature reinforce the dignity of the individual.

Leading CEOs, such as Jim Burke and Ralph Larsen at Johnson & Johnson and Jack Welch at General Electric, consider the infusion of these values as absolutely critical to their company's success. They are constantly striving to create what Walter Wriston, former CEO of Citibank, calls a "marketplace for ideas"—a place where candid, even heated debate can take place around issues, people are open with their ideas, and decisions are made solely on the merit of the underlying ideas. In the words of Jack Welch, they are constantly "pulling the dandelions of bureaucracy," simplifying organizational processes, increasing group and individual autonomy, while providing cohesion through a shared strategy and goals. The objective is to maintain coherent strategic direction while locating critical decisions close to the customer, and enhancing the initiative, commitment, and ownership of people throughout the organization.

The reinforcement of these values requires that corporate leaders be constantly vigilant to organizational deviations, quick to respond—sometimes in seemingly harsh ways because of the high stakes—and highly consistent in their actions. Their actions will speak much more loudly than their words, defining what is truly valued in the organization. In an age when individuals are very cynical about what their organizations and their leaders stand for, consistency takes on increased importance.

The talk of the benefits of increased individualism, shared purpose, and meaning from work should not be taken as soft and "touchy-feely" management. It places extra burdens on leaders—demanding constant diligence and consistency in their actions and the enforcement of high standards of performance. Leaders must be tough taskmasters as well as exemplars of these higher values.

Conclusion

Clearly, the quality of purpose alone is not sufficient to engender a high level of individual fulfillment in a company. It requires constant attention to a multiplicity of factors. But without a purpose valued by the members of the organization, sound management practices will fail to realize the full potential of individual expression and ingenuity.

Each organizational avenue to greater individuality loses its potency if the purpose being served is not valued and does not relate individuals to others in meaningful ways. Because these otherwise very beneficial actions serve hollow ends, they take on a certain emptiness. The opportunity to express one's creativity and take initiative loses its full force if it is not tied to a broader purpose that meaningfully links the individual to others. A constructive sense of self cannot be found just within. One must relate oneself to the world—to nature, to other people, and to society and its institutions. Yet one must do so without losing oneself. Life takes on meaning in the context of its relationship with the world and in influencing it in some positive way through one's actions.

Equally as clear, a corporation does not further individuality by making people dependent on the firm for their identity. The subordination of the self to the corporation, as in William Whyte's organization man, is not the pathway to greater individualism or happiness. Rather, the corporate leader's role is to create an environment in which people's dignity is reinforced and in which they can actualize the self. The leader does this by providing an opportunity to serve ends individuals believe are worthwhile and by creating an environment in which people are encouraged to exercise their creativity and have reasonable autonomy to take the initiative to make their ideas a reality. The corporation then becomes a source of opportunity for personal growth and self-expression.

Organizational members who lack a strong sense of self can be a detriment to morale and performance. They see themselves as a tool to be manipulated by others.[13] Much like Reismann's other-directed person, they seek their identity by trying to please others.[14] An inevitable consequence is hollowness. One's work life has no meaning beyond status and possessions. The shallowness of these measures of worth causes a sense of emptiness and consequent guilt. Guilt arises from the sense of not making the most of one's life. When in reflective moments, people see their life running though their fingers like sand, an emptiness pervades their existence. This numbness and alienation becomes reflected in their work. Management bears a responsibility for creating an environment that nurtures a constructive sense of self. For example, although it is true that some organizational members do not consciously seek to serve others through their work, effective leaders can help open the doors to this possibility by reinforcing the social value of their collective efforts. This reinforcement begins with a meaningful purpose.

We are at a watershed in history. Whereas corporations have long been considered by many people to be degrading of personal dignity and individuality, the enlightened corporation of the future holds the promise of enhancing both. Competitive pressures and the increasing importance of the knowledge worker are moving us in this direction, as are some of the most current management practices. In order to make faster and better decisions, companies are increasing their decentralization, flattening their organizations, removing bureaucratic procedures that stifle initiative and creativity, increasing the use of teams, and granting greater autonomy throughout their organizations. Each of these actions holds the promise of greater opportunities for self-expression. If this promise is realized, corporations will become vehicles for bringing greater meaning to the lives of their members.

But this promise will be lost if the purpose these acts serve is not valued by the members. Of course, quality of purpose alone is not sufficient to engender high levels of individualism in a corporation. The realization will come only with constant attention to the consistency of decisions, actions, and words that unlock the commitment, zeal, and sacrifice of individuals throughout the organization. In this way, enhancing constructive corporate individualism, corporate purpose, and leadership are closely intertwined.

III   *Competing Purposes in the Global Marketplace*

Purpose and Global Competitiveness
  The Realities

A new economic order is in the making. The fall of communism and the economic crisis in Asia of the late 1990s tempt many American observers to proclaim final victory of the U.S. system of shareholder capitalism. Is this conclusion justified or shortsighted economic hubris? What are the realities of international competitiveness?

Today's global marketplace brings companies reflecting distinct national histories and philosophical ideas into direct competition. As a result of these unique heritages, major international competitors adhere to very different ideologies regarding the fundamental purposes of corporations. As they play out on the world's competitive stage, the strategic consequences of differing corporate purposes are placed in high relief.

Of the major world economic powers, only the United States and the United Kingdom have an ideology firmly predicated on the primacy of shareholder wealth maximization. The foundation of the free-market ideologies of the other powers range from Germany's social-market economy to the emphasis on the harmony of corporate and national interests in Japan and Korea. The corporate purposes of many companies from these countries tend to be more directly linked to serving society—or the nation—than are their American counterparts. The philosophical and historical roots of these differences are deep. The competitive consequences are profound. They shape the institutional relationships between industrial firms, shareholders, and capital-market institutions and affect the strategic thinking of managers. The results can be found in the differing strategies, goals, and degrees of willingness to invest in people, plant, and R&D that determine the outcome of the competitive battle.

Recent events cloud our vision of these fundamentals. A brief recap of these events will help bring the basics back into clear view. In the 1980s U.S. competitiveness was rapidly eroding and the country was widely viewed as in a deep competitive crisis. By the end of the decade, the Japanese were celebrating their economic victory over the United States—a victory most of them (as well as many Americans) believed was final. The voices were varied, but the message common. The United States was a decaying economic power. Akiyuki Nosaka, one of Japan's leading novelists, reflected the sentiment of many Japanese when he called America a country of "refugees, a nouveau riche country." Looking at the United States, he said, is like watching "a test run for the decline of the human race." Takuma Yamamoto, the chairman of Fujitsu Ltd., observed, "We have to go out of our way to find American products worth buying." One leading Japanese professor called America a "vegetating nation," while another advised the United States to build on its strengths and "become a premier agrarian power—a giant version of Denmark." Even Japanese government bureaucrats became vocal. Kazuo Ogura, director general of the Cultural Affairs Department in the Ministry of Foreign Affairs, intoned, "There is something wrong with American society. The United States used to be a model for us to emulate, but now that sense is gone."[1] These comments sound somewhat silly today, given the relative performance of the two economies in the 1990s and early 2000s.

Japan's economic fortunes quickly changed. Ten years later, Japan was in recession and experiencing a serious crisis of confidence. Asia was in an economic tailspin, and Europe was preoccupied with its economic union. Rising above this economic din, a chorus of voices can be heard in America celebrating the triumph of the American system of shareholder capitalism. Coupled with the missteps in the Asian economies, the impressive efforts of U.S. companies to increase efficiency, product quality, and focus on the needs of customers have led many observers to conclude that at the beginning of the twenty-first century America had won the competitive battle. The triumph of market-based economies over communism reinforced this sense of final conquest. These victories were widely proclaimed as victories of American ideology. Little recognition was given to the fact that most of the world's free-market economies were based on communitarian capitalism rather than America's shareholder-based capitalism.

Corporate evangelists in the United States began lecturing Asian and European countries on the need to adopt America's ideology. Many American businesspeople, journalists, and academics are, often somewhat paternalistically, recommending the wholesale adoption of the American system in countries as diverse as Japan, Germany, and Malaysia. These would-be advisers are providing the recipes for wholesale change that range from corporate governance practices to shareholder activism, from relationships with employees and sister companies to goals dominated by financial returns for shareholders. But, in the future will the comments of many of these American pundits sound as misguided as the Japanese sentiments of the 1980s?

Such overconfidence and complacency has been the downfall of many a company—witness the American memory chip industry in the 1970s, General Motors in automobiles, and IBM in personal computers—and Japan in the 1990s. Instead of celebrating, this is the very time American business should be questioning its most fundamental assumptions. Between the despair of the 1980s and the hubris of the late 1990s lies the truth.

Self-congratulatory celebration is premature. The United States enters the twenty-first century with nagging problems and a looming threat. The United States lags behind many of its major competitors in savings and in investment in fixed capital and research as a percent of GDP. Its infrastructure is aging, and its educational system is in disrepair. Since the mid-1970s, the country has been failing an ultimate measure of competitiveness—the ability to raise the hourly incomes of its people. The cause can be attributed in part to an ideology that puts returns ahead of growth, consumption ahead of savings, and consequently constrains investment—an ideology with shareholder wealth maximization as its central tenet.

Demographics strongly favor an Asian resurgence. Currently, the continent is home to over half of the world's people and produces a third of the world's output. Both of these figures will increase significantly in coming decades. Over time, rising living standards will bring Asia's share of industrial output more in line with its portion of the world's population. The Central Intelligence Agency predicts that the GDP of East and Southeast Asia and Oceania will be 35 percent larger than that of North America by 2015.[2] When these strong forces are coupled with an increasingly well educated populace and differences in ideology, America will likely once again feel under competitive assault early in the new century.

The New Competitive Realities

In industry after industry, competition is intensifying at a rapid pace throughout the world. This new hypercompetitive reality means that specific competitive advantages in most industries are not sustainable for long periods of time. Powerful forces are at work that increase the importance of cost and quality to competitive advantage and reduce the ability of companies to differentiate their products and services from those of competitors. In many industries, the differential between the low-price leader and the higher-margin, high-functionality, and high-quality producer has collapsed.[3] In a given market segment, many companies that pursue a strategy of differentiating their products from the competition can no longer price much above the low-price leader.

The globalization of markets has affected the intensity of competitive rivalry in three critical ways. First and most simply, more firms from different countries have been brought into direct competitive confrontation. By the simple law of supply and demand, the greater the number of firms competing in a given market, the more intense the rivalry.

Second, these companies often have differing purposes that lead some to primarily emphasize growth, and others to stress return on investment. The resulting patterns of actions produce different strategies—strategies that are prone to misjudgment by competitors because of their contrasting underlying values.

Third, by expanding the absolute size of markets, globalization has increased the importance of economies of scale and scope to competitive advantage. Global market share becomes even more important to capturing the necessary volume to be cost competitive.

As capital increasingly replaces labor in the manufacturing process, more of a manufacturer's costs are fixed, further intensifying the pressure for volume in many industries. In these industries the competitive advantage goes to those companies with the ability and willingness to employ capital in pursuit of marketplace superiority. Also, in countries such as Germany, Japan, Korea, and China, social mores and legal restrictions on layoffs, result in employees becoming largely a fixed cost, adding to the drive for sales volume.

At the same time as these pressures for volume are building, the customer has become more demanding and knowledgeable. This sophistication has resulted in an emphasis on quality and functionality throughout the developed world. The movement to lean manufacturing, which simultaneously reduces costs and increases quality, enables leading-edge manufacturers to service these customer demands well. Consequently, companies must compete rigorously on both cost and product features to gain the necessary volume and market share to reap global scale and scope economies.[4]

As firms increasingly compete globally for brand recognition, evidence indicates that brand is becoming ever more important to competitiveness. However, creating and maintaining global brand loyalty is expensive. Therefore, scale is necessary to amortize this cost across unit volume.

Technical knowledge is proliferating rapidly, leading to increased complexity. Because this knowledge quickly diffuses throughout the world, it is not proprietary for long. As technology swiftly moves into the hands of international competitors, the traditional source of competitive advantage on which many American companies have relied—the technological differentiation of their products—is no longer as sustainable as it was in the past. International competitors have been able to offer high-quality, attractively priced products using the latest technology. The race to create new knowledge gains speed daily. Therefore the pace at which a company can learn and bring knowledge to the market becomes increasingly critical. The level of expenditures on research and development—and particularly on operating-process improvements—becomes especially important. As investment in research and development increases, it becomes more of a fixed cost of competing globally. This further enhances the pressure for scale economies.[5]

These sources of competitive advantage reflect a company's willingness to invest and its ability to create knowledge rapidly. Both of these are heavily influenced by corporate purpose.

America's Competitiveness

The ultimate test of competitiveness, as the President's Commission on Industrial Competitiveness defined it, is the ability, "under free and fair conditions, [to] produce goods and services that meet the test of international markets while simultaneously maintaining or expanding the real incomes of its citizens."[6] America receives a "B-" on this test.

The Stagnating Ability to Increase Citizens' Incomes

The average real hourly earnings of American nonagricultural workers were actually lower in 2000 than in 1969. Adding the employers' contributions to social security and other private benefits, nonfarm employees' real compensation per hour increased less than 0.8 percent per year over this thirty-one-year period. Although job creation has been impressive, it has been characterized by a shift away from higher-wage manufacturing jobs to lower-paying service jobs. Although Americans still enjoy the highest living standards in the world, their living standards have been improving less quickly than the other G-7 countries. As a result, to improve their financial well-being, many families must work longer hours or become two-income households. Even so, the real median money income of American families grew less than 1 percent per year from 1980 to 1999.

In addition, income disparity is increasing—not only in terms of earned income, but also in terms of wealth. From 1983 to 1998, the richest 1 percent of Americans received 53 percent of the total gain in marketable net worth (marketable assets less debt), and the top 20 percent received 91 percent of the total growth in marketable wealth. The remaining 80 percent of the American population was left with only 9 percent of the marketable wealth increase during this period of economic boom.[7]

This stagnation occurred despite prodigious levels of borrowing against the future in the form of gaping governmental budget deficits and substantial increases in private sector debt. Unfortunately, the growing indebtedness has not proportionately increased investments in the future. Instead, the nation's infrastructure has eroded, and much of its capital stock has aged. A large portion of the increase in corporate indebtedness has gone to fund leveraged buyouts or other forms of financial restructuring rather than to finance productive investments in people, plant, and technology.

America's Performance in International Trade

America's problems with competitiveness go beyond its citizens' stagnating real incomes to include large and growing merchandise trade deficits and a languishing share of world trade. Throughout this century until 1971, the country had a positive trade balance. However, large trade deficits became commonplace after 1980. From that year through 2000, its merchandise trade deficit totaled $3.1 trillion. The deficit accelerated through the 1990s, exceeding a staggering $1.0 trillion from 1998 through 2000 alone.

America's share of the world export market eroded significantly from 1950 until the 1987 Plaza Accord produced a sizable depreciation of the dollar, which halted the decline. In the early 1980s—a time when an ever-increasing proportion of the world's manufacturing output was being exported—America's share of the international export market for manufactured goods fell precipitously from 14.1 percent in 1980 to 9.9 percent in 1985. Although America's share of manufactured exports stabilized at around 12 percent in the 1990s, it has yet to prove its ability to regain its 1980 level.

In many key industries critical to the nation's future prosperity (such as aerospace, computer components and peripherals, machine tools and robotics, and scientific and precision equipment), the country's market share continued to erode.[8] From 1985 to 1997, the country's share of world production in aerospace fell from 64.5 percent to 50.7 percent, and its share of the production of communication equipment declined from 28.2 percent to 22.8 percent. In office and computing machinery, although America's share of world production fell from 35.2 percent to 27.3 percent from 1985 to 1991, the dramatic domestic boom in technology investment raised its share to 47.3 percent by 1997. However, the share of exports in this industry fell from 26.2 percent to 17.1 percent over this thirteen-year period. Similarly in drugs and medicines, although the share of world production increased during this time, the share of the export market decreased.

Asian countries experienced steady gains in market share from 1980 to 1997. Taking the high-tech industries of aerospace, office and computing equipment, communications equipment, and drugs and medicines as a whole, Japan's share of world production increased by two percentage points during this period, China's share went from 1.8 percent to 7.2 percent, and South Korea's, Taiwan's, and Singapore's combined share went from 2.7 percent to 8.0 percent.[9]

The U.S. bilateral trade with Japan provides a particularly troubling indication of American competitiveness. The U.S. trade deficit with Japan rose from $9.9 billion in 1980 to $81.3 billion in 2000. The industry-by-industry distribution of the trade surpluses and deficits is even more alarming. Many of the largest U.S. surpluses were in low-tech industries such as food, beverages, tobacco, and raw materials, whereas Japan's surpluses were in the high-tech areas of automobiles, computer peripherals, semiconductors, telecommunications equipment, consumer electronics, and electrical machinery.[10]

The export of services presents a brighter picture for the United States.

The nominal value of service exports tripled during the 1980s and doubled again in the 1990s.[11] America is the leading exporter of commercial services, with a 19.3 percent share of world exports in 2000. However, despite this impressive growth, services still account for only a little over one quarter of the country's total exports. Also, the service exports are heavily concentrated in two related industries—tourism and transportation—which together accounted for 45 percent of all services exported in 2000.

Unfortunately services have not experienced the significant increases in productivity necessary to fuel increased standards of living. In fact, the productivity of the services sector has shown only marginal improvement since 1979.[12] This frustrating lack of productivity improvement highlights the manufacturing sector's continued importance to raising the nation's standard of living.

America's Performance Under the New Competitive Realities

America's international competitiveness in this hypercompetitive environment is dependent on a variety of factors, including the productivity of the workforce, the technological strength of its people, the differences in labor costs, and the magnitude, efficiency, and effectiveness of investments in plant, equipment, and research and development. Corporate purpose affects each of these areas by influencing the nature of corporate goals, management's proclivity to invest, and the motivation of employees.

An examination of the source of the threat to the United States' relative competitive prowess leads to an appreciation of the power and consequences of contrasting purposes. In evaluating today's competitive realities, it is important to keep in mind that Japanese, Korean, and German companies achieved their impressive competitive accomplishments of the last four decades despite formidable obstacles at home. The industrial base of each country was decimated by war. Except for their people, Japan and Korea have no natural resources upon which to build a competitive advantage, and Germany has few. In Japan and Korea, industry continues to carry the burden of management processes that are inefficient, highly bureaucratic, and paternalistic—and, particularly in Korea, often autocratic. Furthermore, Japanese government policies support archaic practices that protect inefficient businesses and sap competition. In Germany, the government's welfare-state policies have limited managerial discretion and imposed high labor costs on companies. Yet despite these burdens, their industries have grown impressively over the last three decades. This performance is a tribute to the potential realized when the human spirit is dedicated to purposes people deem worthwhile.

Productivity. Improving productivity faster than rivals do is essential to maintaining a competitive cost structure. Although American workers remain the most productive workers in the world, their lead has eroded. Increases in U.S. productivity have lagged much of the developed world until the mid-1990s. From 1974 until 1989, Germany's and Korea's average annual labor productivity held fairly steady at 2.3 percent and 6.0 percent, respectively, while Japan's productivity accelerated during the late 1980s to an average annual level of 3.7 percent from 1985 until 1989, up from 2.7 percent between 1974 and 1984. U.S. productivity during this period followed a pattern similar to Japan's, although at lower levels, rising from an average annual rate of 1.3 percent from 1974 until 1984 to 2.4 percent from 1985 until 1989. After receding to 1.8 percent from 1990 to 1995, the average annual U.S. productivity accelerated to 2.5 percent from 1996 until 2001, while Japanese, Korean, and German productivity decreased from earlier levels.[13]

Looking at the manufacturing sector alone presents a somewhat brighter picture. From 1987 to 1998, U.S. manufacturing productivity grew 3.1 percent, whereas Japan's productivity increased 3.8 percent per year and Germany's 3.0 percent per year. U.S. manufacturing productivity increased sharply from 1996 through 1999, growing at an average annual rate of 4.4 percent compared with 3.2 percent and 2.1 percent for Japan and Germany, respectively. This led some economists to declare an era of a "New Economy." However, Robert Gordon, professor of economics at Northwestern University and a leading authority on productivity, calculates that much of America's productivity increase from 1995 to 1999 was attributed to an astounding 41.7 percent increase in computer-manufacturing productivity. He concludes, "the productivity performance of the manufacturing sector of the United States economy since 1995 has been abysmal rather than admirable. Not only has productivity growth in non-durable manufacturing *decelerated* in 1995–99 compared to 1972–95, but productivity growth in durable manufacturing stripped of computers has *decelerated even more.*"[14]

Over the last two decades of the twentieth century, America's productivity growth was adversely affected by a confluence of forces: inadequate levels of investment, slower technological progress, an end to the easy productivity gains from the transformation of farm jobs into industrial ones, the increase in government regulation (particularly those requiring nonproductive investments to protect the environment), and the increasing proportion of the workforce in service and other non-blue-collar jobs.[15] "New economy" or not, one thing is clear: the competitive forces that have reduced employment in manufacturing have consequently lessened this sector's ability to contribute to the higher overall productivity necessary to raise the nation's standard of living and enhance its international competitiveness.

Productivity and the Changing American Workforce. The nature of the American workforce has changed significantly over the last century. Whereas the percentage of those working in agriculture fell to less than half of the workforce in the 1880s, manufacturing peaked at 37 percent of civilian employment in 1946, only to fall precipitously to 22 percent in 1980, 18 percent in 1990, and 14.7 percent in 2000. Those working in service jobs have made up more than half of the workforce since the late 1920s and rose to three-quarters in 2000. A similar growth in service jobs has taken place among America's major international competitors. However, there are notable differences in the pattern. The percentage of the labor force employed in manufacturing also *increased* in all major Asian economies from 1960 to the early 1990s. Over this period, German manufacturing jobs remained high as well, making up approximately a third of total employment throughout the 1980s, but after reunification fell to a quarter of total employment in 2000.

Because of the strength of the service sector, the ability of the U.S. economy to create jobs outstripped that of its major trading partners. From 1980 to 2000 the United States created 36.4 million jobs, whereas Japan and Germany (adjusted for reunification) created only 9.8 million and 1.1 million jobs, respectively. In the 1990s, services generated a net 20.7 million new American jobs, whereas the rest of the economy lost 4.5 million jobs.

The source of new jobs in the United States has shifted away from large corporations to small businesses. Although the sales of the *Fortune* 500 companies accounted for approximately 40 percent of the gross national product in 1991, they provided only 10.9 percent of the nonfarm jobs, down from 18 percent at their employment peak in 1979.[16] Small companies have been the sources of the majority of new jobs created since 1980, and the Small Business Administration predicts that small businesses will create about two-thirds of all new jobs between 1990 and 2005. In the late 1990s, these firms accounted for 63 percent of America's exported products and generated more than half of GDP.[17]

The success of American small business results in part from one of its hallmarks: the business's owners are also its managers, and these owner-managers assume responsibility for the economic and moral performance of their organizations. In many cases, this creates customer-focused companies with a keen sense of responsibility to their employees.

Investment. Historically the level of fixed capital investment in the United States has trailed that of its major trading partners, with the exception of the United Kingdom. For example, from 1986 to 1995, America's real growth in business sector capital stock was half that of Japan.[18] In 1998 the United States' gross fixed capital formation as a percent of GDP was 19.2 percent, compared with Japan's, Korea's, and Germany's 26.8 percent, 29.8 percent, and 21.3 percent, respectively.[19] The U.S. nonresidential fixed business investment as a percent of GDP fell steadily since the 1970s, declining from 12.9 percent in 1980 to a low of 9.9 percent in 1992, before the investment boom in information and communication technologies in the late 1990s created a rebound to 13.1 percent in 2000.

RCA's plight in the television industry provides a prime example of the increased importance of capital investment and global scale economies to sustained competitiveness. The French government through Thompson now owns RCA, the technological leader in the early days of television. Prior to the rise of international competition in the television industry, RCA used its innovativeness, brand strength, and willingness to cut prices to lead the American industry. Rather than compete overseas, the company licensed its technology, receiving over $130 million in royalties by the mid-1980s. However, Japanese competitors used this technology and spearheaded the use of integrated circuits in televisions—a technological change that fundamentally altered the competitive structure of the industry—to eventually dominate the industry.

Integrated circuits increased reliability, reduced the number of components, and cut the labor content of a television. As the customer became aware that the reliability of all brands was improved, price became increasingly more important to the buying decision. The traditional barriers to entry into the United States market began to crumble. Reliability meant that the service network was less important. The weakening of the power of brands meant that marketing and distribution was also less important. The benefits from scale in manufacturing and in R&D, particularly process improvements, became critical cost drivers.

At this point the story takes a strange turn. American manufacturers, such as RCA, saw the inroads the Japanese sets were making in the U.S. market and concluded the reason was the low prices of Japanese sets derived from Japan's labor cost advantage. Given this appraisal, the logical thing to do was to move manufacturing offshore to countries with lower labor costs. This the American companies did.

Oddly, though, at this same time the Japanese began moving their manufacturing to America. Why? The Japanese saw their advantage not as cheaper labor but as their willingness to make heavy investments in capital and people to improve both manufacturing processes and the product. The process and product improvements were skillfully integrated. Fully solid-state sets required fewer parts, and the new integrated circuit technology allowed automatic insertion. By the late 1980s, labor was less than 10 percent of the costs of assembling a television. While the United States was seeking lower labor costs to use with the old manufacturing technology, the Japanese were building innovative plants in the U.S. market that substantially reduced labor costs. By locating manufacturing in the United States, transportation costs and tariffs were reduced. The Japanese built their U.S. position initially in low-cost, high-quality televisions by pricing aggressively and selling through private-label channels. Later they moved to sell their own brand based on an image of quality and reliability. In addition, because the Japanese competed globally, they gained important economies of scale in manufacturing and research and development. The failure of the U.S. industry to compete globally and to make the heavy investments in process and product technology gave the Japanese companies a lead that the Americans never overcame. With the 1995 sale of Zenith to Korea's Goldstar, America no longer had a competitor in the television industry.

The Investment in Knowledge. Learning from its bitter competitive experiences of the 1980s, the United States has moved to strengthen its world leadership in the investment in knowledge (defined as public and private spending on higher education, R&D, and software). From 1991 to 1998 the U.S. average annual investment in knowledge grew 3.9 percent. By 1998 its investment in knowledge represented 6.0 percent of GDP, exceeding the 4.7 percent, 5.2 percent, and 4.2 percent in Japan, Korea, and Germany, respectively, and 3.6 percent for the European Union.[20]

Although the United States rightfully takes pride in its technological prowess as a source of competitive advantage, the historical pattern of research and development expenditures actually presents a somewhat mixed picture. Japan exceeds the United States in the numbers of researchers per capita. Japan and Germany also have traditionally had higher nondefense R&D expenditures as a percent of GDP than the United States, and Japan's lead is particularly striking at 3.0 percent of GDP in 1998 versus 2.2 percent for the United States. Across countries the source of funding, the proportion of expenditures allocated to applied research, and the growth in spending differ significantly. In the late 1980s, contrary to popular perception, the Japanese government provided funding for only approximately 11 percent of all R&D expenditures. By contrast the United States government provided funding for nearly half of all U.S. expenditures in the 1980s, although percentage of federal funding declined throughout the 1980s and 1990s, falling to 26 percent by 2000.[21] Most significantly, Japan allocates a substantially higher portion of its R&D expenditures to applied research than does the United States. Coupled with a high net technology-transfer inflow, Japan is able to access American basic research and bring commercial products to market faster through its commitment to applied research.

Although the absolute level of the U.S. federal government's funding of research has increased substantially since the mid-1950s, its portion of both applied research and development expenditures has been in decline since the 1960s, and the federal share of basic research funding has declined since the late 1970s. Federally funded research and development fell from 1.83 percent of GDP in 1965 to only 0.7 percent in 2000. This reflects an average 1.2 percent per year decline in federal funding for R&D in real terms from 1988 to 2000. Although the real level of government funding for applied research has remained approximately the same since 1984, by 2000 government funding for development had declined 37 percent from its peak in 1987.

Private-sector spending has picked up the slack caused by the reduction in government funding, rising from half of total R&D in 1985 to 68 percent in 2000. As a result, in the 1990s total expenditures grew at a compound rate of 4.9 percent for basic research, 2.4 percent for applied research, and 3.7 percent for development.

The pattern of patent applications provides a less comforting picture. Japan outstrips the leading industrialized countries in new patents.[22] From 1985 to 1998, 46 percent of all U.S. patents were granted to inventors of foreign origin, and those of Japanese origin alone were 21 percent of the total. By 1988, five Japanese companies were among the top ten manufacturers receiving patents. Four of them were in the top five recipients. A decade earlier only one Japanese company, Hitachi, was among the top ten, ranking eighth.[23] By 1998 six of the top ten recipients of U.S. patents were Japanese companies and one (Samsung Electronics) was Korean.

However, the growth of Japanese research has not been met by a significant increase in the export of Japanese technology. To the contrary, Japan remains a large net importer of technology as reflected by trends in patent and other technological trade. Strategically, the Japanese seek to import cutting-edge product technology to which they can apply their superiority in manufacturing process technology. In support of this strategy, in the late 1980s the percent of total R & D expenditures devoted to manufacturing processes in Japan was twice that of the United States.[24]

The United States continues to be the major exporter of technology to the world. In 1990, the United States received $16.6 billion from international patent and license transactions—a figure that doubled by 1998. Meanwhile, Japan, the world's largest importer of technology, expended $6.0 billion on patents and licenses in 1990 but received only $2.5 billion for its technology transfers.[25] From 1988 through 2000, Japanese royalty and license payments to American firms for the use of their inventions and processes tripled to $6.7 billion, whereas the American firms' royalties and license fees for Japanese technology rose from less than $1.0 billion per year to $3.7 billion.[26]

According to the National Science Foundation, these differences have resulted in Japanese dominance of manufacturing and engineering technology in many industries and near-parity with the United States in advanced development. Only in basic research does the United States retain clear overall leadership.

Any company's—and in aggregate, any country's—ability to achieve and maintain technological leadership is dependent on its ability to create knowledge of greater value and with greater speed than its competitors. As we have seen in the early chapters, this ability directly reflects the commitment of its people and the meaning they find in their work, the competitive viability of its strategy, management's willingness to commit capital, and the effectiveness of its way of managing—each of which is heavily influenced by the corporate purpose.

Savings. Savings take on their competitive importance because they tend to be "sticky," staying in the country of origin (thereby affecting the availability and cost of capital). In fact, the correlation of savings with investment and economic growth has been striking across countries.[27] If inadequate domestic levels of savings force companies to turn to offshore sources of capital, the result can be instability and increased risk, since foreign capital tends to be "hot"—moving around the globe in response to short-term events.

A declining savings rate has dampened investment in the United States. From 1950 to 1980, Americans saved between 7 percent and a little less than 11 percent of their disposable personal income annually. However, during the 1980s, the savings rate began a precipitous decline, falling to only 1.0 percent in 2000. This compared quite unfavorably with a personal savings rates of the United States' major international competitors (such as those from Japan, Germany, Korea, and China). For most of the 1990s, Japan's and Germany's savings rates averaged between 12 and 13 percent.

The United States' federal budget deficit, which represents dissavings, compounded the problems created by the low personal savings rate. From 1980 to 1998, the cumulative federal deficit exceeded $3.0 trillion. This large budget deficit, combined with an adverse balance of international trade and a meager savings rate, produced a cumulative current account deficit in U.S. international transactions of $2,461 billion from 1982 until 2000. The current account deficit for 2000 alone was $444 billion, the highest level on record. The need to attract and retain foreign capital of this magnitude required the Federal Reserve to maintain interest rates at high levels compared with those of many of our strongest trading partners. This adversely affected the availability and cost of capital for American businesses. In addition, the interest and dividend payments on this capital go to foreign citizens instead of to Americans, limiting the growth of domestic income and living standards. As a consequence of becoming a net debtor nation, our national economic sovereignty has been compromised. For example, in 1997, in retaliation for U.S. pressures on trade, the Japanese government threatened to push up U.S. interest rates by a wholesale sell-off of U.S. treasury bills.

Cost of Capital. During the 1970s and 1980s, the United States suffered from a cost of capital disadvantage relative to Japan and Germany. Lower real interest rates, higher financial leverage, and particularly in the case of Japan, a higher price/earnings ratio combined to produce Japan's and Germany's lower capital costs. The gap began to narrow in the late 1980s because of declining levels of financial leverage in Japan and Germany, a narrowing of real interest rate differentials, a reduction of Japanese price/earnings ratios, and an increase in American stock prices.[28]

Differences in the cost of capital can significantly affect investment decisions. They affect the comparative returns required on everything from equipment investments to research and development projects. Higher required returns mean that fewer projects meet the return standards. The pernicious competitive effects of cost of capital differences are clear. Other things being equal, companies with the ability and willingness to undertake lower-return investments have a substantial competitive advantage over companies requiring higher returns.

In theory the increasingly efficient global capital markets should lead to equal availability, interest rates, and risk-adjusted cost of equity capital throughout the world. But this has not happened. Just as risk-adjusted returns can differ among businesses within the United States, they can differ even more so internationally. The reasons for this phenomenon, which confounds many economists, go beyond government policies that restrict the free flow of capital. Explanations can be found in differences in corporate purposes and institutional relationships that result in a large portion of savings staying in the home country. If a company's purpose is to serve the national interest, it will only reluctantly move activity offshore, other than sales and marketing. Domestic jobs, exports, and development of the country's technological competence become dominant goals. Similarly, financial institutions with nationalistic values will be hesitant to lend abroad except to further the economic interests of domestic companies.

The pattern of stock ownership and the nature of the relationship between manufacturers and the financial institutions providing their capital can profoundly affect the level of financial leverage common in a country, the level of expected returns on equity holdings, the type of pressures exerted on management by the capital markets, and the proclivity of capital to stay at home. For many foreign manufacturers, their major shareholders are also their major lenders or industrial concerns that have commercial ties with them. Since debt is the main source of external capital, these lenders tend to focus on their borrowers' growth as being in their best interest—it increases the demand for loans and other financial services. For industrial owners, their benefits are derived from increased business dealings generated by growth, not from direct financial returns on their investment. Besides, they have little intention of selling their position in these manufacturers, and thus unrealized capital gains have little importance. Risk is reduced and collateral business benefits increased by the closeness of these relationships. Consequently, capital tends to stay close to home.

The inability of capital to move fluidly across national boundaries is evidenced by the high correlation between savings and investment within individual countries. Martin Feldstein, a Harvard professor and former chairman of the President's Council of Economic Advisors, observes, "Capital may be free to move internationally, but its owners and managers prefer to keep almost all of each nation's savings at home. . . . Much of the capital that does move internationally is pursuing temporary gains and shifts quickly as conditions change. The patient money that will support sustained cross-border capital flows is surprisingly scarce."[29]

Yet, with the increasing fluidity of world capital markets, the underinvestment in applied research and plant and equipment cannot solely be attributed to a lower savings rate. Many American managers are choosing not to fully pursue the funds available in the world markets. Why? The answer rests in large part with differences in corporate purpose, which motivate managers in countries such as Japan, Germany, and Korea to overinvest or for American managers to underinvest, depending on one's perspective.

Investments in People. As countries such as Germany, Japan, and Korea have demonstrated, economic strength is determined by the quality of a country's people—their skills, dedication to hard work, creativity, and commitment. None of these countries had the benefit of plentiful natural resources. Recognizing that their people were their prime resources, they placed a premium on educating them for the demands of the modern technological age and have made a national commitment to technological advancement. This training is seen as key to generating the productivity and quality on which their competitive advantage and future prosperity depend. Hedrick Smith has observed that both Germany and Japan "see each young person's skills as a social asset to be developed for the common good. . . . Each teenager's growth is too important to society to be left just to the individual."[30]

The Japanese and Korean educational systems are both heavily influenced by Confucian principles that emphasize the importance of learning and place a premium on *wa*, or harmony. Elementary education emphasizes socialization, interdependence, and mutual obligation. Although Koreans tend to be more individualistic than Japanese, they both value harmony and teamwork. Both countries' educational systems emphasize math and applied sciences, whether a student is college bound or enters the workforce after high school. In Korea a system of vocational training institutes and technical high schools prepare youths for factory jobs. In both countries, one's academic performance and credentials define social status and opportunity. In Japan's stratified society, high school performance significantly determines one's job and thus future life.

The Japanese school year is 240 days long, and Germany's is 230 days long, whereas in the United States it is only 180 days long. The consequence is that by the time they graduate from high school, Japanese students have been in school the equivalent of four more years than their American counterparts. This means that most Japanese high school students—those destined for blue-collar jobs as well as those destined for college—have the equivalent of American college-level training in math and sciences. For example, most have taken calculus. Given the technological requirements of the modern manufacturing facility with its numerically controlled machinery and team decision making, this knowledge gives the Japanese workforce a decided advantage. As American sociologist and Japanese scholar Thomas Rohlen concluded in his study of Japanese education, "The greatest accomplishment of Japanese primary and secondary education lies . . . in its generation of such a high average level of capability."[31]

Although Japanese companies receive graduates with a sound basic education and invest heavily in training and developing them, Germany expects their new hires to come already trained. The training takes place in a two-track educational system. At age sixteen, students are administered tough exams that channel about two-thirds of them into rigorous apprenticeship programs that typically last three years. The other third are given college-preparation education. The apprenticeship program has deep historical roots in Germany, dating back to the medieval guild system, in which master craftsmen would take on apprentices. As a result of the rigorous apprenticeship program, German students enter blue-collar jobs skilled and ready to work, with little additional training required by the company that hires them. In addition, many German firms run apprenticeship programs for white-collar professionals. These apprenticeship programs are estimated to cost German industry approximately $12 billion per year—a significant investment that indicates the importance placed on the programs.[32]

The results are impressive. Korea's literacy rate of nearly 98 percent is one of the highest in the world. On international math and science proficiency tests, American thirteen-year-olds score significantly below their Asian and European counterparts. For example, on the math test in the 1990s, Koreans and Taiwanese students scored 73, French students scored 64, and Americans lagged behind at 54. Similarly, on the science test Koreans scored 78, Taiwanese 76, the French 69, and U.S. students trailed at 67.[33]

The heavy investment that German, Japanese, and Korean firms make in the development of their personnel at all levels contrasts sharply with the American experience. In the 1980s American companies spent about $30 million per year on the training and development of their employees. However, two-thirds of these expenditures went to college-educated employees, whereas the rest of the workforce received only about $10 million in training. In addition, the training was heavily concentrated. Less than 1 percent of American companies accounted for 90 percent of the expenditures.[34]

Although education and skill levels of employees are important—an edge that Germany, Japan, and Korea enjoy—of equal importance in developed countries are the motivation of the employees and the equipment and processes they are given to do their jobs. Because of the value placed on employees, the investment made in their education, and the security of their jobs, employees in these countries have a greater commitment to their companies than do most American employees. Too many Americans believe senior managers consider them expendable cogs in the wheels of industry. Widespread corporate downsizing only reinforces this view.

The Shape of Competition in the Twenty-first Century

The forces determining competitiveness will continue to evolve. In fact, unrelenting change will be a hallmark of the twenty-first century. The future direction of change will be based on a confluence of fundamental demographic, social, and economic forces—forces that affect the corporation's relationship with its employees, customers, and society. The transformation will be accelerated by the action of competitors—predominantly foreign—who view the rules of the competitive game quite differently than do their American counterparts. Although the future shape of the global competitive threat cannot be precisely predicted, the essence of possible future states of competition can be captured in three different scenarios.

The first scenario depicts an unabated intensity of competitive pressures from those who are currently our most formidable economic adversaries. Companies from countries such as Japan, Germany, and Korea will continue to pursue strategies driven by ultimate ends that are manifested in objectives of growth rather than profit maximization. They will persist in making what to American eyes seem to be unwise investments—unwise because they promise low returns by American standards. Unfortunately for U.S. companies, these investments to capture market share, to increase productivity and quality, to develop people, and to enhance products at a pace that reduces near-term profitability are precisely the actions that increase competitiveness.

The second scenario offers more hope for American business. In essence it levels the competitive playing field by assuming that our principal foreign competitors will evolve to compete much like we do. In this scenario the industrialized societies in Asia and Europe—shaken by the Asia crisis of the late 1990s—will adopt relationships among corporations and institutional shareholders, such as banks and other corporations, resembling the more contentious relationships in the United States today. Self-interested consumerism will be on the rise. The result would be an erosion of savings—and thus the loss of plentiful low-cost capital for investment—and mounting pressure to increase returns to shareholders.

Parenthetically, if this occurs, the internal factors that have driven the intense competitiveness of the latter part of the twentieth century will decline. Humankind will pay a heavy price. The meaning found in work will diminish, and the pace of material progress will slacken appreciably. There can be little argument that the aggressive competition between American, Asian, and European companies has provided a worldwide stimulus to innovation and productivity improvements far beyond the levels that would have been achieved otherwise.

Regardless of what happens in these Asian and European countries, the third scenario sees a new set of competitors emerging. China, Eastern Europe, and possibly Russia, India, Indonesia, and other Asian countries will eventually overcome their internal barriers to becoming modern market-based economies and world-class competitors. Demographics are on their side. The question is one of time and the form their economic systems will take. Undoubtedly this will occur first in selected industries and subsequently expand into a broad range of businesses. But given their socialist heritage, corporate policies in these massive countries are likely to be heavily shaped by social concerns. Examples abound, such as when China faced labor unrest in the mid-1990s, and the government, to defuse the unrest, required banks to increase lending to the affected companies so that they could raise wages.

The consequence will be yet another wave of competition driven by forces that subordinate returns on investment to the aggressive pursuit of growth intended to serve national and social needs. Profits will become increasingly important but will clearly remain a means to these other ends.

The future reality will probably reflect elements of each of these three scenarios. However, although the institutional relationships and cultural values in countries like Germany, Japan, and Korea will inevitably evolve, it is unlikely that this will bring them to a state similar to the United States today. For the foreseeable future, they will retain many of their distinctive characteristics although modified by the forces of social evolution.

Therefore, while America has been struggling to cope with the three consecutive waves of competition from Europe and Asia—beginning first with Germany in the 1960s, Japan in the 1970s, and then the smaller Asian tigers in the 1980s—it faces the prospect of yet another wave with companies driven by visions of corporate purpose even more removed from its own. Consequently, at the dawn of the triumph of market-based capitalism over communism, it is critical that American companies not become smug and complacent. The fall of communism means that new market-based economies will spawn competitors whose views of competition are shaped by deeply embedded socially oriented values. A battle for supremacy is shaping up between product-market-oriented free economies and capital-market-oriented free economies.

The new world economic order is still in the making.

9   **America's Rivals**
     Changing the Rules of Competition

Corporate leaders from America, Europe, and Asia are each guided by different sets of ideas, beliefs, and assumptions derived from their unique national histories and embedded in the social fabric of their countries. These varying ideologies compete in today's global marketplace, shaping individual companies' purposes, influencing the decisions of corporate leaders, and defining their firm's relationships with capital-market institutions. To fully appreciate the long-term strategic significance of America's dominant shareholder-focused ideology of corporate purpose, the competitive consequences of these competing ideologies must be understood.

The competitive forces at work are deep and intense. This battle of ideologies is creating a new synthesis. This synthesis will be forged from the characteristics of each ideology that provide the best promise to be effective across national boundaries, to inspire people, and to guide strategic decisions to create sustained knowledge-based competitive advantages. The global corporate ideology of the future will be neither American shareholder capitalism as currently conceived or nation-centered communitarianism, as in Japan, Germany, and Korea. Both are parochial and will not stand the test of global acceptance. The new global ideology will combine the best elements of the major ideologies to form a new, more competitive whole.

To understand the strength and nature of the forces at work in forging this new synthesis, the ideology and management philosophies related to corporate purpose in Japan, Korea, and Germany will be examined. Each of these countries achieved outstanding long-term competitive performance and, consequently, experienced its own "economic miracle," and then hardships in the 1990s. Each represents a different source of global competition: western Europe, established Asia, and the newly developed Asian "tigers." In addition, because of cultural and historical similarities, Korea provides a glimpse of the form of market-based economy likely to evolve in China over the long term.

A company's corporate purpose usually reflects its home country's dominant ideology. Thus an understanding of the role of corporate purpose is furthered by an appreciation of the concept of ideology. Harvard Business School professor George C. Lodge provides a useful definition of a nation's ideology:

> [Ideology is] a set of beliefs and assumptions about values that the nation holds to justify and make legitimate the actions and purposes of its institutions. . . . Ideology is the collection of ideas that a community uses to make values explicit in some relevant context. The term "values" in this definition refers to timeless, universal, noncontroversial notions that virtually every community everywhere has always cherished: survival, for example, or justice, economy, self-fulfillment or self-respect. The phrase "relevant context" is the collection of phenomena, facts, events, insights, institutions, and forces that affect the community from within and from without: the surrounding reality, the actual environment. Ideology connects the two: values and relevant context.[1]

Ideology (the unconscious pattern of ideas, assumptions, and beliefs that shape our actions) and "rationalization" (the conscious development of a system of ideas to make one's actions logical and consistent within the "relevant context") are close in meaning. The ideology of shareholder wealth maximization has been used by many American managers and academics to rationalize—and simplify—managers' responsibilities and to justify their sometimes self-serving behavior. By focusing primarily on one constituent's needs, managers can rationalize their prerogatives and independence to act in ways that adversely affect other constituents. However, in the process, managers becomes less accountable for their actions. When asked to justify a controversial act, such as corporate downsizing, they can respond, "The shareholders made us do it!" At one level this is an unconscious reaction in defense of the capitalist system. To these managers, the capitalist system has become synonymous with the maximization of profits for the benefit of shareholders. This ideology also provides justification for and legitimacy to management's power.

But capitalism has many different forms. What is critical is how these different forms respond to free-market needs. The American view of capitalism has focused on the capital markets for its rationale—thus the purpose of shareholder wealth maximization. The other countries we will review in this chapter orient capitalism more to the product markets, employees, and the national economy. For them, the heart of capitalism is competition in the product markets to achieve communitarian ends. Thus a drama is playing out on the world stage, pitting capital-market-oriented capitalism against communitarian-oriented economies. Some innovative high-performance companies are forging a new product-market-based ideology that blends the best of these twos major ideologies. (Some companies have been at this work for decades.) Since the critical competition takes place in the product markets, not the capital markets, ideologies emphasizing the marketplace should have a competitive advantage. The competitive victory will go to companies with cultures comprising beliefs and values that marshal the knowledge and ingenuity of their people, spawn employee commitment to and identity with the corporate purpose, enhance managers' willingness to wisely deploy significant amounts of capital, and define institutional relationships in ways that support competitive, growth-oriented strategies.

A significant gulf exists between the American practices, on the one hand, and those of Japan, Korea, and continental Europe, particularly Germany, on the other hand. This gulf is deep and is created by fundamental forces. Two factors have particular power: the philosophical underpinnings of the respective cultures that support their distinctive core values, and the differences in the institutional relationships between industrial corporations and capital-market firms. Both of these forces combine to create different views of corporate purpose.

The home country's philosophical foundations shape the values of the managers and the expectations society places on corporations. In a fundamental sense, these underpinnings define the society's beliefs and assumptions about the relationship of human beings to nature, about the essential human character, and about the relationship of people to each other. From these relationships flow the responsibilities that form the society's view of the shareholders' rights and duties. In most market-based economies of the world, the purpose is based on a communitarian ideology that ties the purpose more closely to society as a whole than to one subset of society, such as shareholders.

The relationship between the company and capital-market institutions significantly influences the nature of the external pressures placed on corporate managers for performance and the definition of performance itself. The most dramatic differences resulting from these varying pressures are the relative emphases placed on the product market versus the capital market, and consequently on growth versus return on investment.

In considering the impact of these issues, one needs to distinguish between ideology and management practices. Ideology is very slow to change. It has the potential to last for centuries. On the other hand, practices—such as unfocused diversification, profitless growth, "cronyism" in relationships between enterprises and financial institutions, and opaque financial reporting—can change fairly rapidly. This is particularly true if managers come to view these practices as counter to the prevailing ideology.

Comparative Corporate Purposes

To understand the origin of the values and institutional relationships embedded in the distinctive ideologies of corporate purpose of companies from Germany, Japan, and Korea—who are among America's most formidable global competitors—we need to begin by examining the historical and philosophical roots in each country.

The Heritage of Feudalism

Germany, Japan, and Korea share a common historical trait—they were relatively late to emerge from a feudal society. Bismarck's unification of Germany in 1871 marked the end of the feudalism that still lingered in many principalities. Japan began to shake off the feudal social structure in 1868 with the restoration of the young emperor Meiji after the overthrow of the 268-year rule of the Tokugawa clan. Not until Japan occupied Korea in 1905 did Korea begin to emerge from the feudal structure of the Yi dynasty, which had existed since 1392.

Although feudalism took different historical forms in these countries, they shared some commonalties. The ruling families or clans owned the real property. Subjects had well-defined rights and duties, such as the right to protection, minimal education, and support, and a degree of benevolent governance. But the duties of individuals were stronger than their rights. The foremost duty was to show loyalty to the ruling family. In all endeavors, the individual's interests were clearly subordinated to the "common good" as defined by the ruler. This arrangement provided a rich legacy of values relative to businesses' role in service of society and of the sacrifice of self-interest to achieve common goals. These beliefs provided the foundation for the subsequent evolution of the cultural values related to business in each of these countries.

Business that began during these feudal times had close relations with the government, often acting as government's economic agent—a legacy that remains to this day in each country. Not only were these countries late to industrialize, but also the communitarian values of feudalism linger—the strong role of the state, the paternalism of leaders, and the dominance of community or national interests over the individual.

The combination of being late to industrialize and the strong national commitment proved a powerful motivation. By appealing to the very real need to catch up, national and business leaders were able to unleash considerable individual motivation to benefit the national interest through serving the company's needs.

The Influence of the Confucian Tradition

Confucian ideals and values have heavily influenced the cultures of Japan and Korea. Confucianism is a humanistic philosophy that emphasizes personal virtue. Its central objective is the creation of a cooperative world in which the individual lives in harmony with others and with society, and society is in harmony with the cosmos. Social harmony, the paramount virtue, is born of mutual trust and responsibility. Confucius believed that this harmony is possible only in a hierarchically ordered society characterized by a high level of interdependence among people predicated on mutual benefit. Individual behavior is shaped by principles associated with clearly defined duties and roles. This thinking has two important corollaries. First, society is viewed as an organic whole, rather than a body of separate and distinct individuals; second, the individual's interest is clearly subordinate to the group's and society's interests.[2]

A virtuous Confucian life is life of disciplined duty to others as defined by one's specific role. For example, superiors in a relationship are expected to be righteous and benevolent, whereas subordinates have a duty to be loyal, respectful, obedient, deferential, and submissive. Living according to this code creates a bond of mutually beneficial relationships. Confucius reflected this belief in his response to a question from a follower who asked, "How may one improve one's character and correct one's personal faults?" Confucius replied, "An excellent question. If a man put duty first and success after, will not that improve his character? If he attacks his own failings instead of those of others, will he not remedy his personal faults?"[3] Duty takes precedence over personal interests.

Confucianism also places great importance on learning. Education is a vehicle for internalizing Confucian values in every individual and thus is a vital part of the path to a virtuous life for ruler and subject alike. Learning also provides the key to fulfilling one's role in society, for through education and continual self-improvement one is better equipped to serve the family and community. In contrast to American society, where education is valued in personal terms as a means of upward mobility and a rewarding career, the Asian emphasis on education is to create a life better able to serve others.

From these beliefs, four sets of principles influence the role of business firms and the way they are managed in Japanese and Korean society. First, corporations should act in harmony with society. They are part of, not distinct from, the organic whole. As a result, there exists considerable national loyalty and ability to identify one's work with the community or national welfare. This has proved to be a powerful source of motivation for hard work, dedication, and often sacrifice to serve corporate goals.

Second, the moral priority placed on the subordination of the individual to the collective interests makes individuals more ready to identify with the firm. Viewing themselves as part of a whole, their lives take on meaning in relationship to the whole. Also, the identification with the whole gives rise to skepticism that individualistic behavior is self-serving. The result in Japanese, Korean, and Chinese cultures has been an abiding focus on achieving social harmony and the belief that harmony is possible only if individual interests are subordinated to those of the group, corporation, and society.

Third, the high value on education and learning has made Japanese and Korean organizations fast to absorb new technology. They are willing to listen, learn, and adapt technological ideas from abroad. Their ability to do so is enabled in part by the high level of knowledge and skill present in workers at all levels.

Fourth, two beliefs—that subordinates should give loyal devotion to their superiors and that children must demonstrate filial piety by showing love, respect, and total obedience to their parents—make an individual more accepting of the principles of hierarchy and of his or her submission to collective interests. The priority placed on family duties has also fostered the familism that permeates Korean—as well as Chinese and Taiwanese—society and businesses. Work is for the honor and welfare of the family. Japan defined the priorities in the duties to others differently. Beginning in feudal times, the emphasis was on loyalty to the ruler. Responsibility to the family was subordinated to the ruler. This duty was subsequently transferred to the nation and to the corporations that serve the ends of the state. These beliefs also help explain why traditional paternalistic attitudes and management practices are still widespread in Asian businesses.

American Occupation

Korea and Japan also were strongly influenced by the United States after the Second World War. Since the war, Koreans particularly have been shaping a new culture that combines the communitarian values of their Oriental heritage with the values of individualism received from the West—first through Christian missionaries and then through the American occupation. This new combination has the potential to generate considerable competitive benefit: a focus on individual initiative and creativity in the harmonious service of valued national ends.

Japan

As recently as 1850 the Japanese lived in almost complete isolation from the rest the world. Japan's transition from feudalism to the industrial age was abrupt and direct. Once the door to Japan was opened, the country began to voraciously acquire Western knowledge and technology. In less than a quarter century, the society was peacefully transformed from an agrarian feudal society to a rapidly industrializing and increasingly urban society in which one's ability was becoming more important to success than one's class or clan.

In the early twentieth century, world economic pressures and political unrest at home gave rise to effective military control of the government, which deliberately fed the fires of nationalism. This nationalism plunged Japan into its darkest days, which ended in devastating defeat and foreign occupation. Yet from these ashes Japan rose to challenge the United States as the world's premiere industrial power.

This rapid evolution from feudalism to world economic leadership cannot be understood without understanding the ideology, the core beliefs of which remained common throughout—beliefs in the value of the subordination of the individual to the common good, of strong group loyalties in service of the group interests, of the value of social harmony, and of the interdependence of people, institutions, and nature. These beliefs shape Japanese corporate competitive behavior today.

The Historical Development of Communitarian Values

The Rise of Centralized Feudalism. In the twelfth century, the dissolution of central imperial rule motivated provincial leaders to band together to protect their interests. Centralized authority gave way to a feudal system similar to that in Europe, held together by the personal loyalties among noblemen who commanded their own military forces. Loyalty—above all the loyalty of subject to the lord or to the clan—was the prime virtue in this system.

In 1600, after a prolonged period of conflict among clans, Tokugawa Ieyasu seized power and established himself as shogun (the chief commander of the emperor's army). He and his descendants were to rule Japan for 268 years. He divided the country between his own domain and those of feudal lords (or daimyo), who were chosen from among Tokugawa's sons, his prior vassals, allies, and even a few of his enemies.

Modern Japanese culture began to take shape under the Tokugawa shoguns. The shoguns seized on neo-Confucian values as a means to maintain order and stability in society and to facilitate effective administration, thus preserving the status quo. Confucian values of loyalty, service, responsibility, discipline, training, and craftsmanship served these ends well and strengthened the bond of loyalty between the samurai and their lord and between the lords and the shogun. By spreading Confucianism, the shogun and daimyo sought to turn their samurai's interests more to peaceful pursuits and to provide the samurai with an education that would make them more effective administrators.[4] As the samurai's role evolved from warriors to administrators of the lord's domain, their education in Confucian classics, which began in their youth, became more important.

Over time real power gravitated from the shoguns to the daimyo and eventually to the samurai bureaucrats. The shoguns and many daimyo became largely aristocratic symbols of authority as the samurai bureaucracy increasingly governed through councils and group decisions.[5] The samurai military virtues of loyalty, bravery, honor, and self-discipline merged with the Confucian values to create a strong commitment to loyal service to the common ends. As a result, from the time of the centralized Tokugawa system on, says Japanese scholar and ambassador Edwin Reischauer, "Confucian schools of philosophy dominated thought and Confucian attitudes pervaded society, until the Japanese in the early nineteenth century had become almost as thoroughly Confucian as the Chinese or Koreans."[6]

During the Tokugawa period, a strong ideology emerged centered on the belief in the importance of maintaining social order, harmony, and loyalty to the state. The ultimate end was the benefit of the society as a whole. The individual was not only subordinated to the collective interest, but in contravention of true Confucian principles, loyalty to the state took precedence over family loyalties. The belief in the priority of the state, which was based on the supreme value of the common good, took a much stronger and unquestioned form than in the West. For "unlike Christians, Japanese did not believe in a transcendent being or value system that could serve as a legitimate basis for challenging the power of the state."[7] These beliefs were accompanied by the development of a clear caste system in which the samurai were at the top of the hierarchy, followed by farmers and craftsmen. Merchants, who were viewed with disdain because of their presumed pursuit of self-interest, were seen as more parasitic than productive and were on the bottom.

To protect their country from possible foreign challenge, the shoguns instituted a self-imposed seclusion from the outside world that was to last until the Meiji Restoration. Christianity, which threatened the belief that the individual's ultimate loyalty should be to the state, was viciously stamped out. Overseas Japanese were prevented from returning to Japan for fear they might reinstitute Christianity. To defend against more secular contaminations, Japanese ships were limited to coastal vessels. The isolation allowed the Japanese to become more culturally homogeneous with strongly shared values (unquestioned loyalty, respect for military leadership, and an affinity for group organization) and to develop a strong sense of national identity. However, cut off from the scientific and industrial development of the West, Japan fell far behind technologically.[8]

Internally, facilitated by the integration of the economy, increasing urbanization, and light taxation, the merchant class grew in power. Great merchant houses, predecessors to the large trading companies such as Mitsui, were developed. This increased power was viewed as a threat to feudal stability and to the selfless values of the samurai, who were largely running the country. Consequently, the shoguns and daimyo took actions designed to restrain the merchants' growing power and to prevent the samurai from being corrupted by the desire for wealth and material pleasures.

Ironically, because trade was despised, it was taxed lightly and indirectly. This placed the burden of taxation on agriculture. Consequently, because the incomes of the daimyo and their samurai retainers were tied to agricultural taxes, they fell increasingly in debt to the urban merchants.[9]

The Meiji Restoration. By the 1860s, Japan was ripe for change. The shogunate was financially weakened, the merchant class continued to grow in influence, and the search for a cure of a general social malaise was focusing increased attention on the desirability of returning to a strong emperor.

Against this backdrop came the incursion of foreign powers. This threat brought into question the legitimacy of the shogun's rule, which was justified largely by his role as the protector of the nation, and laid bare Japan's technological backwardness. In 1853, accompanied by one quarter of the U.S. Navy, Commodore Perry arrived in Tokyo Bay to force Japan to open its ports to American shipping. In 1863 a British fleet destroyed Kagoshima in retaliation for the killing of an Englishman in Yokohama. Again in 1864, Western allies leveled the forts protecting the Straits of Shimonoseki after the Japanese fired on one of their ships. These events shook the Tokugawa regime to its foundations. Fearing colonization, a group of lords overthrew the Tokugawa government in 1868 and seized the royal court in the name of the fifteen-year-old emperor, Meiji.

Although "imperial princes, court nobles, and a few feudal lords" were the titular leaders of the imperial regime, a group of "able, young reformers of largely middle or lower samurai rank" were primarily responsible for the formulation and implementation of policies.[10] Similarly, in the development of the large industrial corporations, the positions of power in state-owned companies went to former samurai. For the most part, these former samurai transferred their feudal values—devotion to the common good, loyalty, courage, and self-sacrifice—to their new roles. Because the samurai's values were thought to make them likely to act like servants of the national interest and because the merchant class entrepreneurs were suspected of placing their personal interests above the common good, government aid flowed more heavily to enterprises owned or managed by former samurai. Thus began a pattern of corporate leadership dedicated to the good of Japanese society and of corporate-government cooperation that continues to this day.

The objective of the new government was clear: to better serve the national interests. The challenges were daunting. The first order of business was to avoid colonization by a predatory foreign power. To be successful, the new leaders first needed to institute government reforms that would replace the old feudal systems with effective central control. Second, they needed to rapidly create a modern industrialized economy. With the policies of the new regime, for the first time in Japanese history the idea of progress began to blossom.

The concern with the common good took precedence over individual rights and due process, for which the new leadership showed little concern. Because individual rights fostered self-interested behavior, they were seen as potential threats to the common welfare. Building on Japan's aristocratic tradition, the government set out to develop an elite dedicated to serving the nation. The ablest young men were selected and assiduously prepared for future leadership roles in companies and in the government bureaucracy. Attempts were made to insulate the elite from pressures from commoners, who were thought to have neither the knowledge nor the motivation to put the national interest first. Those who challenged the desired social order were isolated and punished.[11]

The young former samurai immediately set out to reform the government. Remarkably, the feudal lords peacefully gave up their land in return for government bonds. By 1876 the samurai had been stripped of all their special privileges with a minimum of unrest. The successful abolishment of the clans was replaced with a new system of prefectural government. The dismantling of these feudal privileges, coupled with the development of the management elites and the newfound belief in the idea of progress, put Japan on the path to becoming a society in which status depended not on heredity and class but on the education and achievements of the individual.[12]

To modernize the economy, Japan began a campaign to absorb a great deal of Western technical knowledge. Consistent with the high value Confucianism placed on learning, the leaders searched throughout the West for the best ideas and most modern technology. The high value placed on learning also facilitated the assimilation and application of the technology once Japan received it. The rapid modernization of Japanese industry soon outstripped the skills of the craftsmen, and schools could not keep pace with the changing needs, so corporations instituted their own training programs. The workers' receptivity to training reflected the ingrained values of respect for learning and self-cultivation, values predicated on making the workers greater contributors to the welfare of society as a whole.[13]

The Meiji leaders believed that some industries needed government help to get started and to teach them modern techniques. Regional development banks were established to aid industries important to national development. Strategic industries, such as railroads, telegraph, and steel, were started by the government, and other industries by private capital. However, in keeping with the belief that the businesses would grow faster as private enterprises, most of the government-started companies were later sold to private companies. Since the common good of the nation would be served by rapid economic growth, private ownership of corporations was justified directly by its benefit to society, rather than by individual property rights as in the Anglo-American world.[14] The companies' duties to society were strong and clear. Their purpose was, through rapid growth, to help modernize Japan in order to increase the wealth of the nation, to increase its power internationally, and to provide jobs for an increasingly urban population. In a very real sense, these samurai businessmen saw themselves as industrial warriors—the "saviors of Japan" from the "menace of the West."[15] Japanese scholar Ezra Vogel captures the essence of this sense of purpose:

> From the beginning of Meiji the large companies in key sectors had the view that, while it was permissible to make money and while in a certain sense they had the rights of private ownership, they were bounded by and responsible to the government and national interest. . . . The dominant view was that large companies created with government assistance were not privately owned but were operated for national purposes. The company existed for those working in the company rather than for the bankers and stockholders. . . . Because most of the industrial leaders came from the *samurai* class, it is not surprising that they were prepared to think about the public good and that they worked easily with government officials who shared the same values, attitudes, and class background.[16]

The Rise of Militaristic Nationalism. During World War I, most Asian markets were left open to Japanese exploitation, which enabled rapid growth of Japanese industry. However, the end of the war brought new realities. Renewed competition from European industries curtailed Japan's economic growth. Increasing global economic stagnation and the subsequent depression shrunk international trade and gave rise to nationalistic economic policies that swept across the developed world. This put further stress on the Japanese economy, creating significant hardships for farmers and industrial workers. The result was considerable unrest.

Criticism of the perceived increase in the corruption of Japanese society escalated. The negative influences of the West and of the big-business leaders' cozy relationship with the government were particularly targeted.

The independence of the military from civilian control enabled military leaders to leverage the sense of national crisis into action. Against the backdrop of a widespread feeling of being economically bottled up by the rest of the world, many Japanese eyed a military conquest of China and its large market as a solution to their economic woes. Through a series of contrived incidents, the military found the excuse to invade Manchuria in 1931. The result of the successful conquest was an outpouring of national patriotic fervor, which considerably strengthened the hand of the military leaders. The military leadership used this power to force big business to serve the government's objectives. Clashes with Chinese forces in 1937 led to an all-out war with China, adding fuel to the nationalistic flames. Military officers increasingly were placed in governmental positions, and they eventually dominated the government. Thus, in a span of twenty years, a remarkable transformation had taken place. Without the benefit of a charismatic dictator, a "vague change of mood" was transformed into a significant shift in the balance of power between the civilian government and the military, and subsequently in national policies that eventually led to Japan's involvement in World War II.[17]

The American Occupation. The Japanese emerged from World War II deeply disillusioned with their military leadership, a feeling intensified by the hardships of defeat and the awareness that they had been intentionally deceived by the military propaganda used to generate popular support for war. The public's disillusionment and confusion made them receptive to change. The occupation instituted a program of demilitarization, a new constitution that resolved the old constitution's ambiguities (the emperor was now clearly a powerless figurehead), broke up the *zaibatsu* (the powerful "financial clique" of giant holding companies that controlled Japanese industry) and dispossessed the owning families, confiscated much of the remaining wealth, instituted land reforms that banned absentee ownership of agricultural land, developed laws that encouraged the organization of labor unions, and attempted to reform (i.e., Westernize) the educational system.

Postwar Japan. Despite their disillusionment, the Japanese people had not lost their belief in the moral basis of government, or other Confucian values of loyalty, faith in education and hard work, and the importance of trust and mutual benefit in interpersonal relations. The central beliefs that the public good does not conflict with private interests and that enhancing the nation's wealth would benefit all people helped energize their commitment to rebuilding the country. Duty still took priority over individual rights as individuals subordinated their interests to the common good of the country or company. The result was a widespread sacrificial commitment to the rebuilding of Japan.

The supreme authority given to the common good produced a constancy of purpose that enabled Japan to transform itself over the last one-and-a-half centuries without significant internal conflict. Ezra Vogel recounts this surprisingly harmonious change:

> During the course of modernization, *samurai* gave up their own class privileges, clans went along with their own abolition, tightly knit communities accepted amalgamation into larger units, landlords gracefully yielded property during land reform in exchange for little more than token payments. The Japanese have changed loyalties from clan to nation, from village to town, from family to firm. Yet a basic communitarian ideology that acknowledges the importance of cooperating for the collective good has remained firm throughout. . . . All groups and individuals in the society acknowledge—even take for granted—the desirability of working together for national purposes. Since World War II, the preeminent concern has been reviving the country, bringing the fruits of a high standard of living to all citizens and giving the Japanese a place of honor in the world. . . . The view persists that people are subjects of the nation rather than citizens with inalienable rights, because there are rewards for those who cooperate and benefits are withheld from those who do not, and because they believe that the fate of everyone living on the Japanese islands is closely bound together. . . . Individualism is still not a positive value.[18]

The reconstruction of Japan required the import of massive amounts of foreign goods. The only means to do so was to export goods to generate the necessary foreign exchange. By the end of the occupation, the government bureaucrats and leaders of industry had reached a general consensus on a reindustrialization plan that placed priority on the development of export and import-substitution industries.

After the war, corporate purpose and national purpose, which had been intricately intertwined since feudal days, became one. To this day, the strong, deeply ingrained concern of corporate leaders with the national interest—what Robert Christopher calls "a strong tribal consciousness"—makes them preoccupied with growth.[19] Growth, more than returns on investment, is synonymous with national economic success. Expanding international market share in important industries brings honor to Japan.

The tendency to view things holistically gives most Japanese leaders an intuitive sense that the value of the corporation's total value-producing capacity is more important than the wealth received by any one constituent. Therefore the focus is not on shareholder wealth, but on corporate wealth production in all its facets—growth that provides jobs within the company and expands the businesses of suppliers, products and services that provide greater value to customers, and exports and taxes that strengthen the country. This priority was reinforced by the sources of capital during Japan's rapid-growth years, when capital needs greatly outstripped the cash flow of industry. The necessary external capital was raised primarily through debt, which resulted in much higher debt/equity ratios than those of comparable American companies. Since public equity financing was not an important source of funds, the satisfaction of independent shareholders was not a high priority. In addition, today other members of the *kieretsu* (the business groups that grew to replace the *zaibatsu*) own significant amounts of the outstanding shares. Consequently, a manager's performance is judged by how well the interest of the group is served. The other *kieretsu* members are interested in their own expanding business, and therefore in the growth of their affiliates. Lenders have the same motivation. Thus lenders, major shareholders, and managers alike are focused on growth.

With a holistic simplicity, this purpose of serving the national interest through economic growth becomes one with serving the interests of employees. The individual and the corporation share the same ultimate end—the common good. The common good is captured first at the company level. The company is valued as an institution in and of itself and is worthy of eternal survival. By serving the company well, an employee participates in this "eternal good." The company is also a group of people in which each individual participates in a web of relationships and mutual responsibilities. The Japanese are fully aware that the resulting duties may require personal sacrifice. But to a significant degree, a person's self is defined by his or her relationships, not independently of them. An important aspect of this group orientation is the company's responsibility to create and maintain a sense of community among employees. Isamu Yamashita, former chairman of Mitsui Zosen (Mitsui Engineering and Shipbuilding Company), puts this responsibility in historical perspective:

> After World War II, when Japan began reindustrializing, people started to flock to the big industrial complexes, and the old sense of geographic community largely broke down. In a very real way, we in industry spoiled the old community life of Japan, and something had to replace it. So in today's Japan, companies like ours are the new communities, and their managers have a responsibility to create conditions in which people can enjoy a community life. Above all, of course, we managers have the overriding responsibility of keeping the community alive.[20]

The company also serves society—principally Japanese society. This service brings added meaning to the work of employees.

Japanese employment practices reflect the interconnection of corporate purpose, growth objectives, and employee welfare. Japanese companies have long viewed people as their most valuable assets—not an unreasonable assumption for enterprises located on islands devoid of significant natural resources. Therefore they have developed policies to ensure the development and retention of skilled people. The seniority-based compensation system provides monetary rewards determined by length of service. Thus personal financial rewards are deferred to the latter part of an employee's career—an incentive for talented people to stay with one company. The tradition of lifetime employment was a privilege designed to attract the highest caliber of talent in a scarce market, to reduce labor unrest, and to make employees more receptive to change. The greater stability in the workforce has enabled Japanese companies to make substantial investments in the training and development of people. These investments are unlikely to walk out the door. The employment security, which rests on the widely recognized corporate responsibility to employees, reduces resistance to change, thus making the training pay off in more rapid (although incremental) innovation.

These policies also reinforce the corporate focus on the objective of growth. The compensation system based on seniority requires growth to keep costs down. Only through growth can the percentage of younger, lower-paid workers in the workforce be maintained or increased. Slow growth means rising labor costs. Lifetime employment practices convert labor into a fixed cost. Thus, in economic slumps, cutting back production is not financially attractive. The result is pressure to maintain production volume by reducing prices.

These practices have fostered a strong work ethic. Each individual has a responsibility and duty to contribute fully to the achievement of the corporate ends. The cultural importance placed on the group enhances the power of group acceptance and approval. Because personal relationships and mutual loyalty define the self in Japan, the drive to serve shared ends is intensified. Similarly, the social pressures on slackers are strong.

Much has been written in recent years about the "new human beings"—the younger generation of Japanese now entering the workforce with more seemingly individualistic values. Although they generally place increased emphasis on a better quality of life and are frustrated by bureaucratic practices such as the seniority system, which stifles creativity and individual initiative, their complaints are more with management practices than with the core values that are pillars of the Japanese ideology. Experience indicates that within a year or two of entering the workforce most of these "new human beings" behave in general accordance with the traditional values of their older coworkers. Only time will tell whether a more sustained assault on the outmoded management practices will result in lasting change.

Japan's past success in international markets has often been attributed to "Japan Inc."—the collaboration between government and business to create highly competitive, and subsidized, industries. Although the government's direct aid to businesses has been significantly less than most critics think, there is a set of values that underlie the relationship of business and government that facilitate a cooperative association that historically has been highly beneficial to Japanese industry. First, the ends of government and business are common—the welfare of the nation and its people. Second, the government bureaucracy attracts the best and brightest people who are assumed to work selflessly for the national interest. This gives the bureaucracy—ministries such as the Ministry of Finance (MOF, the most powerful ministry in

Japan) and the Ministry of International Trade and Industry (MITI)—a moral authority and a competence that enhance its influence. Elected politicians do not enjoy a similar august public opinion. They are perceived to be driven by self-interest and to be heavily influenced by special interests. The consequence is that the power to control initiatives, such as deregulation, rests more with the bureaucracy than with the prime minister or the diet.

The MOF and MITI have traditionally worked closely with industry sector associations and business leaders to develop policies designed to enhance the international competitiveness of Japanese firms. The aid to businesses targeted for expansion or change traditionally has come through implicit guarantees of bank loans, tax incentives, and occasionally subsidies to motivate or enable companies to do what they otherwise would have been unable or unwilling to do.

The Corporate Purpose of Japanese Companies

Japan's historical and philosophical heritage is reflected in today's corporate purpose of many of its leading companies. The purpose is based on the primacy of the common good, as the company leaders define it.

The quality and power of their purpose has enabled Japanese companies to offset many of their antiquated managerial practices that sap their competitiveness. Most companies are overstaffed at the managerial level, have elaborate bureaucratic management processes that surpass the most Byzantine American organizations, and have norms that discourage individual thinking and preoccupy managers with trying to avoid personal embarrassment. Yet many Japanese firms have grown to be among the most competitive in the world. How can this be, given these managerial handicaps?

Part of the answer lies in the power of purpose to infuse the corporation with value and to guide a consistent pattern of decisions to form a highly coherent strategy and reinforce competitiveness (often at the expense of financial returns). A dominant theme in the purposes of these companies is some form of service to society. Ideally, in the Japanese context, serving society has three prongs: serving customers with products and services that enhance their lives, providing material wealth to the nation and communities, and enhancing the welfare—material and spiritual—of employees. This union of interest—nation, company, employee, and customer—provides the context and direction for decisions that should produce outstand-

ing competitive results, other things being equal. Focusing on the total
wealth-producing capacity of the company—wealth for customers, employees, communities, nations, and yes, investors—reflects the value of harmony.
In the strategic domain, there is not a conflict among these constituents,
unlike the conflicts embedded in an ideology that juxtaposes the shareholder
against customers and employees. Harmony and constancy in purpose leads
to constancy in strategy—the ability to sustain long-term investments that
enhance the essential core competencies of the organization.

The purpose of the typical Japanese company has allowed it to focus
on the product market almost exclusively, undistracted by capital-market
concerns or pressures. This concentration of attention and effort has been
critical to its long-term competitive success. Strategic concerns dominate
financial ones. Profits must be sufficient to fuel growth and make the investments necessary for competitive success, but they need not be "maximized."

This purpose is institutionalized in the ownership structure and corporate governance in Japanese companies. The lenders and most corporations that own stock in a company, who are often part of the *keiretsu*, seek
benefits in the form of expanded business with the company, not in direct
financial returns on their investment. The focus is on growth, or indirectly
on the total value-producing capacity of the firm they own.

At the level of individual motivation, employees in Japan clearly do
often sacrifice their self-interest for the perceived good of the organization.
Part of this may be due to social pressure within the group. However, most
managers speak with conviction regarding the importance of their company's
products and services to society, the sense of mutual responsibility among
employees, and therefore the social importance of their work. There are few
complaints about having to compromise doing the right thing for the sake of
the shareholder or even in order to increase profits. Time and again, profits
are referred to as an important means to achieving the company's other
objectives, most of which can ultimately be measured by growth.

It is not unusual to hear Japanese managers, when talking about the
priorities guiding their decisions, to stress the importance of the firm's survival. This sentiment is often enshrined in time-honored statements of beliefs
and corporate songs. For example, Toshiba's company song ends with the
verse, "May Toshiba prosper for all eternity." With this belief, it is not a
stretch to see one's own work, no matter how lowly, to be contributing to
something worthy of eternity. Life takes on added significance both because

of the quality of the corporate cause and because of the personal participation in something that might be eternal—something certainly more permanent and meaningful than the individual life. Devotion to the corporate cause intensifies. What is "right" in decision making becomes clearer.

The desire for the firm to survive "eternally" when linked to the social quality of its unchangeable purpose places a longer time frame on decisions. Shinji Sakai, president and CEO of Toyota Motor Sales, USA, reflects on the Eastern spiritual orientation embodied in Toyota's purpose:

> From the oriental or Buddhist point-of-view, the length of time is much longer. So, in our philosophy there are some things that are definitely unchangeable. We view a company just like a human being. It has a life, it has a meaning and it has to be treated as such. And so just like human life, there has to be something within the company that is very consistent, unchangeable.[21]

This view reinforces the emphasis on growth. Sakai explains, "Steady continuous growth is not a Toyota or a single company's philosophy, but it is the underlying unchangeable human concept that we believe in. Though I am not a strong practitioner of religion, this is the Buddhist type of thinking that most of us believe in."[22]

Similarly, the mutual responsibility between employees and between employee and company reinforces a sense of loyalty, fosters a commitment to the common endeavors of the group, and influences decisions. Employees benefit from growth and from jobs secured by the organization's competitive advantage. Since the individual is likely to be with the firm throughout his or her work life, and since the seniority system defers financial rewards until later in the individual's career, the time perspective incorporated into decisions becomes long term. If the firm's duty is to ensure the workers a lifetime of meaningful employment, then the employees have the mutual obligation to give their utmost.

Japanese companies have a tradition of annual speeches by the CEO to welcome new employees. At one such speech, Akio Morita, the person most credited with Sony's success, stressed the employees' responsibility to ensure that they find meaning in a work life devoted to the company's ends:

> We did not draft you. This is not the army, so that means you have voluntarily chosen Sony. This is your responsibility, and normally if you join this company we expect that you will stay for the next twenty or thirty years.

> Nobody can live twice, and the next twenty or thirty years is the brightest
> period of your life. You only get it once.
>
> When you leave the company thirty years from now or when your life is
> finished, I do not want you to regret that you spent all those years here.
> That would be a tragedy. I cannot stress the point too much that this is
> your responsibility to yourself. So I say to you, the most important thing in
> the next few months is for you to decide whether you will be happy or
> unhappy here.[23]

The expected mutual commitment is a deep one.

In many leading Japanese companies, corporate purpose defined in
terms of the social value of the firm's economic activities becomes inextricably linked with the mutual responsibilities to employees. The balancing point
between the interests of employees, customers, and society differs somewhat
across these companies. But in most firms, the company and employees are
one—the company cannot be distinguished from the network of relationships among the employees who constitute it.

Often this holistic view of the employees and the firm's external
responsibilities to society dates back to the company founders or early
CEOs who were critical to the corporation's success. Konasuke Matsushita,
the founder of Matsushita Electric Industrial Company, was fond of saying,
"Matsushita makes people before it makes profits." The company's purpose
is grounded in the founder's conviction that a company is indebted to society for its existence. Arataro Takahashi, Konasuke Matsushita's alter ego in
the company and former chairman, gives this account of the transformation
of the founder's thinking about the company's purpose:

> Until 1932, Mr. Matsushita was one of those businessmen who strove
> to make his business bigger in order to make more profits. But he came
> to doubt that idea. Was he right, he asked himself, only to worry about
> profits? After much thought, he came out with a new policy, which had
> three principal goals: to improve the living conditions of the people, to
> improve the general welfare of the society, and to further the national
> interest.[24]

The expression of the company's purpose, which was originally articulated
by Konasuke Matsushita a few years after starting the company, remains
alive today as the "Basic Management Objective." It states, "Recognizing our
responsibilities as industrialists, we will devote ourselves to the progress and
development of society and the well-being of people through our business

activities, thereby enhancing the quality of life throughout the world." In his 1997 welcoming speech to new employees, Yoichi Morishita, president, urged each employee to make Matsushita's management philosophy his or her own. He said,

> As we approach the new century, Matsushita Electric's Basic Business Philosophy will continue to emphasize "devotion to progress and the development of society." Matsushita Electric, through the efforts of all its employees, will strive to be a company that:
>
> 1. Places the needs of our customers first
> 2. Creates value
> 3. Is a global enterprise
> 4. Creates an environment in which employees can make the fullest use of their abilities.

For Masaharu Matsushita, chairman, this means "every phase of our business must reflect a devotion to the customer and thinking from the customer's point of view."

Kazuo Inamori, the founder of Kyocera and one of Japan's most respected entrepreneurs, tells of his awakening to the awareness of Kyocera's responsibility to its employees and how this duty must be integrated with Kyocera's purpose:

> One year after I founded Kyocera, I realized that I had started something outrageous. Eight of us started the company to prove that the technology we developed could be accepted by society. But before long, several young people we had hired demanded that we guarantee their future income!
>
> I had to seriously ponder the question, "What is an enterprise?" I was in no position to guarantee *anybody's* future livelihood, not even my own family's. Still, these employees were entrusting their future to our company. There was no way that we could betray the expectations of our employees, who were basing their lives on their jobs with us. Three days and nights of impassioned discussions made me change Kyocera's corporate mission. We shifted our priority from technology to employees.
>
> *Kyocera's management rationale is to provide opportunities for the material and intellectual growth of all our employees, and, through our joint effort, contribute to the advancement of society and mankind.*
>
> Our business shall strive first to provide opportunities for our employees. Building on this, we shall jointly contribute to the progress of technology, society, and mankind. I believe these are the only worthwhile objectives of our business.[25]

To Inamori, "The principle of business is to please people. We must certainly make our outside customers happy. And we must please our internal customers, too—the other employees and departments who depend on us."[26] In essence, Kyocera's corporate purpose is to serve customers—those who buy the company's products—and the people who devote their lives to the design, manufacture, and sale of the products.

Toyota Motor Corporation exemplifies the competitive power of a constant corporate purpose. Toyota's experience also indicates how globalization poses a challenge to a nation-focused purpose.[27]

Risaburo and Kiichiro Toyoda wrote the original statement of "The Toyoda Precepts" in 1935 to codify founder Sakichi Toyoda's five basic tenets of management. From the outset, Toyota's purpose was to serve the development of Japan. The first objective was to contribute "to the development and welfare of the country by working together, regardless of position, in faithfully fulfilling your duties." In another precept, Toyota employees were also asked to "be kind and generous; strive to create a warm, homelike atmosphere"—an appeal to the creation of a sense of community historically so highly valued in Japanese society. The other three precepts dealt with values expected to guide individual behavior: "be at the vanguard of the times through endless creativity, inquisitiveness and pursuit of improvement"; "be practical and avoid frivolity"; and "be reverent, and show gratitude for things great and small in thought and deed."

The 1935 precepts remained unchanged until 1963, when they were recast as "Toyota Corporate Policies." The statement expressed three ends: "to contribute to the growth of the Japanese economy; to obtain a reputation for 'Toyota quality'; and to expand the business to achieve world recognition of Toyota." Becoming recognized for its quality would serve the nation by expanding the demand for Toyota's products and also would enhance Toyota's reputation. The company's reputation is a central concern of Toyota executives to this day, reflecting the value they place on Toyota as an institution and possibly the holistic identification of self with the company.

Revised statements were again issued in 1983 and 1989. Each was more elaborate in expressing the values guiding the company in achieving its ends. The ends changed in one important aspect—the focus on social benefit expanded beyond Japan, reflecting the growing importance of Toyota's foreign sales. In 1983, the statement said "make a vigorous contribution to the economy, both in Japan and worldwide." In 1989 the statement was amended to say, "contribute to economic growth and greater quality of life through responsible corporate citizenship in every corner of the globe."

Toyota's internal struggle to become a global company is very evident in the 1992 "Guiding Principles at Toyota." Of the seven principles, six contained words and phrases referring to global responsibilities, such as "world," "global," "people everywhere," "people around the world," "community of every nation," and "global management." In the introduction to the Guiding Principles, Chairman Shoichiro Toyoda, recognizing the significant impact the increasing globalization was having on Toyota, rephrased Toyota's purpose: "Toyota always has been a company devoted to enhancing the quality of life for people around the world by providing useful and appealing products. . . . I want to call on everyone at Toyota to take part individually and collectively in reinforcing our corporate identity as a company where the greater good of society is the first consideration in all endeavors." Shoichiro Toyoda, in discussing the Guiding Principles in a Toyota newsletter, adds, "A Japan-oriented perspective is simply not appropriate in this global era."[28]

Two constant themes resonate through the years at Toyota and are deeply embedded in the premises that guide management decisions. The first is that Toyota exists to serve society directly through its actions in producing products. Initially the focus was on serving Japan's industrial development. In practice, this priority exists to this day, although the words and genuine intent are to serve people in all corners of the globe. When a decision presents a dilemma in choosing among conflicting aims, the chosen alternative is usually the one most favorable to Japan.

The second consistent theme is the emphasis on growth as the dominant operative goal. Growth serves economic development, enhances Toyota's global reputation, and benefits employees—all key Toyota objectives. It also is a measure of the company's success in providing cars that customers value. Chairman Shoichiro Toyoda and President Tatsuro Toyoda explain the linkage of growth to the achievement of Toyota's purpose:

> *Growth is good.* It is essential to economic and industrial vitality. But growth without purpose is no good for anyone.
>
> Our purpose at Toyota is to provide customers with quality products at affordable prices. And we believe in doing that in ways that contribute to economic and industrial vitality in the countries and communities where our customers live.

This is not altruism. It is simply a matter of recognizing that our own long-term interests coincide with the interests of people and companies in the markets we serve.[29]

In the 1990s, the strong yen and the weak Japanese market placed Toyota's profits under stress. For the first time in many managers' memory, the level of profitability became an important consideration in decision making. Yet growth remained the dominant objective. Motosuke Tominaga, director, Toyota Motor Corporation, explains:

Toyota's highest corporate objective is always how to grow and how to sustain growth. We have assumed responsibilities for shareholders, for the community, for employees, for dealers, and we have assumed the responsibility to keep the company running in good shape. This translates to continuous growth.

The question I get asked most is, "[On] which side does the company stand: profit oriented or sales-growth oriented?" Actually, we need both, but the profit is needed at a level so that we can continuously grow. We have to have some profits to invest for future growth, to meet our social obligations in the Japanese and the worldwide community. We can do all these only if we can maintain our steady growth in the world market.[30]

Other senior Toyota managers echo the linkage of growth and corporate purpose, and the secondary, facilitating role of profits:

Although we are facing a very severe situation in short-term profit, future growth is still considered the general objective. Being selfish is not acceptable to Toyota. We have to do many things to contribute to the society. In the automobile industry, about three-quarters of the world population is not enjoying the benefits of having a car. Our motto and our big role are to provide them with the benefits of owning a car.

Toyota needs to make a continuing contribution to the society. It has an obligation to the society that it has to meet. Continuous growth allows us to be responsive to the social needs of Japan and to the worldwide communities. After that, of course, we have to make a profit, so profit is secondary. We need profit for investment to make the product for future growth. So the profit amount may be different from year to year, but the minimum profit is needed so that it can be invested to assure us to make the good products that the customers want in the future.[31]

None of Toyota's statements of guiding principles since 1935 mentioned profit until 1992, when it was identified as a corollary to the princi-

ple "pursue growth through efficient global management." Profits are necessary to fund growth, but they are not ends in themselves.

As Toyota's profits declined in the early 1990s, the increased emphasis on profit was driven not only by a concern for its effect on the company's
ability to grow, but also by the indirect effect on the nation of Japan.
Because Toyota is a bellwether for the Japanese economy, Toyota managers
feel a specific responsibility. If Toyota should operate at a loss or have to lay
off permanent workers, the negative repercussions would be felt throughout
the economy. It would be a major blow to the confidence of business executives, consumers, savers, and investors alike. Therefore, Toyota's purpose
relative to serving Japan demands the maintenance of a minimum level of
profitability.

In his research, Shankar Basu chronicled two difficult decisions that
highlight Toyota's purpose and related operational goals in action. The first
decision involves the allocation of Camry production between Japan and the
United States. It illustrates a fundamental dilemma Japanese (and Korean)
companies face as protectionist pressure mounts and costs become increasingly important to competitiveness. Political and economic pressures motivate them to move manufacturing offshore—either to lower-labor-cost countries or closer to the end markets—but traditional values have focused on
service to the national society. For example, building manufacturing capability in the United States would mean more American jobs rather than
Japanese jobs. Values now conflict. Service to the nation has been brought
into tension with the desire to "enhance the quality of life of people around
the world" and to demonstrate the superiority of the company, its people,
and its nation through competitive dominance.

In the early 1990s, Toyota had to decide whether to move Camry production out of the Tsutsumi plant in Japan, which produced six different
models of automobiles for worldwide distribution, to the TMMU plant in
Kentucky, which produced only Camrys. As automobile sales declined in
Japan, the domestic demand for Camrys dropped precipitously. In the United
States, however, Camry demand was growing impressively. The TMMU
plant was operating at its two-shift capacity of 273,000 units, and because
of its favorable cost structure was exporting approximately 24,000 cars. Sales
in the United States were being constrained by the lack of capacity.

In 1994, 97,612 Camrys were exported from Japan to the United
States. Because of the sharp rise in the yen, these exported cars cost much

more than those manufactured in the Kentucky plant. In addition, because of trade friction between Japan and the United States, Toyota was operating under voluntary restraints that limited its total exports.

Moving approximately one hundred thousand units of production to the United States, which the American managers strongly recommended, would have increased Camry sales, lowered costs, significantly increased profits, and given Toyota more slack under the voluntary restraints to import other models. Economically, the choice was clear—expand U.S. production. But Toyota management chose not to. In fact, TMMU was not authorized to hire any new employees, which prevented the addition of a third shift, and until December 1993 TMMU was not allowed even to work employees overtime. As a consequence of the decision, Toyota lost an estimated fifty thousand units of Camry sales in the United States in both 1993 and 1994.[32]

Why was this choice made? Two principles overrode the other compelling economic considerations. First, Toyota felt greater responsibility to its permanent workers in Japan. An abrupt transfer of production would threaten the jobs of the permanent workers at the Tsutsumi plant. Because of declining Japanese demand, Toyota had already terminated the contracts of approximately three thousand seasonal workers in Japan. Given the uncertainty regarding future global automobile demand, Toyota managers also did not want to add new American employees to whom they would have a future responsibility. Keeping these new workers on during a downturn would adversely affect Toyota's performance.

The second principle was the negative effect on Japan such a transfer of production would have, particularly if Toyota would eventually need to lay off permanent employees. The direct economic effects are clear. But there is also the presumed indirect effect a one-hundred-thousand-unit reduction in production would have on the confidence of the public in the Japanese economy.

The second critical decision involved restructuring the white-collar workforce throughout Japan. Motivated by a 60 percent decline in net income from 1990 to 1993, the company decided to address the low productivity of white-collar workers. This was an issue also important to the company's long-term global competitiveness. Toyota management had long realized that its managerial workers were less productive than were those in the United States.

The seniority-based promotion system coupled with large annual hires of new university graduates had clogged the middle-management ranks. There were too many managers, and there was too little room for advancement. Consequently, many were underemployed, and younger employees were frustrated by their prospects for career advancement. To address these problems and increase administrative productivity, the company took several actions, including initiating a slowdown in hiring recent college graduates, instituting a voluntary early retirement program, reducing work hours from 180 per month to 160, canceling bonuses, and reducing wages.[33] But when these steps failed to produce the desired efficiencies, a program (code named "Business Reform") was instituted to cut the white-collar head count by 20 percent. The primary targets were people in administrative, sales, and overseas-related jobs at headquarters.

The typical American company, once the decision was made, would have laid off these individuals as soon as practical. This action would provide earlier, and therefore larger, financial benefits. But this is not what was done at Toyota. Not a single person was laid off. Some employees were given the option of being transferred to suppliers or dealers, and 4 percent chose to do so. The other 16 percent were removed from their jobs and redeployed, primarily to areas dealing with new initiatives—to new markets, new products, and new business development, and to reengineering projects.

The reasons for forgoing the financial benefits of simply laying off the redundant white-collar workers are similar to those that drove the Camry production-allocation decision: the company's obligations to their employees and the impact the layoffs would have on the Japanese economy. Managers also indicated that they were concerned that Toyota would "lose face" if there were layoffs.

These decisions demonstrate the priority Toyota continues to place on its responsibilities to the nation and to its employees. These priorities are consistent with the purpose of serving the common good, as Toyota's leaders perceive it. Even though the company's purpose expresses a duty to society globally, there is a managerial finger on the scale to achieve a balance among responsibilities that favors Japan. The result is a committed workforce, a traditional willingness to make investments in the company's long-term future without concern for maximizing profitability, and an intuitive understanding of the importance to society of the company's total value-producing capacity. These attributes form the bedrock of Toyota's competitive advantage. The company could not have been a leader in the development of lean manufacturing if it had not established an environment of enormous trust with its employees.

The essence of these stories is repeated in other leading Japanese companies. Corporate purpose places priority on nation, employees, and customers ahead of financial returns. Corporate objectives and critical strategic decisions reflect this priority.

South Korea

The rise of South Korea to become the world's eleventh-largest economy is strongly tied to the cultural values that drive it. Modern Korean culture is an unusual blend of what to Western eyes are conflicting values: individualism adopted from the West, vibrant nationalism fueled by the Japanese occupation, and traditional Confucian beliefs regarding the subordination of individual interests to community needs. By integrating these values and then leveraging them through a highly educated and motivated workforce, Korea was able to span the entire industrial revolution in three decades—from textiles to semiconductors.

The relatively small size of the domestic market and the lack of natural resources meant that rapid growth could come only through export. Therefore, almost from the outset of its industrialization, Korean products had to be competitive in the world market. The strategy to become the low-cost producer in specific manufacturing industries required the development of the necessary competencies to be competitive on price and quality.

The industrial development of Korea was carried out by a small group of large conglomerate corporations called *chaebol*. The senior managers of the *chaebol* share long-standing close personal relationships, and most of these companies are controlled and led by the founding families. All *chaebol* are relatively new enterprises. Of the four largest *chaebol*, LG (formerly Lucky-Goldstar) and Hyundai were established in 1947, Samsung in its present form began in 1951, and Daewoo was not created until 1967. By the late 1990s, the sales of these four *chaebol* accounted for nearly half of Korea's GDP and exports.

A key to the *chaebol*'s success has been their usefulness to the government as an instrument for economic development. Through close cooperation with the government galvanized by a common nationalistic fervor, these companies have been the central force in the economy's development.

The *chaebol* were favored because of the belief that centralized efforts would make more efficient, more timely, and lower-risk use of Korea's scarce resources and would be more conducive to government influence. Government bureaucrats, who, like their counterparts in Japan, were highly competent scholar-aristocrats, channeled resources—sometimes preferentially—according to five-year plans. The first plan targeted import substitution, and subsequent plans evolved from the export of labor-intensive light-industry goods, to heavy-industrial goods, and finally to high-tech products. The government set export targets for individual firms and provided them with strong incentives, including low-cost loans, tax breaks, and protection from foreign competition in domestic markets. In response, the *chaebol* made prodigious investments in the Korean economy and for the most part reinvested their profits in Korea. However, in the mid-1990s, driven by the high domestic wage rates (manufacturing wages were 50 percent higher than in Hong Kong) and by the rapid globalization of their major industries, the *chaebol* began making significant foreign direct investments. To cope with the high wage rates, the *chaebol* are continually shifting their emphases to higher-value-added products requiring sophisticated technology.

In recent years, Korea has been accumulating technological skill at a rapid rate. Technology initially was imported primarily from Japan and the United States, but in recent years Korean companies have been substantially increasing their own R&D expenditures. At the outset, this increase was to catch up with foreign competitors, but now the objective of many Korean industries is to surpass them. The investment in this endeavor has been impressive. By 1998 Korea ranked just behind Sweden and the United States among all OECD countries in its investment in knowledge as a percentage of GDP.[34] Consider Korea's rapid inroads into the dynamic random access memory chip (DRAM) market. At the end of the 1990s, Samsung was the world leader in DRAM semiconductors, and LG and Hyundai were among the world's top ten DRAM manufacturers. Korean memory chip manufacturers outinvested their American and Japanese competitors by a sizable margin. In 1995 Korean companies were reinvesting an astonishing 30 to 50 percent of their semiconductor revenues in new plant and equipment, compared to only 15 percent for the Japanese.[35] Driven by an obsession with beating the Japanese, Samsung spent prodigious amounts—many billions of dollars—on semiconductor development, multimedia and telecommunications products, and thin-film-transistor liquid-crystal-display screens (LCDs) for laptop computers. Its strategy has been to obtain technology through alliances with and acquisitions of U.S. and Japanese companies and to invest heavily to dominate markets in next-generation products such as cellular phones, personal digital assistants, multimedia products, and LCDs. Under the banner "The Leader for the 21st Century the World Will Notice," Samsung's ambition is to become one of the world's ten largest "technological powerhouses" and within electronics alone to be one of the world's top five electronics companies.[36] A new twenty-seven-year-old molecular biology recruit sees the purpose of this strategy as being "for the betterment of mankind."[37]

Daewoo Group represents both the best and worst aspects of the Korean *chaebol*. It became Korea's second-largest *chaebol* and is symbolic of the investment excesses to which many of them went to achieve growth. Founded in 1967 by Kim Woo-Choong, by 1997 the original eighteen-thousand-dollar investment had grown into the world's twenty-fourth-largest company, with sales of $71.5 billion, larger than Siemens, Hitachi, Chrysler, Du Pont, Mobil, or Procter & Gamble.[38] By 1998, Daewoo accounted for an astounding 10 percent of Korea's GDP and 13 percent of its exports. In addition, Daewoo companies and their suppliers employed approximately 2.5 million Koreans.[39]

These results were produced by aggressive investment in unfocused diversification, low—or possibly nonexistent—profits (the accounting for profits at all *chaebol* is suspect, and Daewoo's have proved to be misleading), and consequently large amounts of debt. Daewoo's disparate businesses spanned automobiles, machinery, shipbuilding, electronics, construction, financial services, and trading.

In 1999, under pressure from the government for economic reform of all *chaebol* and from creditors for increased security for their $47 billion of debt (of which, $10 billion was held by foreign institutions), Daewoo agreed to a sweeping restructuring of its businesses and Chairman Kim resigned, eventually fleeing the country to avoid prosecution on fraud charges associated with the company's deceptive accounting practices. A number of companies were targeted to be sold, and Daewoo Motors declared bankruptcy.

Daewoo's restructuring represented a watershed in Korean development. Banks and other lenders became more discriminating in their lending practices, forcing greater transparency on corporations. The *chaebol* no longer absorbed almost all of the country's capital. Consequently, funds began to flow increasingly to smaller companies. With time, because of the cultural mix of individualistic values and the importance of serving the broader interests of society, these new realities might produce a significant rise in innovation and entrepreneurial activity within Korea—taking the country to its next level of competitiveness. To understand this new potential competitiveness, one needs to understand the depth of its roots in Korean culture and psyche.

Daewoo's Kim Woo-Choong reflects many of the values of Korean society, combining Christian beliefs received from his mother, a respect for traditional Confucian values, and an intense sense of nationalism. He is a complicated man. He coupled his passion for Korean economic development with a brash overconfidence stemming from Daewoo's success and the accompanying accolades. The result was a high-rolling hubris. He truly believed he knew best what was right for Korea, had a vision of Daewoo's role in the nation's development, and would not be deterred in this quest. The nobility of the ends began to justify the means. Accounting practices, however deceptive, became a means to attract more capital to Daewoo to fund its ever-greater role in Korea's destiny. He saw the Asian Crisis as an opportunity to gain share from his competitors. As they retrenched, he rolled the dice, expanding rapidly and accumulating massive amounts of new debt in a short period. As the crisis deepened, cash flow evaporated and lenders became more circumspect, eventually forcing Daewoo into de facto receivership and Kim into exile.

Yet, despite his failings, Kim Woo-Choong had a keen insight into the Korean character and was in many ways an embodiment of that character. This tragic individual reflected the best and worst of Korean executive leadership. For that reason, his views, which from all indications were sincerely held, provide particular insight into the Korean managerial mind and into the reckless limits to which driven competitors such as he can—and do—go. It is against people like Kim that other global companies must compete. Therefore, on the following pages, Kim Woo-Choong's commentary will be used to provide a Korean chief executive's view of the cultural context of a Korean corporation's purpose.

Major Cultural Influences

The Yi Dynasty (1392–1910). Confucianism has had a greater influence on life in Korea than in either Japan or China, owing in large part to the Yi dynasty's relentless promotion of Confucianism during its 518-year rule. For the Yi rulers, Confucian values represented the ideal path to achieving social harmony and maintaining public order. Consequently, Confucianism was mandated to be taught in all schools, and until 1894 aspiring public servants were required to take a national examination based largely on Confucian classics. These steps helped institutionalize Confucian principles as the foundation for society's traditional ways.[40] With its emphasis on family and hierarchy, the agrarian society was unified more by a Confucian ethic than by a national spirit. Nationalism had to await the cruelty of the Japanese occupation to be awakened.

The Yi dynasty's neo-Confucian beliefs held that the only legitimate source of wealth and power was public office. Confucian principles took a particularly dim view of commerce and industry, which were "despised as occupations unfit for men of virtue."[41] With Korea's more recent rapid introduction of capitalism, the failure to create a strong moral foundation has perpetuated the low social standing of businesspeople.

Korea's Confucian roots have instilled lasting competitive benefits in Korean companies, benefits derived from a commitment to education, respect for superiors, and dedication to one's work and society. The results are highly skilled workers who cooperate well with others in order to better serve Korean society. As a result of the importance placed on education, Kim observes,

> Korean workers could be trained to manufacture quality products, and technology could be transferred and absorbed without difficulty. Even through times of dire poverty, our ancestors retained the great tradition of providing the best education possible for their children. The fact that a country which had virtually nothing could become the developed nation that we have today is the result of our highly-educated manpower and our thirst for knowledge.[42]

Bearing witness to the strong influence of the Confucian value of education, Korea has the largest number of doctoral degrees per capita of any country in the world—a fact that has facilitated the country's rapid absorption of advanced technology.

Japanese Occupation. Japan occupied Korea in 1905 and formally annexed it in 1910. Thus began a period of brutal rule that was made particularly harsh by the Japanese sense of superiority. The Japanese exploited the Koreans to serve Japanese national aspirations. To serve these interests, Japan set out to rapidly industrialize Korea, building infrastructure and introducing modern industrial techniques. The industrialization accelerated Korea's urbanization and eroded the agrarian society that was the custodian of the traditional values. By 1937, in an attempt to further assimilate the Koreans into Japanese culture, the occupiers mandated that only the Japanese language be used in the schools, and they forced Koreans to change their names to Japanese names.

To overcome resistance to their rule and to maintain social order, the Japanese overtly appealed to Confucian values. This tactic was an attempt to demonstrate the unity of ideals and the common cultural heritage between Japan and Korea and to rationalize Japanese rule in terms of Korean tradition.[43] By appealing to the Confucian sense of hierarchical order and the primacy of society's interests, the Japanese hoped to convince the Koreans that their community interests rested in serving the economic interests of "greater Japan" and that Japanese and Koreans shared similar spiritual aims.[44] Even Japan's military conquests of Manchuria and China were presented to the Koreans as a defense of Confucian morality.[45]

Not only did Japan's colonization reinforce traditional Confucian values, particularly the subordination of the individual to collective interests and the loyalty to a bureaucratic hierarchy, but it also had another critically important effect. The Japanese occupation significantly increased Korean patriotism. Koreans were infused with a determination to prove that they are not inferior to the Japanese and to "get even" for Japan's past transgressions. Initially this took the form of slogans to catch up with Japan economically, but these have been increasingly replaced with "beat Japan." An obsession with beating Japan runs deep throughout Korean industry. This obsession has powerfully influenced the purpose of Korean *chaebol*, which became partners with the government in realizing the nation's destiny.

Korea's history and the continuing military threat from North Korea make Koreans preoccupied with survival. This preoccupation gives urgency to their national development efforts.

For many managers of Kim Woo-Choong's generation, their common experience gives them a profound sense of destiny and responsibility. They were born during the cruel Japanese occupation, were adolescents during the Korean War that killed many of the older men, and were the first generation in years to receive a university education. Chairman Kim speaks passionately about the responsibility his generation inherited because of the Japanese occupation and the powerful motivation behind this responsibility:

> We Koreans have had an extremely powerful motivation—to break the shackles of tragedy and poverty for ourselves and for our descendants.
>
> [Our generation was] the first, after the long Japanese Occupation, to have our own nation, to have the freedom to speak and write our own language. We were also the first to have our own educational system, and to complete a modern education. We were, as a result, the first to establish solid individual identities, and armed with determination, the first to go out and make contributions in our respective social areas. It was our generation, armed with solid determination, which literally worked like crazy and sacrificed so that we could greatly shorten the period required for the nation to mature to the point where it is now standing on the threshold of becoming an advanced nation.
>
> It was up to my generation to achieve what other generations had accomplished for other nations. We were determined to leave something for future generations, something besides poverty and devastation. People my age had a historical sense of mission, and we were determined to bear any sacrifice to make this dream come true. This is still the case, even for many younger Koreans.[46]

Daewoo's Kim believes these essential elements of Korea's success are present in other East Asian countries as well:

> The reason for Asian success is a simple one: the will and determination of the peoples of these countries to work hard for a better life and a better nation. In Korea during the 1960s, the passion to establish a rich and strong country inspired the diligence of the people, as captured by our slogan at the time, "We, too, can prosper." The development of this region [is not] the result of rationalism that comes from combining long-time accumulated experience and advanced theories as is the case in the West. Asia's success is almost entirely the result of human effort driven by desperate will.[47]

American Occupation and the Advent of Individualism. The introduction of Western values into Korean society began with concerted Protestant missionary activity in the late nineteenth century. Along with Christianity came Western—primarily American—ideals of individualism, which the Koreans adapted to their communal way of life. In part this was done through strong, closely knit congregations. Protestantism flourished in Korea during the American occupation after World War II.

The Christian concept of stewardship melded well with the Confucian values of loyalty to the group and state and influenced the Korean view of property rights. In the words of Kim Woo-Choong, "Christianity talks about the 'sense of stewardship,' the sense that whatever you have during this life is not yours but something that you have been entrusted with. This carries with it a responsibility to take care of what you have and to use it properly for others."[48]

Because of the American occupation and the Korean War, which took fifty-two thousand American lives, America has had considerable influence on Korean values. The American presence introduced values of individualism, free enterprise, equality, and democratic political institutions into Korean culture. These ideals were embodied in the Korean constitution and promoted in primary school textbooks. The ideals of individualism have found particularly receptive ears among young Koreans. In part this is because individualism promises to free them from the constraints imposed on their personal progress by the traditional hierarchical order. Yet most Koreans retain a healthy skepticism of too much individualism, equating individualistic behavior with selfishness. This feeling extends to a widely held ambivalence regarding the accumulation of personal wealth.[49] There is a belief—often justified—that gains are ill-gotten, through collaboration with the Japanese during the occupation and more recently through bribes and secret government favors.

Creating a New Cultural Hybrid

In present-day Korea, most educated, urban middle-class Koreans consider themselves "strongly individualistic."[50] These individualistic tendencies potentially clash with Korea's traditional Confucian ideals and rekindled nationalism. What is emerging is a culture that rationalizes these two sets of values—one that ties the values of individual expression, initiative, and personal development to the service of the common good. This new ideology is influencing corporate purpose, the way Korean firms are managed, the relationship of individuals to their firms, and therefore the competitiveness of the firms. If successful, the new ideology will blend the best features of Korea's traditional culture with the benefits of creativity and initiative derived from the values of individualism.

The blending of these traditions has resulted in values of achievement, individual fulfillment, perseverance, and loyalty, and an optimistic national-ism approaching xenophobia. In the final analysis, however, "the interests of the community take precedence over those of the individual."[51] During times of seemingly ever-present national crisis, the government has successfully appealed to the sacrifice of individual desires for the common good. In the financial crisis of 1997, the government received millions of dollars worth of jewelry and gold voluntarily donated by citizens to help shore up the coun-try's financial reserves.

The Korean workforce is steeped in the traditional Confucian values of mutual responsibility and self-development in the service of a common cause. Consequently, workers are disciplined and dedicated to hard work, driven by two principal motivations. First, they believe that their sacrifices will lead to a better life for their children. Second, this is their way of con-tributing to social harmony and the betterment of Korean society in general. However, at the management level, the Confucian deference to authority often results in Korean companies being managed in a highly authoritarian manner, with the chairmen being the greatest offenders. This authoritarian-ism stifles ideas and innovation. Fortunately for the Koreans, in today's mar-ketplace, technology transfers across national boundaries more readily than do ideology and nationalistic values. They can license technology from abroad and leverage it by applying the benefits of their ideology in the areas of learning, hard work, and willingness to invest.

In most *chaebol* these beliefs foster a corporate purpose that integrates service to the common good with a drive to increase the power and prestige of the company. The desire for corporate power and prestige has two primary origins. First, these are mostly family-controlled companies, and the family's reputation and power increase along with the company's. In fact, there is vig-orous competition among the *chaebol* for bragging rights within Korea. Sec-ond, as in Japan, employees identify with the company and believe it wor-thy of a long life, which requires continual growth. Not only is growth necessary to keep the company from dying, but also it reflects favorably on the organization's worthiness and reputation. In practice, as in Japan, the drive for growth and size reinforces actions that serve the common good.

Korea has benefited substantially from what some critics have described as "profitless growth." Growth, not returns on investment, has been the prime objective of *chaebol* leaders. With government-subsidized, low-cost debt available to the *chaebol*, they were less concerned with the availability and costs of capital than with developing the opportunities to invest it. As a result, the returns on capital have been quite low for Korean companies—in 1996 the average return on equity for the thirty largest *chaebol* was only 3 percent—but their ability to capture market share in a wide variety of industries has been impressive and a boon to the living standards of the average Korean and to national development.

Seeking a better understanding of the influence of capital-market considerations on strategic decision making, the author once asked Chairman Kim Woo-Choong what Daewoo's cost of capital was. He looked at me as if that was a very dumb question. After a pause, he said he could borrow all the funds he needed at 11 percent before taxes. I then asked about his cost of equity capital—an even dumber question. Although he replied that his dividends were about 1 percent of his equity, it was evident he had not thought much about the cost of equity. Kim's replies indicate a very different view of capital from that of the typical American CEO. Kim was vitally interested in investment opportunities and the availability of capital to undertake them. He considered the cost of capital Daewoo's out-of-pocket cost—not an expected rate of return derived from the capital asset pricing model. This view enabled him to rationalize the extremely aggressive spending that eventually triggered the events that led to the dismantling of the Daewoo Group. Regardless of how misguided some of Kim's actions may seem, the reality is that American managers must compete with the Kims of the world. From his perspective, this was the best way to create one of the largest companies in the world (only six U.S. companies reported larger revenues in 1997) and to help Korea become a world industrial power.[52]

Similar to Japanese companies, *chaebol* exhibit a significant sense of responsibility to their employees. This responsibility is displayed in benevolent paternalistic practices, such as lifetime employment and seniority promotion systems. Many companies stress Confucian themes of harmony and mutual benefit. For example, LG promotes harmony as its core principle. Consequently, even though LG has been a leader in restructuring its managerial ranks, it, like Toyota, accomplished significant change through retirements and the transfer of people to new growth businesses rather than layoffs. Kim Young-Chan, who managed LG's restructuring effort, reflects on the company's commitment to its people, saying, "Our chairman has a firm belief we should not cut labor to increase profits."[53] As in Japan, people take precedence over profits. Korean employees have clearly benefited. Helped along by militant unions, wages increased at an average compound rate of 17 percent per year over the twenty years up to 1996.

The confluence of values represented in the purposes of Korean *chaebol* provides significant competitive advantages. Purpose linked to the common good of Korean society focuses the company on economic expansion, which can best be achieved by devoting undivided attention to the product markets with the objective of maximizing long-term growth. Returns need to be sufficient to fund the growth and underwrite the business and financial risk. The strategic intent of "beat Japan" also provides a highly motivational rallying cry that fosters loyalty and gives direction to actions. The Confucian-like atmosphere of mutual benefit and the call for harmony reinforce loyalty. These benefits, coupled with a highly educated workforce, are critical ingredients to executing effective strategies in the knowledge-intensive businesses of tomorrow, particularly those requiring heavy capital investment.

Korea's considerable competitive success has not been without some difficulties. The right balance between these cultural streams is not easily achieved. Daewoo's Kim expresses considerable concern over "the trend towards greater egocentrism at the expense of concern for the nation and society," and the increasing satisfaction with short-term "small achievements" and "immediate comfort" rather than "having a fighting spirit to overcome difficulties and to succeed in the long run."[54]

Also, the heavy emphasis on growth has led to unfocused diversification. The lack of relatedness among many of the *chaebol*'s businesses has hampered the *chaebol*'s ability to develop core competencies applicable to different core businesses and has diffused scarce senior-management attention. The government in recent years has been attempting to get each *chaebol* to focus on a few core businesses and divest the rest. However, until the Daewoo breakup, they had limited success, even though they offered tax incentives and other inducements.

The *chaebol* have thrived on the availability of government-subsidized debt. However, as the *chaebol*'s operations have become more globalized and their foreign direct investments have increased, the social benefit of this lower-cost capital does not necessarily remain in Korea. Consequently, these government subsidies are less likely to play as significant a role in the future, particularly as the financial system is restructured in response to the economic crisis of the late 1990s. Fortunately for them, the *chaebol* have been weaning themselves from the need for this assistance.

Antiquated, autocratic management practices are a significant handicap to every *chaebol*, although some, like LG, have been more progressive than others. But none of the practices have enabled the *chaebol* to harness the full benefit of the individualism that resides in the Korean people. For example, the seniority system contradicts the meritocracy that is central to the ideals of individualism and stifles creativity and initiative. The autocratic treatment of subordinates undermines the message of mutual respect and benefit and discourages the expression of individual ideas. Also, the ad hoc autocratic style of some chairmen is not conducive to the formulation and execution of coherent, consistent strategies. Furthermore, the refusal of some *chaebol* to place professional managers in the most senior positions undermines the quality of management. These are significant problems, some of which have cultural roots. But many *chaebol* are actively working to overcome them. However, until they do, they will act as a drag on the competitive benefits inherent in most *chaebol*'s purpose.

The Future Asian Competitive Threat

The Asian competitive threat of the past pales in comparison with the potential of an Asia that combines the traditional communitarian beliefs of loyalty and service to the common good with Western practicality, increased individualism, and the associated creativity and initiative. This potential hybrid culture promises to combine high levels of motivation, commitment, and even self-sacrifice with a focus on competitiveness through individual initiative and creativity. If sustained, this hybrid will undoubtedly prove to be highly successful in the marketplace. Korea provides a window on this potential.

Two countries—Taiwan and China—with very different political ideologies but with interrelated histories and many common social values, provide insights into the potential future nature of Asian competition. Both call for the subordination of individual interests to causes beyond the self—to the family in Taiwan and to the welfare of the state and national society in China.

Taiwan

The ideology underlying Taiwanese business is similar to Korea's: a dominant communitarian ideology with strong underlying individualistic tendencies. The recent histories of the two countries have remarkable similarities. Both countries were heavily influenced by Chinese culture, particularly Confucian thought. Japan colonized Taiwan ten years earlier than it did Korea (from 1895 to 1945). After World War II, both countries were considerably influenced by American values.

Familism has had an even stronger influence on the structure of the Taiwanese economy than it has had in Korea. The result has been a more fragmented economy with an emphasis on less capital-intensive light industries. Like mainland China, where families traditionally were the dominant economic units, the bulk of Taiwanese companies are family-owned and managed. Yet this strong family influence does not undermine the communitarian responsibilities firms have to the society and individuals have to the family. "The imperial Chinese assumption that the family owes unlimited duties to the state remains in the background as a principle" in Taiwan.[55] Within families, the emphasis is on duties, particularly of one generation to another, rather than on rights. This sense of duty affects business decisions. The family and company funds are usually intermingled. Typically, as much money as possible is left in the company—in part for the benefit of future generations—and the family draws on the company's funds only as needed.[56] The result is a high proclivity to invest, not unlike the frugality associated with the traditional "Protestant ethic" in the West.

China

Arguably, China poses the most significant international competitive threat for the first quarter of the twenty-first century. It is undertaking significant reforms of its economy with the national objective of maintaining an average annual growth rate of 6.5 percent for the next quarter century. If successful, China will become a $5 trillion economic superpower, surpassed only by the United States and Japan.[57]

To achieve these ambitious objectives, in 1997 President Jiang Zemin announced plans to consolidate the 305,000 state-owned enterprises (SOEs), focusing primarily on the 118,000 industrial enterprises. In the late 1990s, the SOEs were in a clear state of crisis: half of all SOEs were operating at steadily increasing losses, and the combined income of all SOEs was in deficit. In part, this crisis was the result of the heavy social burden placed on these companies in the form of high taxes, benefits for employees (including health care, housing, and education), and requirements to continue to pay surplus workers, who represented as much as 20 percent of the workers. These companies employed about two-thirds of the 170 million urban workforce but produced only one-third of the gross industrial output.

"Township and village enterprises" have faired better than the SOEs. These organizations are backed by local government but are market-oriented with a mixture of public, private, and collective ownership. They have grown rapidly to represent over 40 percent of China's industrial output and employ 120 million workers.[58]

To respond to the SOEs' crisis, the government plans to merge companies in key sectors, such as electronics, telecommunications, steel, chemicals, and aviation, to create one thousand large companies capable of competing in free global markets. These companies will be patterned after the Korean *chaebol* and will continue to work in close cooperation with the government. These new large companies will continue to be state-controlled and state-subsidized, although some might be opened to domestic and possibly foreign ownership. Those not consolidated will be sold to employees or foreign investors. The mission of these *chaebol*-like companies will be to expand the economy and thereby improve Chinese living standards and strengthen the nation. Presumably they will have ready access to capital and by competing in global markets will be forced to improve their technological and managerial skills. If these reforms are successful, the SOEs could emerge as powerful world competitors, driven by an ideology quite different from that of the United States.

China's restructuring will only add to an impressive arsenal of potential competitive advantages. A massive domestic market offers Chinese companies the prospect of a protected fortress within which to develop the technological prowess, sales volume (and thus manufacturing cost advantages derived from economies of scale and the learning curve), and financial resources with which to launch aggressive attacks on global markets. The country's 40 percent savings rate, the highest of any industrialized Asian country, provides approximately $400 billion in capital each year. The almost unlimited supply of low-cost labor means that it will not face rising labor costs as early in its development as did countries such as Japan and Korea. China has nearly 300 million people who earn less than one dollar a day. As these people migrate to the industrial workforce over the next twenty years, they will keep the lid on wages.

Reinforcing these economic and government forces is a tradition of placing the common good ahead of individual self-interest—a tradition derived from two millennia of imperial dynasties (some benevolent Confucian-based rulers, others ruthless despots) and from communist rule. Throughout Chinese history, business organizations have served the state-defined common good and also, prior to communism, the benefit of the family. This heritage has produced a society where, as one China scholar observed, "the primary values are communitarian, but underneath, most of their secondary values are highly individualistic."[59] This combination of values, as in Korea, represents the potential to produce a society where corporate purpose is focused on serving the common good and the means for doing so are energized by individualistic tendencies.

As China moves from Deng Xiaping's market-driven socialism to Jiang Zemin's vision of a "complete market system," the focus will be on growth that generates jobs and further develops the economy. This focus means that companies will be growth- and export-oriented and will compete by very different rules than is common in the West, particularly in America. This mixture of purpose, goals, and capabilities could have potentially severe competitive consequences for China's rivals. The principal threat to the country's development plan is the potential for social and political unrest precipitated by popular demands for greater democracy or massive unemployment resulting from the consolidation of the SOEs and requiring previously protected companies to fend for themselves in a market economy.

This powerful confluence of competitive factors (socially oriented corporate purposes, large domestic market, abundant capital, low-wage labor, and individualistic tendencies), when combined with a national mandate to grow, gives China the potential to become a very formidable competitive juggernaut. In many ways, the past "economic miracles" of Japan and the Asian Tigers are harbingers of a more intensely competitive future global marketplace.

The "Asia Crisis" and the Sustainability of Ideology

Beginning in 1997, economic problems swept Asia. The crisis is indicative of the intensifying competitive pressures brought on by China's development, of many Asian companies' proclivity to overinvest, and of the world capital markets' willingness to facilitate—if not encourage—this investment.

Although these problems surfaced first in Thailand, they became most visible in Korea, in part because of Korea's standing as the eleventh largest industrialized nation. The crisis was quickly attributed to a variety of underlying causes. In Korea, the paramount explanation was the cozy relationships between government, business, and financial institutions characterized as "Korea Inc." or "crony capitalism," which resulted in a government-dominated industrial policy and excessive borrowing by companies, and the absence of shareholder activism to hold managers accountable for their firms' financial performance.[60] As a result of this analysis, many observers were quick to predict a wholesale change in the structure of the Korean economy—changes that would fundamentally alter the country's ideology, making Korea resemble the United States. Similar arguments were also raised regarding Japan and other Asian countries.

This analysis fails to distinguish adequately between five separate forces: the country's core ideology, the government's role in the economy, the role of the large companies, the influence of increasing global competition, and the impact of fluid (some would say hot) international capital. Although government policies and corporate practices are likely to change, there is little reason to believe there will be far-reaching changes in the ideologies underlying the corporate sectors of the Korean, Japanese, and other Asian economies. In fact, the Korean economy's response to these traumatic events provides convincing evidence of the fundamental underlying strength of the Korean ideology. To the surprise of most Western analysts, the shock to the Korean economy did not last long. Displaying impressive resilience, after plummeting 6.7 percent in 1998, Korea's real GDP rebounded sharply to grow at an average annual rate of 9.8 percent in 1999–2000.

The root causes of the crises are straightforward and are not a direct consequence of these countries' ideologies. In the case of Korea, the causes are fivefold: (1) excessive borrowing, (2) unfocused diversification, (3) razor-thin operating margins produced by aggressive pricing to gain market share, (4) rising wages, and (5) the need to compete with the Chinese onslaught in the global marketplace. These causes are similar to the problems facing other Asian countries. The Korean government's policies, which pushed large amounts of capital through the banking system, encouraged the extremely high debt/equity ratios of Korean companies. With the availability of low-cost debt supported by implicit government guarantees and an imperative to help industrialize the nation, Korea's large conglomerates, or *chaebol*, diversified into a dizzying array of unrelated businesses, both horizontally and vertically. This urge to diversify was also fed by the value corporate leaders placed on size for its own sake. Not only was size an indication of how well the company was serving the national imperative to industrialize rapidly, but it also enhanced the power and prestige of the *chaebol* and their executives in the Korean society and indirectly of Korea as a nation throughout the world. However, this diversification spread corporate resources thinly. To grow rapidly, Korean companies priced aggressively and undertook investments that barely covered the out-of-pocket cost of debt, much less the overall cost of capital. The resulting low profit margins provided a slim cushion for mistakes or unexpected economic events. To maintain labor peace and to aid in the development of the country, wages rose rapidly. Consequently, when new Asian competitors—particularly China—began competing with Korea in the world market, many businesses within the *chaebol* found themselves caught between their own high wages and their competitors' low prices, which in part were a reflection of their lower wages. Preexisting profit margins provided an inadequate cushion for such a battle.

Although these fundamental underlying causes had lingered for years in Asia, the crisis was precipitated by runaway financial institutions lubricated by funding from excessively optimistic foreign investors and a ferocious intensification of competition for exports. Compounding the problem were accounting practices that obscured the real value-supporting loans. Tempted by the readily available low-cost capital, many businesses took the money and made unwise investments.

The crisis was the culmination of years of hedging by commercial banks and other investors who borrowed short term at low interest rates in the United States and Japan and used these funds to buy high-rate short-term notes from banks in Korea and other South East Asian countries. The Asian banks then lent the funds domestically for long-term investments. Many of these industrial and real estate investments provided inadequate cash flow to service the debt. Consequently, the crisis in part can be viewed as the result of a lack of due diligence by the world's money center banks. By the end of 1996, loans from European, American, and Japanese institutions to East Asian money center banks exceeded $700 billion. In addition, many Asian countries were running trade deficits, causing external short-term debt to exceed foreign exchange reserves. In Thailand and Indonesia short-term debt was approximately twice their reserves, and in Korea it was over three times.

Two events triggered the collapse. First, concerned about rising interest rates in Japan, Japanese banks began to pull their loans out of Asian countries. Second, China's aggressive program to grow its economy through exports put intense pressure on other Asian competitors. Prices for goods fell, which further reduced cash flow. As investors and currency traders began withdrawing funds from these countries, the value of the Asian currencies plummeted. The reduced value of these currencies increased the size of the outstanding external debt, and a vicious cycle was in place.

The three most likely reforms in response to these realities—changes in the banking system (which will lead to more open capital markets and reduced availability of low-cost debt), less governmental protection and regulation of domestic markets, and increased transparency in reporting corporate performance—will only sharpen the competitive edge of most corporations over the long term. However, the values, assumptions, and beliefs underlying the motivations to pursue growth and to invest aggressively run deep. Although they may be modified to meet the new realities, they will not readily change in fundamental ways. Undoubtedly returns will continue to be subordinated to growth as managers strive to serve the national economy, their fellow employees, and the company itself. Corporate managers will likely raise profitability to levels deemed necessary to generate the cash flow required to fulfill these broader objectives, but profits will remain a means to these ends. However, companies are likely to become more focused on what they consider to be their key businesses, divesting many unrelated, nonstrategic businesses.

Some companies had pushed returns down to extreme levels, and this will be remedied. Efforts to increase profitability will make the companies more selective in their investments. Increased transparency will make managers more accountable for performance. However, the new equilibrium in returns is likely to continue to be considerably below that required by typical American competitors to cover their theoretical cost of capital. As a consequence of these changes, key businesses will receive more resources from operating cash flow and more management attention. To increase innovation, competitive agility, and efficiency, the way of managing in many Asian companies is likely to evolve to reflect greater subunit autonomy, more openness to the ideas of subordinates, and more merit-based performance measurement.

All these factors will aid the companies' long-term competitiveness.

However, a wholesale revamping of ideologically based economic relationships is unlikely to occur anytime soon.

Germany

As with Asian companies, history and a confluence of economic, political, and social institutional relationships reinforce and help embed socially minded corporate purposes in the German society. A vibrant nationalism, close coordination between business and government, the codetermination that marks management and labor relationships, strong corporate links with banks, and the weak influence of nonbank shareholders each focus German executives' attention on the social consequences of their actions. One German scholar observes, "Government, business, and labor in Germany have sought and found legitimacy for their actions by fulfilling the needs of the community as their first priority. Satisfying the needs of the individual was perceived as being secondary."[61] This system has resulted in considerable competitive success, creating the world's second largest exporting nation (and by far the largest in terms of exports per capita or exports as a percentage of GDP).

The roots of the social responsibilities felt by German business leaders are deep, as is a commitment to quality and service in their products. A long tradition of close cooperation and coordination between business, government, and labor, which manifests a sense of being "social partners," marks Germany's distinctive view of corporate purpose. These attitudes are rooted in necessity and nationalism. As W. R. Smyser notes,

> [Germans are] very conscious of being in a small country that can only survive if all work together. Germans have a sense of being collaborators in a common enterprise even as they may compete for their place within it or may argue ceaselessly about the specific policies that the enterprise should pursue. . . . The concept of private initiative operating within a public framework lies firmly imbedded in the conscience of West German managers. They believe in the link between a cooperative society and individual freedom and in the implications of this for self-restraint as well as for competition.[62]

These beliefs strongly shape the corporate purpose of most German firms. What emerges is a purpose with a social conscience focusing on a company's contribution to the wealth of German society.

This strong sense of responsibility takes the form of social concern for employees, an emphasis on the creation of quality jobs, and attention to the impact of business activity on the local community.[63] Growth, a dominant objective of German business, serves each of these ends well. Consistent with these concerns, a 1993 Economics Ministry report identified the virtues of "consciousness of responsibility, humanity and compassion, reliability, loyalty, punctuality, decisiveness and creativity" as the foundation for making Germany a leading industrial nation.[64] Even during the economic problems of the 1990s—brought on by the cost of reunifying Germany, the world's highest unit-labor cost, and stresses associated with the creation of the European monetary union—no mainstream business, government, or labor leader advocated abandoning these values. To the contrary, the soul searching caused by these events reinforced the commitment to these values.

Robert Bosch, the founder of Robert Bosch GmbH, Germany's ninth-largest corporation, is an exemplar of these values. His motto, "Better to lose money than trust," guided his decisions. He treated the company's workers as if they were part of his family, developing housing projects and hospitals for them and their families.[65] His paternalism is reflective of much of German business tradition.

The stress on an improved standard of living, good jobs, and other social concerns, coupled with the limited size of the German market, creates a need to expand through competitive exports. German industry has been quite successful in this endeavor. Indeed, although the German economy is only one quarter the size of the U.S. economy, the size of its exports of goods approaches that of the United States. German exports consistently exceed those of Japan.

A Brief History

A look at German history and tradition gives an understanding of the depth to which the values underlying corporate purpose are ingrained in German society, and therefore in its managers.

Philosophically, German thought has been heavily influenced by Georg Wilhelm Friedrich Hegel (1770–1831). Hegel's idea of the dialectic, in which thesis and antithesis resolve themselves in synthesis, has shaped German thinking about the economy. Hegel's synthesis is not a compromise between two opposites. Rather, it is a combination that contains elements of both, but supersedes them to create something of a higher order. Because of these ideas, Germans more readily accept the concept of the constructive coexistence of opposites. This acceptance can be found in the potentially conflicting notions of the "social-market economy," codetermination, and other factors that bring such a high level of order to German society. It is not unusual for Germans to think of workers, management, shareholders, the government, and communities living in some form of constructive synthesis.

Hegel, like Rousseau before him, believed that because government is the reflection of the general will, it is superior to any business or individual interest. In fact Hegel was convinced that the individual could find fulfillment and freedom only as a citizen of a strong state. Therefore, the individual's right to property is subordinated to the general will as reflected in the commands of the state. Laws alone determine ownership, not some idea of natural rights. Private rights should be subject to social control.[66] In this view, corporations are embodiments of the general will, and consequently their claims are superior to the individual's (i.e., superior to the shareholder's or the manager's interest).[67] Although the individual's property rights were subordinated to the general will, Hegel considered them nevertheless essential to an individual's freedom. Since a person's will is externalized through the acquisition and use of property, the absence of rights to property would curtail the individual's self-realization and freedom.[68] Common ownership would not enable the individual to use the property according to his or her purposes. Hegel's ideas reinforce the beliefs in the responsibility of the corporation to act in accordance with the general will and in the subordination of the individual to that purpose.

Over the years, German leaders have used Hegel's ideas regarding property rights to justify the subordination of private rights to the demands of a potentially totalitarian state. This justification led to a tradition of state superiority over individual property rights and was used to rationalize some of the acts of the Prussian autocracy and the Nazi state.

Germany's Industrialization. Until well into the nineteenth century, the German principalities were largely feudal in nature and autonomous. Property was owned by the ruling families. The economies were based on guild and craft production that emphasized quality. Economic necessities of these relatively small principalities caused them to focus on exports to maximize the sales of their products, and thereby the welfare of their citizens. Consequently, close relationships developed between the business owners and the local and state governments. As industrial power became concentrated in the wealthy families, particularly in the northern German states, business took on an aura of Prussian paternalism.

Being late to industrialize (Germany was nearly seventy-five years behind Britain and fifty years behind the United States), there was a widely acknowledged need to catch up. After Otto von Bismarck unified the country in 1871, the industrial leaders, in cooperation with the state, developed policies that enabled the country to leapfrog into the industries that would dominate the early twentieth century. Banks, large corporations, and cartels played the leading roles in this transformation.[69] This strategy proved quite successful. As Alfred Chandler has documented, from 1913 to 1973 Germany consistently had more corporations in chemicals, primary metals, electrical machinery, and general machinery than did Great Britain or the United States.[70]

During this period the state acted as the steward of industrial properties collectively owned by the private sector and the state, as well as state-owned rail, power, and communications industries. The state ensured that these enterprises served the interests of the German people.

The German welfare state also had its beginnings under Bismarck. Concerned about the radical demands of the increasingly militant workers' unions and the growing political strength of the rival Social Democratic Party, he began to develop a system of social welfare to preempt both forces. These policies were designed to make workers beneficiaries of Germany's increasing industrialization, thus promoting social cohesion. With the government promoting social legislation, the militant trade unionists soon learned that through the state's political action they could often obtain what they could not win from corporate management.

From Bismarck on, the state had an increasingly active role in the economy. The government's intrusion into the economy reached its peak under the fascist Nazi regime. However, this legacy of government-business cooperation and paternalistic concern for employees and communities lives on today. Reunification served to reinforce these tendencies. East Germany was even more strongly influenced by the paternalistic traditions of Prussia than was West Germany. In addition, East Germans' forty-five years under communism made them excessively reliant on the government and gave them no experience in how free markets work. Even after reunification, a poll found that 57 percent of East Germans believed "socialism was a good idea that was badly implemented."[71]

Creating the Social Market Economy. The Nazi abuses discredited the central government as the dominant economic actor. Consequently, after World War II a new system was needed. Ludwig Erhard, West Germany's first minister of economics and successor to Conrad Adenauer as chancellor, provided the new system with his ideas regarding a "social market economy" (*Soziale Marktwirtschaft*). The system was based on the principles of free competition in open markets, the right to private property, a minimum of state involvement, and welfare programs that would make competition socially productive. This system was market-based and free from state domination, but it had a "human face."[72] Nevertheless, beginning in the 1970s, the state gradually became more interventionist.

Germany's economic miracle can be attributed in large part to its social-market economy and the related distinctive institutional arrangements that enable stiff competition among firms to take place, competition governed by a widely accepted set of principles embedded in a traditional German concept of *Ordnung*, or "order." *Ordnung* connotes a systematic view in which "all things are part of a whole, and must be evaluated in terms of their effects on that whole. All elements share the whole, and are in turn shaped by it. All depend on it, as it depends on them. . . . The government's function is to preserve the system, against abuse by the participants but mainly against itself."[73] The individual and the system affect, and protect, one another.

Ordnungspolitik, which makes this synthesis possible, is a system "of measures and institutions which impart to competition the framework, rules and machinery of impartial supervision which a competitive system needs as much as any game or match if it is not to degenerate into a vulgar brawl. . . . This presupposes mature economic discernment on the part of all responsible bodies and individuals and a strong impartial state."[74] *Ordnungspolitik* implies a social contract in which managers can pursue competitive advantage while accepting their responsibilities to employees and the community.

Beyond cooperation between business and government, two other institutional relationships are central to German competitiveness and shape the corporate purpose of its firms: the close relationships of industrial firms to the German banks and the consensus-based interaction of management and labor captured by the concept of codetermination. These represent "a set of political and social institutions which have primacy over the operation of the market. But—and this is an essential feature of the German model—this primacy is not vested in the state. First and foremost it is vested in the law itself, respect for which is stronger in Germany than in any other European country."[75]

The Ownership and Structure of the Corporate Sector

The heart of the German industrial sector is the *Mittelstand*, medium-sized companies, 80 percent of which are privately held. *Mittelstand* headquarters are scattered widely across Germany and are typically based in communities where their owners and employees live. The result is a heightened sense of responsibility and attachment to both employees and the community that some have likened to patriarchies. Most of these owner-managed companies have close relations with their local banks and take a particularly long-term view of their business, unhampered by return on investment targets or concerns about raising capital.

Even among the large corporations, many are privately owned.[76] Out of an estimated 380,000 companies, there are only about 700 publicly owned companies listed on a German stock exchange.[77] Since most German companies are privately held, owners and managers exercise strong control with little influence from other external capital-market forces, and there is a significant unity of purpose between the owners and the firm, reflecting a responsibility to German society.

For publicly owned German companies, the most significant and influential ownership positions are typically held by banks, other industrial corporations (many firms own shares in each other), and state and federal governments. The banks stand out as having the greatest influence. German banks own approximately 9 percent of all domestically listed shares, but own significantly more of the large companies.[78] A study by the German Monopolies Commission found that the large universal banks own 10–25 percent of forty-eight of the one hundred largest firms, 25–50 percent of forty-three others, and more than half of nine of these firms.[79] In addition to their direct ownership, German banks hold shares on deposit for other shareholders. In practice, they vote not only their own shares but also those for which they are the depository. This gives them effective control over approximately 50 percent of the listed shares.[80] The most powerful bank, Deutsche Bank, owns more than 10 percent of seventy companies, including 28 percent of Germany's largest industrial company, Daimler-Benz. Deutsche Bank executives sit on four hundred boards of directors.[81] German corporate law requires over 75 percent of all shareholders to approve changes in a public company's capital structure (for example, the issuance of new shares or new bonds). Thus a 25 percent ownership position (or at least a 25 percent voting right) forms a blocking minority. Consequently, a bank or group of banks can form a blocking minority with considerable negative control.[82]

Typically, the banks, other corporations, and government entities that are shareholders are primarily interested in the long-term competitiveness of the firms they own. They have long-standing and often close business relationships with the firms in which they are investors. As in Japan, instead of seeking to profit from the sale of their equity holdings in these firms, banks and corporate shareholders look to the firms in which they own common stock as a source of future business. For banks, the largest proportion of their investment in a firm is normally in loans, not equity. In fact, German companies have greater indebtedness than their U.S. counterparts and are even more reliant on short-term debt than are the Japanese. Except for the usually meager dividends, banks' shareholdings provide little prospect for returns until they are sold— something the banks normally do not do. The banks practice long-term "relationship banking," and therefore their paramount interests are increases in loans, cash management services, foreign exchange transactions, and other banking services. For shareholders that are industrial companies, it is their commercial ties—as suppliers, distributors, or customers—that govern. As a consequence, their principal focus is on the long-term growth of the commercial relationships with the companies they own, not on current returns on these investments. For the government owners, their constituents' interests are paramount. These are truly long-term investors, each with a greater interest in the firm's growth than on direct returns on their investments.

The stability among banks and borrowers, buyers and suppliers, and unions and managers is a source of considerable competitive strength. The stability of the workforce enables German companies to invest heavily in skills and training without concern that these "assets" will move to another company. Commitment among employees to the company—and pride in the firm's accomplishments—fosters loyalty, hard work, and a constructive concern for the company's future. The relationship among buyers and suppliers encourages close working relationships that can reduce cost and increase innovation. The close relationship with banks ensures availability of capital and lessens concerns about short-term earnings volatility. Each of these relationships contributes to long-term thinking.

As a result of their strong relationships with and ownership of industrial firms, banks have a larger role in management decisions than they do in America. Through their role on supervisory boards, they can be quick to remove poorly performing executives. However, they are also a source of considerable stability that allows managers to take a long-term view.

Codetermination

Another principal structural determinant of German corporate purpose is the relationship between the workers and management, which is predicated on consensus decision making. In part owing to Germany's rich historical guild and craftsman tradition, managers have considerable respect for good workers. Because of this tradition and a system called *Mitbestimmung* (codetermination), consensus, not conflict, marks the relationship between management and labor unions. This alliance—forged from mutual respect and systematic integration—creates a formidable barrier to the exercise of influence by nonbank shareholders. Both management and labor want profits reinvested, not distributed as dividends. In the words of one German union leader, "We want investment and management wants investment, while capital interests want dividends. We do not press our wage demands to the point where management has no money left to reinvest. The most secure jobs are those in a modern factory."[83]

Codetermination gives workers extensive consultative powers. One vehicle for this is the workers' council (*Betriebsrat*), which by law is made up exclusively of workers. Although it has no direct control, it gives workers a voice in operational issues directly affecting them. Another vehicle for worker participation is the supervisory board (*Aufsichtsrat*). The supervisory board, on which the workers and shareholders are equally represented, oversees management. The chair, who is selected by the majority of the shareholders' representatives, has the deciding vote in the event of a tie. Since public shareholdings are widely distributed, these shareholders play a minor role in corporate governance.

Years of consultation between labor and management have generated a greater appreciation of each other's, as well as the shareholders', interests. The result is considerable stability. For example, there have been only four contested takeovers in Germany from 1945 to 1994.[84] Also, Germany loses far less working time to strikes than nearly any other industrialized country.

The result is that "German firms are closer to parliamentary democracies, run by company boards, specialists on those boards and trade unions. . . . The *Mitbestimmung* system gives unions a stake in ensuring that the demands of their members do not put firms and industries in jeopardy. It turns workers and managers from opponents into partners."[85]

The relationship between management and workers goes beyond employee involvement in governance and the promotion of high wages. Together, corporate management and labor unions set national employment policy.[86] Management places considerable emphasis on jobs, reflecting German society's preoccupation with employment. Firms also spend up to 15 percent of their net incomes on apprenticeship training programs. Increased skills promise increased productivity, which serves the firms' interests well.

German tradition and structural relationships weave a socially conscious purpose into the fabric of firms. Much like many Asian firms, German companies see themselves as part of a whole—an image captured by the concept of *ordnung*. German firms exist to serve this whole: their employees, communities, banks, other related industrial companies, and nation. They do this by creating wealth for their communities through better jobs and more competitive products. They take pride in their image in the community. To serve this purpose, they focus on growth and are constantly searching for foreign markets for their products. They can be fierce international competitors. German companies tend to shun price competition and instead compete on trying to make their products the world's best through a relentless focus on product quality, service, and productivity.

Wrestling with Change

With the fall of the Berlin Wall in 1990 and the subsequent reunification of Germany, West Germany took on a great responsibility. The new nation had to absorb a bankrupt economy with severely outdated infrastructure and plant, and 16 million people with an average standard of living only one fifth the West's. Also, substantial gross transfers had to be made to the former East Germany—DM200 billion in 1995 alone.[87]

While the government was preoccupied with making reunification successful, the German economy weakened. In the hypercompetitive world of the 1990s, relying on excellence of a product without adequate regard to costs proved insufficient grounds for competitive advantage. The demands placed on companies by government and labor pushed many companies' cost structures to noncompetitive levels. German companies were struggling under the burden of extensive government regulations, high social taxes, the highest corporate tax rate of any large industrialized country, tough work rules, and government protection of certain industries.

Although the German people have enjoyed considerable benefits from the social-market economy system—they have the highest hourly wages in manufacturing ($26.93 in 2000 compared to $20.89 in Japan and $19.20 in the United States), the shortest workweek, and the longest vacations of any major industrial country—these benefits have gradually eroded Germany's competitiveness. Noncash benefits paid to employees—the "second wage"—add 80 cents to every dollar of basic wages.

The escalating wages and heavy social burden on corporations had predictable results. Germany became an unattractive location to manufacture. German companies, for the first time in a significant way, began moving production overseas. Foreign companies also began to cut their investments in Germany. Germany's share of world merchandize exports also fell from a peak of over 12 percent in 1987 to just under 9 percent in 2000, a level approximating Germany's market share in the early 1980s. These factors combined to push the unemployment rate to the highest level since immediately following World War II.

These events shook all of Germany's "social partners," leading to a new nationwide consensus in the late 1990s that economic reforms were necessary. Although proposals to reduce welfare spending, deregulate certain industries, and reduce corporate taxes had the support of business, political, and some labor leaders, none were advocating a dismantling of the communitarian foundation of the German economy.

Despite their vocal public protests against moves toward "pure capitalism" and the rejection of "long-held social values," labor leaders increasingly recognize that further increases in wages, benefits, and restrictive work rules threaten the future of high-paying German jobs.[88] Some recent agreements reflect this change in thinking. For example, in 1997 unions agreed to pay cuts of up to 10 percent for troubled chemical companies. Also, during the recession of 1993, Daimler-Benz reached an agreement to contain wage increases and to cut its workforce by seventy-two thousand jobs (20 percent) through generous severance payments and government-subsidized early retirements. The chief labor representative of Daimler-Benz's supervisory board commented afterward, "We know that we have the highest wages and are the most privileged in terms of working hours. It's also clear to us that we can only maintain this standard of living if we become more productive. There's no contradiction in saying we as labor must save costs."[89] Also, to achieve more cost-competitive labor agreements, corporations are beginning to move away from industry-wide pattern bargaining agreements to company-specific agreements. The initiatives for most of these moves, which often entail labor concessions, have started at the plant level, where union leaders and workers recognize the need for changes if their jobs are going to be secure in the future. As the CEO of one of Germany's leading companies observes, "The German worker is making a sacrifice."[90] As a result of these "sacrifices," unit labor costs, which rose at a 4.6 percent compound annual rate in the 1980s, grew only 1.3 percent per year in the 1990s.

There is general agreement within the country that the key to Germany's historical competitive strength rests in the cooperation among labor, management, and government to achieve common objectives—the welfare of the German people. As companies look forward, they recognize that the ability to develop and apply knowledge will be increasingly important. The positive aspects of the current system—a sense of the whole, loyalty, commitment, and long-term thinking—will become increasingly important. What is needed is a reduction in welfare expenditures and less burdensome regulations to enable corporations to more agilely and cost-effectively serve the common good. If the emerging consensus is transformed into action and the shackles that have hindered German companies for more than a decade are removed, Germany will be an even more formidable competitor than it has been in the past.

Lessons from America's Competitors

Germany, Japan, and Korea are blazing new competitive and ideological territory. Each in its own way is struggling to create new ways of managing that blend the best of the cultural attributes of individual creativity and initiative within the company while maintaining a communitarian corporate purpose focused on responsibility to employees, customers, communities, nation, or global society. Each of these countries—as well as China—is taking concrete steps to reduce the government's role in business, making its companies more responsive to the product market.

Although each of these countries has its own unique history, philosophical traditions, and institutional relationships between industrial companies, capital-market firms, and the government, they all share many commonalities that point to corporate purposes with a significantly different character than the Anglo-American shareholder-oriented view of purpose.

All have a strong sense of nationalism that deeply moves many individual employees. As Fukuyama observes, "The nationalist is primarily preoccupied not with economic gain, but with recognition and dignity. . . . The recognition one seeks, however, is not for oneself as an individual, but for the group of which one is a member."[91] Nationalism consequently has significant implications for purpose. Recall the call for personal sacrifice to build a prosperous Korea, and Toyota's aim for world recognition and for the development of Japan. German executives are steeped in a tradition of strong national sentiment and corporate service to German society. Corporate purpose that resonates with the wellsprings of nationalism in individual workers can unleash astonishing levels of commitment to the common cause. Clearly, it can be misused, as it was in Japan and Germany in the grotesque misadventures that eventually led to World War II and the virtual destruction of each country. But this history underscores the motivational power of nationalism. In today's society, corporations channel this motivation in constructive directions.

However, reliance on nationalism as a unifying motivational force has severe limits in a world of global competition. It does not travel well beyond national boundaries. Clearly, service to one country provides little motivation to employees in another country. Leaders in these countries who understand this reality expand their rhetoric and their actions to a focus on customers and employees worldwide or to global society.

Companies in each of these countries have a strong commitment to their employees. In Japan, the company often is not distinguished from its employees. The employees are the company. Both Korean and Japanese companies demonstrate Confucian characteristics of seeking harmony between the employee and the company. German companies often feel their first responsibility is to their employees' welfare and have formed a social partnership with labor. These commitments and attitudes result in a reciprocal loyalty between managers (the company) and employees that can have significant competitive benefits. People work harder, are more focused on achieving the common ends, and are more likely to put aside self-interest to serve the common cause.

As opposed to the Anglo-American model of adversarial relations between business and government, each of these countries has close, cooperative relationships between government and business. The benefits include the availability of low-cost capital, protection of domestic markets from international competition, and tax incentives.

The ownership of corporations in each country is held closely by founding families, other industrial concerns, and/or banks. The resulting relationships put the emphasis on growth and insulate corporate managers from the pressure exerted by independent capital-market institutions for higher returns on capital.

The combined effect of nationalism, an employee focus, cooperative government relations, and owners who seek benefits in the form of the greater commercial ties, is a managerial holism that focuses on long-term competitive success. The result is an intuitive emphasis on expanding the total value-producing capacity of the corporation. A focus on improving the welfare of employees creates loyalties and stability in workforce relationships that are critical to the creation of knowledge. Freed from excessive concerns about return on capital, managers have a greater willingness and ability to invest heavily in the businesses in which they seek to compete. The long-term growth and corporate reputation is stressed, rather than quarterly earnings and discounted present values (today's value) of investments. To achieve growth, companies in each of these countries have emphasized exports. In order to compete in global markets, they have had to develop highly competitive skills and to invent or adopt world best practices.

When working properly, these forces lead to a laserlike focus on the product market, undistracted by undue pressures from independent capital-market institutions. This focus has been central to the competitive strength of these companies. The product market is understood, if only intuitively, to be the generator of all tangible wealth. Growth, greater value added, and consequently lower costs are central to their strategies.

The economic successes of these countries should not be a surprise. Their ideologies have resulted in a willingness of managers—some would say a recklessness—to invest substantial amounts in the pursuit of growth and to foster close, reciprocal relationships with employees. In each country, corporate leaders take great pride in their company's reputation and contribution to national welfare. The strong obligations to the welfare of their country and their employees are brought into harmony with the long-term competitive interests of the company through the pursuit of growth. The harmony is strengthened in practice because individuals find self-worth and fulfillment by participating in causes that are clearly useful to society. By providing opportunities for individual initiative and creative self-expression through work—something the Japanese and Koreans particularly are trying to improve—and opportunities to identify closely with their communities by serving worthwhile ends that clearly benefit society—something companies in each of these countries strive to do—these companies are developing powerful, people-based competitive capabilities. Unleashing and directing their employees' latent human potential for the service of corporate ends generates commitment, loyalty, and workforce stability—factors essential to rapid creation and deployment of knowledge.

But for each of these countries, this work is still in progress (and for China, it is just beginning). The problems confronting them as they enter the twenty-first century are largely the consequences of too much government involvement in business, shaky banking systems, archaic management methods that unduly restrict human creativity and initiative, and in the case of Korea, unfocused diversification by the *chaebol*. Steps are actively being taken in these countries to address these problems. An important part of the unfinished work in these countries is freeing businesses from government regulation and subsidies. When this happens, businesses will be more at the mercy of free-market competitive pressures, requiring a further emphasis on efficiency and innovation. These reforms will be slow in the making because of the political power of many of the groups whose special interests would be adversely affected. However, competitive realities demand reform, lest the economies lose competitiveness and the national standards of living stagnate or decline.

This analysis is not to suggest that the United States should emulate any of these countries. Instead, it is to provide an understanding of critically important competitive forces that are at work in the global economy. There are deep and long-standing differences in the ideologies among these countries and the United States. These ideologies lead them to compete by very different rules with different scorecards. The competitive consequences are profound. Those who predict that these countries will soon adopt a form of shareholder capitalism similar to the system that is prevalent in the United States underestimate these ideologies' deep roots in values, history, and philosophical ideas. They will not change soon, and they will not significantly change over time unless the ideology fails in the marketplace. Such failure is unlikely, however. A great experiment is under way to enable greater individualism within firms and to harness it to serve communitarian ends. The quest is for a realization of the essential harmony of the deep human need to identify constructively with worthy ends beyond the self and to express the self creatively—to live a life that makes a difference. Work can do this.

If the experiment is successful, the greater human potential that will be unleashed will have major competitive implications. Innovation will increase and costs will decline, as some leading American and Japanese companies have already demonstrated. The result is an ever more free and competitive market economy capable of producing a considerable increase in the value received by customers and employees alike.

CONCLUSION   *The Lessons for Leadership*

10   Infusing Purpose
A Moral and Strategic Responsibility of Leadership

All great things are done for their own sake.
　　—*Robert Frost*

It is the oldest lesson in the world. Succeeding generations always forget it. Unless you're customer-focused, you go out of business.
　　—*Walter Wriston*[1]

At the heart of effective corporate leadership rests the responsibility to define, promote, and defend a meaningful overarching purpose of corporate activity—one that ennobles those who serve it, stimulates individual commitment, and brings unity to cooperative action. This responsibility is at once strategic and moral.

Infusing the Company with Purpose: A Strategic Responsibility of Leadership

The leader is responsible for corporate performance—a responsibility that embodies duties to customers, employees, shareholders, and communities. To be successful in the highly competitive marketplace of the future, companies will have to be increasingly agile, responsive, and able to excel at innovating efficiently and rapidly. Each of these characteristics is embedded in the capabilities and motivations of the company's people—its human capital. Consequently, companies will require leaders with unparalleled ability to unleash the creativity and initiative of their members.

These conditions for strategic success cannot flourish in an environment where the top-down exercise of authority or the heavy use of often-stifling formal processes are relied on to provide direction. Innovation, efficiency, and speed necessitate a high level of autonomy throughout the organization. Rapid decision making based on detailed knowledge of customer needs and the relevant technologies requires decentralized authority. Responsibility for performance must accompany this autonomy. Self-direction replaces the formal sources of direction of top-down authority and formal management processes. For this self-control to be effective, each individual needs a clear understanding of how his or her responsibilities fit with the company's purpose, mission, and strategies. This understanding and direction begins with the guidance provided by the priorities embodied in a shared sense of purpose.

Alignment Born of a Certain Harmony

The leader is responsible for providing this direction—for creating a certain harmony among the realities of the marketplace and the firm's defining characteristics—its purpose, mission, strategies, goals, and values. Without a purpose that fosters coherence and concord among the firm's raison d'être, strategy, and values, discord will reign within the firm. A customer-focused purpose makes this harmony possible.

This purpose guides organizational leaders in making extremely important, and often subtle, distinctions regarding some of the most fundamental dilemmas of corporate life. These dilemmas include whether to orient the organization primarily toward the product markets or the capital markets; whether profits are ends or means; how best to resolve tensions between actions to secure competitiveness and those to generate higher returns and between long-term and short-term performance; and how to place customers' priorities ahead of employees without treating employees as means to the customers' ends.

By its very nature, strategy is product-market oriented; consequently, only a purpose of serving the customer is directly aligned with strategy. This purpose also helps to ensure that operational goals are consistent with and supportive of the strategy. This is quite unlike a shareholder-focused purpose, which calls for financially dominated goals that internalize the capital market's priorities within the firm and that can be at cross-purposes with a product-market-oriented competitive strategy.

Infusing strategy and operational goals with a customer-focused purpose also helps to align individual motivations and aspirations with the firm's strategic mission and objectives. The primary emphasis on the product market unites individual actions with strategy, creating the coherence of interests, goals, and values essential to outstanding performance. This coherence reduces counterproductive internal conflicts and tensions that can sap competitiveness; it is an essential ingredient for creating an organization with a constructive culture built around strong shared values. Like a highly efficient machine, the critical parts of an organization—its people, tangible resources, strategy, and shared values—work together with a minimum of friction. And they are concentrated on delivering a maximum effort to where it counts—to providing target customers with a higher perceived value at a lower delivered cost than competitors.

In contrast, a shareholder-oriented purpose can sow the seeds of tension throughout the organization—from product-market strategies designed to serve capital-market ends, to specific actions to create, produce, deliver, and service the firm's products governed by financial goals. Caught in this conflict, individuals often find their personal values at odds with corporate ends. Confusion and dissonance often exist in these companies over whether generating financial returns or creating customer value is more important.

Defining and communicating corporate purpose is not the responsibility of CEOs, boards, and senior corporate managers alone. Leaders at all levels can and should infuse collective effort in their organizational units with a worthwhile purpose. The objective is to create a powerful common understanding of the priorities guiding each person's actions. In companies seeking to maximize shareholder wealth, subunit leaders face the added challenge of creating a meaningful customer-focused purpose for their unit while buffering the unit from the shorter-term profit pressures that so often accompany a shareholder-focused purpose. Successfully meeting this challenge requires courage and vigilance to maintain consistency in words, decisions, and processes to form a pattern that communicates the value of serving customers and creating the foundation for future competitive advantage.

Defining Corporate Purpose:
A Moral Responsibility of Leadership

Institutional integrity—like individual integrity—is derived from a coherence and wholeness of moral values and actions. Outstanding leaders work tirelessly to build their organizations' character. An essential step in this effort is the promotion and implementation of a corporate purpose that, by bringing a moral quality to collective ends, forms the cornerstone of institutional integrity. A customer-focused purpose can do this. By their deeds, these leaders make the quality of the firm's cause real, thus creating an ideal to which individual actions can aspire.

Building a moral organization begins with the faith that in constructive environments individuals will strive to do what is right. Recognizing that the highest moral aspirations, which are potentially the strongest and most enduring, often lie latent in many people's work lives, the leader seeks ways to energize these motivations. A meaningful purpose can help do this.

The leader also understands that if left unrealized, these latent motivations can create frustration and alienation. Work loses its intrinsic meaning and value—it becomes merely a way to make money or to further one's professional career. When the corporate purpose is of no real personal value to employees, the company becomes what Philip Selznick calls an "expendable tool" for achieving these extrinsic material ends. When people use the organization as a tool, rampant self-interest sows the seeds of politicized dissention, conflicting goals, and eventual apathy.

Without a positive belief in the fundamental motivations of people, a manager is more likely to impose strict control processes to curb deviant behavior, take a much greater top-down role in making decisions, and build the corporate staff to extend his or her influence. This centralization of power and increased bureaucratization of decision making is the opposite of what is needed to build a high-performing organization and is also corrosive of moral aspirations. In addition, attempts to manipulate desired behavior through material rewards and measurement and control systems lack the power of intrinsic rewards to direct and motivate behavior.

The assumption of responsibilities—not curtailing or abrogating them—builds character. Increased responsibilities enhance a person's sense of duty, dignity, and achievement and foster greater creative self-expression. Consequently, effective leaders not only delegate responsibility, but also create environments that motivate and enable people to assume greater responsibility.

The morality of individual action springs from its positive effect on the lives of others. Consequently, the leader should link individual achievement to a corporate purpose that embodies meaningful ends worth striving to achieve. A customer-focused purpose does just that; it brings a unity, coherence, wholeness, and significance to operational goals, personal accomplishment, and the ultimate corporate ends.

Not Treating Employees as Means

In keeping with Judeo-Christian principle and Immanuel Kant's moral imperative, no person should be treated as a means to any other end. People are ends in themselves. Yet their ingenuity and hard work are essential to providing value for customers, shareholders, and society. This tension creates one of the most perplexing moral dilemmas facing corporate leaders in a capitalistic society: how to achieve outstanding performance without treating people as means to achieving it.

This dilemma can be resolved only if individual organizational members personally value the purpose of their work. Only when the corporation's and the individual's purposes of work are one can he or she be led in the service of corporate ends without being used as a means to these ends. Achieving this harmony between the corporation's purpose and the employees' interests activates the basic human desire to serve other people and causes beyond oneself. Serving the purpose is part of who they are. When they act in the company's interest, they are furthering their own ends as well.

The simple fact is that people identify much more closely with (and their work is more directly related to) creating value for customers than with producing wealth for shareholders. The substance and quality of a customer-focused purpose provides the glue that binds the firm's members together and forms that certain harmony among strategy and individual values upon which outstanding competitive performance is grounded.

This is one reason why most outstanding leaders can give their firm's people an importance rivaling the customer. These leaders intuitively understand that when people knowingly contribute to valued ends beyond themselves, they expand and enrich their sense of self. Consequently, the conflict between people's self-interest and subordinating this interest to the service of others is a false dichotomy. In serving others, people are better able to overcome their sense of separateness and find meaning for their own lives from the quality of their relationships directly with others and through serving a noble cause benefiting others. Their heightened commitment to the cause motivates them to a fuller realization of their potential. The end is personally worth sacrificing their narrowly defined self-interest. As a consequence, and somewhat paradoxically, when people are treated as an end, not as a means, they normally create more value for others as well.

Raising Moral Aspirations

As any manager can attest, the workplace raises ethical dilemmas that challenge one's moral fiber. Managers can create work environments that intensify these challenges or minimize them. Constructive leaders assume responsibility for creating environments in which the moral aspirations of people are raised, not corrupted. In fact, achieving outstanding competitive performance is integrally connected to the leader's ability to do so. When this occurs, the organization is more cohesive, direction is clearer, responsibility more readily assumed, and motivation greater. Unfortunately, too many managers lack the courage, understanding, or conviction required to achieve this state. In the resulting void, forces are unintentionally created that test and often erode the character of their subordinates.

Echoing Maslow's words, "What a man *can* be, he *must* be," the constructive leader creates an environment that stretches and motivates followers to achieve a high level of moral and creative development. In essence, the leader acts to enable—indeed encourage—followers to move to higher levels of moral development.[2] Peak moral reasoning occurs when actions are based on the concept of social utility (the greatest good for the greatest number), and on universal, logical ethical principles affirming "respect for the dignity of human beings as individual persons."[3] Serving a worthwhile corporate purpose and behaving toward those in and outside the organization in ways that further the common good and mutual benefit reinforce these highest stages.

As people grow to think and act in this way, narrow self-interest is transformed into an interest that connects the individual more closely with other human beings. Because the self is defined primarily through relationships with others, by working cooperatively with colleagues to serve the needs of customers, the individual's sense of separateness is replaced by a greater connectedness with fellow employees and with customers.

To create this enabling environment, the leader must forge an organization in which people are challenged to achieve high standards of performance in the pursuit of a worthy purpose beyond themselves; where each individual's work possesses a certain dignity; where decisions are made in an atmosphere of mutual trust, openness, and candor and ideas are valued on their merit; where people enjoy constructive degrees of autonomy and the freedom and encouragement to exercise their creativity and individual initiative; where they are offered ample opportunities for personal growth and achievement and are given the resources needed to fulfill the responsibilities entrusted to them; and where they feel a sense of community bound together by a common purpose and values respecting the dignity of each individual. The foundation of this environment is a shared and valued purpose that instills employees with the conviction that they can simultaneously shape the corporate destiny and pursue their vision for their own life.

As people become less self-possessed, a new relationship to work and to the company develops. Their loyalty, commitment, and diligence increase. Consequently, behavior conducive to the spread of trust becomes more prevalent. As these values become woven into the organizational fabric, corporate performance is enhanced. An ethic of mutually beneficial responsibilities and of service to a valued purpose fosters a sense of connectedness and community. The ability to trust others to do the right thing increases organizational unity. The spirit of belonging to a "family" or "team" brings added satisfaction from achieving common worthwhile ends through cooperative efforts. In addition, these conditions promote respect for new ideas and a willingness to assume responsibility for results. Direction is given to decisions, so that they are more likely to be in harmony with valued ends and less likely to be compromised by narrow self-interest.

To have this uplifting effect, strategy, shared values, and action must be tied to purpose. As an executive of a leading health care company observes, "When values are not tied to the vision or mission, they float and become somewhat irrelevant."[4] At their finest, these are moral responsibilities. They profoundly influence the lives of the people touched by the corporation and enhance the firm's ability to contribute value to society.

The distinguishing characteristics of outstanding leadership—what James MacGregor Burns calls "transforming leadership"—are the leader's ability to understand employees' values, motivations, and higher needs, as well as the leader's own, and the ability to get followers to act to achieve goals embodying shared values and motivations. The "fundamental act" of leadership, Burns writes, is "to induce people to be aware or conscious of what they feel—to feel their true needs so strongly, to define their values so meaningfully, that they can move to purposeful action."[5] By successfully energizing people's higher needs and values, the leader can profoundly affect their moral aspirations and character. By seeking to satisfy the followers' higher needs and aspirations, the leader "engages the full person of the follower" and serves as "an *independent force in changing the makeup of the followers' motive base through gratifying their motives*."[6] By consistently reinforcing how these needs and values are grounded in a worthy corporate purpose, the conditions are created for people to ennoble themselves. Although leaders can do little to ennoble others directly, they can create the enabling environment. By responding constructively to this environment, people transform and ennoble their lives. As their work rises above a narrowly self-interested "career" or "job" to become a "calling," they have taken a critical step toward the self-transcendence that the psychologists and theologians have linked to a fully developed, self-actualized adult life.

This self-transcendence has a critical strategic implication—it fosters greater knowledge creation. By lowering the barriers between the self and the other (be it a person or an idea), individuals become more open to ideas of others and more willing to share ideas of their own. This openness and candor is essential to high levels of knowledge creation.

When a leader sets out to create an atmosphere of purpose-centered, values-based, mutually beneficial responsibilities, the moral aspirations and behavior of both the leader and the led are raised to higher levels. The result, Burns explains, has "a transforming effect on both. Perhaps the best modern example [of this transforming leadership] is Gandhi, who aroused and elevated the hopes and demands of millions of Indians and whose life and personality were enhanced in the process."[7] It is this dynamic process of transformation that ultimately makes leadership moral.

A leader's own level of moral conduct and aspiration is enhanced by the constant striving to set the example, to communicate the collective aspirations, and to reinforce them through consistent daily actions. Reflecting on his years teaching leadership at West Point, Colonel Larry Donnithorne concluded, "The roots of sound leadership are in ideals: moral principles (such as justice and beneficence), high-minded values (loyalty, integrity, consideration for others), and selfless service."[8] Being an exemplar of these ethical aspirations places new demands on leadership.

Not all members of the organization will respond initially to the leader's exhortations. However, many will—and will do so with enthusiasm because they see their own values reflected in the company and their personal integrity being enhanced in the process. When the leader aspires to a higher level of moral behavior and demands the same of followers, a virtuous cycle of increasing aspirations occurs. Each level of higher moral behavior inspires

yet more moral behavior. Of course, not all employees will have an intense experience of oneness with the corporate purpose and values. However, the commitment and enthusiasm of those who do will invariably have a positive influence on others. Peter Drucker has observed that as the performance of organizational "stars" increases, the gap between these outstanding performers and the average performer in an organization tends to remain constant. The "stars" pull up the average person's performance. The same is true of moral aspirations. Raising the moral aspirations of a small key group of individuals is contagious.

Consequently, exemplars of these values are needed throughout the organization. Fortunately this kind of leadership creates a new cadre of leaders. Followers who are energized and elevated by the substantive purpose of this relationship and who become more active in the pursuit of the common goals, often become leaders of character themselves.

Trust-instilling behavior builds highly cooperative, mutually beneficial relationships with customers and suppliers that can have important competitive effects. With trust comes greater loyalty and a level of mutual understanding that facilitates commercial transactions. The reduced friction and lessened need for formal mechanisms to protect the company's interests in these relationships lowers the cost of doing business, enhances reaction speed, and reduces risk.

Defining the Purpose:
Six Steps to Arriving at a Mission of Meaning and Value

Individuals have a strong need to understand and find meaning in the purpose of their work. They cannot think about their relationship to the organization in value-free ways. Their substantial personal investment in this relationship demands justification. They "crave an explicit statement of value—a perspective on what counts as being true, beautiful and good."[9] Absent leadership, they define the value and meaning of their relationship to the company on their own—often in idiosyncratic or cynical ways. When developed in a leadership vacuum, these definitions can conflict from individual to individual, undermining group cohesion and commitment.

Consequently, the leader must assume responsibility for developing and guiding the process by which the organization defines a common purpose that is valued by a broad cross section of employees. To ensure that others see the chosen purpose as worthy of their commitment, the process needs to be carefully designed and thoughtfully executed. The resulting purpose needs to be clear, simple, and consistent with the principal activities of the organization and its strategy and mission. The leader's responsibility is to ensure that the corporate purpose is aligned with the values of individual contributors and to make it *their* purpose for serving the company.

Recognizing this inherent drive for meaning and value, the leader should design a series of "challenge sessions" in which he or she challenges the organization to define its collective purpose and make explicit the values, assumptions, and beliefs on which it rests. This process should begin at the top of the organization and, as quickly as possible, be extended sequentially to lower levels of the organization. These discussions, if open and candid, will address the most fundamental moral issues underlying group existence and each individual's work.

The challenge-session process, which consists of six steps, should begin with the top corporate management group. Although in some environments the discussion will be more free-ranging and more frank with the help of an independent facilitator, the CEO should usually play this role—particularly if the organization (and especially the CEO) has a history of valuing independent thinking and candor. What is essential is that people feel free to express their deepest values and beliefs regarding the organization's reason for being and the logic behind these ideas. Therefore at the outset the CEO should encourage individuals to think for themselves and to challenge commonly accepted ideology, conventional wisdom, underlying assumptions, and what others might believe. In companies that have not had similar discussions in the past, the executives are often surprised to find how much their own thinking—which they often consider unique because it doesn't follow the traditional ideology or is "too humanistic" and "soft"—has in common with that of their colleagues.

Step One. The first goal of the challenge sessions is to develop a complete list of alternative constructs of purpose that people have in their minds. These ideas should be put forth without analysis or evaluation. If the organization has an existing statement of purpose, the CEO can begin as Jim Burke did at Johnson & Johnson, asking people to challenge the validity of the existing purpose. He confronted the senior executives saying, "The Credo statement in 150 or 200 of our locations hangs on the wall at least. If the Credo doesn't mean anything, we really ought to come to that conclusion or rip it off the walls and get on with the job. I think if it is seen as an act of pretension, it is not only valueless but it's negative."[10]

The debate should be framed to ensure a breadth of discussion. Individuals should be encouraged to give their personal answer to the meaning they derive from working for the company, what they consider to be the ultimate ends of that work, and how these ends fit with the realities of the competitive marketplace. It is at once a discussion of high moral principles, pragmatic economic ideas, and personal values. The objective is to find the common ground among the three. To begin the discussion, the leader can simply ask the following question:

- Why does our company exist? What is its primary purpose for being?

Step Two. Initially, the suggested reasons for the company's existence are likely to range widely, from "to make a profit," "to produce goods and services," "to maximize the wealth of shareholders," "to serve customers," and more generally, "to serve all of its constituent's needs" or "to serve society." These constructs of purpose should be divided into two groups—those statements that describe the current reality within the company and those that define a desired normative state—by asking the following two questions:

- Based on the company's pattern of words and actions, what would an outside observer say our purpose *is*?
- What *should* our purpose be?

Step Three. Once all ideas are on the table and are identified as either descriptions of reality or statements of aspiration, the following questions should be asked regarding each aspirational purpose:

- Why should the specific end be given priority? What is the underlying justification?
- Why is it a desired purpose?
- Is it an ultimate corporate purpose, or is it a subset of a more fundamental purpose?

This last question should be repeated until the purpose connected to a particular point of view can no longer be driven to a more fundamental level. For example, if the stated purpose is "to make a profit," the response might be, "For what purpose should we make a profit?" If the answer is to maximize shareholder wealth, then the follow-up question could be, "Why should our most foundational end be to serve the shareholder?" Eventually someone is likely to answer something to the effect, "The shareholders are owners, the corporation is their property, and we as managers are agents in ensuring that their property rights are realized." But the questioning should not stop here. The managers need to be able to express why the shareholders' property rights should be given supremacy. The answer for this purpose, as for any other, rests in its presumed benefits to society. In essence, the assumption is that seeking to maximize shareholders returns guides the allocation of capital to its highest use, as measured by returns, which should maximize the wealth of society in general.

An issue that often arises in the discussions is whether the purpose should call for balancing the interests of key constituents or whether it should express an explicit priority among these interests. The balancing argument is seductive, since it does not require managers in the group to grapple with the vexing trade-offs they face in the daily reality of their work. For this reason, it is fatally flawed as a purpose. The issue of balancing constituents' interests should be probed by asking the following questions:

- How should conflicts between the interests of these constituents be resolved?
- What guidance does such a definition of purpose provide to specific decisions?
- When a particular decision embodies conflicting interests among constituents, will individuals throughout the organization be left to apply their own varying personal values in making the decision or will they resolve the conflict by making the decision that they believe best reflects the measurement and reward systems? Is either one what we want them to do?

Managers are usually fairly quick to realize that despite the public relations merits, in practice a purpose calling for "balancing all constituents' interests" provides little direction and has an inherently vacuous nature.

Step Four. Once the fundamental rationale for each aspirational purpose is established, the probing should then turn to its effects on people and performance. At this point, the discussion typically begins to congeal around two concepts of corporate purpose: to maximize the returns to shareholders or to serve the needs of customers. The issue then becomes which purpose should dominate. To resolve this conflict, three lines of questioning should be pursued.

The first line of questioning puts into perspective the relative contributions of employees, customers, and shareholders. It tends to weaken the rationalization for placing first priority on shareholders (but can raise the point of "why not the employees").

- Which constituency makes the greatest contribution to performance, bears the greatest accountability for performance, and assumes the greatest risk and responsibility for failure?

The second line of questioning focuses on the implications the alternative purposes have for strategy and performance:

- Does the purpose provide constructive and useful direction to decision making? Is the direction resulting from this purpose conducive to maximizing the organization's long-term competitiveness? Is our future competitiveness more dependent on our financial or human capital?
- Does this purpose energize the firm's ability to learn and create new, competitively valued competencies?
- Does this purpose reinforce the firm's strategy and give it added value? Which purpose defines a set of priorities that is most consistent with the firm's strategy? Is the essence of our strategy focused on the customer, the shareholder, or the employee? What are the consequences if our purpose does not provide the same focus as does our strategy?
- Can individuals throughout the organization relate their daily contributions to this purpose in a meaningful way?

The third line of questioning personalizes the implications of different priorities by asking each manager these questions:

- What end has the greatest value to you, and why?
- Will the purpose be a stimulus to commitment? Does it represent a cause that you and others will see as worthy of personal commitment and loyalty?

The decision can then be brought to a head by asking this question:

• When there is a conflict among these constituents' interests, whose interest should receive greater weight?

When the group reaches a definition of purpose irreducible except for religious or metaphysical explanations, the process can end, but not until then. Most companies elect to stop here, short of formally attaching this definition to the service of God's will—although the leader should ensure that the debate over purpose is open to such essential elements. For many people, absent these fundamental ideas, the debate will seem constrained. Some companies, such as ServiceMaster, choose to make this belief central. ServiceMaster's ultimate purpose is "To honor God in all we do." To accomplish this, their operative objectives are "to help people develop, to pursue excellence, and to grow profitably." Johnson & Johnson's Burke, reflecting on the importance of this issue in his company's "Credo Challenge" sessions, remarks: "We argued over every word including the elimination of the word 'God.' At the end it said, 'So help me God,' and I have got to tell you, so help me God, that that was the most controversial issue in the whole business."[11]

Although these questions might seem like an orderly march through a well-defined agenda to a predetermined outcome, in reality the discussion is usually quite wide-ranging—philosophical as well as emotional. There is no need to rush to an end. The full range of discussion might take one or two days to reach its conclusion. At Johnson & Johnson, the debate among senior corporate executives took twelve hours.

The result should be a clear, simple statement of the company's ultimate priority that will provide the foundation for statements of vision, mission, strategy, and related objectives. An open process will help to ensure that the purpose is one that all managers understand, that they appreciate its underlying rationale, and that they believe it was developed by an objective and fair process.

Step Five. From these senior management discussions should emerge a draft statement of purpose. Using this statement as a starting point, this same process should then be repeated at descending organizational layers until all managers have been included. To convey the importance placed on the development of a shared purpose, representatives of senior management—and as frequently as possible the CEO—should conduct the meetings. To reach all levels of employees, video conferencing with the CEO or videotapes of the CEO (possibly including excerpts from the senior management debates) may be helpful. Managers should be asked to challenge the draft statement of purpose, change it, or commit to it. The emphasis should be on the challenge. If people's varying ideas of corporate purpose are not fully and fairly discussed, the process is in danger of being seen as a sham. Rather than providing the benefits of a clear shared purpose, cynicism regarding the purpose and senior management's manipulative intent is heightened. If this occurs, the results are very likely to be detrimental rather than beneficial.

Effective challenge sessions can generate highly emotional and energetic debate. The issues are considered fundamentally important because they involve people's own beliefs and values relative to work. For some, it touches fundamental issues related to the meaning of their work—and thus their lives.

For Johnson & Johnson's James Burke, the company's "Credo Challenge" process was so important that it took nearly two years, during which either Burke or David Clare, the COO, eventually "sat with every manager in the company worldwide." These were powerful sessions precisely because people were "forced to think about what *business* was all about and what *they* were about and whether or not they could live with the principles we espoused." Burke explains,

> When you ask them to start challenging the statements inherent in the Credo and they have to begin to deal with the conflicts and trade-offs in those issues, they come alive in ways that you can't make them come alive on any other issues that they deal with, because you are dealing with the fundamental morality of the institution for which they work. They bring to that institution their own set of beliefs and their own set of convictions. If you can't provide an environment that is consonant with their set of convictions, I have got to believe they are not going to be as productive as if you can. And if they can contribute to that environment—test it, challenge it, and feel comfortable with it—then they are going to give more to it than our competitions will. I really believe . . . that the long-term success of the corporation is deeply wrapped up in these issues.[12]

Step Six. Once the purpose challenge sessions are completed, the responsibility for drafting the new purpose statement rests with the leader. The draft statement should then be discussed with the senior management team and additional refinements, if any, made.

Obviously, this process is very time-consuming. But the time spent is indicative of the importance of the outcome. A clear, understood, and shared purpose represents one of the most significant and efficient means a corporate leader has to influence the direction of decisions made by people who are closer to customers and technologies. The challenge process not only acts as an excellent vehicle to communicate the purpose, but also should enhance every participant's understanding of the logic and values underlying the purpose, and of senior management's commitment to it. Deeper and more widespread commitment to the purpose results.

Living the Purpose

The leadership challenge does not end with the articulation of an agreed-upon purpose. Leaders must make the purpose live in the daily decisions of people throughout the company. This requires constant and consistent communication of the purpose, taking actions that reinforce the purpose and enhance people's understanding of its substance and importance. The leader must also be vigilant to address quickly and directly the cynicism that corporate statements of principle often arouse. The best antidote to cynicism is constancy of behavior in accordance with the espoused purpose.

The importance of achieving consistency and coherence among the purpose, the firm's strategy, the way of managing, and the resulting goals was discussed at length in earlier chapters. Sometimes the leader's actions to enhance the power of purpose are subtle and symbolic.

Using Symbolism to Infuse the Purpose

The most effective corporate leaders use symbolism and metaphors to clarify and reinforce the purpose's influence on strategy and organizational character. Hewlett-Packard has its "Bill and Dave" stories and Wal-Mart its "Sam" stories that reinforce the companies' fundamental purposes.

For example, one often-told story at Hewlett-Packard reinforces the company's commitment to its people. David Packard returned to the company from serving as U.S. deputy secretary of defense to find a $100 million long-term debt offering in the final stages of development. It would be the company's first significant amount of long-term debt. The funds were to be used to finance the company's rapid growth. He immediately killed the proposed borrowing and asked managers to implement cost-reduction initiatives to generate the necessary capital. He made his reasoning clear. Hewlett-

Packard (HP) had a primary commitment to its people and to its customers. The HP employees were the source of the innovation that served customers so well. They represented a fixed cost that would be maintained during an economic downdraft. The company's obligation to meet this fixed cost should not be compromised by the contractual fixed cost associated with servicing debt. Reinforcing HP's value of independence, Packard also wanted to avoid capital-market influence on company decisions.

Similarly, Bill Hewlett, when presented with a newly developed instrument he found unexceptional and poorly designed, smashed it in front of the engineers in the laboratory, calling it a "hunk of junk." Again the message is clear. Reflecting the words of Hewlett-Packard's formal statement of principles, the company's "central purpose" is "to satisfy real customer needs" by providing "products and services of the highest quality and the greatest possible value to our customers," which "meet or exceed their expectations." The instrument failed this test.

At times the symbolism may be simple, but the message powerful. When Jan Carlzon took over SAS, he began to revitalize the company by shifting the focus from having the most advanced aircraft fleet with the lowest operating costs to providing the business traveler with greater value. He symbolized the change by repainting the aircraft and providing flight crews and ground personnel with new uniforms. When the company's on-time performance improved dramatically, he gave each employee an expensive watch with an aircraft on the second hand. In both a strategic and symbolic move, he mothballed four new Airbuses purchased by prior management. To be effective, the new, larger planes would have required a hub-and-spoke system. This system would have inconvenienced the business travelers who wanted the frequent nonstop flights the older DC-9s enabled. Clearly, aircraft superiority was no longer central to SAS—service to the business traveler was.

Carlzon used the catchy phrase "moments of truth" to capture the new direction. Customer satisfaction was the result of numerous brief encounters with frontline personnel. The sum of hundreds of these "moments" would differentiate SAS from its competitors. In a radical decentralization, each person was to do what he or she considered to be best for the customer. Given the autonomy to do what they thought was right, the frontline people, with considerable enthusiasm and initiative, revolutionized the interface with customers. During his first year as CEO, Carlzon spent nearly half of his time with frontline personnel, a practice that reinforced his strategic message. The turnaround in performance was remarkable in both its speed and magnitude. Within two years, SAS had become the most punctual carrier in the world and was selected as the "airline of the year" by *Air Transport World* and the best airline for the business traveler by *Fortune*. The enhanced value for the customer did not come at the expense of profitability. As he embarked on his turnaround, Carlzon hoped to produce $50 million of profits by the third year. To his pleasant surprise, the human ingenuity and effort unleashed by the focus on serving the customer created $80 million of profits after only one year.[13]

In a similar effort to bring the critical message to the frontline personnel, Sam Walton made it a priority to visit as many Wal-Mart stores as possible each year. He would assemble the store's "associates" for a talk begun with the "Wal-Mart" cheer. As the associates gathered for one such session, Walton said, "Northeast Memphis, you are the largest store in Memphis, and you must have the best floor-cleaning crew in America. This floor is so clean— let's sit down on it. I thank you. The company is so proud of you, we can't hardly stand it."[14] The messages were unmistakable. The customer was top priority, serving the customer was noble work of intrinsic value, and each associate's contribution was important—whether it was cleaning the floor or managing the store. They were serving a worthy cause and the dignity and contributions of each individual associate should be respected.

Attracting and Retaining High-Caliber Personnel

Building a strong organization begins with the recruitment and retention of high-caliber people at all organizational levels. Outstanding leaders agree that character is more important than technical skills. By "recruiting to the mission," they look for people who possess the attributes to become leaders, share the organization's basic values, and will find meaning and satisfaction in serving the company's purpose. Character is the bedrock upon which leadership is built. And high-performance companies require leaders throughout the company who are capable of promoting the purpose and strategy and eliciting high levels of performance from others.

Jack Welch explains the importance of this process for General Electric:

> In our view, leaders, whether on the shop floor or at the tops of our businesses, can be characterized in at least four ways.

The first is one who delivers on commitments—financial or otherwise—and shares the values of our Company. His or her future is an easy call. Onward and upward.

The second type of leader is one who does not meet commitments and does not share our values. Not as pleasant a call, but equally easy.

The third is one who misses commitments but share the values. He or she usually gets a second chance, preferably in a different environment.

Then there's the fourth type—the most difficult for many of us to deal with. That leader delivers on commitments, makes all the numbers, but doesn't share the values we must have. This is the individual who typically forces performances out of people rather than inspires it: the autocrat, the big shot, the tyrant. Too often all of us have looked the other way—tolerated these "type 4" managers because "they always deliver"—at least in the short term. And perhaps this type was more acceptable in easier times, but in an environment where we must have every good idea from every man and woman in the organization, we cannot afford management styles that suppress and intimidate. Whether we can convince and help these managers to change—recognizing how difficult that can be—or part company with them if they cannot, will be the ultimate test of our commitment to the transformation of this Company and will determine the future of the mutual respect and trust we are building. . . . We know now that without leaders who "walk the talk," all of our plans, promises, and dreams for the future are just that—talk.[15]

A meaningful purpose helps attract, motivate, and retain high-caliber people. The president and CEO of the largest business unit of a leading health care company directly links the idealism of the company's purpose to the type of person the company seeks to attract and to the motivation of these people once at the company:

There is a lot of idealism within our organization in terms of improving the health delivery system, to improve the quality of care and cost-effectiveness, to manage the health of populations by being proactive, and providing programs that do not wait for people to get sick but try to keep them healthy. This idealism believes if we keep people healthy when possible and provide the highest-quality appropriate service when they are ill, then we will also have the most cost-effective health system. This is what drives everybody that is really good in this business. When I recruit people, a philosophical orientation toward this concept is a key factor. Do the right things drive this person? It has heightened people's belief that we all can really make a difference.[16]

A senior vice president at the same company adds,

> We are dealing with the health of the people who make up this country. So there is a call to a greater objective beyond selling some commodity. And I think that is why people are here. There is a feeling of pride in advancing people's health. Personal monetary gain is part of it, but particularly today, it is the opportunity to build something of value. I am a builder and get satisfaction in doing so.[17]

Once a person is part of the company, high-performance firms make a conscious effort to indoctrinate them in the firm's purpose, its values, and its priorities. One leader likened this acculturation process to an "inoculation." It does not take for everyone—and some of these people will leave the organization, usually within a short period of time. But for others it begins a period of healthy performance in which they have immunity to the temptations to take expedient, but morally corrosive, actions. They rise to the defense of the organization's values and ends that they hold dear. Screening new employees and candidates for internal promotion based on character and alignment with the corporate purpose increases the probability they will find enhanced meaning for themselves in serving corporate ends.

Creating an Environment of Respect for the Individual

All people seek dignity and respect. High-caliber people demand it. Consequently the leader must work diligently to create a norm of respect for individuals at all organizational levels and in all jobs. Respect for the dignity of individuals originates with work that is grounded in serving a valued common cause, and it is reinforced by the example set at the top. Because of the cause's significance, all work that contributes to it is noble. The shared cause requires that others respect each individual's work and that each person's contributions be considered significant—just as it was for the janitor that cleaned the floors at Wal-Mart.

The leader enhances the satisfaction of personal achievement by creating an environment that grants appropriate levels of autonomy and recognizes individual accomplishments. This recognition enables people to identify and appreciate their own unique contributions to serving the firm's purpose—to see their "tracks in the sand," as one CEO expresses it. Respect for individual dignity is also furthered by the leader's vigilance in rooting out

those who do not treat others with respect. Once offenders have been identified, the leader can coach them, giving them the chance to learn and change.
But if they do not respond, then they must be removed from the firm before
their actions metastasize throughout the organization.

An environment of mutual respect is motivating. By its very nature,
this environment fosters a celebration of individual achievement and is the
key to unlocking an important door to increased creativity. Respect for individual dignity demands respect for each person's work, no matter how basic,
and for ideas on their merit, no matter from whom they come. It fosters a
greater sense of connectedness to others in the organization and to the company's purpose. A sense of connectedness leads to a sharing of ideas, to seeking the input of others, and to offering help freely when asked. Respect for
the individual also forms the bedrock for trust throughout the organization.
Authenticity and sincerity cannot thrive without mutual respect. The value
of individual dignity is also an effective antidote to the often well intentioned
paternalism that can degenerate into degrading patronization.

An openness to and a respect for ideas, when combined with the
greater sharing of ideas that flow from a sense of connectedness, produce the
ferment from which new, innovative syntheses arise. Toyota's development
of lean manufacturing—which first revolutionized the automobile industry
and then spread to other industries—could only have been developed in an
environment of enormous trust born of mutual respect. The same is true for
3-M's and Hewlett-Packard's remarkable track records in new product
development.

The Courage to Govern

The call to place the customers' interests ahead of shareholders' typically raises questions regarding corporate governance and the responsibilities of boards of directors. Although the separation of management from
ownership and the rise of institutional investors as corporate owners raise
specific concerns, the fundamental issues are not new. Since the inception of
the modern American corporation, some companies have been managed for
the primary benefit of shareholders, others for customers, and a few for
employees.

Today's debate over corporate governance should be framed by three
realities. The first reality—now, as in the past—is that strong competitive

performance resolves most, if not all, governance dilemmas. History and the evidence presented in Chapter 1 show that in the long term shareholders are likely to benefit most from companies with a customer-focused purpose. Historically, companies whose founders made customers the firm's first priority have grown to positions of dominance in their industries, companies like HP, IBM, Johnson & Johnson, Procter and Gamble, Merck, and Wal-Mart. In addition, they have generally enriched the lives of those individuals associated with them.

The second reality is that debate over corporate governance is focused on a small minority of companies that are performing far below their potential. Deriving general lessons for most companies from these outlying underachievers should be done with great care and caution.

The third reality is that the legal responsibilities of board members are broadly defined, giving them considerable discretion to do what they consider right for the firm's long-term competitiveness. The U.S. Constitution grants the states, as one of their sovereign rights, the right to incorporate petitioning organizations. Initially, the state charter of incorporation was a closely guarded concession. However, the expansion of commerce in our nation's early years created competition among states to capture the fees and taxes derived from having companies domiciled in their jurisdictions. States courted corporations by offering more liberal laws applying to incorporation and to directors' responsibilities and liabilities. "In this contest, 'liberal' meant that directors would not be held to the same tight standards as trustees, the so-called prudent man rule. Instead, directors were expected to exercise the *duty of loyalty* and *the duty of care*, and their conduct was judged according to *the business judgment doctrine*."[18] The "duty of care" requires directors to exercise due diligence in the discovery of information and in considering all reasonable alternatives before making a decision. The "duty of loyalty" requires directors to avoid potential conflicts of interest with their responsibilities to the company and its shareholders. As long as directors fulfill their dual duties of care and loyalty, courts do not challenge their decisions.

In response to a wave of hostile takeovers, by 1994 thirty-eight states enacted laws empowering directors to consider the interest of stakeholders other than shareholders. This trend to protect boards and managers followed a 1987 U.S. Supreme Court decision that ratified certain antitakeover laws.[19] One secondary consequence of this trend was pressure on Delaware courts.

Incorporation fees and taxes fund approximately 20 percent of Delaware's state budget. Faced with a possible migration of corporations out of Delaware to states with laws more favorable to managers, the Delaware courts began to liberalize their interpretation of the state's laws.[20]

The business press also plays a widening role in corporate governance. In articles regarding egregious corporate or management behavior or poor performance, the media increasingly identify board members by name. This attention can have a powerful effect in encouraging individual members to fulfill their responsibility. The result can be intensified board diligence and willingness to act.

Ultimately, the solutions to the issues of corporate governance rest with individual board members and corporate leaders. If they possess the courage to do the right thing, to speak out when necessary, and to be evaluated objectively on their performance, concerns regarding effective governance evaporate. Ironically, the values so often praised within a corporation, such as independent thinking, candor, and openness, are frequently absent from the norms of the boardroom. This lack means that more boards need to regularly evaluate not only the CEO's performance but also their own performance as an effective governing body and as individual directors. In a 1998 Korn/Ferry survey, only a third of the boards had such an evaluation process for the board and only 19 percent for individual directors.[21]

The Courage to Lead

At the conclusion of a series of lengthy group discussions of the issues addressed in this book, an accomplished senior executive expressed a common frustration: "Why are common sense and practice so different?" His frustration was that defining a purpose worthy of personal commitment, focusing people in the organization primarily on achieving product-market competitiveness and total value creation, specifying a role for the capital markets appropriately reflective of their contributions, and the creation of an environment in which people can find meaning in their work all seem like common sense. Yet in practice organizations rarely achieve this alignment. Why? The answer usually lies in a failure of the courage to lead.

Going against a deeply embedded ideology—in this case, shareholder wealth maximization—requires courage. This ideology is reinforced by the fact that stock price and accounting returns on investment are the most visible measures of performance. It is strengthened further by the business press, which accepts largely without question shareholder returns and short-term profitability as *the* defining measures of successful corporate leadership. Other measures are simply too complicated—and often too difficult to determine—to be useful in brief articles or television clips. The pressures in the equity markets and the press to conform to conventional wisdom form obstacles along the path to outstanding long-term performance.

Effective leaders overcome these obstacles because they have the courage to do what is right for the company in the long term. These acts of courage are often moral acts requiring the leader to put the cause ahead of career, effectiveness ahead of popularity—in essence, to subordinate self-interest to the common interest. In all purposive organizations, "One must be comfortable to risk one's career to keep principles alive."[22] The leader becomes an exemplar of courage and principle.

The first step in illuminating a path others will trust and follow is defining a clear, widely accepted purpose. The effective leader artfully uses the energizing value of purpose to bring real meaning and value to strategic initiatives throughout the firm.

In the pursuit of this purpose, leaders must have the courage and self-understanding to be honest and candid both with themselves and with others. This character goes beyond traditional norms of honesty. It requires facing reality squarely and getting others to do the same. Communication must be clear and frank. Effective leaders do not try to "spin" or blur the changes required to achieve strategic objectives. Employees, members of the board of directors, and shareholders need—indeed have a right—to know where the corporation is headed and the anticipated challenges along the way. This is a foundational step in creating organizational commitment and flexibility to change. It also serves to attract shareholders who understand the firm's strategy and will act like true owners rather than short-term speculators.

The leader must have the courage to deal constructively with uncertainty. This entails the proactive commitment of resources—people and capital—in the face of uncertainty. This also requires the courage to protect the firm's most critical asset—its people and the knowledge-creating capability they represent—when the company is pressured by the capital market and the media for returns higher than are consistent with its strategic objectives. Similarly, the leader should avoid the seduction of seeking "good press" today at the expense of doing what is best for the long-term health of the enterprise.

Once the direction is set and clearly communicated, the leader must have the courage to stay the course when confronted with unjustified criticism, no matter how much it may sting. Yet the leader must also possess the courage to listen openly to ideas and opinions from all quarters—from other managers, directors, capital-market functionaries, and the press—and to accept and act constructively on justified criticism. This is the essence of the courage to face reality. Steadiness is born of courage, as is the willingness to risk again and again in order to bring forth outstanding performance from the organization.

Leaders should avoid the tempting trap of confusing people's personal loyalty to them with a more enduring loyalty to the organization's cause. Leaders must make critical decisions that are often unpopular. Examples abound. Jan Carlzon at SAS, Jack Welch at GE, and Lou Gertsner at IBM all took unpopular actions when they assumed leadership of their companies. Their focus was not on creating loyalty to themselves but on renewing attention to their companies' strategies. Loyalty to a person does not have the endurance or directional power of loyalty to one's own values or to a cause. When leaders infuse a company with value, it becomes a strong, enduring institution valued for itself by its members.[23] This value is directly derived from the worth attributed to the ends the company serves. When the cause becomes institutionalized, it forms the grounds for loyalty that has permanence and transcends individual personality.

The Leader as Taskmaster

In their role as taskmasters, effective leaders set and maintain high standards of principle and performance, holding people accountable for meeting their goals and removing people (even high performers) whose actions betray the company's core values. Acting on their faith in the individual to do what is right to meet the standards, they demand a high but achievable level of personal stretch. This stretch brings personal growth. Attaining objectives once thought impossible generates a sense of accomplishment and deep satisfaction that enhance one's sense of self-worth.

Courage is contagious. When there is a genuine commitment to the purpose, people have a greater willingness to overcome their natural reluctance to risk personal relationships and personal credibility by challenging the ideas of others and the organization's conventional wisdom. When the purpose has personal meaning and value for them and they see it threatened by actual or potential events, they are likely to speak out. A conviction of purpose creates a greater willingness to confront others, grasp previously unforeseen opportunities, and raise controversial ideas to achieve the valued end. The result is a greater openness and candor in the decision-making process, which serves to make better and faster decisions.

Combating Complacency

A customer-focused purpose, with its product-market orientation, also helps combat one of the greatest threats to high-performing organizations—the complacency and hubris that often flow from success. Successful leaders recognize what Winston Churchill wisely observed: "Success is never final." They are able to infuse their organizations with this feeling. They do it largely by grounding the need for improvement and change to the constantly evolving customer needs and ever-present competitive threat. As long as there is a threat from a potential competitor, they do not rest, nor do they allow their people to rest.

Successful leaders heighten the recognition for the need for change by continually focusing people's attention on marketplace realities and the importance of the organization's high aspirations. A customer-oriented purpose is what gives these events and aspirations meaning and power at the personal level. This commitment contrasts sharply with the compromised awareness of needed product-market changes resulting from a focus on financial returns prompted by a shareholder-oriented purpose.

By stretching people to ever-higher levels of achievement, leaders not only attack complacency—that archenemy of change and competitive performance—but also create an environment conducive to personal development and achievement. Personal growth requires not only the acquisition of new skills, but also the opportunities to use them in new and creative ways. Growth comes from experience. The greater the stretch, the greater is the learning—and also the greater the risk of failure. Consequently, it is important for the leader to ensure that all managers are tolerant of failure when the act was well reasoned and diligently executed. The message should be "Mistakes are okay, but learn from them. You should not make the same mistake twice." This lesson, which begins at the top of the organization, is one Johnson & Johnson's Jim Burke learned early in his career with the company. He had overseen the development of a line of children's medications that were safer and easier to use. But the line failed, in large part because the consumer associated the Johnson & Johnson name with products that were not as strong as those of competitors. Burke came in the office one morning to find a message from General Robert Johnson asking to see him. Knowing the subject would be the failed product line, Burke went to the meeting with some trepidation. But instead of chastising him for the failure, "the General" congratulated him for his efforts, saying, "What business is all about is making decisions, and you don't make decisions without making mistakes. Now, don't ever make that mistake again, but please make sure you make other mistakes."[24]

Conclusion

We are in the midst of the tumultuous confluence of two transformational events. The first is the rapid globalization of business that is creating a Darwinian struggle among competing ideologies. These ideologies shape the prevalent corporate purpose in different countries and affect the degree of individualism fostered by the customary way people manage. The second event is a rapid change in the coin of competitive advantage from labor costs and capital to knowledge. In this battle, some ideologies will prove superior to others. The victors will be the companies that liberate and raise the human spirit. Consequently, a prime responsibility of corporate leadership is to guide firms to the superior ideology—one that will forge knowledge-based competitive advantages.

A select group of leading American companies has shown the way to a new synthesis of the best of the competing ideologies. At its core are management practices that enhance constructive individualism within the firm and a communitarian purpose that links people in meaningful ways to the society of which they are part. These pathfinders have not subordinated their companies' broader responsibilities to the rights of shareholders. Instead, these pioneers (some who have been at this work for decades) have pursued a purpose dedicated to the customer. Recognizing their significant responsibilities to their employees, they have developed a way of managing that heightens the mutual respect, individual expression and initiative, and moral aspirations of their people. This emphasis on respect for the individual coupled with a corporate purpose that people find worthy of commitment creates an environment in which people are able to find increased meaning for their lives through work. The self-transcendence resulting from this dedication to a cause beyond oneself coupled with the widely shared value placed on this end makes the organization's marketplace for ideas an open, cooperative, and vibrant one. Knowledge creation is substantially enhanced as a consequence. Aided by this synthesis, these exemplary companies' successes have endured decades of competition.

Some Asian and European companies are following this lead. Although their cultural point of departure is quite different, they are seeking a similar synthesis. Their major challenges are to create a work environment conducive to greater individuality, to ensure that their purpose has been broadened to have a global relevance, and to avoid succumbing to the call to adopt American-style shareholder capitalism.

A Purpose with Global Relevance

To be effective in an increasingly diverse and globalized world, corporate purpose must be capable of traveling well across cultures and national boundaries. This transportability begins with a corporate purpose that is recognized by diverse peoples as valid and worthy of their commitment. The purpose must contribute to forging unity out of diversity. Companies that make themselves efficient marketplaces for different ideas bound together by common ends and shared core values will have the greatest global reach and superior competitive performance. The new combinations arising from the melding of varying ideas will make these companies the most innovative as well. As ServiceMaster's chairman, Bill Pollard, observes, "It is the acceptance of difference with a commitment to common purpose and mission that allows for both homogeneity and heterogeneity. The firm then can harness the energy and creativity of difference to produce results."[25]

Hewlett-Packard's leaders found that transporting its corporate culture to countries with distinctly different traditions required them to distinguish between the permanence and immutability of its values and the adaptability of its objectives and practices. For example, in HP's Korean joint venture with Samsung, strong Korean values regarding respect for and deference to authority conflicted with aspects of the "HP Way," such as respect for the individual, participative management, and open communication. Samsung requested that local management practices be the norm in the joint venture. However, after some discussion, managers in the United States and Korea were persuaded to retain the central aspects of HP's values and objectives.[26]

HP management communicates the concept of varying permanence by three concentric circles. At the center are core end values, such as HP's purpose, and values guiding interpersonal behavior, such as honesty and respect for the individual. These values do not change across cultures. The next circle contains the objectives embodied in the mission and strategy, which change only in response to marketplace needs. The outer circle represents the practices, such as using titles when talking to others in the Korean organization, which can be modified to adapt to the cultural practices of a particular country. The shared values and common purpose provide unity. Direction to decisions is aided by the values and objectives embodied in the purpose, mission, strategy, and objectives. The result is a company that retains its distinctiveness across the globe—a distinction that enhances its competitiveness—yet has the flexibility to adapt to practices that are not in conflict with its core values.

Economic Reform—A Caution

HP's experience provides a valuable lesson for countries, such as Germany, Japan, and Korea, as they consider restructuring their economic relationships and practices. They need to exercise caution in selecting the changes to pursue. The din of advice to accept wholesale the American system of shareholder capitalism coupled with a crisis of confidence in many of these countries set the stage for overreaction—discarding the good aspects of their current system along with the bad. These countries' business and political leaders must be discriminating in their choices of change. Just as there is much that needs to be changed—for example, increasing transparency in reporting, reforming the banking system, and reducing government protection of uneconomic practices and industries—there is also much that is good about these other systems. The importance many place on employees fits a world of knowledge-based competition well. Their purposes grounded in the social good, rather than shareholder wealth maximization, are competitively beneficial. These purposes traditionally have allowed these companies to have a laserlike focus on their product-market strategies for developing long-term competitive advantage without undue capital market distractions. However, to reflect global-market realities, the purposes need to be expanded beyond myopic nationalism to a focus on worldwide customers. A substantial increase in shareholder rights a la the predominant U.S. ideology poses a danger to competitive performance. It is also difficult to contain, as a few people, driven by greed, can pervert the system to their, not society's, advantage. Once out of the bottle, it is very difficult to put this genie back in.

Business leaders in these countries can also significantly affect their company's performance by revamping their management practices to create a work environment conducive to constructive individualism.

The Growing Responsibilities of Corporations: An Issue of Global Legitimacy

As corporate power grows and corporations increasingly become prime instruments for constructive social change, they also will be less subject to central state control. These corporate-based social changes will be controlled by executives who lack explicit training in such affairs and do not enjoy the legitimacy of being placed in their positions of power by a democratic process. Consequently, managers' inherent authority to act will be questioned more and more. Therefore getting the purpose right—one that is in harmony with society's needs—and aligning corporate actions with this purpose will be increasingly critical. The effective leader needs the courage, determination, and persistence to promote, defend, and communicate a clear purpose that can legitimatize the firm's actions in society's eyes. Corporations must be seen as serving the betterment of society. Failing to achieve such alignment of needs and actions, the future legitimacy of corporate leaders will be undermined to the detriment of both corporate performance and society's needs.

A customer-focused purpose reinforces the perceived authority of an increasingly powerful management to act, whereas the narrow constituency of a shareholder-focused purpose tends to undermine it. Because a customer-focused purpose works to unleash greater human creativity and initiative and to expand a firm's capacity to create *total value* through increased product-market competitiveness, its pursuit can add to management's legitimacy. Without this legitimacy, corporations risk becoming seen by many as a corrupting influence. The resulting social dissatisfaction could well damage corporations' abilities to perform and realize their immense positive potential.

An Ideology for the Twenty-first Century

Too many American corporations are entering the twenty-first century with an ideology forged in the eighteenth and nineteenth centuries. In fact, that outmoded ideology is becoming increasingly dogmatic. Measurement systems based on current or historical shareholder wealth creation, such as EVA, are sweeping across American companies. Layoffs have become a readily accepted form of good management practice—so commonplace that they are no longer very newsworthy. The American companies caught up in this trend are moving further away from the ideologies held by most of the rest of the world. This shortsighted dogmatism is accompanied by complacency and overconfidence similar to what has doomed many high-performing companies in the past. The sentiment is often expressed that America's shareholder capitalism has achieved the final victory, and it is only a matter of time until this ideology sweeps the world. This is dangerous arrogance. It ignores both the deep cultural roots of the other free-market ideologies and the inherent long-term competitive advantages associated with a customer-focused purpose.

This ideology cannot last. It will wither under attack from firms with more competitive purposes and from an American society that will increasingly grow to question the validity of such an ideology. Furthermore, because of its lack of significance and relevance across cultures—and perceived imperialistic character in some cultures—it is not well suited for a globalized world.

The ideology of corporate purpose that will dominate the twenty-first century will be one that has legitimacy and acceptance within society, unleashes latent human potential, generates greater total value, and, in a globalized world, travels well and intact across cultural boundaries. Only one purpose meets these requirements—serving customer needs while placing a high priority on the employees' development and satisfaction.

Guided by a constructive, widely shared purpose, the corporation can be a positive moral force in the future. If led well, corporations can become a source of valued products that enrich lives, opportunities through work that yield individual self-realization and bring increased meaning to life, and economic performance that increases society's wealth. If led poorly, they will be a source of increasing personal alienation and frustration—oppressive of the human spirit and of its highest aspirations. The choice of corporate purpose defines the difference.

Reference Matter

Notes

Introduction

1. Albert Einstein as quoted in John Gardner, *On Leadership*, 11.
2. Lew Platt, in a speech to Hewlett-Packard's executive conference, July 19, 1993.
3. Pascale and Athos, *Art of Japanese Management*, 81.
4. Drucker, *Management: Tasks, Responsibilities, Practices*, 61.
5. Ibid., 78.
6. Barnard, *Functions of the Executive*, 86 and 94.
7. Ibid., 87.
8. Selznick, *Leadership in Administration*, 90.
9. Ibid., 63 and 65.
10. Ibid.
11. Andrews, *Concept of Corporate Strategy*, 79.
12. Badaracco, *Knowledge Link*.
13. World Trade Organization (WTO), "World Trade in 1999."
14. Kahn, "China's Overcapacity."
15. Kuhn, *Structure of Scientific Revolutions*, 175.
16. Chandler, *Visible Hand*.

Chapter 1

1. Collins and Porras, *Built to Last*, 56.
2. Some corporations become extensions of their nation's will, as has often been the case in Japan and Korea. In these cases, the independence from their home country is greatly diminished.

3. Kotter and Heskett, *Culture and Performance*. In Kotter and Heskett's research, the strength of an individual company's culture was based on the independent evaluations made by senior executives of their competitors. A strong culture was associated with affirmative responses to questions such as these:

1. To what extent have managers in competing firms commonly spoken of a (company name) "style" or way of doing things?
2. To what extent has the firm both made its values known through a creed or credo and made a serious attempt to encourage managers to follow them?
3. To what extent has the firm been managed according to long-standing policies and practices other than those of just the incumbent CEO?

No attempt was made to judge whether or not the cultures were constructive.

4. For readers interested in learning more of this early history, see Chandler, *Visible Hand*.

5. Although it is not practical to do so, ideally "value creation" should be measured net of all costs involved in the corporation's activities, including their impact on the environment, the health of communities, and the stress and despair of workers and their families.

6. Walton, *Sam Walton*, 183.

7. Ibid.

8. Ibid., 252.

9. Ibid., 252–53.

10. Ibid., 253.

11. Here the concept of sustainable growth is useful because of its simplicity. Barring outside financing through new equity issues or an increase in the proportion of debt in the capital structure, a company cannot sustain a growth rate greater than its return on equity times the percentage of income retained after dividends. Of course, increasing the debt/equity ratio will enable a firm to grow faster than its retained return on equity; but once the higher target debt/equity ratio is reached, the growth once again will be constrained by the retained return on equity. Because of the increased financial leverage, the return on equity (and therefore the sustainable growth rate) will be higher than before the increase. Communication of this simple concept reinforces the understanding of the need for profits to fund growth and investment.

The formula for sustainable growth is

$$(1 - P)(1 + \frac{D}{E})(ROI - i\frac{D}{I})$$

Where P is the dividend payout rate, D/E is the debt equity ratio, ROI is the return on total capital, I is the interest rate on corporate debt after taxes, and D/I is the ratio of debt to total capital. If the debt/equity ratio is constant, then the sustainable growth rate is simply the product of the return on equity times the retention rate (1 - P).

12. Collins and Porras, *Built to Last*, 56.
13. Lincoln, *Lincoln's Incentive System*, 30.
14. Ibid., 161.
15. Ibid., 161–63.
16. "How Lincoln Motivated Men," *Civil Engineering* (January 1973): 76–84.
17. Barnard, *Functions of the Executive*, 154.
18. Drucker, *Management: Tasks, Responsibilities, Practices*, 59–60.
19. The Clorox Company, 1993 Annual Report, 8.
20. Drucker, *Practice of Management*, 12.
21. Adam Smith, *Wealth of Nations*, 98.
22. Ellsworth, "Capital Markets," 172 and 181.
23. Berle and Means, *Modern Corporation*, vii–viii.
24. Ibid., viii.

Chapter 2

1. Shaw, "Epistle Dedicatory,"in *Man and Superman*, xxxi–xxxii.
2. Auletta, *Art of Corporate Success*, 123.
3. Ibid.
4. Data compiled by Challenger, Gray, and Christmas, Inc.
5. Tichy and Charan, "Interview with Jack Welch," 120.
6. Nussbaum, "I'm Worried About My Job!"
7. Ibid.
8. Fisher, "Morale Crisis," 71–2.
9. An International Survey Research Corporation survey reported in Lee, "Trust Me."
10. O'Reilly, "The New Deal," reporting on the results of surveys conducted by Sirota & Alper Associates.
11. Maharaj, "Layoffs," C1.
12. See Cappelli, *New Deal at Work*, 122–24.
13. "Give Them That Old Time Ambition," *Training* (February 1992): 74.
14. A study by the American Management Association, reported in Henkoff, "Getting Beyond Downsizing," 58; and a survey by Watson Wyatt Worldwide, reported in Hilsenrath, "Many Layoffs," A2.
15. Henkoff, "Getting Beyond Downsizing," 58.
16. Hilsenrath, "Many Layoffs," A2.
17. Fisher, "Morale Crisis," 70.
18. Reich, *Work of Nations*, 173.
19. Badaracco, *Knowledge Link*.

20. Hirschman, *Exit, Voice, and Loyalty*, 30, 98–99.

21. Royce, *Philosophy of Loyalty*.

22. Andrews and Withey, *Social Indicators of Well-Being*, 286. Other studies confirming the weak correlation between income levels and happiness include Campbell, *Sense of Well-Being*; Duncan, "Does Money Buy Satisfaction?"; Freedman, *Happy People*; Inkeles and Diamond, "Personal Development and National Development"; and Veroff and Kulka, *Inner Americans*. These and other studies are reviewed in Lane, *Market Experience*, 524–33. Also see Myers, "Funds, Friends, and Faith."

23. This section draws in part from Badaracco and Ellsworth, *Leadership*, 68–71.

24. Volf, *Work in the Spirit*, 72.

25. Tilgher, *Work*, 16–17.

26. Weber, *Protestant Ethic*, 80.

27. Tilgher, *Work*, 49.

28. Weber, *Protestant Ethic*, 160.

29. Genesis 1:26–30.

30. Rodgers, *Work Ethic*, xi.

31. Volf, *Work in the Spirit*, 50.

32. Adam Smith, *Theory of Moral Sentiments*, 153–54.

33. Adam Smith, *Wealth of Nations*, 625.

34. Marx, *Selected Writings*, 78–79.

35. Volf, *Work in the Spirit*, 59.

36. *Grundrisse der Kritik der Politischen Okonomie*. Berlin, Diez, 1974, p. 387, as quoted in Volf, *Work in the Spirit*, 63.

37. Rodgers, *Work Ethic*, 11–12.

38. Ibid., 12.

39. Rodgers, *Work Ethic*, 35. The Lincoln quote originally appeared in *The Collected Works of Abraham Lincoln*, ed. Roy P. Basler, 3 vols. (New Brunswick, N.J.: Rutgers University Press, 1953–55), 3:462, 478–79.

40. Rodgers, *Work Ethic*, 35. The Rockefeller quote originally appeared in "John D. Rockefeller on Opportunity in America," *Cosmopolitan* 43, 1907, 372.

41. Rodgers, *Work Ethic*, 14.

42. Work committees brought together elected representatives of the workers and managers to discuss common problems and grievances.

43. Rodgers, *Work Ethic*, 59.

44. Schor, *Overworked American*, 35.

45. Ibid., 45.

46. "Due Diligence," *The Economist*, August 24, 1996, 48.

47. Berger, "Problem of Work," 212.

48. John Paul II, "Centesimus Annus," 6.

49. John Paul II, "Encyclical Laboren Exercens," sections II.6 and II.9.

50. Freud, "Civilization and Its Discontents," in *Complete Psychological Works*, 21:101, as quoted in Neff, *Work and Human Behavior*, 88.

51. Freud, "Civilization and Its Discontents," as quoted in Meakin, *Man and Work*, 4.

52. Freud, *Complete Psychological Works*, 21:8.

53. Freud, *Civilization and Its Discontents*, 80.

54. Menninger, "Work as Sublimation," 6:170–82, as quoted in Neff, *Work and Human Behavior*, 94.

55. As quoted in Meakin, *Man and Work*, 5.

56. Frankl, *Man's Search for Meaning*, 121.

57. Ibid., 133.

58. *Introjection* is the unconscious incorporation of attitudes or ideas into one's personality.

59. Maslow, *Farther Reaches of Human Nature*, 42, 46, 291, 293, 296–97, and 300.

60. Csikszentmihalyi, *Flow*, 92 and 209.

61. Ibid., 216–17.

62. Bellah et al., *Habits of the Heart*, 66.

63. Fromm, *Sane Society*, 164.

64. Mill, *Autobiography*, 286, as quoted in Singer, *Meaning in Life*, 103.

65. Singer, *Meaning in Life*, 92–93, 97, and 99.

66. John W. Gardner, *Self-Renewal*, 100, 102–3.

67. Russell, *Conquest of Happiness*, 211 and 214.

68. Ibid., 215.

69. Schumacher, *Good Work*, 4.

70. Ibid., 122.

71. John W. Gardner, *Self-Renewal*, 94.

72. Ibid., 99.

73. Collier, "Business Leadership."

74. Pollard, *Soul of the Firm*, 32.

75. Goodman and Goodman, *Communitas*, 153.

76. Fromm, *Sane Society*, 159.

77. Csikszentmihalyi, *Flow*, 160.

78. Ibid., 92.

79. Yankelovich, "Work Ethic," 6.

80. Lublin, "Worker Productivity."

Chapter 3

1. In broadest terms, a strategy is a pattern of commitments, objectives, and decisions that define a company's fundamental purpose for existing, what business it is

to be in, how it will compete in that business, and the functional policies necessary to create and sustain the desired competitive advantage. The strategy's objective should be to provide the highest possible perceived value to the final customer at the lowest possible delivered cost.

2. Barnard, *Functions of the Executive*, 138.

3. Hamel and Prahalad, *Competing for the Future*.

4. Collins and Porras, *Built to Last*.

5. Hamel and Prahalad, *Competing for the Future*, 202–11.

6. "Behind the Scenes of 'HP Directions in the '90s,'" *FYI* (Hewlett-Packard Company newsletter).

7. Occasionally, vision statements will also proclaim the shared values defining how organizational members choose to behave in their dealings with one another and with people outside the organization. However, what is of interest to an understanding of purpose is vision's relationship to end values.

8. Lew Platt, in remarks made to the Hewlett-Packard executive conference, July 19, 1993.

9. Hewlett-Packard Company newsletter.

10. Collins and Porras, *Built to Last*, 46 and 74.

11. Ibid., 56 and 57.

12. Senge, *Fifth Discipline*, 206 and 209.

13. Hamel and Prahalad, "Strategic Intent," 64. For a fuller description of strategic intent see *Competing for the Future*, by the same authors.

14. Collins and Porras, *Built to Last*, 91ff.

15. Ibid., 94.

16. Ibid., 9.

17. Hamel and Prahalad, "Strategic Intent," 67.

18. Ibid., 64–66.

19. Toyota Motor Corporation document reproduced in Basu, "Concept of Corporate Purpose," 85.

20. Hamel and Prahalad, *Competing for the Future*, 228.

21. Bartlett and Ghoshal, "Changing the Role of Top Management," 81.

22. For one such study of the performance record of diversification efforts, see Porter, "From Competitive Advantage."

23. Inamori, *Passion for Success*, 65.

24. Prahalad and Hamel, "Core Competence," 83.

25. Ibid., 86.

26. Reichheld, *Loyalty Effect*.

27. Hewlett-Packard company documents.

28. For a fuller description of Johnson & Johnson's response to the Tylenol poi-

soning crisis and the customers' reaction, see Campbell and Nash, *Sense of Mission*, 151–54; and *Corporate Ethics: A Prime Business Asset.*

29. James Burke, in a presentation at the Harvard Business School, December 1983.

Chapter 4

1. Howard, "Values Make the Company."
2. Watson, *A Business*, 5–6.
3. Barnard, *Functions of the Executive*, 82.
4. Bartlett and Ghoshal, "Changing the Role of Top Management," 81 and 88.
5. Ibid., 82.
6. To facilitate year-to-year learning, the out years actually remain constant over a five-year period. For example, from 1995 to 1999, the out years would remain 2000 and 2005. In 2000, the out years would change to 2005 and 2010. In this way, year-to-year changes in expectations regarding the strategic business unit's competitive position and industry attractiveness are not obscured by changing target dates.
7. Badaracco and Ellsworth, *Leadership*, 50, 61, 136–37.
8. Ibid., 85.
9. Presentation by James E. Burke at Harvard Business School, December 1983.
10. House and Price, "Return Map," 93.
11. Simon, *Administrative Behavior*, 223–24.
12. Kaplan and Norton, *Balanced Scorecard.*
13. Reichheld, *Loyalty Effect*, 221–23.
14. Kaplan and Norton, *Balanced Scorecard*, 101–3. For more details on Hewlett-Packard's break-even time concept, see House and Price, "Return Map."
15. Kovar, *Decision-Making Environment.*
16. Paine, "Sears Auto Centers."
17. The 202 companies in the Kotter and Heskett study were ranked in quintiles of cultural strength. Within this sample, the eighty-eight companies for which the expressed nature of the corporate purpose could be determined were then identified by the quintile in which they fell in the total sample. See Kotter and Heskett, *Corporate Culture and Performance.*

Chapter 5

1. Ellsworth, "Capital Markets," 179.
2. Korn/Ferry International, *Board of Directors Twenty-first Annual Study*, 1994, 21.
3. EVA is a registered trademark of Stern Stewart & Company.
4. Ip, "With Dow 9000 Nearby, Stocks Get Boost."

5. The capital charge is simply the company's risk-adjusted cost of capital times the aggregate amount of capital employed. Some companies use cash flow instead of adjusted operating profits and adjust capital employed to account for inflation and differences in depreciation and asset lives. However, the basic principles remain the same.

6. Yoffie, "Global Semiconductor Industry," 1.

7. The return on capital is calculated based on long-term capital net of cash and securities and on income before interest and dividends earned on the cash and securities.

8. Drucker, "Pension Fund Revolution."

9. Frederick F. Reichheld uses this analogy of multiple gauges in arguing for an integrated scorecard in *The Loyalty Effect*, 218.

10. McTaggart, Kontes, and Mankins, *Value Imperative*, 16.

11. Hamel and Prahalad, *Competing for the Future*, 151.

12. Ibid., 167.

13. For example, see Thurow, *Head to Head*; Thurow, *Future of Capitalism*; Porter, "Capital Disadvantage"; and Ellsworth, "Capital Markets."

14. Poterba, "Stock Market Wealth."

15. Dorfman, "Analysts Devote More Time."

16. Laderman, "Wall Street's Spin Game," 152.

17. Ibid., 154.

18. Ibid., 148.

19. Nocera, "A Whole New Ball Game," *Fortune*, July 24, 2000, 82. These data are based on ratings tracked by Zacks Investment Research on approximately six thousand companies.

20. See Reichheld, *Loyalty Effect*, 168–74, for a description of some of Bain Capital's investment activities.

21. Buffett, *1989 Annual Report*, Berkshire Hathaway, 14. The company did away with regular mailings of quarterly reports in 1998, posting them to the Internet instead. To receive a mailed, printed report, shareholders must make a specific request.

22. Buffett, "An Owner's Manual."

23. Ibid.

24. Ibid.

25. New York Stock Exchange, *Fact Book for 1991* and *Fact Book for 2000*.

26. Reichheld, *Loyalty Effect*, 162.

27. "Will Money Managers Wreck the Economy?" *Business Week*, August 13, 1984, 89.

28. Jaffe, "Talk with John Templeton."

29. "Will Money Managers Wreck the Economy?" *Business Week*, August 13, 1984, 87.

30. Reichheld, *Loyalty Effect*, 162.

Chapter 6

1. For an excellent account of this evolution of thought, see Hirschman, *Passions and Interests*.

2. The concept of the Sabbatical Year embodied the Old Testament view of property. Every seventh year, land was to be allowed to go fallow by its owners to allow the poor to reap its benefits, loans were to be forgiven, and slaves were to be set free and furnished liberally from the owners' own flock, seed, and wine. See Exodus 23:10–11, Exodus 21:2, and Deuteronomy 15:12–15. Even more radical was idea of the Year of the Jubilee, which held that every fiftieth year there should be a proclamation of "liberty throughout the land." All property, except city dwellings, was to be returned to its original owners in keeping with God's command to Moses, "The land shall not be sold in perpetuity, for the land is mine; for you are strangers and sojourners with me" (see Leviticus 25:10–31). Unsurprisingly, there is little evidence these principles were widely practiced.

3. Plato, *Dialogues of Plato*, p. 24.

4. Ibid., 23. For Socrates and Plato the improvement of the soul came from virtue—the care for wisdom and truth. Virtue is knowledge. Socrates argued that to know the good is to do the good, since "no one does evil voluntarily." Wrongdoing is due only to the lack of knowledge of the good.

5. Plato, *Republic*, bk. 4, 422.

6. Plato, *Republic*, bk. 8, 550.

7. Plato, *Republic*, bk. 6, 485.

8. Plato, *Republic*, bk. 3, 415 E.

9. Aristotle, *Politics*, bk. 2, 5. 1263b.

10. Aristotle, *Politics*, bk. 2, 1263 a and b.

11. Aristotle, *Politics*, bk. 1, 9, 1258a.

12. Seneca, *Ep.* 14, *LCL*.

13. Vernon Bartlett, "Idea of Property," 100.

14. Grace, *Concept of Property*, 150.

15. Gonzales, *Faith and Wealth*, 215.

16. Deane, *Ideas of St. Augustine*, 107.

17. Grace, *Concept of Property*, 151.

18. Ibid., 21.

19. Aquinas, *Summa Theologica*, vols. I–II, q. 72, art. 4.

20. Grace, *Concept of Property*, 23.

21. Aquinas, *Summa Contra Gentiles*, vol. III, 121–22.

22. Aquinas, *Summa Theologica*, vol. II, q. 66, art. 2.

23. Aquinas, *Summa Theologica*, vol. II, q. 32, art. 5. Reproduced in Grace, *Concept of Property*, 24, and Aquinas, *Summa Theologica*, vol. II, q. 66, art. 2.

24. Randall, *Making of the Modern Mind*, 89–90.

25. Hirschman, *Passions and Interests*, 129.

26. Ibid., 130.

27. Adam Smith, *Wealth of Nations*, 388–89.

28. This definition combines those presented in Weber, *Protestant Ethic*, 79, and Grace, *Concept of Property*, 27. St. Paul, in I Corinthians 7:17, says, "Only, let every one lead the life which the Lord has assigned to him, and in which God has called him."

29. Weber, *Protestant Ethic*, 80–81.

30. Ibid., 70.

31. Tillich, *History of Christian Thought*, 269.

32. Ibid., 271.

33. Ibid.

34. Randall, *Making of the Modern Mind*, 139.

35. As quoted in Weber, *Protestant Ethic*, 175.

36. C. B. Macpherson develops the term "possessive individualism" in *The Political Theory of Possessive Individualism*.

37. Randall, *Making of the Modern Mind*, 381–82.

38. Ibid., 381.

39. Hirschman strikingly documents this evolution of thought in *The Passions and the Interests*.

40. Spinoza, *Tractatus Theologico-politicus*, as quoted in Hirschman, *Passions and Interests*, 13.

41. Machiavelli, *Discourses*, bk. 1, chap. 68.

42. Hirschman, *Passions and Interests*, 16.

43. Macpherson, *Possessive Individualism*, 269.

44. Hobbes, *Leviathan*, 99.

45. Macpherson, *Possessive Individualism*, 264.

46. Hobbes, *Leviathan*. From these ideas he made a major departure from past thinking. Without relying on divine right, tradition, or justice, he justified an absolute and undivided sovereign and deduced the source of the individual's obligation to the state. Hobbes's covenant between the self-perpetuating sovereign and the governed provided a middle ground between the authoritarian governments of the past and the democracies of the future.

47. Locke, *Second Treatise*, chap. 2, 4.

48. Ibid.

49. Ibid., chap. 2, 6.

50. Macpherson, *Possessive Individualism*, 269.

51. Locke, *Second Treatise*, chap. 5, 27.

52. This verse reads, "As for the rich in this world, charge them not to be haughty, nor to set their hopes on uncertain riches but on God who richly furnishes us with everything to enjoy." In verses 18 and 19, Paul adds, "They are to do good, to be rich in good deeds, liberal and generous, thus laying up for themselves a good foundation for the future, so that they may take hold of the life which is life indeed."

53. Locke, *Second Treatise*, chap. 5, 27.

54. Locke, *First Treatise*, 42.

55. Locke, *Second Treatise*, chap. 5, 37.

56. Ibid., chap. 9, 124.

57. Macpherson, *Possessive Individualism*, 263–64.

58. Ibid., 3 and 269.

59. Wood, "Influence of the Reformation," 165–66.

60. Ibid., 166.

61. Dr. Samuel Johnson defined deism in his 1755 *Dictionary* as "the opinion of those that only acknowledge one God, without the reception of any revealed religion." A Deist is a person "who follows no particular religion but only acknowledges the existence of God, without any other article of faith."

62. Tillich, *History of Christian Thought*, 265.

63. Franklin, *Advice to a Young Tradesman*.

64. Franklin, "Way to Wealth."

65. Weber, *Protestant Ethic*, 51.

66. Thomas Jefferson in an October 28, 1775, letter to Rev. James Madison.

67. Adam Smith, *Wealth of Nations*, 324–25.

68. Adam Smith, *Theory of Moral Sentiments*, 71.

69. Adam Smith, *Wealth of Nations*, 423 and 594.

70. Ibid., 594–95.

71. Ibid., 98.

72. Ibid., 325.

73. Ibid., 324.

74. Ibid., 322, emphasis added.

75. Adam Smith, *Theory of Moral Sentiments*, 3.

76. Ibid., 354.

77. Ibid., 124–25.

78. Adam Smith, *Wealth of Nations*, 651.

79. Adam Smith, *Lectures*, 320.

80. Schlatter, *Private Property*, 240.

81. Hume, *Essays*, 189, quoted in Schlatter, *Private Property*, 242.

82. Hume, *Treatise of Human Nature*, bk. 3, pt. 2, 2.

83. Bentham, "Principles of Morals and Legislation," 65.

84. Bentham, *Theory of Legislation*, 111.

85. Mill, *On Liberty*.

86. Mill, *Principles of Political Economy*, 218, from Schlatter, *Private Property*, 249.

87. Schlatter, *Private Property*, 250.

88. Niebuhr, *Children of Light*, 116.

89. Boorstin, *Americans*, 154.

90. Bell, *Cultural Contradictions of Capitalism*, 71–72, 84.

91. Farney, "Chaos Theory," A1, A8.

92. Kristol, *Two Cheers for Capitalism*, 262.

93. Berle and Means, *Modern Corporation*, 8–9.

94. Robert E. Lane, in *The Market Experience*, 9, defines happiness as "a more or less enduring and comprehensive emotional state" and "life satisfaction" as "more of a judgment, a cognitive appraisal of one's life."

95. Lane, *Market Experience*, 3 and 6.

Chapter 7

1. Berlin, *Four Essays on Liberty*, 131.

2. Abraham Maslow considers the relatedness to others and involvement in causes outside of oneself as key elements of self-actualization. See his *The Farther Reaches of Human Nature*.

3. Paulsen, *Immanuel Kant*, 82.

4. Hoover, *American Individualism*, 9–10 (italics in original).

5. Bellah et al., *Habits of the Heart*, 334.

6. Fromm, *Sane Society*, 41.

7. Bellah et al., *Habits of the Heart*, 84.

8. Ibid., 150–51.

9. Ibid., 144.

10. Carnegie, "Gospel of Wealth," 14.

11. Crittenden, *Beyond Individualism*, 13.

12. Schumpeter, *Capitalism, Socialism, and Democracy*.

13. Fromm, *Sane Society*, 181.

14. Reismann, *Lonely Crowd*, 23.

Chapter 8

1. Helm, "Scorn for America."

2. National Intelligence Council, "Global Trends 2015."

3. For examples of these forces at work, see Cooper, *When Lean Enterprises Collide*.

4. Cooper, *When Lean Enterprises Collide*.

5. For a more complete discussion of the increased pressures for volume, see Ohmae, *Borderless World*.

6. President's Commission on Industrial Competitiveness, *Report of the Commission on Industrial Competitiveness*, vol. 1, p. 6.

7. Wolff, "Where Has All the Money Gone?" Wolff defines "marketable wealth" as the current value of all marketable assets less debts. It excludes consumer durables such as cars and some forms of retirement wealth, which the author claims do not "materially alter the picture."

8. United States Central Intelligence Agency, *Handbook of Economic Statistics*, 156; and National Science Board, *Science and Engineering Indicators—2000*.

9. National Science Board, *Science and Engineering Indicators—2000*, appendix table 7–4.

10. United States Department of Commerce, International Trade Administration, "U.S. Commodity Trade."

11. United States Department of Commerce, International Trade Administration, "U.S. Foreign Trade Highlights: 1996."

12. *Wall Street Journal*, using data provided by Morgan Stanley & Co. and the U.S. Labor Department.

13. OECD and U.S. Bureau of Labor Statistics.

14. "The New Economy: Work in Progress," *The Economist*, July 24, 1999, 22.

15. "The Prospect for Productivity," *The Economist*, February 17, 1990, 25.

16. "Small Business, Small Beer," *The Economist*, July 25, 1992, 31.

17. Alvarez, "Small Business."

18. United States Central Intelligence Agency, *Handbook of International Economic Statistics*, 1996.

19. OECD, *STI Review No. 27: Special Issue on New Science and Technology Indicators*, December 2001.

20. OECD, *STI Scoreboard 2001*.

21. Economic Planning Agency, *White Paper on the Japanese Economy*, August 7, 1990; and National Science Foundation, "National Patterns of R&D Resources."

22. Comparing the patent numbers for Japan and the United States can be somewhat misleading. Japan's patent system is not based on comprehensive patents as the U.S. system is. Thus multiple patents are often issued in Japan in cases where only one patent would be needed in the United States.

23. "Top Ten Corporations Receiving U.S. Patents," *Wall Street Journal*, October 4, 1988, B4; and "American Patents," *The Economist*, October 28, 1989.

24. Mansfield, "Industrial R&D," 226.

25. *The Economist*, August 22, 1992.

26. Helm, "Foreign Firms with Deep Pockets"; and United States Department of Commerce, *Survey of Current Business*, April 2001.

27. Banks, "Why George Bush Wants to Bring IRAs Back"; and Feldstein, "Global Capital Flows."

28. Federal Reserve Bank of New York staff estimates and Farrell and Holden, "U.S. Has New Weapon," 73.

29. Feldstein, "Global Capital Flows."

30. Hedrick Smith, *Rethinking America*, 134.

31. Rohlen, *Japan's High Schools*, 322.

32. Glouchevitch, *Juggernaut*, 130.

33. United States Department of Commerce, *Competing to Win*, 33.

34. Marshall and Tucker, *Thinking for a Living*, 69.

Chapter 9

1. Lodge and Vogel, *Ideology and National Competitiveness*, 2–3.

2. Brandt, "Korea," 210 and 211.

3. *Analects*, reproduced in Huston Smith, *Religions of Man*, 241.

4. Warren W. Smith Jr., *Confucianism in Modern Japan*, 231.

5. Reischauer, *Japanese*, 67–68.

6. Ibid., 214.

7. Vogel, "Japan," 143.

8. Reischauer, *Japanese*, 68–70.

9. Ibid., 71–72.

10. Ibid., 81.

11. Vogel, "Japan," 150, 153, 154.

12. Reischauer, *Japanese*, 83.

13. Vogel, "Japan," 152.

14. Ibid., 147.

15. Reischauer, *Japanese*, 190.

16. Vogel, "Japan," 148–49.

17. Reischauer, *Japanese*, 100.

18. Vogel, "Japan," 169, 155–56.

19. Christopher, *Japanese Mind*, 255.

20. Quoted in Christopher, *Japanese Mind*, 234.

21. Basu, "Concept of Corporate Purpose," 123.

22. Ibid., 122.

23. Morita (with Reingold and Shimomura), *Made in Japan*, 145–46.

24. Cruikshank, "Matsushita," 55.

25. Inamori, *Passion for Success*, 63.

26. Ibid., 66.

27. Recent research conducted by Shankar Basu, a vice president of Toyota Industrial Equipment, provides insight into the linkage of Toyota's purpose to its objectives and strategic decisions. See Basu, "Concept of Corporate Purpose." This research is the source for much of the data upon which the following account of Toyota is based.

28. "A Toyota for the 21st Century," *Toyota Management Forum* (October 1992): 2.

29. Toyota Motor Company, *1993 Annual Report.*

30. Basu, "Concept of Corporate Purpose," 129–30.

31. Tokuichi Uranishi, general manager, Corporate Planning Division, and Hiromasa Neishi, general manager, Overseas Planning Division, as quoted in Basu, "Concept of Corporate Purpose," 138 and 139.

32. Basu, "Concept of Corporate Purpose," 162.

33. Ibid., 147.

34. OECD, *STI Review No. 27: Special Issue on New Science and Technology Indicators*, December 2001.

35. Chao and Hamilton, "Bad Times."

36. Nakarmi and Neff, "Samsung's Radical Shakeup"; Nakarmi, Kelly, and Armstrong, "Look Out, World."

37. Glain, "Korea's Samsung."

38. "Fortune's Global 500," *Fortune*, August 4, 1997, F-2.

39. "The Death of Daewoo," *The Economist*, August 21, 1999, 58.

40. Warren W. Smith Jr., *Confucianism in Modern Japan*, 167.

41. Brandt, "Korea," 213.

42. Kim, *Hard Work and Leadership*, 16 and 123.

43. Warren W. Smith Jr. *Confucianism in Modern Japan*, 167.

44. Brandt, "Korea," 216.

45. Warren W. Smith Jr., *Confucianism in Modern Japan*, 181.

46. Kim, *Hard Work and Leadership*, 5–6, 50, and 155.

47. Ibid., 176–77.

48. Kim, *Every Street*, 181–82.

49. Brandt, "Korea," 217 and 219.

50. Ibid., 208.

51. Ibid., 224.

52. "The Fortune Global 500," *Fortune*, August 3, 1998, F-2.

53. "South Korean Manufacturing: The Giants Stumble," *The Economist*, October 18, 1997, 68.

54. Kim, *Hard Work and Leadership*, 139; and Kim, *Every Street*, 40.

55. Winckler, "Statism and Familism on Taiwan," 182.

56. Ibid., 183.

57. Clifford et al., "Can China Reform Its Economy?"

58. "China's State-Owned Enterprises: Beijing Rules," *The Economist*, May 3, 1997, 55.

59. Winckler, "Statism and Familism on Taiwan," 173.

60. It should be noted that it was not just domestic Korean banks that did the lending. International banks also made significant loans to Korean companies.

61. Allen, "Germany," 80.

62. Smyser, *Economy of United Germany*, 41, 42, and 69.

63. Glouchevitch, *Juggernaut*.

64. Benjamin, "German Study," A10, reporting on "Securing the Future of German Competitiveness," Economics Ministry, 1993.

65. Glouchevitch, *Juggernaut*, 55–56.

66. Schlatter, *Private Property*, 257.

67. Ibid.

68. Ibid., 256–57.

69. Allen, "Germany," 81–82.

70. Chandler, *Scale and Scope*, 21–23.

71. "A Survey of Germany," *The Economist*, May 21, 1994, 27.

72. Smyser, *Economy of United Germany*, 131.

73. Ibid., 133.

74. Wilhelm Ropke, an economist, quoted in "Germany in Transition," *Daedalus* (Winter 1994).

75. "A Survey of Germany," *The Economist*, May 21, 1994, 4.

76. Germany has two kinds of corporations: those that are privately owned and unlisted (the *Gesellschaft mit beschrankten Haftung* or GmbH) and those that are publicly owned and listed on a German stock exchange (*Aktiengesellschaft* or AG).

77. Michael T. Jacobs, *Short-Term America*, 69.

78. Because the shares of most German companies are held in bearer form, it is difficult to determine ownership patterns precisely.

79. See Shirreff, "Bankers as Monopolists," for a discussion of the ownership structure as found by Monopolies Commission.

80. Kester, "Governance, Contracting, and Investment Horizons."

81. Thurow, *Head to Head*, 34.

82. Glouchevitch, *Juggernaut*, 75.

83. Ibid., 114.

84. "A Survey of Germany," *The Economist*, May 21, 1994, 4.

85. Ibid., 4 and 8.

86. Glouchevitch, *Juggernaut*, 106.

87. "Is the Model Broken," *The Economist*, May 4, 1996, 17.

88. Steinmetz, "Germans Falter."

89. Gumbel and Choi, "Germany Making Comeback."
90. Woodruff, "German Worker."
91. Fukuyama, *End of History*, 201.

Chapter 10

1. Simon and Button, "What I Learned."
2. Kohlberg, *Psychology of Moral Development*.
3. Ibid., 215.
4. Arnold Hebert, interviewed by author, June 20, 1994.
5. Burns, *Leadership*, 44.
6. Ibid., 20.
7. Ibid.
8. Donnithorne, *West Point Way*, 11.
9. Howard Gardner, *Leading Minds*, 55.
10. Johnson & Johnson company videotape on the initial "Credo Challenge" meeting.
11. James Burke in a presentation at the Harvard Business School, December, 1983.
12. Ibid.
13. Carlzon, *Moments of Truth*; and Bartlett, Elderkin, and Feinberg, "Jan Carlzon."
14. Huey, "Most Successful Merchant."
15. General Electric Company, "1991 Annual Report," 5.
16. Jeff Folick, interviewed by author, September 1, 1994.
17. Arnold Hebert, interviewed by author, June 20, 1994.
18. Lorsch with MacIver, *Pawns and Potentates*, 7.
19. Monks and Minnow, *Corporate Governance*, 38. The case referred to is *CTS Corp. v. Dynamics Corporation of America*.
20. Ibid., 35 and 209.
21. Korn/Ferry International, *25th Annual Board of Directors Survey*, 1998.
22. Donnithorne, *West Point Way*, 114.
23. Philip Selznick made a similar observation nearly a half century ago in *Leadership in Administration*.
24. Smith and Tedlow, "James Burke," 8.
25. Pollard, *Soul of the Firm*, 36.
26. Rogers and Beer, "Human Resources at Hewlett-Packard."

Bibliography

Abegglen, James C. *Kaisha, The Japanese Corporation.* New York: Basic Books, 1985.

Allen, Christopher S. "Germany: Competing Communitarianisms." In *Ideology and National Competitiveness: An Analysis of Nine Countries,* ed. George C. Lodge and Ezra F. Vogel. Boston: Harvard Business School Press, 1987.

Alvarez, Aida. "Small Business: A Vital Building Block to Economic Growth." *Economic Perspectives,* vol. 3, no. 1 (February 1998): 11.

Amsden, Alice H. *Asia's Next Giant: South Korea and Late Industrialization.* New York: Oxford University Press, 1989.

Andrews, Frank M., and Stephen B. Withey. *Social Indicators of Well-Being: Americans' Perceptions of Life Quality.* New York: Plenum Press, 1976.

Andrews, Kenneth R. *The Concept of Corporate Strategy.* Homewood, Ill.: Irwin, 1987.

Aquinas, Thomas. *Summa Contra Gentiles,* vol. III. Trans. Dominican Fathers. London: Burns, Oates, and Washbourne, 1923.

———. *Summa Theologica,* vols. I–II. Allen, Texas: Christian Classics, 1981.

Ardagh, John. *Germany and the Germans: An Anatomy of Society Today.* 3rd ed. New York: Penguin Books, 1995.

Aristotle. *The Politics.* Trans. T. A. Sinclair and Trevor J. Saunders. London: Penguin Books, 1981.

Auletta, Ken. *The Art of Corporate Success.* New York: Penguin Books, 1985.

Badaracco, Joseph, and Richard R. Ellsworth. *Leadership and the Quest for Integrity.* Boston: Harvard Business School Press, 1989.

Badaracco, Joseph L., Jr. *The Knowledge Link*. Boston: Harvard Business School Press, 1991.

Banks, Howard. "Why George Bush Wants to Bring IRAs Back." *Forbes*, August 21, 1989, 68–69.

Barnard, Chester. *The Functions of the Executive*. Cambridge: Harvard University Press, 1938.

Bartlett, Christopher A., K. W. Elderkin, and B. Feinberg. "Jan Carlzon: CEO at SAS (A)," Harvard Business School Publishing, Case Number 9-392-149, 1992.

Bartlett, Christopher A., and Sumantra Ghoshal. "Changing the Role of Top Management: Beyond Strategy to Purpose." *Harvard Business Review*, November–December 1994.

Bartlett, Vernon. "The Biblical and Early Christian Idea of Property." In *Property: Its Duties and Responsibilities*. New York: Macmillan, 1922.

Basu, Shankar. "The Concept of Corporate Purpose and Its Linkage to the Key Objectives and Strategic Decisions at Toyota Motor Corporation," doctoral dissertation, Claremont Graduate School, 1996.

"Behind the Scenes of 'HP Directions in the '90s.'" *FYI*, Hewlett-Packard Company newsletter.

Bell, Daniel. *The Cultural Contradictions of Capitalism*. New York: Basic Books, 1976.

Bellah, Robert N., Richard Madsen, William M. Sullivan, Ann Swidler, and Steven M. Tipton. *Habits of the Heart: Individualism and Commitment in American Life*. New York: Harper & Row, Perennial Library, 1986.

Benjamin, Daniel. "German Study Cites Challenges to Competitiveness." *Wall Street Journal*, September 2, 1993.

Bennis, Warren G., and Burt Nanus. *Leaders: The Strategies for Taking Charge*. New York: Harper & Row, 1985.

Bentham, Jeremy. *The Theory of Legislation*, ed. C. K. Ogden. London: Routledge & Kegan Paul, 1931.

———. "An Introduction to the Principles of Morals and Legislation" (originally published in 1824). In *Utilitarianism and Other Essays*, ed. Alan Ryan. Harmondsworth, Middlesex, England: Penguin Books, 1987.

Berger, Peter L. "Some General Observations on the Problem of Work." In *The Human Shape of Work*, ed. Peter L. Berger, pp. 211–39. New York: Macmillan, 1964.

Berle, Adolf A., and Gardiner C. Means. *The Modern Corporation and Private Property*. Rev. ed. New York: Harcourt, Brace and World, 1967.

Berlin, Isaiah. *Four Essays on Liberty*. Oxford: Oxford University Press, 1969.

Boorstin, Daniel J. *The Americans: The Colonial Experience.* New York: Random House, 1958.

Brandt, Vincent S. R. "Korea." In *Ideology and National Competitiveness: An Analysis of Nine Countries*, ed. George C. Lodge and Ezra F. Vogel. Boston: Harvard Business School Press, 1987.

Buffett, Warren. *1989 Annual Report*, Berkshire Hathaway.

———. "An Owner's Manual." *1997 Annual Report*, Berkshire Hathaway.

Burke, James E. Presentation at Harvard Business School, December 1983.

Burns, James MacGregor. *Leadership.* New York: Harper & Row, 1978.

Campbell, Andrew, and Laura L. Nash. *A Sense of Mission: Defining Direction for the Large Corporation.* Reading, Mass.: Addison-Wesley, 1992.

Campbell, Angus. *The Sense of Well-Being in America.* New York: McGraw-Hill, 1981.

Campbell, Joan. *Joy in Work, German Work: The National Debate, 1800–1945.* Princeton, N.J.: Princeton University Press, 1989.

Cappelli, Peter. *The New Deal at Work.* Boston: Harvard Business School Press, 1999.

Carlzon, Jan. *Moments of Truth.* Cambridge, Mass.: Ballinger, 1987.

Carnegie, Andrew. "The Gospel of Wealth" (originally published in 1889). In *The Gospel of Wealth and Other Timely Essays*, ed. Edward A. Kirkland. Cambridge: Harvard University Press, 1962.

Chandler, Alfred D. *Strategy and Structure: Chapters in the History of the American Industrial Enterprise.* Cambridge: MIT Press, 1962.

———. *The Visible Hand: The Managerial Revolution in American Business.* Cambridge: Harvard University Press, Belknap Press, 1977.

———. *Scale and Scope.* Cambridge: Harvard University Press, 1990.

Chao, Julie, and David P. Hamilton. "Bad Times Are Just a Memory for DRAM Chip Makers." *Wall Street Journal*, August 28, 1995, B5.

"China's State-Owned Enterprises: Beijing Rules." *The Economist*, May 3, 1997, 55.

"Chips on Their Shoulders." *The Economist*, November 1, 1997, 62.

Christensen, C. Roland, Kenneth R. Andrews, and Joseph L. Bower. *Business Policy: Text and Cases.* 4th ed. Homewood, Ill.: Irwin, 1978.

Christopher, Robert C. *The Japanese Mind.* New York: Simon & Schuster, 1983.

Clifford, M. L., D. Roberts, J. Barnathan, and P. Engardio. "Can China Reform Its Economy?" *Business Week*, September 29, 1997, 118.

Collier, Abram T. "Business Leadership and a Creative Society," *Harvard Business Review*, January 1968, 155.

Collins, James C., and Jerry I. Porras. *Built to Last: Successful Habits of Visionary Companies.* New York: HarperCollins, 1994.

Cooper, Robin. *When Lean Enterprises Collide*. Boston: Harvard Business School Press, 1995.

Corporate Ethics: A Prime Business Asset. New York: Business Roundtable, 1988.

Creel, H. G. *Confucius and the Chinese Way*. New York: Harper & Row, 1960.

Crittenden, Jack. *Beyond Individualism: Reconstructing the Liberal Self*. Oxford: Oxford University Press, 1992.

Cruikshank, Jeffrey. "Matsushita." *Harvard Business School Bulletin* (February 1983): 55.

Csikszentmihalyi, Mihaly. *Flow: The Psychology of Optimal Experience*. New York: Harper & Row, 1990.

Cyert, Richard M., and James G. March. *A Behavioral Theory of the Firm*. Englewood Cliffs, N.J.: Prentice-Hall, 1963.

D'Aveni, Richard A., with Robert Gunther. *Hypercompetition: Managing the Dynamics of Strategic Maneuvering*. New York: Free Press, 1994.

Deane, Herbert A. *The Political and Social Ideas of St. Augustine*. New York: Columbia University Press, 1963.

"The Death of Daewoo." *The Economist*, August 21, 1999, 58.

De Pree, Hugh D. *Business as Unusual: The People and Principles at Herman Miller*. Zeeland: Herman Miller, 1986.

De Pree, Max. *Leadership Is an Art*. New York: Dell, 1990.

Donaldson, Gordon, and Jay W. Lorsch. *Decision Making at the Top*. New York: Basic Books, 1983.

Donnithorne, Larry R. *The West Point Way of Leadership*. New York: Currency Doubleday, 1993.

Dorfman, John R. "Analysts Devote More Time to Selling as Firms Keep Scoreboard on Performance." *Wall Street Journal*, October 29, 1991, C1.

Drucker, Peter F. *The Practice of Management*. New York: Harper & Row, 1954.

———. *Management: Tasks, Responsibilities, Practices*. New York: Harper & Row, 1973.

———. *The Unseen Revolution: How Pension Fund Socialism Came to America*. New York: Harper & Row, 1976.

———. "Reckoning with the Pension Fund Revolution." *Harvard Business Review*, March–April 1991, 112.

"Due Diligence." *The Economist*, August 24, 1996, 48.

Duncan, Otis Dudley. "Does Money Buy Satisfaction?" *Social Indicators Research*, no. 2, (1975): 267–74.

Economic Planning Agency. *White Paper on the Japanese Economy*. August 7, 1990.

Ellsworth, Richard R. "Subordinate Financial Policies to Corporate Strategy." *Harvard Business Review*, November–December 1983, 170–82.

———. "Capital Markets and Competitive Decline." *Harvard Business Review*, September–October 1985, 171–83.

Erikson, Kai, and Steven Peter Vallas, eds. *The Nature of Work: Sociological Perspectives*. New Haven, Conn.: Yale University Press, 1990.

Farney, Dennis. "Chaos Theory Seeps into Ecology Debate, Stirring Up a Tempest." *Wall Street Journal*, July 11, 1994, A1 and A8.

Farrell, Christopher, and Ted Holden. "The U.S. Has a New Weapon: Low-Cost Capital," *Business Week*, July 29, 1991, 72–73.

Feldstein, Martin. "Global Capital Flows: Too Little, Not Too Much." *The Economist*, June 24, 1995, 72–73.

Fisher, Anne B. "Morale Crisis." *Fortune*, November 18, 1991, 70–80.

Fletcher, George P. *Loyalty: An Essay on the Morality of Relationships*. New York: Oxford University Press, 1993.

Frankl, Viktor E. *Man's Search for Meaning*. New York: Washington Square Press, 1984.

Franklin, Benjamin. "Advice to a Young Tradesman." (Originally published in 1748.) In *The Autobiography and Other Essays*. New York: New American Library, 1985.

———. "The Way to Wealth." (Originally published in 1757.) In *The Autobiography and Other Essays*. New York: New American Library, 1985.

Freedman, Johnathan. *Happy People*. New York: Harcourt Brace Jovanovich, 1978.

Freud, Sigmund. *Standard Edition of the Complete Psychological Works*, vol 21, ed. James Strachey. London: Hogarth, 1966.

———. *Civilization and Its Discontents*. Ed. James Strachey. New York: Norton, 1962.

Friedberg, Aaron L. *The Weary Titan: Britain and the Experience of Relative Decline, 1985–1905*. Princeton, N.J.: Princeton University Press, 1989.

Fromm, Erich. *The Sane Society*. New York: Fawcett World Library, 1955.

Fukuyama, Francis. *The End of History and the Last Man*. New York: Free Press, 1992.

Gardner, Howard. *Leading Minds*. New York: Basic Books, 1995.

Gardner, John W. *On Leadership*. New York: Free Press, 1990.

———. *Self-Renewal: The Individual and the Innovative Society*. Rev. ed. New York: Norton, 1981.

General Electric Company. "1991 Annual Report."

Gerlach, Michael L. *Alliance Capitalism: The Social Organization of Japanese Business*. Berkeley: University of California Press, 1992.

de Geus, Arie. *The Living Company*. Boston: Harvard Business School Press, 1997.

Ghoshal, Sumantra, and Christopher A. Bartlett. *The Individualized Corporation*. New York: Harper Business, 1997.

"Give Them That Old Time Ambition." *Training* (February 1992): 74.

Glain, Steve. "Korea's Samsung Plans Very Rapid Expansion into Autos, Other Lines." *Wall Street Journal*, March 2, 1995, A1.

Glouchevitch, Philip. *Juggernaut: The German Way of Business: Why It Is Transforming Europe and the World*. New York: Simon & Schuster, 1992.

Gonzales, Justo L. *Faith and Wealth*. New York: Harper & Row, 1990.

Goodman, Paul, and Percival Goodman. *Communitas: Means of Livelihood and Ways of Life*. New York: Vintage Books, 1960.

Gore, Charles, and others. *Property: Its Duties and Rights*. New York: Macmillan, 1922.

Grace, Frank. *The Concept of Property in Modern Christian Thought*. Urbana: University of Illinois Press, 1953.

de Grazia, Sebastian. *Of Time, Work, and Leisure*. New York: Twentieth Century Fund, 1962.

Greenleaf, Robert K. *Servant Leadership: A Journey into the Nature of Legitimate Power and Greatness*. New York: Paulist Press, 1977.

Gumbel, Peter, and Audrey Choi. "Germany Making Comeback, with Daimler in the Lead." *Wall Street Journal*, April 7, 1995, A6.

Hamel, Gary, and C. K. Prahalad. "Strategic Intent." *Harvard Business Review*, May–June 1989.

———. *Competing for the Future*. Boston: Harvard Business School Press, 1994.

Handy, Charles. *The Age of Unreason*. Boston: Harvard Business School Press, 1990.

———. *Beyond Certainty*. Boston: Harvard Business School Press, 1996.

Helm, Leslie. "In Japan, Scorn for America." *Los Angeles Times*, October 25, 1991, A1.

———. "Foreign Firms with Deep Pockets Test U.S. Labs." *Los Angeles Times*, November 6, 1994, D1.

Henkoff, Ronald. "Getting Beyond Downsizing." *Fortune*, January 10, 1994.

Herzberg, Frederick. *Work and the Nature of Man*. Cleveland, Ohio: World, 1966.

Herzberg, Frederick, Bernard Mausner, and Barbara Block Snyderman. *The Motivation to Work*. New York: Wiley, 1959.

Hilsenrath, Jon E. "Many Layoffs Hurt Companies More Than They Help." *Wall Street Journal*, February, 21, 2001.

Hirschman, Albert O. *Exit, Voice, and Loyalty: Responses to Decline in Firms, Organizations, and States*. Cambridge: Harvard University Press, 1970.

———. *The Passions and the Interests*. Princeton, N.J.: Princeton University Press, 1977.

Hobbes, Thomas. *Leviathan*. (Originally published in 1651.) London: Penguin Books, 1985.

Hoover, Herbert. *American Individualism*. New York: Doubleday, Page, 1923.

House, Charles H., and Raymond L. Price. "The Return Map: Tracking Product Teams." *Harvard Business Review*, January–February 1991, 92–100.

Howard, Robert. "Values Make the Company: An Interview with Robert Haas." *Harvard Business Review*, September–October 1990, 134.

"How Lincoln Motivated Men." *Civil Engineering* (January 1973): 76–84.

Huey, John. "America's Most Successful Merchant." *Fortune*, September 23, 1991, 54.

Hume, David. *Treatise of Human Nature*. (Originally published in 1740.) Ed. T. H. Green and T. H. Grose. London: Longmans, Green, 1878.

———. *Essays, Moral, Political, and Literary*. Vol. 2. Ed. T. H. Green and T. H. Grose. London: Longmans, Green, 1875.

Inamori, Kazuo. *A Passion for Success*. New York: McGraw-Hill, 1995.

Inkeles, Alex, and Larry Diamond. "Personal Development and National Development: A Cross-Cultural Perspective." In *The Quality of Life: Comparative Studies*, ed. Alexander Szalai and Frank M. Andrews. Beverly Hills, Calif.: Sage, 1980.

Ip, Greg. "With Dow 9000 Nearby, Stocks Get Boost As Corporate America Tightens Its Belt." *Wall Street Journal*, March 23, 1998, C1.

"Is the Model Broken?" *The Economist*, May 4, 1996, 17.

Jacobs, Michael T. *Short-Term America*. Boston: Harvard Business School Press, 1991.

Jaffe, Thomas. "A Talk with John Templeton." *Forbes*, January 25, 1988, 84.

Jefferson, Thomas. October 28, 1775, letter to Rev. James Madison.

John Paul II. "Encyclical Laboren Exercens" ("On Human Work"), September 15, 1981.

———. "Centesimus Annus" ("The 100th Year," an Encyclical on the 100th Anniversary of Pope Leo XIII's "Rerum Novarum"), 1991.

Joyce, Patrick, ed. *The Historical Meanings of Work*. Cambridge: Cambridge University Press, 1987.

Kahn, Joseph. "China's Overcapacity Crimps Neighbors." *Wall Street Journal*, July 14, 1997, A10.

Kant, Immanuel. *The Philosophy of Kant*. Ed. Carl J. Friedrich. New York: Modern Library, 1949.

Kaplan, Robert S., and David P. Norton. *The Balanced Scorecard*. Boston: Harvard Business School Press, 1996.

Kester, W. Carl. "Governance, Contracting, and Investment Horizons: A Look at Japan and Germany." A paper prepared for the Capital Choices Conference, a joint project of the Council on Competitiveness and the Harvard Business School, March 1991.

———. *Japanese Takeovers: The Global Contest for Corporate Control*. Boston: Harvard Business School Press, 1991.

Kim Woo-Choong. *Every Street Is Paved with Gold: The Road to Real Success*. New York: William Morrow, 1992.

———. *Hard Work and Leadership: The Daewoo Recipe for Success*. Seoul: Daewoo Group Planning and Coordination Office, 1992.

Kohlberg, Lawrence. *The Psychology of Moral Development*. San Francisco: Harper & Row, 1984.

Kono, Toyohiro. *Strategy and Structure of Japanese Enterprises*. London: Macmillan, 1984.

Korn/Ferry International. *Board of Directors Twenty-first Annual Study*. 1994.

———. *25th Annual Board of Directors Survey*. 1998.

Kotter, John P., and James L. Heskett. *Corporate Culture and Performance*. New York: Free Press, 1992.

Kovar, Donald G. *The Decision-Making Environment of the Capital Investment Approval Process*. Doctoral dissertation, Claremont Graduate School, 1986.

Kristol, Irving. *Two Cheers for Capitalism*. New York: Basic Books, 1978.

Kuhn, Thomas S. *The Structure of Scientific Revolutions*. 2nd ed. Chicago: University of Chicago Press, 1970.

Laderman, Jeffrey M. "Wall Street's Spin Game." *Business Week*, October 5, 1998, 148–54.

Lane, Robert E. *The Market Experience*. Cambridge: Cambridge University Press, 1991.

Lauk, Kurt J. "Germany at the Crossroads: On the Efficiency of the German Economy," *Daedalus*, vol. 123 (Winter 1994): 57–83.

Leavitt, Harold J. *Corporate Pathfinders*. New York: Viking Penguin, 1986.

Lee, Chris. "Trust Me." *Training* (January 1997): 28–37.

Lincoln, James F. *Lincoln's Incentive System*. New York: McGraw-Hill, 1946.

Lincoln, James R., and Arne L. Kalleberg. *Culture, Control, and Commitment: A Study of Work Organization and Work Attitudes in the United States and Japan*. Cambridge: Cambridge University Press, 1990.

Lipman-Blumen, Jean. *The Connective Edge: Leading in an Interdependent World*. San Francisco: Jossey-Bass, 1996.

Locke, John. *Two Treatises of Government*. Cambridge: Cambridge University Press, 1960.

Lodge, George C. *The New American Ideology*. New York: Knopf, 1975.

———. *The American Disease*. New York: Knopf, 1984.

Lodge, George C., and Ezra F. Vogel, eds. *Ideology and National Competitiveness: An Analysis of Nine Countries.* Boston: Harvard Business School Press, 1987.

Lorsch, Jay W., with Elizabeth MacIver. *Pawns and Potentates.* Boston: Harvard Business School Press, 1989.

Lublin, Joann S. "Trying to Increase Worker Productivity, More Employers Alter Management Style." *Wall Street Journal*, February 13, 1992, B1.

Machiavelli, Niccolo. *The Discourses.* Ed. Bernard Crick. London: Penguin Books, 1970.

Macpherson, C. B. *The Political Theory of Possessive Individualism.* Oxford: Clarendon Press, 1962.

Maharaj, Davan. "Layoffs: A Company's Strategy of First Resort." *Los Angeles Times*, November 22, 1998.

Mansfield, Edwin. "Industrial R&D in Japan and the United States: A Comparative Study." *American Economic Review*, vol. 78, no. 2 (May 1988): 223–28.

Marshall, Ray, and Marc Tucker. *Thinking for a Living: Education and the Wealth of Nations.* New York: Basic Books, 1992.

Marx, Karl. *Selected Writings.* Ed. David McLellan. Oxford: Oxford University Press, 1977.

Maslow, Abraham H. "A Theory of Human Motivation." *Psychological Review* 50 (1943): 370–96.

———. *The Farther Reaches of Human Nature.* New York: Viking Penguin Books, 1971.

Maslow, Abraham H., with Deborah C. Stephens and Gary Heil. *Maslow on Management.* New York: Wiley, 1998.

McKinsey Global Institute. "Capital Productivity." Washington, D.C., 1996.

McTaggart, James, Peter Kontes, and Michael Mankins. *The Value Imperative.* New York: Free Press, 1994.

Meakin, David. *Man and Work.* New York: Holmes & Meier, 1976.

Menninger, Karl. "Work as Sublimation." *Bulletin of the Menninger Clinic* 6 (1942).

Mill, John Stuart. *Principles of Political Economy.* Ed. W. J. Ashley. London, 1909.

———. *Autobiography.* In *John Stuart Mill: A Selection of his Works*, ed. John M. Robson. New York: Odyssey Press, 1966.

———. *On Liberty.* (Originally published in 1859.) Ed. Gertrude Himmelfarb. London: Penguin Books, 1974.

Mintzberg, Henry. *The Rise and Fall of Strategic Planning.* New York: Free Press, 1994.

Monks, Robert A. G., and Nell Minnow. *Corporate Governance.* Cambridge, Mass.: Blackwell Business, 1995.

Morita, Akio, with Edwin M. Reingold and Mitsuko Shimomura. *Made in Japan*. New York: E. P. Dutton, 1986.

Murphy, R. Taggart. *The Weight of the Yen*. New York: Norton, 1996.

Myers, David G. "The Funds, Friends, and Faith of Happy People." *American Psychologist* (January 2000): 56–67.

Nakarmi, Laxmi, Kevin Kelly, and Larry Armstrong. "Look Out, World—Samsung Is Coming." *Business Week*, July 10, 1995, 52–53.

Nakarmi, Laxmi, and Robert Neff. "Samsung's Radical Shakeup." *Business Week*, February 28, 1994, 74.

National Intelligence Council. "Global Trends 2015: A Dialogue About the Future with Nongovernment Experts." December 2000, 35.

National Science Board. *Science and Engineering Indicators—2000*. Arlington, Va.: National Science Foundation, 2000 (NSB-00-1).

National Science Foundation. "National Patterns of R&D Resources, 2000: Data Update." March 2001.

Neff, Walter S. *Work and Human Behavior*. New York: Atherton Press, 1968.

"The New Economy: Work in Progress." *The Economist*, July 24, 1999, 22.

New York Stock Exchange. *Fact Book for the Year 1991*.

———. *Fact Book for the Year 2000*.

Niebuhr, Reinhold. *The Children of Light and the Children of Darkness*. New York: Charles Scribner's Sons.

Nocera, Joseph. "A Whole New Ball Game." *Fortune*, July 24, 2000.

Nonaka, Ikijiro, and Noboru Konno. "The Concept of 'Ba': Building a Foundation for Knowledge Creation." *California Management Review* (Spring 1998): 40–54.

Nonaka, Ikijiro, and Hirotaka Takeuchi. *The Knowledge Creating Company*. New York: Oxford University Press, 1995.

Novak, Michael. *The Spirit of Democratic Capitalism*. New York: Simon & Schuster, 1982.

Nozick, Robert. *Philosophical Explanations*. Cambridge: Harvard University Press, Belknap Press, 1981.

Nussbaum, Bruce. "I'm Worried About My Job!" *Business Week*, October 7, 1991, 94–97.

Ohmae, Kenichi. *The Borderless World*. New York: HarperBusiness, 1990.

O'Reilly, Brian. "The New Deal: What Companies and Employees Owe One Another." *Fortune*, June 13, 1994, 50.

Paine, Lynn Sharp. "Sears Auto Centers (A)," Harvard Business School Publishing, Case Number 9-394-010, 1994.

Pascale, Richard Tanner, and Athos, Anthony G. *The Art of Japanese Management*. New York: Simon & Schuster, 1981.

Pascarella, Perry. *The New Achievers: Creating a Modern Work Ethic*. New York: Free Press, 1984.

Paulsen, Friedrich. *Immanuel Kant: His Life and Doctrine*. Trans. J. E. Creighton and Albert LeFevre. New York: Unger, 1963.

Pfeffer, Jeffrey. *Competitive Advantage Through People*. Boston: Harvard Business School Press, 1994.

———. *The Human Equation: Building Profits by Putting People First*. Boston: Harvard Business School Press, 1998.

Plato. *Dialogues of Plato*. Trans. B. Jowett, ed. Justin D. Kaplan. New York: Washington Square Press, 1950.

———. *The Republic*. Trans. B. Jowett. New York: Random House.

Pollard, C. William. *The Soul of the Firm*. New York: HarperBusiness, 1996.

Porter, Michael E. *Competitive Advantage: Creating and Sustaining Superior Performance*. New York: Free Press, 1985.

———. "From Competitive Advantage to Corporate Strategy." *Harvard Business Review*, May–June 1987, 43–59.

———. "Capital Disadvantage: America's Failing Capital Investment System." *Harvard Business Review*, September–October 1992.

Poterba, James. "Stock Market Wealth and Consumption." *Journal of Economic Perspectives*, Spring 2000.

Prahalad, C. K., and Gary Hamel. "The Core Competence of the Corporation." *Harvard Business Review*, May–June 1990, 79–90.

President's Commission on Industrial Competitiveness. *The Report of the President's Commission on Industrial Competitiveness*. January 1985.

"The Prospects for Productivity." *The Economist*, February 17, 1990, 25.

Randall, John Herman, Jr. *The Making of the Modern Mind*. Cambridge, Mass.: Houghton Mifflin, 1940.

Reich, Robert B. *The Work of Nations*. New York: Knopf, 1991.

Reichheld, Fredrick F. *The Loyalty Effect: The Hidden Force Behind Growth, Profits, and Lasting Value*. Boston: Harvard Business School Press, 1996.

Reischauer, Edwin O. *The Japanese*. Cambridge: Harvard University Press, 1981.

Reismann, David. *The Lonely Crowd: A Study of the Changing American Character*. New Haven, Conn.: Yale University Press, 1950.

Rodgers, Daniel T. *The Work Ethic in Industrial America, 1850–1920*. Chicago: University of Chicago Press, 1978.

Rogers, Gregory C., and Michael Beer. "Human Resources at Hewlett-Packard (A) and (B)," Harvard Business School Publishing, Case numbers 9-495-051 and 9-495-052, 1995.

Rohlen, Thomas R. *Japan's High Schools*. Berkeley: University of California Press, 1983.

Royce, Josiah. *The Philosophy of Loyalty*. 1924.

Russell, Bertrand. *The Conquest of Happiness*. New York: Horace Liveright, 1930.

Sathe, Vijay. *Culture and Related Corporate Realities*. Homewood, Ill.: Irwin, 1985.

Schein, Edgar H. *Organizational Culture and Leadership*. San Francisco: Jossey-Bass, 1985.

Schlatter, Richard. *Private Property: The History of an Idea*. New Brunswick, N.J.: Rutgers University Press, 1951.

Schor, Juliet B. *The Overworked American*. New York: Basic Books, 1991.

Schumacher. E. F. *Good Work*. New York: Harper & Row, 1979.

Schumpeter, Joseph. *Capitalism, Socialism, and Democracy*. New York: Harper & Row, 1946.

Scitovsky, Tibor. *The Joyless Economy: An Inquiry into Human Satisfaction and Consumer Dissatisfaction*. New York: Oxford University Press, 1976.

Selznick, Philip. *Leadership in Administration*. New York: Harper & Row, 1962.

——. *The Moral Commonwealth*. Berkeley: University of California Press, 1992.

Senge, Peter M. *The Fifth Discipline*. New York: Currency Doubleday, 1990.

Shaw, George Bernard. "Epistle Dedicatory to Arthur Bingham Walkley." In *Man and Superman: A Comedy and a Philosophy*. New York: Brentano's, 1905.

Shirreff, David. "Bankers as Monopolists." *Euromoney*, March 1987, 71.

Simon, Herbert A. *Administrative Behavior*. 3rd ed. New York: Free Press, 1976.

Simon, Ruth, and Graham Button. "What I Learned in the Eighties." *Forbes*, January 8, 1990: 103.

Singer, Irving. *Meaning in Life: The Creation of Value*. New York: Free Press, 1992.

Slywoltzky, Adrian J., and David J. Morrison. *The Profit Zone*. New York: Times Business, 1997.

"Small Business, Small Beer." *The Economist*, July 25, 1992, 31.

Smith, Adam. *The Wealth of Nations*. Ed. E. Cannan. New York: Modern Library, 1937.

——. *Lectures on Justice, Revenue, and Arms*. In *Adam Smith's Moral and Political Philosophy*. Ed. Herbert W. Schneider, 281–335. New York: Hafner Publishing, 1948.

——. *The Theory of Moral Sentiments*. Amherst: Promeheus Books, 2000.

Smith, Hedrick. *Rethinking America*. New York: Random House, 1995.

Smith, Huston. *The Religions of Man*. New York: Harper Perennial, 1986.

Smith, Warren W., Jr. *Confucianism in Modern Japan*. Tokyo: Hokuseido Press, 1959.

Smith, Wendy K., and Richard S. Tedlow. "James Burke: A Career in American Business (A)," Harvard Business School Publishing, Case no. 9-389-177, 1989.

Smyser, W. R. *The Economy of United Germany: Colossus at the Crossroads*. New York: St. Martin's, 1992.

"South Korean Manufacturing: The Giants Stumble." *The Economist*, October 18, 1997, 68.

Steinmetz, Greg. "Germans Falter in Struggle to Regain Competitive Edge." *Wall Street Journal*, June 12, 1997, A14.

"A Survey of Germany." *The Economist*, May 21, 1994, 27.

Thurow, Lester. *Head to Head: The Coming Economic Battle Among Japan, Europe, and America*. New York: William Morrow, 1992.

———. *The Future of Capitalism*. New York: William Morrow, 1996.

Tichy, Noel M., and Ram Charan. "Speed, Simplicity, Self-Confidence: An Interview with Jack Welch." *Harvard Business Review*, September–October 1989, 112–20.

Tilgher, Adriano. *Work: What It Has Meant to Men through the Age*. Trans. D. C. Fisher. London: Harrap, 1931.

Tillich, Paul. *A History of Christian Thought*. Ed. Carl E. Braaten. New York: Simon & Schuster, 1967.

de Tocqueville, Alexis. *Democracy in America*. Vols. I and 2. (Originally published in 1835 and 1840). Ed. Phillips Bradley. New York: Vintage Books, 1990.

"Top Ten Corporations Receiving U.S. Patents: Japanese Manufacturers Grow More Inventive Than Their U.S. Rivals," *Wall Street Journal*, October 4, 1988, B4.

"A Toyota for the 21st Century." *Toyota Management Forum* (October 1992): 2.

Toyota Motor Company, *1993 Annual Report*.

United States Central Intelligence Agency. *Handbook of Economic Statistics*, 1994.

———. *Handbook of International Economic Statistics*, 1996.

United States Department of Commerce. *Competing to Win in a Global Economy*. September 1994.

———. *Survey of Current Business*. April 2001.

United States Department of Commerce, International Trade Administration. "U.S. Foreign Trade Highlights: 1996."

———. "U.S. Commodity Trade with Top 80 Trading Partners, 1996–2000."

Veroff, Elizabeth Douvan, and Richard A. Kulka. *The Inner Americans: A Self-Portrait from 1957 to 1976*. New York: Basic Books, 1981.

Vogel, Ezra F. "Japan: Adaptive Communitarianism." In *Ideology and National Competitiveness: An Analysis of Nine Countries*, ed. George C. Lodge and Ezra F. Vogel. Boston: Harvard Business School Press, 1987.

Volf, Miroslav. *Work in the Spirit*. New York: Oxford University Press, 1991.

Von Krogh, Georg, Kazuo Ichijo, and Ikujiro Nonaka. *Enabling Knowledge Cre-*

ation: How to Unlock the Mystery of Tacit Knowledge and Release the Power of Innovation. New York: Oxford University Press, 2000.

Vroom, Victor H. *Work and Motivation.* New York: Wiley, 1964.

Walton, Sam. *Sam Walton, Made in America: My Story.* New York: Doubleday, 1992.

Watson, Thomas, Jr. *A Business and Its Beliefs.* New York: McGraw-Hill, 1963.

Weber, Max. *The Protestant Ethic and the Spirit of Capitalism.* Trans. Talcott Parsons. New York: Charles Scribner's Sons, 1930.

———. *The Religion of China: Confucianism and Taoism,* Trans. and ed. Hans H. Gerth. Glencoe, Ill.: Free Press, 1951.

"Will Money Managers Wreck the Economy?" *Business Week,* August 13, 1984: 89.

Winckler, Edwin A. "Statism and Familism on Taiwan." In *Ideology and National Competitiveness: An Analysis of Nine Countries,* ed. George C. Lodge and Ezra F. Vogel. Boston: Harvard Business School Press, 1987.

van Wolferen, Karel. *The Enigma of Japanese Power: People and Politics in a Stateless Nation.* London: Macmillan, 1989.

Wolff, Edward N. "Where Has All the Money Gone?" *The Milken Institute Review,* vol. 3., no. 3 (third quarter, 2001): 34–43.

Wood, H. G. "The Influence of the Reformation on Ideas Concerning Wealth and Property." In *Property: Its Duties and Rights,* Charles Gore and others. New York: Macmillan, 1922.

Woodruff, David. "The German Worker Is Making a Sacrifice." *Business Week,* July 28, 1997, 46.

World Trade Organization (WTO). "World Trade in 1999."

Yankelovich, Daniel. *New Rules: Searching for Self-Fulfillment in a World Turned Upside Down.* New York: Random House, 1981.

———. "The Work Ethic Is Underemployed." *Psychology Today,* May 1982, 6.

Yoffie, David B. "The Global Semiconductor Industry, 1987." Publishing Division, Harvard Business School, 1987.

Zaleznik, Abraham. *Human Dilemmas of Leadership.* New York: Harper & Row, 1966.

———. *The Managerial Mystique: Restoring Leadership in Business.* New York: Harper & Row, 1989.

Index

accountability, 44, 55, 118–19, 137, 265, 351

accounting practices: *chaebol* and, 294, 308; performance measures and, 147–48

Adenauer, Conrad, 314

Age of Reason, 197–204

American Federation of Labor, 76

America's competitors: lessons from, 320–23; problems facing, 323–24. *See also* Asian countries; China; Germany; global competitiveness; Japan; South Korea

Analog Devices, 126

Andrews, Kenneth, 8–9

Anglo-American ideology: future competitiveness and, 56, 162–71, 323–24; individual fulfillment and, 222; as logically flawed, 157; measurement of wealth-producing capacity and, 157–62; as outdated, 52–56, 214–25, 357; product-market vs. capital-market orientations in, 3, 104–7, 112–13, 266, 267; property rights heritage and, 52–56, 214–25; rationalization and, 265; resource allocation decisions and, 171–76; shareholder diversity and, 176–80; shareholder rights and responsibilities and, 182–225. *See also* individualism; property rights ideology; shareholder-focused purpose

Aquinas, Saint Thomas, 182–83, 190–91

Aristotle, 69, 187–88, 199, 215

"Asia crisis," 303–10

Asian countries: American economic strength and, 244–45; Asian crisis and, 306–10; capital markets in, 147–48; competitive pressures from, 16–18, 303–6; foundations of ideologies in, 267–70. *See also* China; Japan; South Korea

Asian Tigers, 16, 265, 306

aspirations, human, 83–88, 332–35

aspirations, strategic, 95, 96–103, 109

Athos, Anthony, 5

AT&T, 41

Augustine, Saint, 69, 189–90

authority, as source of influence, 2